How to Study in College

ELEVENTH EDITION

Walter Pauk
Cornell University, Emeritus

Ross J. Q. Owens

WADSWORTH
CENGAGE Learning·

Australia · Brazil · Japan · Korea · Mexico · Singapore · Spain · United Kingdom · United States

WADSWORTH
CENGAGE Learning·

How to Study in College, Eleventh Edition
Pauk, Owens

Editor-in-Chief: Lyn Uhl

Director, Developmental Studies: Annie Todd

Executive Editor: Shani Fisher

Media Editor: Amy Gibbons

Editorial Assistant: Erin Nixon

Brand Manager: Jennifer Levanduski

Market Development Manager: Joshua Adams

Marketing Coordinator: Nicole Pavlu

Senior Marketing Communications Manager: Linda Yip

Rights Acquistions Specialist: Shalice Shah-Caldwell

Manufacturing Planner: Sandee Milewski

Art and Design Direction, Production Management, and Composition: PreMediaGlobal

Cover Designer: Riezebos Holzbaur/ Tim Heraldo

Cover Images: ©wavebreakmedia ltd/ Shutterstock (top); ©Robert Kneschke/ Shutterstock (left); ©Catherine Yeulet/ Photos.com (bottom)

For product information and technology assistance, contact us at **Cengage Learning Customer & Sales Support, 1-800-354-9706**

For permission to use material from this text or product, submit all requests online at **www.cengage.com/permissions.** Further permissions questions can be emailed to **permissionrequest@cengage.com.**

Library of Congress Control Number: 2012955262

ISBN-13: 978-1-133-96078-2
ISBN-10: 1-133-96078-2

Wadsworth
20 Channel Center Street
Boston, MA 02210
USA

Cengage Learning is a leading provider of customized learning solutions with office locations around the globe, including Singapore, the United Kingdom, Australia, Mexico, Brazil and Japan. Locate your local office at **international.cengage.com/region**

Cengage Learning products are represented in Canada by Nelson Education, Ltd.

For your course and learning solutions, visit **www.cengage.com**

Purchase any of our products at your local college store or at our preferred online store **www.cengagebrain.com**

Instructors: Please visit **login.cengage.com** and log in to access instructor-specific resources.

Printed in the United States of America
1 2 3 4 5 6 7 16 15 14 13 12

Contents

To the Instructor of the Eleventh Edition

Students who are seeking help are not primarily interested in theory, and most of them have little patience with merely inspirational talk. They want practical instruction on how to succeed academically. They want something that they can readily understand and apply and that works. After a week of classes, they discover that the hit-or-miss tactics that got them through high school are grossly inadequate and inefficient at the competitive college level. So they turn to us for help.

Let's then teach these students proven techniques for studying and learning. *How to Study in College* is brimming with exciting techniques, based on widely tested educational and learning theory, that have already helped myriad students. But the tail of theory is never allowed to wag the practical, feet-on-the-ground dog. While theory is always implicit and is sometimes given in enough detail to explain the rationale behind a particular technique or reassure the skeptic, it is never presented without explicit applications and never used simply as exhortation. After all, the person who needs penicillin is hardly cured by learning the history of antibiotics!

Because it is so crucial that students learn for the long term, we are wholeheartedly against techniques that stress mere memorization. Such techniques fill the mind with "knowledge" that melts away after a test and leaves learning still to be done. The techniques presented in this book result in real learning. And real learning, like a real diamond, lasts.

Finally, no textbook—no matter how complete or current—is truly useful if it is boring, confusing, or excessively difficult to read. We have worked hard to keep this book well organized and clear, maintaining a conversational tone so that reading it is like having a sincere, person-to-person chat.

What's Different in the Eleventh Edition?

The eleventh edition marks some important updates to trusted chapters and features along with some key structural changes, all of which are designed to make the text even more valuable and authoritative.

New! Chapter 1 Makes the Key Link Between Goal-Setting and Concentration

The book's first chapter combines the best of the previous edition's chapters on goal-setting and concentration into a single chapter that establishes the essential link between these important long- and short-term academic activities. Not simply a melding of two older chapters, "Concentrate on Reaching Your Goal" incorporates exciting new insights from the field of cognitive science that have proven to make both goal-setting and concentration more rewarding and successful.

New! Updated Chapter on Stress Management

The eleventh edition's chapter on stress management adds important techniques for managing stress that take advantage of recent discoveries in brain science.

New! Chapter Devoted to Listening Skills

One of the most important yet largely underappreciated skills is listening. The eleventh edition devotes an entire chapter to this vital component of academic success, focusing on the special challenges of listening and offering some concrete strategies for getting the most out of oral presentations.

New! Updated Vocab-u-ladders

The end-of-chapter word connection puzzles have been updated to provide additional word origin insights and incorporate vocabulary taken directly from the chapters they accompany.

New! Tantalizing Chapter Teasers

Each chapter opener now includes several intriguing clues to fascinating facts from within the chapter, designed to pique interest and add an extra motivation to keep reading.

Valuable Features Retained

Although the enhancements to the eleventh edition make for an even more compelling and effective text, many of the most helpful and popular elements from the previous edition have been retained in this one.

- **Concept Maps.** Concept maps continue to provide a graphical means of summarizing chapter content. Before students read a chapter, the maps supply advance organizers, which, according to David P. Ausubel, make it easier to learn and remember material in the chapter itself. After students have read the chapter, the concept maps provide a bird's-eye view, showing that chapter's main concepts with linking lines that establish relationships.
- **Marginal Questions.** The blue marginal questions that make *How to Study in College* distinctive among study skills textbooks remain, as do the outside margins, which not only make room for these printed questions but also make it easier for students to annotate the text on their own.
- **It's Your Q.** Although most of the book's paragraphs are accompanied by marginal questions, a few questions in each chapter have been replaced by "It's Your Q" boxes that encourage students to formulate and write in their own marginal questions.
- **Skill Tags**. The blue-and-white Skill Tags that accompany each chapter subsection highlight the eight core skills—*focusing, overviewing, reframing, summarizing, planning, questioning, clustering,* and *self-direction*—that underlie all the book's topics, tips, and techniques and provide another helpful way of reframing the book's content.
- **Vocabulary in Action.** This end-of-chapter section provides three distinct approaches to vocabulary enrichment: "Say What?" quotes an eclectic array of thinkers and leaders and asks students to use context to pinpoint the meaning for some of the words they use; "Vocab-u-ladder" employs a word puzzle to encourage students to explore the derivations of words and their relationships; and "Back-story" takes a key word directly from each chapter, spotlighting its fascinating and sometimes surprising history.

Ancillary Materials

This edition is supported by several ancillaries that are designed to reinforce and enrich the basic book:

The **Student Companion Site** includes practice quizzes, flashcards, exercises, glossary of terms, and additional resources to help students be successful in their course. Students can access this free website at www.cengagebrain.com.

The **Instructor's Companion Site** includes a downloadable **Instructor's Manual** that provides you with quick access to information on preparing your syllabus, extra multiple-choice questions for each chapter, and discussion questions, and reproducible masters relating to the concepts found in the text. **PowerPoint Slides** for each chapter of the eleventh edition are also accessible through the Instructor Companion Website. Use these slides to enhance any classroom presentation.

Access the **Instructor Companion Site** by logging into your account at http://login.cengage.com.

College Success Factors Index (CSFI) 2.0 is an online survey that students complete to assess their patterns and behavior in ten factors that are specific to succeeding in the classroom/campus: Responsibility/Control, Competition, Task Planning, Expectations, Wellness, Time Management, College Involvement, Family Involvement, Precision, and Persistence. The CSFI is a perfect assessment tool for tracking your students' success in the course. For more information about this resource, visit http://www.cengage.com/success/csfi2.

The **College Success Planner** is an annual planner available as a package item with this textbook. This 18-month planner assists students in making the best use of their time both on and off campus.

An additional service available with this textbook is support from **TeamUP Faculty Program Consultants**. For more than a decade, our consultants have helped faculty reach and engage first-year students by offering peer-to-peer consulting on curriculum and assessment, faculty training, and workshops. Consultants are available to help you establish or improve our student success program and provide training on the implementation of our textbooks and technology. To connect with your TeamUP Faculty Program Consultant, call 1-800-528-8323 or visit www.cengage.com/teamup.

For more in-depth information on any of these items, talk with your sales rep, or visit www.cengage.com.

Acknowledgments

Sincere words of thanks go to those who are permanently linked to this book: the late Henry F. Thoma and Ian D. Elliot.

Sincere thanks also go to the contributors of material in previous editions: Professors Harrison A. Geiselmann, Kenneth A. Greisen, and Jane E. Hardy, all of Cornell University; Professor William G. Moulton of Princeton University; Professor James A. Wood and Dr. Nancy V. Wood, both of the University of Texas at El Paso.

In addition, Walter Pauk remembers the valuable contributions made by Professors Mike Radis and Ron Williams of Pennsylvania State University as well as Professor Carol Kanar of Valencia Community College.

Ross Owens is especially grateful to the Neier family (Tara, Gary, and Terry), Yun Wang, Kirsten R. Johnson, and Carlton Vogt, dear friends all, who provided valuable support during the challenging but rewarding process of revising this edition. Finally, as always, deepest thanks go to Walter Pauk himself, a loyal friend and wonderful mentor, who remains the embodiment of this book's plain-spoken, clear-thinking, well-meaning wisdom.

At Cengage Learning, we would like to thank Shani Fisher and Joanna Hassel for their editorial support of our work. We would also like to thank Pooja Khurana, Prashanth.K and Margaret Bridges for their time and contributions in seeing this new edition to its completion.

We would also like to thank the reviewers of previous editions, as well as these reviewers of the present eleventh edition, for their helpful suggestions:

Julia Beyeler, University of Akron-Wayne College
Pamela Price, Mercer County Community College
Paula Westdorp, Kellogg Community College
Paul White, Lakeland College
Janet Zupan, University of Montana-Missoula

And finally, in this edition, as in the ten previous ones, Walter Pauk offers very special thanks to his students:

"I am eternally grateful to my many students who have taught me much—so that I may pass on a little more to others."

W. P.
R. J. Q. O.

To the Student

Why waste time reading a book about study when you could be studying instead? If you're like many students, you are both anxious to learn and impatient to succeed. You want a book that provides the answers you need, techniques that you can actually use, and, most of all, that doesn't waste your time. We understand this feeling and, over the course of more than five decades, have written and refined *How to Study in College* with exactly this sort of purpose in mind.

And yet, this is not a simple test-passer, paper-writer, grade-getter kind of book. That sort of quick-fix approach can be very appealing and it may get you over one hump, but unless your skills are solid and your learning is permanent you'll find yourself repeatedly climbing the same hill. *How to Study in College* is organized from top to bottom in a way that should make it easy to learn, use, and remember. It provides you with tips, techniques, and strategies that are supported by research and that you can use again and again, and it is designed with features that reinforce the very lessons you are learning. In short, you'll not only be reading a book that teaches but also one that practices what it preaches!

How This Book Is Organized

What does it take to be a successful student? Imagine the power of being able to answer that basic question in a single, simple, memorable phrase. It might not always make things easier—studying still takes effort—but it would make them clearer and a lot less intimidating.

Becoming a successful student involves building a strong study skills foundation before gaining, retaining, and ultimately explaining information. That's right. That's the seed from which this entire book has grown. Build a base for information and then gain it, retain it, and explain it. All of the book's 14 chapters branch out from this single idea and have been clustered beneath these basic steps.

Part I: Building a Foundation. Even if it's made from sturdy and resilient materials, a tall tower will still topple if it's built upon a rickety base. In the same way, the gaining, retaining, and explaining you do in college must rest on a firm foundation of basic skills. Incidentally, these are skills that will be invaluable at college but should also serve you well at home, in your career, and for the rest of your life. You don't need to be a college student to benefit from knowing how to focus (**Chapter 1**), control your time and organize your space (**Chapter 2**), handle pressure (**Chapter 3**), and build and maintain your vocabulary (**Chapter 4**).

Part II: Gaining Information. How can you possibly know all there is to know? The world is awash with information. It's out there. You just have to go out and get it. But how? First of all, you need to know how to read. If that sounds obvious or even ridiculous, you may need to rethink what you know about reading. The truth is, there's no "one size fits all" method of reading. The way you read should be adapted to *what* you read. That's the topic of **Chapter 5**. Of course, reading is just one channel of communication. In fact, all of us spend more time listening than reading. And in college, much of that listening is done in lectures. That's why **Chapter 6** is devoted to bringing lectures to life. Even if it were possible to understand and digest every piece of information you read and hear, it still wouldn't be wise. Time is short and not all information is created equal. Therefore, you need to be able to focus on the valuable information. **Chapter 7** helps you decide which information is worth keeping and which can be discarded. Finally, not all information comes in the form of words. And not all students learn best by using words. **Chapter 8** explores the other channels of communication we use in our efforts at understanding.

Information is everywhere. You need a plan for going out and getting it.

Part III: Retaining Information. When we talk about *retain it*, we're dealing with another important *–ain* word: your brain. As you'll learn in Part III, your brain's working memory only has room for roughly seven items at once. You can't possibly hold on to a semester's worth of information in the working memory of your brain. Not even close. What's more, the things you keep in working memory evaporate, fast. If you can't quickly find a place to store them, they'll be gone in a matter of minutes. Perhaps forever. The *retain it* section of this book will tell you how to hold on to information more or less permanently. Your primary storage areas will be your long-term memory and your notes. In **Chapter 9**, you'll find out more about how the memory works and learn the things you can do and shouldn't do if you want your memories to last. In **Chapter 10**, you'll learn how to retain valuable information by taking notes efficiently and effectively, using a simple, time-honored system that should work in almost any situation. **Chapter 11** shows you how to read those notes, make sense out of them, and then turn them into a part of your permanent knowledge.

Part IV: Explaining Information. In an ideal world, retaining information would be its own reward. You know, learning for learning's sake. But that's not how college works. In college your performance is measured with grades. The grades you receive depend upon how well you can "show what you know," that is, how successfully you can take the information that you've retained during the semester (and often before) and explain it. The most common kind of explaining in college comes in the form of tests and exams. That's the topic of **Chapter 12**. It provides you with systems, tips, and techniques for translating what you've gained into a test score that you can be proud of. **Chapter 13** focuses on another way of explaining—discussions. Depending on the course, class participation or online discussion threads can play an important role in your grade. But more importantly, you may not know how well you understand something until you have had an opportunity to discuss it with others. You'll learn how to prepare for discussions and how to perform in them in a way that benefits both your understanding of your subject and helps your grade. Finally, **Chapter 14** tackles the writing of research papers. Although it may seem like a specialized skill, as this chapter will demonstrate, much of what you'll need to explain in a paper draws on other skills that you've had a chance to develop and refine up to this point.

You earn your grade based on your ability to explain what you've gained and retained.

How This Book Is Designed

Everything about *How to Study in College* is focused on helping you to become a successful student. This mission goes beyond the text of the book and includes the elements that make up the book's design. The at-a-glance table of contents, the concept maps, the chapter checkups, and the marginal questions all act as tools to help you gain, retain, and explain the information in this book. In addition, the "Vocabulary in Action" section at the end of each chapter reinforces the idea that building your vocabulary should be a lifetime pursuit and not just a one-shot deal, while the Skill Tags found at the start of each chapter subsection reinforce that the dozens of strategies, tips, and techniques in this book are all built on a foundation of eight basic skills.

At-a-Glance Table of Contents

How to Study in College includes the sort of detailed table of contents (TOC) you'd expect to find in almost any textbook. It begins on page iii and extends over several pages. But the book includes another "at-a-glance" TOC inside the front cover that lists the book's 4 parts and 14 chapters and briefly explains the purpose of each part. The at-a-glance TOC is a concentrated version of the book that helps you to gain, explain, and retain the book's contents more easily. The psychological effect of being able to see the book's entire contents on a single page can be dramatic and highly beneficial. Suddenly a book of more than 400 pages becomes more manageable and easier to grasp. Instead of operating in isolation, each important idea can be fit into the overall framework of the book's organization.

Chapter Topics

Most chapter textbooks have titles, but that title doesn't always tell you clearly what the chapter's about. That's why each chapter in *How to Study in College* has both a title *and* a *topic*. The topic is a one- to three-word phrase—like Organization, Comprehension, or Critical Thinking—that cuts to the very heart of the chapter's subject matter, providing a succinct summation of its focus and making it just a little easier for you to stay on track as you progress through the book. Like the Skill Tags that accompany the chapter subsections, the chapter topics are designed to make each chapter's purpose even clearer.

Concept Maps

Textbook chapters aren't whodunits. Surprises can be fun, but there should be no mystery about how textbook chapters are organized or where they are leading. That's why each chapter in *How to Study in College* gives away the plot at the very beginning. It opens with a map that shows you right up front the topics the chapter will be covering and, just as importantly, how they relate to each other.

These maps should prove helpful in gaining the gist of each chapter before you begin reading—especially if you are a visually oriented learner—and make it easier to review and tie things together after you've finished a chapter.

Use them to survey each chapter before you begin reading. Look at the map as a whole and then note the concepts that make up the map. If you haven't noticed already, the map's top concept is the name of the chapter. Now note how the concepts connect. Turn each concept into a question; the topics connected below each concept should provide a broad outline of the answer.

Use them to review the chapter once you've finished it. Flip back to the front of the chapter and look at the map again. By now each topic name should be more meaningful than it was before you started reading the chapter. Test your knowledge of the chapter's concepts by covering the map and then drawing your own version from memory.

Chapter Checkups

The end-of-chapter questions are designed to teach, not test; you'll find no trick questions and no traps to lead you to an incorrect answer. Take each question at face value and answer it to the best of your ability. Use any incorrect answers you give as opportunities to reread the pertinent portion of the chapter. By rereading and rethinking the question and answer, you will greatly strengthen your understanding of the entire concept. Answers to these questions are available online.

Marginal Questions

If you've already flipped through this book, then you have almost certainly noticed something a little unusual about it. Running along the left side of each page in the marginal area that is blank in most books is a series of questions, one for almost every paragraph.

Why questions? Questions are what make learning come alive. They activate inert facts and turn them into vibrant ideas. If questions aren't a key component of your studying, you may not be truly learning. The book's marginal questions can help you in a number of ways. They provide the following:

1. **Concrete examples** of how each textbook paragraph can be seen as the answer to a question. We don't just tell you to do it. We show you how it's done!
2. **Added motivation** for understanding the book's important ideas. Before you read each paragraph, ask yourself the question in the margin and then set a mini-goal of answering it as you read. If you can answer the question, you'll feel encouraged by the knowledge that you're grasping the ideas in your reading.
3. **A ready-to-use recipe** for reviewing each chapter. You can efficiently do a recap of the important ideas on each page by covering the text with a sheet of paper, asking yourself the marginal questions, and then checking your responses against the actual text.
4. **Navigational cues** that make it easier to go back and pinpoint particular points in a chapter. If you need to return to a chapter to look up a specific passage or confirm a particular fact, the marginal questions will provide additional signposts that point you to the information you are searching for.
5. **Practice!** Not all of the paragraphs have marginal questions. (See "It's Your Q" below.) That's no oversight; it's done for a reason. With questions above and below you, you'll have examples and context to help you fill in the blanks with your own marginal questions as you work at perfecting this vital part of the learning process.

It's Your Q

The Q System uses marginal questions to encourage active reading. In each chapter, most but not all of the paragraphs are accompanied by marginal questions. At the end of each chapter, the "It's Your Q" component encourages you to go back and test your ability to come up with your own marginal questions for the chapter paragraphs that don't already have them. Look for the "It's Your Q" boxes sprinkled throughout each chapter's margins and test your ability to apply the Q System yourself by pinpointing the paragraph's main idea and then writing in a question that will serve as a cue (Q) for that idea.

Say What?

Also at the end of every chapter, you'll find "Vocabulary in Action," a three-part section devoted to vocabulary building. "Say What?" features quotations from notable thinkers and leaders. In each quotation, one or more words are italicized and you are asked to select from one of three words that most nearly reflects the meaning of the italicized word. This is not a test; rather, the purpose is to expose you to words in a real-world context. You may select unfamiliar words for further study. Familiar words will provide reinforcement for your existing vocabulary.

Vocab-u-ladder

The second part of "Vocabulary in Action" provides an entertaining way of reinforcing a fundamental truth about words. Rather than operating in isolation, all words are connected. "Vocab-u-ladder" starts with a keyword from the chapter and challenges you to use a series of clues to create a chain of words that at first glance don't seem to be related.

Backstory

When you learn the histories of words they can acquire a new and deeper significance. That's the goal of "Backstory," the third and final part of "Vocabulary in Action." Backstory takes key words from each chapter and provides the fascinating and sometimes surprising histories of their origins. Once you learn the story behind the word "deadline," for example, it's unlikely that you'll ever view another due date in quite the same way again.

Why do we devote so much of a book about study skills to words? Because when it comes to gaining, retaining, and explaining, nothing is more important. A wide and precise vocabulary is really the main ingredient or quality that provides all of us with the endless ability for better thinking and judgment, not just in studying but in all phases of life—personally, socially, and professionally.

Skill Tags

There's another important element included in this book. In addition to the questions that run alongside most of the paragraphs, there are blue-and-white labels accompanying many of the chapter's subheadings. These are the Skill Tags, the basic building blocks from which the book has been constructed. They alert you to the skill or skills involved in that part of the chapter. For example, reviewing a lecture (see "Relive Your Lectures," p. 277) uses the core skills of *overviewing, summarizing,* and *questioning*; changing your time habits (see "Change Your Time Habits," p. 41) uses *self-direction* and *reframing*.

Although the book has 4 parts, 14 chapters, and well over 100 sections and subsections, all the lessons, strategies, tips, and techniques in *How to Study in College* rely on just 8 core skills: *focusing, overviewing, reframing, summarizing, planning, questioning, clustering,* and *self-direction*.

1. **Focusing.** Focusing is the ability to zero in on what's important to the exclusion of everything else. This can mean concentration, of course, but it also includes setting goals, separating main ideas from supporting details, and choosing valuable facts from among irrelevant ones.
2. **Overviewing.** Overviewing is a key part of preparation. It involves taking a broad, big-picture look at information to establish the key points and interrelationships that might not be as readily apparent from closer examination. It is the ability to identify the framework or skeleton of information. This creates "advance organizers" that make it easier to arrange and retain more specific information.
3. **Reframing.** While overviewing builds a framework, reframing changes that frame. It is the ability to process the same information from different angles, approaches, or contexts. This can mean adapting quickly to new and changing information or "translating" information from one form, such as words and numbers, into another, such as images. It is also that core skill behind reflection.
4. **Summarizing.** Summarizing means condensing information. Determining the main idea of a paragraph, page, article, or book involves the skill of summarizing. So does reciting, your most powerful defense against forgetting.
5. **Planning.** Planning uses a predetermined system or procedure to approach a particular problem, task, or period of time. Creating lists, budgets, and schedules requires planning, but so does any regular study skills strategy you may use, such as the Cornell System for note taking.

6. **Questioning**. Questioning epitomizes active learning. It doesn't necessarily involve skepticism—although it certainly can—as much as it entails engaging in a dialogue with information that would otherwise seem inert.

7. **Clustering.** Clustering is the ability to organize or connect things in meaningful patterns. This means sorting and categorizing both ideas and files, for example, but it also includes thinking of reading assignments in terms of phrases, paragraphs, pages, or chapters, depending on which pattern best suits your purposes at the time. It also involves connecting old familiar information to new, unknown information.

8. **Self-direction.** Self-direction is the ability to act on your own, to set your own agenda, and to be the ruler of your own fate. It includes setting goals, cultivating your own interests and motivation, as well as listening to your "inner voice."

See how you rate with each of these eight fundamental skills. Take the online assessment to determine which skills you excel in and which skills may require additional attention. (Go to www.cengagebrain.com.) With this newfound knowledge, read through the text as you normally would but pay attention to the Skill Tags that accompany the chapter subheadings.

Use your assessment to study more effectively. If, for example, you learn from the assessment that you're good at focusing or relating new information to old but have a difficult time reframing or planning, the knowledge of what your strengths are and where your weaknesses lie can mark the first step to your study success. Skill Tags act as signposts to the skills you need to focus on. They provide an opportunity to sharpen your skills and then use what you know to become a more successful student.

The Value of Reframing

After looking over your answers to the online Skill Tags assessment, you may be thinking, "It's true. I have a hard time finding my old notes, but that's the way I've always been. How can I possibly change?" Or you may believe, for example, that jumping right in and reading a new assignment without surveying it first works better for you because you can save some time and maintain your momentum. These ways of thinking probably feel comfortable, but they may have created blind spots in your view of studying. To get a sense of how blind spots can limit you, try to solve the problem shown in Figure 1. Odds are that a blind spot will prevent you from solving it. Yet once you see the solution, you'll probably say, "How easy! Why didn't I think of that tactic myself?"

The Nine-Dot Problem (Figure 1) not only demonstrates a point, but it is also an excellent learning device. For instance, although very few students have solved the puzzle, they nevertheless have learned the value of reframing. Reframing means remaining flexible enough to look at things from a different angle. If you can break out of the conventional-thinking mold and let your mind rove more freely, you're more likely to be open to more innovative and imaginative approaches to solving problems.

Figure 1

The Nine-Dot Problem
Connect these dots by drawing four straight lines without taking your pencil from the paper and without retracing any lines. The solution appears on page xxiii.

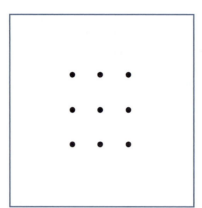

The Power of Planning

It might seem like a big contradiction to suggest that successful students need to be both flexible *and* systematic, but it's true. Being systematic is an important aspect of planning. Without a system, a problem such as the one in Figure 2 can make your head spin.

But if you plan your approach to a problem like this—that is, if you use a system—it can be relatively easy to solve. Drawing a simple grid provides a system for keeping track of the information you know about Anna, Bonita, Carlo, and Derek and the fruits they have brought. Planning can organize information in a way that makes it much clearer. Figure 4 provides the system.

Figure 2

The Lunchtime Problem
Match each student to the fruit that he or she brought for lunch.

Anna, Bonita, Carlo, and Derek each brought a piece of fruit for lunch. The fruits they brought were an apple, a banana, a grapefruit, and an orange.

Bonita's fruit isn't red.
Anna brought a citrus fruit. So did Derek.
Derek's fruit isn't orange.

Which student brought each fruit?

Take Advantage of This Book's Additional Resources

Many of this book's important skills and systems are enriched and brought to life on our website. You'll have an opportunity to boost your vocabulary skills with electronic flash cards, to test your knowledge and comprehension with additional questions, and to customize and print out your own copies of the time- and task-based schedules discussed in Chapter 2. You can also learn more academic strategies in online supplementary chapters on studying foreign languages, studying literature, studying science and mathematics, and using a computer for school. To visit the *How to Study in College* companion website, visit www.cengagebrain.com.

Take Advantage of Your School's Resources

College or university website.   It's a rare college these days that doesn't have a website. What sort of information do these sites contain? That's going to vary widely, depending on the college. Some have simply converted the text of their college catalog into an online form. Others provide elaborate and interactive repositories of information that keep you up-to-date on a variety of college news and often enable you to conduct some transactions that might otherwise need to be done by mail, over the phone, or in person. Regardless of the scope of your college's site, it is often a good place to start. Check the site's FAQs (Frequently Asked Questions) to see if your concern has already been addressed.

College catalog.   General information about your college's requirements, policies, programs, and services appears in the college catalog. Even if your college provides this information on its website, it still helps to have a hard copy of the catalog handy during the first weeks of classes to remind yourself of requirements and deadlines to be met.

Student handbook.   The student handbook provides information about your school's procedures, regulations, and code of conduct. It may also describe the school's requirements for good academic standing and graduation. For details or for specific department requirements, consult your department office or your academic adviser.

Admissions or registrar's office.   You can find answers to questions about grades, transcripts, and college requirements in the admissions or registrar's office. Admission to college and registration for courses begin with this office.

Figure 3
Answer to the Nine-Dot Problem
Begin at the top left corner and follow the arrows.

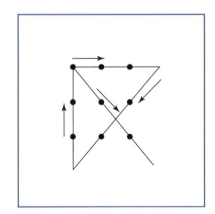

Figure 4
**Answer to the
Lunchtime Problem**
Using a simple grid
makes it much easier
to sort out the puzzle's
clues.

Draw a grid that lists the students in the rows and the fruits in the columns. Mark an x in a box each time you can conclude that a student could not have brought the fruit to lunch. Put a ✓ in a box when you can conclude which fruit a student has brought. (Superscripts next to each mark tell us the statement number that allowed us to draw each conclusion.)

	Apple	Banana	Grapefruit	Orange
Anna	x^2	x^2	x^3	$\checkmark^3$
Bonita	x^1	$\checkmark^2$	x^2	x^2
Carlo	$\checkmark^2$	x^2	x^2	x^2
Derek	x^2	x^2	$\checkmark^3$	x^3

1. Bonita's fruit isn't red.
2. Anna brought a citrus fruit. So did Derek.
3. Derek's fruit isn't orange.

- Statement 1 tells us only that Bonita did not bring the apple.
- Statement 2 tells us that Bonita and Carlo could not have brought either the grapefruit or the orange. Because we already know that she didn't bring the apple, that leaves the banana for Bonita and the apple for Carlo.
- Statement 3 solves the mystery of whether Anna or Derek brought the orange. Because we know that Derek's fruit *isn't* orange, that means he brought the grapefruit and Anna brought the orange.

Office of financial affairs.   For answers to questions about scholarships, loans, and grants, contact the financial affairs office. You will come here to pay fees and fines and to pick up your checks if you are in a work-study grant or program. If you want a part-time job on campus for which you must qualify on the basis of your financial status, you will fill out application forms in this office.

Career development and placement office.   If you want help choosing a major or setting a career goal, contact the career development and placement office. People in this office can administer various interest, personality, and skills assessment tests to help you determine the kind of work for which you are best suited. They can help you find jobs on and off campus. Some career development centers sponsor on-campus recruitment, inviting businesses to interview prospective graduates and aiding them in submitting applications and résumés. After graduation, you can file a résumé in the placement office if you want your school's help with landing a job.

Academic advising office or counseling department.   Academic and guidance counselors can help you with everything from choosing the right course to solving personal problems that prevent you from meeting your academic goals. The academic office or counseling department may be part of the admissions office, or it may be a separate department. In many colleges, students are assigned to an adviser or a counselor who follows their progress throughout their college careers.

Student health center.   If you become ill, you can go to a doctor at the health center. The health center may have a pharmacy and may provide a limited amount of hospital care. Some mental health services may be available through this center, through the office of a school psychologist or psychiatrist, or through a peer-counseling group. The health center may also refer students to an agency outside the college.

Student government association.   Working with the dean of students, the student government association sponsors student activities such as intramural events, dances, special-interest organizations and clubs, and other social and academic events. (Joining a club or taking part in campus events is a good way to meet other students who share your interests.) In addition, your student government may publish a weekly bulletin or a student handbook that summarizes college requirements and resources.

Student publications.   The college newspaper or literary magazine offers contributors unique opportunities for self-expression and provides readers with information and entertainment. Serving on the editorial staff of one of these publications may also fulfill some journalism or English requirements.

Learning lab or skills center.   You may turn to the learning lab or skills center for help in improving your study, reading, writing, math, or computer skills. Whether you are required to spend time in a lab because of your performance on a college skills assessment test or you choose to go on your own, take full advantage of the opportunity to gain the skills you need.

Special student services.   Veterans, students with physical or learning disabilities, minority students, international students, and students who are economically disadvantaged may need the special assistance of a trained support group to meet their academic goals. If you think you qualify for these services, ask your counselor or adviser about them. Your college may also offer services such as off-campus residence listings.

Athletics office.   A listing of the college's athletic programs and events is available in the athletics office. This is the office to visit if you are interested in participating in sports.

Resident assistant.   For on-campus students, resident assistants (RAs) can be a great source of information about campus services. Although RAs are not professional counselors, they have recently been through many of the experiences you're undergoing and can probably direct you to the campus office best suited to your needs.

Final Words

Our ultimate goal in this book is to provide you with tools, skills, and systems that will lead to self-sufficiency. Or, as Ralph Waldo Emerson once expressed it: "The best service one person can render another person is to help him help himself."

Building a Foundation

Your success as a student who can effectively gain, retain, and explain information must rest on a strong foundation of skills that will serve you well through college and beyond. Like the basic courses that act as springboards for advance study, learning to focus your efforts, get organized, strengthen your resiliency, and build your vocabulary should provide a sturdy base on which you can build your academic success. This part will help you to:

1 **Concentrate on Reaching Your Goal**

2 **Use Your Time and Space Effectively**

3 **Learn How to Handle Stress**

4 **Extend Your Word Frontier**

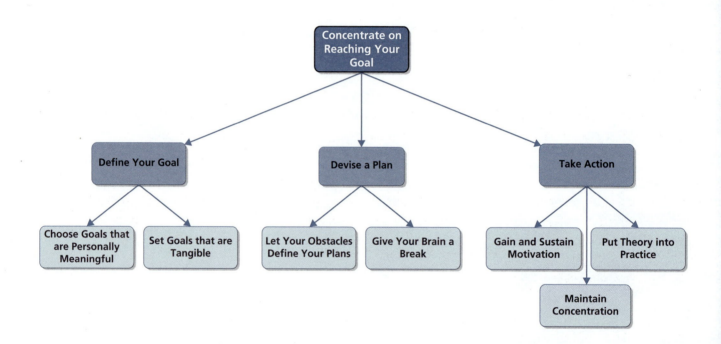

Concentrate on Reaching Your Goal

There's something deep inside each of us that yearns for fulfillment. We were meant for something to which our nature inclines. But what? No one really knows. So, you yourself must dig. Dig—but for what? Start by digging for happiness. Ask "What kind of work would I be happiest in? Doesn't it make sense that every day's work should be a joy?" In this chapter, you can begin to focus your life as you read how to

- **Define Your Goal**
- **Devise a Plan**
- **Take Action**

In this chapter

▶ More than 50 years old, it's still considered by many to be the gold standard for goal-setting. (p. 4)

▶ How bad news could spell good news for reaching your goals. (p. 11)

▶ A quick way to lower your IQ by as many as 15 points. (p. 28)

So much of college hinges on a single word: focus. Your success or failure will often depend on your ability to simply stay on track, use the power and precision of concentrated action to zero in on your aspirations, and chart an unwavering course toward your destination. But who sets that track and where is it going? That's for you to decide. To effectively concentrate on reaching your goal—whatever it may be—you need to sharpen your focus by defining that goal, devising a plan, and, ultimately, taking action.

Define Your Goal

What is the purpose of a goal?

Where are you headed? That's the question that your goal is designed to answer. Imagine throwing ingredients into a mixing bowl without any idea of what you are making. Think of running around on the basketball court with no knowledge of the object of the game. The best cooks and the best basketball players know what they are doing and why they are doing it. They have a clear idea of where they are headed. In short, they have a goal in mind.

What kinds of things can be considered goals?

Although winning a basketball game and baking a cake can both be seen as goals, it can be easier to think of your goal as a kind of destination. A lot of our common expressions use this idea. "Making it to the top," "climbing the corporate ladder," and even "reaching for the stars" portray the goal as a place in the distance that you are trying to reach. Of course, some goals really *are* destinations. When American pioneers declared that their goal was "Pike's Peak or Bust" and tacked signs to their wagons that said so, they were talking about an actual destination hundreds of miles to the west and more than 14,000 feet above sea level. When John F. Kennedy made the moon the country's goal in 1961, he was aiming for a destination that was about 238,900 miles out into space. Although Pike's Peak has long since been reached and climbed, climbing a mountain remains a vivid metaphor for reaching one's goal, and although President Kennedy's speech was delivered more than half a century ago, to this day it remains one of the best examples of a clearly defined goal that was achieved through planning and action.

How do you define your own goal?

Defining your own goal isn't easy. Nor should the process be treated casually. The goal you choose should be personally meaningful enough to inspire you and yet tangible enough that you can tell with certainty when you've achieved it.

Choose Goals That Are Personally Meaningful

SELF-DIRECTION — FOCUSING

What are the risks of having no goal?

Goals bring meaning to life; otherwise, life can be aimless. Viktor Frankl's research revealed these stark data:

When 60 students were asked why they had attempted suicide, 85 percent said the reason had been that "life was meaningless."[1]

How do goals relate to purpose?

Goals and purpose breathe meaning into life. Goals and purpose form the psychological underpinnings of our individual lives. There's power in purpose, as shown in this excerpt:

> We cannot have deep and enduring satisfaction unless we have self-worth. We cannot have self-worth unless our lives are an earnest attempt to express the finest and most enduring qualities that we are aware of. Purpose is an important condition for an enduring satisfaction with life.[2]

You can't simply pull a goal off the shelf like a can of peas. It should be set by you and should reflect your personality and your passions.

Set Your Own Goals

What was Thoreau's advice?

The nineteenth-century American writer, philosopher, and naturalist Henry David Thoreau famously wrote:

> If a man does not keep pace with his companions, perhaps it is because he hears a different drummer. Let him step to the music which he hears, however measured or far away.[3]

How can you bring meaning into your life?

This doesn't mean, as some have suggested, that you need to be an outcast or iconoclast or that you have to live alone in the woods of Walden Pond, as Thoreau once did. Many people who are intricately woven into the fabric of society still manage to adhere to ideals that they have sharpened and defined on their own. To bring meaning into your life, you must decide on your own goal. Avoid the trap of surrendering to the expectations of others instead of pursuing a goal that is personally meaningful.

What role should friends and family play in your goals?

This doesn't mean that you shouldn't discuss your goals with friends and family. It is helpful to ponder their thoughts and advice. But process these through your own brain cells and heart cells, and then make a decision, which must be your very own. Above all, set your own pace instead of marching along with the crowd.

Resist the Tug of the Crowd

What happens when people think as a crowd instead of individually?

When you become part of the crowd, your individual thinking is replaced by crowd psychology. Here's how Gustave Le Bon, a French social scientist, described crowd psychology:

---

[1] Viktor Frankl, an Austrian psychiatrist and psychotherapist, created the theory of Logotherapy, which states that a person's primary motivation is his or her search for meaning in life.
[2] Richard J. Leider, *The Power of Purpose* (San Francisco: Berrett-Koehler Publishers, 1997), p. 35.
[3] Henry David Thoreau, *Walden and Resistance to Civil Government*, 2nd ed. (New York: W. W. Norton, 1992), p. 217.

The most striking peculiarity presented by a psychological crowd is the following: Whoever be the individuals that compose it, however like or unlike be their mode of life, their occupations, their character, or their intelligence, the fact that they have been transformed into a crowd puts them in possession of a sort of collective mind which makes them feel, think, and act in a manner quite different from that in which each individual of them would feel, think, and act were he in a state of isolation.[4]

What did Gould observe about the psychology of a crowd?

Le Bon's observations about crowds were adopted and furthered by Edson Gould, one of the most respected names on Wall Street, who used this easily visualized example to illustrate how the individual is almost powerless to resist the powerful magnetism of the crowd:

You're *alone* in an empty movie theater and hear the cry of "fire." You look around, see no flames, smell no smoke, you *calmly walk* to the nearest exit. But, repeat the same cry of "fire" (again without flames visible or the smell of smoke) in a *crowded* theater and once the *crowd* starts *running* for an exit, you'll find *yourself running*, too. That's crowd psychology.[5]

What should you guard against in crowd psychology?

Don't let crowd psychology rob you of your independence or your freedom to think and decide individually. In sum, preserve yourself as a sovereign individual so that, for better or for worse, you are the ruler of your career and destiny.

Find Goals That Motivate You

Although choosing your own goal is important, any goal can be difficult to achieve if you aren't sufficiently motivated.

What is the difference between performance goals and learning goals?

Psychologists divide our goals into two basic types: performance goals and learning goals. With performance goals, the reward is *extrinsic*. It's the grade you get, the money you make, or the praise you receive. With learning goals, the reward is *intrinsic*. It's the learning itself, the quenching of your curiosity or the perfecting of certain skills and above all the satisfaction you derive. Students with performance goals seek to pass the test. Students with learning goals want to master the material.

Which type of goal is the better motivator?

Although it might seem that performance goals are the best kind of goals to have in college—after all, the diploma and any honors you may receive are based on your grades—scientific research tells a surprisingly different story. Students who set performance goals may be driven less by the prospect of success and more by an effort to avoid failure. They are often risk averse, don't mind cutting corners, and are apt to study just enough to pass the test and no more. Furthermore, they are more likely to struggle with problems such as boredom or procrastination. The goal becomes a technicality instead of an inspiration. In contrast, students who establish learning goals are

[4]Quoted in Dan Sullivan, *The Chartist* (December 30, 1997), p. 4.
[5]Quoted in Edson Gould, *Findings and Forecasts* (New York: Anametrics, 1974).

highly motivated to succeed. They usually study longer because they actually enjoy it, view tasks as challenges, don't typically fear failure, and consider mistakes as an opportunity to learn.

How has money affected the way we define goals?

Everyone, it seems, is out to make money. Look at the crowds thronging the racetracks, the casinos, the state lotteries, and even the frequently bubbling stock market. Apparently this "money idea" has steadily seeped into the career goals of students. According to a poll conducted by consulting firm KPMG (Klynveld, Peat, Marwick, Goerdeler), New York, three out of four college students expect to become millionaires.[6] And yet numerous studies show that beyond a certain level, money may actually diminish happiness instead of increasing it.[7]

What advice does John Rau give his students?

The siren song of money may be difficult to ignore, but is it really the key to happiness or the true mark of success? John Rau, who has been the CEO of three corporations, dean of Indiana University's business school, and no stranger to success himself, offers a straight-shooting sanity check for students who are thinking of sacrificing quality in the pursuit of quantity. "Unless you're doing the stuff you like," he cautions, "you can burn out."[8]

What does Dr. Williams conclude about defining your goals?

In line with Rau's succinct pronouncement, Dr. David G. Williams pulls no punches. Few people know more about "burnout" than medical doctors. After years of treating people who were experiencing burnout, Dr. Williams wrote this compelling article on choosing a career that will enhance the possibilities of living a healthier life.

What Do You Want to Be When You Grow Up?

If you're like me, the last time someone asked you this question was quite some time ago. Most of us guys probably responded with something like a fireman, forest ranger, cop, race car driver or even the President. I'm not being sexist (I'm not even sure there was such a word when someone last asked me the question), but if you're female you probably answered the above question with occupations like a model, flight attendant, school teacher or movie star. You chose these answers because at the time you thought these endeavors would be enjoyable. You could visualize being happy. Maybe a more appropriate question than "What do you want to be when you grow up?" would have been "What would make you happy?" And since the answer to this question changes throughout your life, it's a question we really need to ask ourselves more often.

When was the last time you actually got away by yourself and seriously thought about what you needed to be happy? Maybe it's time to do so.

---

[6]Pamela Sebastian, *The Wall Street Journal* (March 25, 1999), p. A1.
[7]Sonja Lyubomirsky, "Can Money Buy Happiness? New Research Reveals That Reminders of Wealth Impair Our Capacity to Savor Life's Little Pleasures," *Scientific American* (August 10, 2010), http://www.scientificamerican.com/article.cfm?id=can-money-buy-happiness
[8]Quoted in Hal Lancaster, "Managing Your Career," *The Wall Street Journal* (May 6, 1997), p. B1.

As hectic as life has become, we see happiness as a luxury. Surveys have shown that most people really don't believe it's possible to be happy the majority of the time. They think that true happiness is an unobtainable goal. It's an unpredictable, fleeting sensation over which one has little control. But accepting this idea, that you have no or little control over your own happiness, can have serious health consequences. Happiness is just as important, if not more so, to good health as proper nutrition and adequate exercise. Happiness is a powerful healing force. On the opposite side of the coin we have stress. There seems to be an inverse relationship between stress and happiness. In other words, less happiness leads to more stress. And stress can be an extremely powerful destructive force. Stress is one of the best examples of the power the mind can have over the body.

In animal studies, French researchers at the University of Bordeaux have recently shown that depression and anxiety in adults can be a direct result of placing the mother under stress prior to birth. Stress causes the adrenal glands to produce more of the "stress hormone," corticosterone. Corticosterone easily passes from the mother to the fetus through the placenta. Consistently high levels of corticosterone desensitize brain receptors, altering the feedback system and making it more difficult to shut down the excess corticosterone production. After birth these receptors in the brain remain desensitized, which can lead to suppression of the immune system, depression and anxiety later in life. *(J Neurosci 96;15[1 Pt1]:110-6.)*

In an amazing study recently performed at Columbia University, New York, researchers found that young girls who suffer from undue stress grow up to be 5 cm. (2 in.) shorter than their happier contemporaries. Stress stunts their growth by depressing the levels of growth hormone in the body.

Volumes have been written on the detrimental effects of stress. And while I won't bore you with all the detailed research here, stress has been linked to everything from asthma and cardiovascular disease to cancer and practically every disease in between. The point to be made here is that happiness replaces and counteracts stress. Probably more than any other single factor, discovering and acting on what makes you happy can improve both the quality and length of your life.

Over the next few hours, days and weeks, I urge you to invest some time in seriously deciding what you want out of life. What would make you happy? I am not talking about what would make you happy for a moment or a day, but instead, what you want and need to be happy for the long term. I can assure you it will be one of the most productive things you will ever do.

Discovering what it would take for you to be happy is, without a doubt, one of the most powerful tools you'll ever possess. It defines your basis for living. It gives you a purpose and provides the answers to life's day-to-day problems. It almost miraculously provides direction at each of life's crossroads. It crystallizes and clarifies your day-to-day goals and activities. It allows you to focus your talents and energies toward achieving the rewards that are most important to you.

If you can't honestly verbalize what you *need* to make you happy, you're going to wander aimlessly throughout life. The clock keeps ticking whether you decide to answer "what would make me happy" or not. Instead of participating and reveling in life, you end up simply reacting to situation after situation. You unquestionably embrace the idea that your own happiness is out of your control. You then begin to believe that it will suddenly appear just as soon as someone or something in your life changes. Unfortunately, that's like playing the state lottery. Your chances of getting hit by lightning are far better than finding real happiness and meaning in your life.

Most of us (I'm as guilty as anyone, if not more so) have a tendency to take life much too seriously. When we were younger it was easier to be less serious. It reminds me of a Bob Dylan song, in which he says, "If you ain't got nothing, you ain't got nothing to lose." The older and more responsible we become, the more we feel we have to lose. We begin to perceive changes in our lives as risks rather than opportunities. As such, we try to avoid change. But in reality, change is not something over which we have any control.

I'm sure you've heard the saying that there are only two things you can count on: death and taxes. Well, there are actually a couple more. One is that your surroundings will change. Technology changes. Weather changes. People change. Everything changes. Always has. Always will. Accept it. Accept the fact that people and situations are *always* going to be changing throughout your life. Fighting change is like swimming against the current in a river. You're so busy trying to keep your head above water that you never get a chance to see or enjoy what's on the bank. The quicker you accept the fact that everything will change, the quicker you can get out of the water. You can sit on the bank, relax for a moment and evaluate your surroundings. In a life that's always too short, you can then decide how best to spend your remaining time. This brings up the other thing you can always count on—the God-given, human ability to make choices.

Through changes in your thinking, your actions and your lifestyle, you can choose to live your life in a state of unhappiness or in a state of happiness. It's totally up to you.

Although it was several decades ago, I remember sitting at my desk in Mrs. Benger's first-grade class back in Friona, Texas. Above the chalkboard there were two large handwritten signs. One read, "Act the way you want to be and soon you'll be the way you act." It's probably one of the more lasting lessons I've learned in life thus far. (The other sign said, "One who thinketh by the inch and talketh by the yard should be kicketh by the foot." [I'm still working on that one.])

Before you can "act the way you want to be," and before you can expect to find happiness, you must answer that one simple question. "What would make me happy?" It's a difficult question, probably the most difficult you'll ever have to answer. Getting the answer will require some time and serious thinking. Strangely, there's no right or wrong answer. And even stranger is the fact that only you know the answer. Don't think of this as some kind of test. Nobody is going to give you a grade or set any time limits. The only way you can really fail is aimlessly wandering through life and simply not answering the question at all.

So "What do you want to be when you grow up?" "What would make *you* happy?"

Dr. David G. Williams, "What Do You Want to Be When You Grow Up?," *Alternatives for the Health Conscious Individual* 6, no. 15 (September 1996), pp. 119–120. Copyright © 1996, Mountain Home Publishing. Reproduced with permission of Healthy Directions.

Set Goals That Are Tangible

What do you need to make your goal tangible?

Goals you choose yourself should motivate and inspire you to reach the fulfillment that all of us seek in some form or fashion. But inspiration is just the beginning. The goal you set should also be tangible. It must be firmly rooted in reality, something you can readily visualize and clearly define, so that when you see it in the distance you will recognize it and when you get there you will know it.

Visualize Your Goal

In what way does a goal go beyond a statement?

A goal is much more than just a simple statement. Actually, it's a vivid dream that has been mentally acted and reenacted. What lawyer hasn't first imagined presenting a closing argument to judge and jury? What business executive hasn't imagined outlining an exciting plan to staff members seated around the board of directors' table?

What is Peale's explanation of imaging?

Although *imagined* is generally used to denote imagination, in his landmark book *Positive Imaging*, Norman Vincent Peale used the word *imaging* to convey a much deeper concept:

> Imaging consists of vividly picturing, in your conscious mind, a desired goal or objective, and holding that image until it sinks into your unconscious mind, where it releases great, untapped energies.[9]

How does imaging your goal affect it?

So, if we think deeply enough and image vividly enough about what we want to do with our lives, our whole being can be energized. Peale, who is one of the most widely read inspirational writers of all time, goes on to say:

> There is a powerful and mysterious force in human nature that is capable of bringing about dramatic improvement in our lives. It is a kind of mental engineering. ... In imaging, one does not merely think about a hoped-for goal; one "sees" or visualizes it with tremendous intensity. Imaging is a kind of laser beam of the imagination, a shaft of mental energy in which the desired goal or outcome is pictured so vividly by the conscious mind that the unconscious mind accepts it and is activated by it. This releases powerful internal forces that can bring about astonishing changes in the life of the person who is doing the imaging.[10]

What does recent scientific research say about Peale's pronouncements?

Although Peale was an author and motivational speaker, not a scientist, recent scientific research largely supports his contentions about the power of imaging and its

[9]Norman Vincent Peale, *Positive Imaging*. Copyright © 1982. Published by Revell, a division of Baker Publishing Group. Used with permission. http://www.bakerpublishinggroup.com
[10]Ibid.

benefit in setting and achieving goals. In numerous studies, psychologists have found that a particular type of imaging known as *mental contrasting* significantly improves your chances of achieving your goals.[11]

What is mental contrasting?

Mental contrasting uses two types of imaging known as *indulging* and *dwelling* one after the other in order to reflect on your goal.[12] Indulging is similar to what Peale suggests. It involves vividly imaging a positive future where you are achieving your goal. Dwelling is quite different. It involves imaging the present in a largely negative light.

How does mental contrasting work?

Few of us have trouble vividly imaging a positive future, but a negative present? Although the prospect may sound depressing, the outcome is actually the opposite. If you think of your goal as a destination, it's obviously important to have a clear idea of where you're headed, whether that means getting into medical school, starting your own business, running a marathon, or losing weight. But it's equally important to know where you're starting from. Mental contrasting provides a "reality check." As Edwin Locke and Gary Latham, pioneers in the study of goal-setting, explain, "...the setting of goals is first and foremost a discrepancy-creating process. It implies discontent with one's present condition and the desire to attain an object or outcome."[13] If your goal is running a marathon, for example, but right now you can barely walk around the block without feeling winded, that is important to know. What mental contrasting does is to bring the obstacles standing between you and your goal into sharper relief. Once you recognize these obstacles—you have to pass organic chemistry, you need to learn how to write a business plan, you have to increase your ability to run long distances, or you need to resist a second helping at dessert time—you suddenly have a basis for devising a concrete plan for achieving your goal! Brain measuring technology found heightened brain activity among those subjects who use mental contrasting, while the brain activity of those who simply indulged showed no more activity than resting.[14] Imagining yourself as a doctor or cutting the ribbon outside your new store or crossing the finish line at the Boston Marathon or fitting into a fashionable pair of slacks may make you feel good—in fact it's almost guaranteed to make you feel good—but by itself it's not going to do much to help you reach your goal. What's worse, it may even prevent you from reaching it!

How can indulging without dwelling prevent you from reaching your goal?

Although our types of goals can be dramatically different, all of us pursue goals to receive some sort of reward—everything from personal satisfaction to the respect of our peers to good grades or mountains of money. When you imagine achieving your goal, it usually

---

[11]P. M. Gollwitzer and G. Oettingen, "Planning Promotes Goal Striving." In K. D. Vohs and R. F. Baumeister (Eds.), *Handbook of Self-Regulation: Research, Theory, and Applications*, 2nd ed. (New York: Guilford, 2011).

[12]Ibid.

[13]E. Locke and G. Latham, "*New Directions in Goal-Setting Theory,*" Current Directions in Psychological Science 15, no. 5 (2006): pp. 265–268.

[14]Gollwitzer and Oettingen, "Planning Promotes Goal Striving," p. 179.

makes you feel good. It's a reward in and of itself. And therein lies the problem. Studies have shown that if you imagine reaching your destination without thinking about where you're starting from, you may lose the incentive to even set off on the journey at all.

Define Your Goal Clearly

What are the elements of clearly defined goals?

The pioneers' pursuit of Pike's Peak and the U.S. determination to reach the moon in less than a decade both provide inspiring examples of clearly defined goals. As the wagons neared Pike's Peak, the settlers could see the unmistakable outline of the mountain looming ahead of them. As NASA engineers and astronauts worked tirelessly on their ambitious space program, they could step outside on almost any night and gaze up in the sky at their destination. Neither group had any illusions about the difficulty of reaching their goals, but at the same time they had the confidence and determination to keep going until they got there. Small or large, academic or interplanetary, the most successful goals are specific, challenging, and achievable (Figure 1.1).

How do you know if your goal is specific enough?

A goal should be specific enough that you can tell when you've reached it, or if you haven't yet reached it, how close you are to getting there. In general, that will include something you can measure as well as some sort of time limit. If, for example, you simply set yourself a goal of "Running a lot," how will you know when you've reached your goal? On the other hand, if you set a goal of running 30 miles in a week, each day you'll be able to see how much you've accomplished and how much farther you need to go. Every mile you add to your weekly total should sustain your motivation as you draw closer and closer to your goal. This sort of approach isn't limited to running, of course. If you set yourself a goal of "Studying economics," you are settling for a goal as indistinct and unrewarding as "Running a lot." But if you resolve to jot down or highlight the main ideas from Chapter 5 of your economics textbook before 9 P.M., you will have established a very clear goal. Each main idea that you find in your chapter will move you closer. And when the clock strikes 9, you will know without a doubt whether you've reached your goal or not.

Rewards provide the motivation for every goal. Sometimes that reward is a good grade or some other form of recognition from your instructor or peers. In the working world, it may be money, praise, a promotion, or a combination of all three. These are known as extrinsic motivations because they come from outside of you. But motivations can be intrinsic as well. They can come from inside. In fact, psychologists have found that the most powerful motivators are intrinsic ones, such as the satisfaction that comes from a job well done. For many students, the sense of accomplishment they get from perfecting their skills, learning something new, or achieving a challenging goal provides the primary reward. In general, the harder the goal, the greater the reward. Raising the stakes, challenging yourself to rise to the occasion, will often lead to increased effort, focus, and commitment. On the other hand, if a goal isn't challenging enough, the reward may not be adequate and you may not be sufficiently motivated to pursue it.

IT'S YOUR Q

Figure 1.1
The Sky's the Limit. President Kennedy's ambitious lunar goal remains a model for goal-setting to this day.

A FAMOUS GOAL, PLAN, AND ACTION

The <u>G</u>oal

First, I believe that this nation should commit itself to achieving the goal, before this decade is out, of landing a man on the moon and returning him safely to earth.

President John F. Kennedy
before a joint session of Congress
May 25, 1961

The <u>P</u>lan

The Mercury Program:	Each rocket would send a single astronaut into space.
The Gemini Program:	Each rocket would send two men into space to orbit the earth, to practice docking with other spacecraft, and to test human beings' ability to withstand prolonged periods in space.
The Apollo Program:	Each rocket would send three men into space in order to leave the earth's orbit, to orbit the moon, and eventually to land on the moon and explore it.

The <u>A</u>ction

The United States sent twenty manned flights into space between May 1961 and June 1969. In July 1969, eight years and two months after President Kennedy set the country's original goal, astronauts Neil Armstrong and Edwin "Buzz" Aldrin set foot on the moon and returned safely to earth.

Why do goals need to be achievable?

Goals can be specific and challenging but they also need to be achievable. An unrealistically difficult goal can actually backfire, leading to anxiety and discouragement instead of increased motivation. Students who find themselves cramming for a test are all too familiar with this situation as they attempt to do a semester's worth of work in just a day or two. The same applies to couch potatoes who set themselves a first-week goal of running 10 miles a day. Setting unachievable goals is usually a recipe for disaster and can often be worse than having no goal at all.

How can you tell if your goals are achievable?

The mental contrasting you used to envision your goal and its obstacles is also an excellent tool for determining whether that goal is achievable at all. The clearer those obstacles are, the better your sense will be of exactly what you need to do in order to overcome them. If your goal requires money you don't have, you may need to consider getting a part-time job or applying for a scholarship. If it means you need to pass a subject where you've traditionally had troubles, you may need to visit the campus tutoring center in search of assistance. In most cases, clearly identifying these impediments and arriving at strategies for overcoming them will be both liberating and motivating. On the other hand, if after mental contrasting you determine that your obstacles are not simply challenging but truly insurmountable, your goal is probably unachievable and you should give some thought to defining a more realistic goal. That conclusion may be discouraging in the short run, but in the long run it will save you considerable heartache and time.

What does Peale say about defining clear goals?

Once again, motivational author Norman Vincent Peale demonstrates an uncanny ability to anticipate the scientific evidence of goal-setting experts, offering advice that sounds remarkably like what psychologists have since concluded about the most effective goals:

> I suggest that you write down what you want to do with your life. Until you write a goal, it is only a wish; written, it becomes a focused objective. Put it down on paper. When it is on paper, boil it down to a single sentence: what you want to do, exactly when you intend to start (which should be right now), exactly when you plan to achieve your goal. Nothing fuzzy or hazy. Everything sharp and clear and definite. No reservations or qualifications. Just one strong, simple, declarative sentence.... I want you to make half a dozen copies of that sentence and put them where you'll see them at least three times a day. I want that pledge to sink down through all the levels of your conscious mind and deep into your unconscious mind, because that is where it will unlock the energies that you will need to achieve your goal.
>
> If setting worthy goals is the first step on the road to success, the second is the belief—the conviction that you are capable of achieving those goals. There has to be in your mind the unshakable image of yourself *succeeding* at the goal you have set yourself. The more vivid this image is, the most obtainable the goal becomes.
>
> Great athletes have always known this. The high jumper "sees" himself skimming over the bar; the place-kicker in football keeps his head down as he kicks, but in his mind's eye he holds the mental picture of what he wants to happen in the next few seconds.... The more intensely he images this before it happens, the higher his confidence in himself and the better his chances of making it happen.[15]

Devise a Plan

How does your plan relate to your goal?

If you think of your goal as your destination, then a plan can be seen as the route that will take you there. Coming up with a plan is like charting a course. You need to know where you are starting, where you are heading, and where you plan to stop along the way. Most goals will have several possible plans. The challenge comes in choosing the best one.

[15]From Norman Vincent Peale, *Positive Imaging*. Copyright © 1982. Published by Revell, a division of Baker Publishing Group. Used with permission. http://www.bakerpublishinggroup.com

How can you choose the most efficient plan?

The most efficient plan is the most economical. It's a balancing act between what you need and want and what you are able to pay. Paying, as far as a plan is concerned, doesn't always mean money. It can also mean time and energy. For example, a one-week plan for reviewing your notes is "too expensive" if the test is only two days away. In the same way, a plan that forces you to stay up all night will often cost too much because what you gain in knowledge you will lose in sleep. The most efficient plan will meet your goal without being too costly.

What sort of plans are the best?

The best plans aren't always obvious from the outset. For example, many students approach an exam by answering questions as soon as they receive the test. Given the time limit, that plan may seem to make sense, even though it's actually a bad idea. The most efficient strategy is to read the exam directions, look over all the questions, and even come up with a time plan before answering a single question. The first plan is fast but reckless, whereas the second is steady and dependable. Now you have a more structured and efficient approach to test taking. (For more on this plan, see Chapter 12.) When you make an effort to devise a systematic plan, you will usually gain more benefits than you would with a hastily drawn up strategy.

How does flexible thinking affect your plan?

Devising the best plan can require flexible thinking. For example, when you look at a map, you may conclude—as commercial airline navigators once did—that the best way to get from Amsterdam to Tokyo is to head in an easterly direction along what is known as the Mediterranean route. But look at a globe instead of a map, and your perspective may change. Rather than heading east on the Mediterranean route, commercial planes going from Amsterdam to Tokyo now fly north! That's right. They take what is known as the "polar route," flying over the North Pole to Alaska, and then west to Tokyo—for a savings of roughly 1,500 miles! The lesson is this: After you've decided on a goal, work vigorously to accomplish it, but keep looking for ways of achieving the goal more efficiently, perhaps from a different angle. This approach is sometimes known as *reframing*.

What are the best plans for your own personal goal?

Good plans may not work for every goal, and plans that work for most people may not always work for you. That's why the best way to come up with a plan for success is to balance wise advice with your own experience. This book is full of plans for success and tricks of the trade. All of them have been proven to work, and most should work for you. Use trial and error to determine which plans work best for you, and be prepared to adapt some plans to better fit your needs. Even the best plans can fail if they are used too rigidly. Allow a little breathing room. If things go wrong, don't give up. Adjust and keep on going (Figure 1.2).

Let Your Obstacles Define Your Plans

SELF-DIRECTION — PLANNING

How do you implement your own personal plans?

If you've already used mental contrasting to establish your goal, you've taken the first important step in defining your plan. One of the benefits of mental contrasting, in addition to giving you a realistic sense of the obstacles that stand between you and your goal, is that it also provides a natural way to begin creating plans for reaching that goal.

Figure 1.2
A New Way to View G.P.A.

THE <u>GPA</u> OF SUCCESS

<u>G</u>OAL—should reflect your wants and needs. Make it large and ambitious without being vague. Write it down!

<u>P</u>LAN—lists the route you plan to take in order to reach your goal. It should be efficient and specific. Good advice and personal experience combine to create the most effective plans.

<u>A</u>CTION—brings your goal and your plan to life. Requires confidence, self-discipline, and a power over procrastination.

Each obstacle you define requires a plan for overcoming it. If, for example, you set a goal of getting accepted into medical school in four years, you might encounter the following obstacles:

- I don't have the money to afford the cost of medical school.
- Pre-meds are required to take organic chemistry, and I'm terrible at chemistry.

Each of these obstacles should provide a logical starting point for devising a plan. For example, in the first instance, you might devise a plan to investigate possible scholarships or grants to make up for the money you don't have for medical school. Or you might make plans for finding a part-time job. If you find that a particular course is standing between you and your goal, a trip to the tutoring center might be part of a winning plan.

Give Your Brain a Break

SELF-DIRECTION — PLANNING

Where in the brain does most of our rational thinking occur?

Most of the "college-type thinking" you do takes place in a surprisingly small part of your brain. The activities that we typically associate with rational thought—memorizing, recalling, understanding, deciding, and concentrating—are all handled by the prefrontal cortex (PFC). And yet there isn't a lot of room in there. According to David Rock, author of *Your Brain at Work*, if you liken the capacity of your PFC to a cubic foot of space, then the capacity of the rest of your brain would be about the size of the Milky Way.[16]

How do the limitations of the prefrontal cortex affect our thinking?

This tight squeeze sharply limits the pieces of information you can handle at once. When things get too crowded in there, something automatically gets squeezed out, a fact that not only creates problems for your memory (see Chapter 9) but makes sticking

[16]David Rock, "Your Brain at Work," *Google Tech Talk* (November 12, 2009), http://www.youtube.com/watch?v=XeJSXfXep4M (accessed May 25, 2012).

to your goals even more challenging. But space constraints aren't the only drawback of your PFC. It's also limited when it comes to energy. There's ample scientific evidence that willpower—psychologists call it self-regulation—is the cognitive equivalent of a gas-guzzler, burning up your PFC's fuel—glucose—at an alarming rate. When the tank runs dry, your willpower sputters and stalls. As Florida State University cognitive psychologist Dr. Roy Baumeister explains, "We have a limited bucket of resources for activities like decision making and impulse control and when we use these up, we don't have as much for the next activity."[17]

How can you reach your goal without relying on the prefrontal cortex?

The bottom line is this: if you want to be sure of sticking to your goal, you can't count on willpower alone. In fact, your long-term plans for reaching your goal are likely to be the first casualty of an overloaded brain. Do your goals a favor and give your brain a break by automating or outsourcing your plans.

Automate Your Plans

How can you automate your plans?

You can automate your plans by transforming them into habits. Unlike ordinary goals, such as "I will not order an ice cream sundae!" habits don't rely on willpower or on any of the other traditional conscious reasoning functions that reside in the PFC. In fact, one reason why bad habits can be so hard to break is because they are largely automatic. Habits are stored routines for everything from tying your shoes to biting your nails. Instead of clogging up the crowded PFC, they live in a region of the brain called the *basal ganglia*, where they have plenty of room to spread out.[18]

How do habits work?

Habits are typically activated by some sort of cue. For example, putting on your shoes may activate the habit of tying them, while feeling nervous or bored may serve as the cue that triggers the habit of biting your nails. In either case, although you may be vaguely aware of what you're doing, you aren't consciously focused on it. That's why you can tie your shoes while thinking about something else or even while carrying on a conversation. The same applies to biting your nails.

IT'S YOUR Q

You can turn your goals into habits by duplicating the process that habits follow. Take a subgoal, such as "I will study my vocabulary cards," and associate it with a specific cue, such as waiting in line. Using what psychologists call an *implementation intention*, you create an "if-then plan," such as "If I find myself waiting in line, then I will pull out my vocabulary cards and study them." Whereas habits are developed over time by repetition of certain actions, if-then plans can be initiated immediately. Or, as Peter Gollwitzer, one of the pioneers in the study of implementation intentions, explains it, "Apparently, implementation intentions create instant habits."[19]

[17]David Rock, *Your Brain at Work* (New York: Harper Business, 2009), p. 9.
[18]Ibid., p. 38.
[19]Peter M. Gollwitzer, "Implementation Intentions: Strong Effects of Simple Plans," *American Psychologist* 54 (1999): pp. 493–503.

Why won't goals alone suffice?

The problem with goals alone, no matter how admirable, is that they seem to lack the all-important cue. Dozens of experiments have shown that the addition of a cue makes a crucial difference. For example, in one famous study when students were given the goal during the time they had off after Christmas of writing a report on how they spent their Christmas Eve, students who used implementation intentions were three times as likely to complete their report than those who relied entirely on the goal. Keep in mind that both groups of students had the identical goal. The only difference for the more successful students is that not only did they have a plan for reaching that goal, but they attached it to a specific time and place during the vacation period. The time and place were the cue! As it happened, that seemingly minor addition had a major impact. What's more, the fact that the report was assigned during a time that is traditionally filled with distractions and temptations is a testament to the strength of implementation intentions for achieving your goals![20]

Outsource Your Plans

How do you outsource your plans?

Automating your plans will ease the burden on your PFC by moving them to a different, more spacious part of your brain where they have the potential to become instant habits. Of course, there's another option, which is to bypass your brain altogether by outsourcing your plans, taking them out of your head and typing them into a dedicated document that you keep close at hand, adding them as items on a list, or incorporating them into your weekly schedule. The chapter that follows will provide you with numerous outsourcing options.

Take Action

What is action?

Goals and plans won't do you any good unless you take some action. Action is the engine that gets you to your destination. Without action, goals and plans are moot. You can decide you want to finish a book, and you can even plan the pages that you need to read each day, but until you actually start reading, all your preparations will be pointless. In the same way, the goal to reach the moon and the plans for the spacecraft were impressive, but they didn't come to life until the first rocket left the launch pad and headed into space.

What are the keys to taking action?

You've got a goal and plans for meeting it, but how do you get started and keep going until you reach your destination? The keys to taking action are the ability to gain and sustain your motivation, to maintain your concentration, and, finally, to put theory into practice by taking the first big step in pursuit of your own personal goal.

[20]Peter M. Gollwitzer and Veronika Brandstaetter, "Implementation Intentions and Effective Goal Pursuit," Journal of Personality and Social Psychology 73 (1997): pp. 186–199.

Gain and Sustain Motivation

SELF-DIRECTION — PLANNING

IT'S YOUR Q

All motivation is essentially driven by two basic goals: maximizing rewards and minimizing danger.[21] As humans, we possess a hardwired drive to pursue so-called primary rewards, such as food, and possess an equally strong motivation to avoid those dangers that threaten our lives, such as man-eating lions. The challenge with long-term goals is that the danger of straying from them may not be as obvious as an angry lion, while the rewards that come from pursuing them may take a long time to arrive. In fact, one of the reasons why procrastination is such a powerful impediment is that it offers instant tangible rewards at the abstract expense of endangering long-term goals. Without a strong and sustained sense of motivation, it can be difficult to see why studying hard to pursue the distant goal of getting into law school, for example, is superior to the immediate pleasure of closing your books for the night and going out for a pepperoni pizza instead. In order for your long-term goals to be able to compete with innumerable promises of immediate gratification, you need a strategy for sustaining your motivation. The solution is to shorten the delay and increase the frequency of your goal's rewards by setting subgoals, monitoring your progress, and celebrating your successes.

Set Subgoals

How do you set subgoals?

Almost any long-term goal can be divided up into a series of subgoals, which in turn can be further divided. Like your main goal, your subgoals should be challenging, specific, and achievable. Passing a test can be a subgoal if, for example, it is part of a larger goal of graduating with an engineering degree or getting into medical school. So can completing a homework assignment or even finishing a chapter before dinnertime.

How do subgoals help?

Notice in a basketball game how the crowd cheers and the scoring team's pace quickens each time a basket is made. Everyone knows that one basket by itself won't win the game, but when the score is added up, each basket can prove to be crucial. The same is true in school. Although no one has gained success by virtue of a single test or paper, these little victories will add up and help you move toward your long-term goal. In the meantime, subgoals provide the encouragement you need to cheer yourself on and quicken your pace. Computer game designers are well aware of this tendency, which is why these games are often divided into levels. Each time you reach the next level, you feel good and are motivated to continue.

Why does reaching a subgoal increase your motivation?

The motivation you feel with each little victory is actually part of a chemical change. Achieving a goal, even a minor one, triggers your brain's own reward mechanism by producing dopamine, a neurotransmitter associated with pleasure. In addition, dopamine increases your ability to focus, aids memory consolidation, and activates the desire for new challenges.[22]

[21]Rock, *Your Brain at Work*, p. 105.
[22]Hara Estroff Marano, "Procrastination: Ten Things to Know," *Psychology Today* (August 23, 2003), http://www.psychologytoday.com/articles/200308/procrastination-ten-things-know

www.cengage.com/success/Pauk/HowToStudy11e

Monitor Your Progress

What is the benefit of monitoring your progress?

Measurement aids monitoring and enhances motivation. Charity fundraisers frequently use the image of the steadily rising thermometer to display how their goal of raising money is going. Similarly, some fitness programs breathe life into the occasionally grueling goal of accumulating mileage from walking, running, or swimming by plotting it on a map that allows participants to do all their exercising close to home and yet still be able to claim that they have piled up enough miles to travel across their state, the country, or even around the world. What's appealing—and ultimately, motivating—about these approaches is that they take relatively abstract aspirations and turn them into something tangible that makes progress easy and even fun to follow. You can take a similar approach to reaching your goals by choosing any number of ways to monitor your progress.

Outsource Your Plans

How does outsourcing your plans increase motivation?

If you've outsourced your plans (see p. 18), you've not only eased the strain on your brain, but you've also created an excellent tool for monitoring your progress and sustaining your motivation. Lists and schedules provide a visual representation of how you're doing and how much more you have left to do before you reach your goal. Crossing an item off on your list or marking each day on your calendar when you've met your goals is almost sure to encourage you to keep the momentum going. If you're keeping track of your progress on your computer, consider using colors to pack an additional visual punch: red for tasks you still need to do, green for those you've completed. Use your imagination to come up with your own visual representations of your goal pursuit.

Take Tests and Quizzes

What is the value of tests and quizzes in reaching your goal?

As ominous as they may seem to some students, tests and quizzes are wonderful for monitoring your progress. In fact, the more quizzes the better, both for your motivation and for your ultimate success. If for some reason you're in danger of not meeting your goal or subgoal, the sooner you discover this the better. A disappointing grade will alert you to a need to make some adjustments, while a good grade can provide a tangible payoff for all the hard work you've done so far. Either outcome is almost certain to increase your motivation. As psychologist and best-selling author Dr. Daniel Goleman explains, even a setback lights up a portion of the brain that reminds us just how good it will feel to finally reach our goal.[23]

What should you do in a course where there aren't many tests or quizzes?

If tests and quizzes aren't a frequent component of your plans, consider creating your own tests to help measure your progress. Or go online or check your local bookstore to see if there are already some practice tests available for your class. You can find commercially made flashcards for a wide variety of subjects. Of course, each time you recite

---

[23]Dan Goleman, "Motivation: What Moves Us?," *Psychology Today* (December 28, 2011), http://www.psychologytoday.com/blog/the-brain-and-emotional-intelligence/201112/motivation-what-moves-us

your notes (see Chapter 11) you are administering a kind of mini-quiz that provides a real-time assessment of how you're doing.

Use Mental Contrasting

How does mental contrasting aid monitoring?

There's no reason why you can't continue to benefit from the mental contrasting (see p. 11) you originally used to define your goal and establish your plans. Take a moment to "image" your goal once more and contrast it with your present situation. Not only will visualizing in this way refresh the image of your goal, but by contrasting it you should get a clearer sense of how far you've come. And if it doesn't seem as though you've progressed as far as you would've liked, it might provide an opportunity to adjust or rethink your plans so your progress comes more readily.

Celebrate Your Success

What is the benefit of celebrating your success?

Achieving your goals and subgoals will often act as their own reward, but that doesn't mean you can't devise additional ways to enhance that effect and celebrate your success. The way in which you celebrate each milestone doesn't have to be excessive, but it can be helpful and motivational to take a few minutes or even an evening to reward yourself for a job well done before returning to work.

Take Breaks

How does taking a break celebrate success?

Taking regularly scheduled breaks as you work is good for both motivation and, as we'll see in Chapter 9, your memory. Take a five-minute break every half hour or a ten-minute break every hour. Each timeout will provide a modest opportunity to celebrate the progress you've made since the last break, before you return to work, encouraged and refreshed, and motivated to push on to the next break.

Treat Yourself

What sorts of treats are appropriate for celebrating success?

Break up a long session of studying with a healthy snack or plan to go see a movie, watch a video, or meet friends for a meal at the end of a productive week or day. Another possibility would be to buy yourself a book or a magazine you enjoy. As long as you strive to keep the reward proportional to the accomplishment (don't take the night off as a reward for one hour's hard work, for example), there's really no limit to the ways in which you can treat yourself for reaching a milestone in pursuit of your goal. What you consider a treat is entirely up to you. Whatever you do, make a point to establish a connection between the goal you've achieved and the treat you've received. The prospect of a reward, no matter how small, should help to keep your motivation high.

What is the connection between motivation and concentration?

The motivation you maintain by setting subgoals, monitoring your progress, and celebrating your success sends dopamine into your brain that not only makes you feel good but also encourages concentration. Why? Because your brain likes the feeling, wants more, and focuses on getting it. But what if you aren't motivated to begin with? Just as motivation can promote concentration, concentration can lead to motivation.

Maintain Concentration

What is concentration?

Concentration is focused thinking. Just as light waves can be focused into a single powerful beam—a laser—concentration can focus the power of your thoughts, enabling you to think with greater precision and penetrate difficult ideas. Watch a quarterback as he focuses on getting a pass to an open receiver, even while linebackers rush in on him from several directions. That's concentration! Or as world-famous tennis star Serena Williams once put it, "If you can keep playing tennis when somebody is shooting a gun down the street, that's concentration." Of course, concentration isn't limited to sports. Have you ever become so absorbed in your textbook that you find yourself actually "talking" to the author? Have you ever been studying your notes so intently that when you finally look up, you realize that hours have passed since you last checked the clock? That's concentration!

How valuable is concentration?

Humans have long recognized the power of concentration. American poet and essayist Ralph Waldo Emerson wrote that "Concentration is secret of strength," while management consultant Peter Drucker singled it out as "the key to economic results." Novelist Kurt Vonnegut called total concentration "the secret to success in any human endeavor," while legendary book editor Michael Korda described it as "the magic key that opens the door to accomplishment."

What makes concentration elusive?

As powerful as it can be, concentration has an elusive quality. In fact, if you were thinking deeply about a subject and suddenly realized that you were concentrating, at that very moment you would have broken your concentration. Just as sustaining motivation for a long-term goal can be a challenge, maintaining prolonged, undivided focus can be difficult to achieve. After all, in normal circumstances there are dozens of things competing for your attention. Thoughts and ideas constantly bang, rattle, and knock on the door of your consciousness, trying to gain entry.

How does Figure 1.3 illustrate concentration?

Figure 1.3 provides a vivid illustration of the natural tendency to divide attention. As you gaze at this picture, you'll probably discover that your visual focus is shifting

Figure 1.3
A Goblet or Two Profiles?

every few seconds so that you first see a goblet, then two profiles, and then the goblet again. Once you're aware of both images, it is difficult for your eyes to focus on one and ignore the other. Similarly, it is hard for your mind to focus on one idea at a time. People who can focus exclusively on the task before them have a much better chance of completing that task more quickly and accurately than those who divide their attention even when they don't mean to do so.

How do you maintain concentration?

Trouble concentrating may come from external distractions, such as sights or sounds that compete for your attention; from internal distractions, such as worries or daydreams; and from multitasking, which can splinter your concentration into unproductive pieces. Once recognized, these obstacles to concentration can be overcome.

Reduce External Distractions

What is an external distraction?

Anything that stimulates your senses and in the process disrupts your concentration can be considered an external distraction. Study halls and living quarters are overflowing with such distractions, with everything from banging doors to baking bread. To work in a way that is compatible with concentration, you need the proper environment as well as the right equipment.

Select the Proper Environment

What elements make up a proper study environment?

Your study environment should be used exclusively for study. In addition, it should be quiet and well lighted. You can take your work to a place that is already designed for study, or you can create your own study environment.

What is the best environment for studying?

Find a Workshop You'd be hard-pressed to find an environment more suitable for high-quality concentration than a library. It offers a minimum of nonacademic distractions, a quiet atmosphere (usually as a matter of policy), and sufficient lighting. Get in the habit of studying at the library right away, on the first day of class. Even the walk to the library can be used productively as a review session or a refreshing break.

Why is it important to use your study area for studying only?

Whether you choose to work in the library or somewhere else, make sure your study area is reserved for studying. Psychologists emphasize that a conditioning effect is created between you and the desk: If you nap or daydream a lot while sitting at the desk, the desk can act as a cue for napping or daydreaming. By the same token, if you read or work in bed, you make it difficult to work energetically and fall asleep easily. To avoid this negative conditioning, use your desk only for studying. When you feel the urge to nap or daydream, leave your desk to nap or daydream elsewhere.

What other steps can you take to ensure a proper study environment?

Your study area should be your workshop, a place where you feel secure and comfortable. You can ensure that you have the proper environment for study and concentration if you minimize visual distractions, avoid or eliminate distracting noises, refrain from playing music, tune out text messages and the Internet, control the impulse to be disrupted by distractions, and provide the area with plenty of light.

Minimize Visual Distractions   A sheet of notes or a page from a textbook can seem dull compared with a glimpse of a softball game being played on a nearby diamond or a view of gently falling snow. To improve your chances of concentration, avoid competition for your eyes' attention. Study by a window so you can take advantage of the natural light, but keep your head turned away from the potentially distracting view. Of course, not all visual distractions lie on the other side of the windowpane. If your study area contains photographs you're liable to look at, gadgets you're likely to fiddle with, or books you'll be tempted to pick up and read, remove them until you have completed your work.

What can you do to eliminate noise when you study?

Eliminate Noise   If you need a quiet spot for efficient study, do your utmost to find one. Noise can be one of the most serious obstacles to effective study. Nothing is more wasteful than going over the same paragraph again and again because the noise makes it impossible to absorb what you are reading. If the library is the right place for you, make an effort to study there whenever you can. If you study at home, achieving quiet can sometimes be as simple as closing a door or inserting earplugs.

How does music affect concentration?

Turn Down the Loud Music   When studying, loud music, especially vocal music, can break your concentration. To keep your concentration from bouncing between the music and your books, you expend energy that could be put to better use. However, some students can tolerate music better than others. If you find music nonintrusive, then instrumental music—played softly—could potentially form a pleasing background, and such a background can actually muffle some external, intermittent noises.

What can you do to prevent e-mail and the Internet from becoming distractions?

Tune Out Messaging and the Internet   Avoid the temptation to surf the Web or constantly check messages by keeping your screen out of your line of sight and your phone out of range. If you are working on your computer, log out of e-mail and limit your Web surfing to the work at hand. If you're expecting important e-mail, set a timer for an hour or so, and work without interruption before checking. When the timer goes off, check for mail, then start the timer again. Do the same for text messages. Or simply let them wait until after you're done.

What does the spider technique involve?

Try the Spider Technique   A vibrating tuning fork held close to a spider's web sets up vibrations in the web. After the spider makes a few hurried investigations and finds no fly in the web, it learns to ignore the vibrations. The next time you are studying in the library and the door opens, don't look up. Controlling your impulse to look up will disturb your concentration the first few times. But very soon, like the spider, you'll learn to ignore these external disturbances.

Use the Right Equipment

What is the most important piece of concentration equipment?

Because proper lighting is an important component of your study environment, the right light should head your list of equipment to promote concentration and reduce external distractions.

What is the best kind of light for studying?

Find the Right Light Regardless of whether it's fluorescent or incandescent, the best light for studying is bright, even, and steady (remember B, E, and ST).

Bright. The emission of light is measured in lumens. For studying, you need at least 2,500 lumens. That's a lot. Two compact fluorescents of 25 to 30 watts each or two incandescent 100-watt bulbs will meet that requirement.

Even. Shadows in your work area or "hot spots" caused by glare will tire your eyes and make concentration difficult. Get rid of glare by shielding your lamp with a shade and by using a light-colored, nonglossy blotter on your desk. Eliminate shadows by using two lamps, fluorescent light, or diffuse light.

STeady. A constant flicker will undermine concentration. If you use fluorescent light, compact fluorescent bulbs are less likely to strobe than traditional fluorescents. If you are using incandescent light, make sure the bulb is screwed in properly.

What are the drawbacks of studying under bad light?

Good lighting makes for good studying. By contrast, poor lighting causes eyestrain, general tension, headaches, and sleepiness—irritations that interfere with concentration. If you study under good light but your eyes still bother you, have them examined by an ophthalmologist or optometrist. Clear and comfortable vision is essential to good studying.

What is the pencil technique?

Use a Pencil to Catalyze Concentration A technique that does not fail is the simple, humble *pencil technique*. The technique is this: *Whenever you are working to learn, study with a pencil in hand.* And use it! For example, if you are reading a textbook chapter, stop after several paragraphs and very briefly, in your own words, write down the key points made by the author. If, after reading several paragraphs, you find that no words come to you, you have no recourse but to go back and read the passage again. This time, read with determination and concentration to make sure you learn the key points. The secret: Activity promotes and almost ensures concentration. The pencil provides the activity!

What is the best kind of chair for promoting concentration?

Find the Right Kind of Chair Forget anything you may have heard about the virtues of a straight-backed, hard-seated chair. Use a comfortable, well-cushioned chair. Staying awake or falling asleep does not depend on your chair; rather, it depends primarily on your method of study, your attitude and self-discipline, the light, the room temperature, and, of course, how much sleep you've been getting. A hard, often uncomfortable straight-backed chair can't take the place of these basic requirements.

How does a
bookstand influence
concentration?

Use a Bookstand An extremely practical piece of equipment is a bookstand—not a bookshelf or bookends, an actual stand placed on your desk that holds the book in a tilted position and holds the pages down for you. A bookstand can give you a feeling of readiness to study and eliminate the distraction of continually holding the book open.

What other equipment
can be helpful for
concentration?

Keep Other Equipment Nearby Make sure you have what you need close at hand so you can continue to study without interruption. Depending on the classes you are taking and your personal preferences, that may mean a dictionary, a calculator, a clock, a calendar, paper, notebooks, paper clips, tape, rubber bands, pencils, pens, erasers, and index cards. If you make it a habit to keep your desk well stocked, you won't derail your concentration with unplanned emergency trips to obtain necessities.

Discourage Internal Distractions

What are internal
distractions?

Internal distractions are distractions that *you* create: daydreams, personal problems, anxiety, indecision, forgetfulness, and unrealistic goals. These distractions are as disruptive as the sights, sounds, and smells that make up the external variety, even though in this case the only one aware of them is you. Because internal distractions come from within, you have the power to eliminate or at least control them.

Use a Concentration Scoresheet

How does the
concentration
scoresheet discourage
distractions?

Whenever you catch your mind wandering, keep score by putting a check mark on a sheet of paper. The mere act of doing this actually distracts you from your distraction and reminds you to get back to work. The concentration scoresheet works by encouraging self-observation. Making note of your breaks in concentration—when they happen, how often they occur, and what triggers them—will help you realize just how intrusive the lapses are and will enable you to gradually eliminate them.

Put Stray Thoughts on a Worry Pad

What is the purpose
of a worry pad?

There are times when the concentration scoresheet isn't enough. When a persistent worry threatens to completely undermine your concentration, write it down on your worry pad with the idea that you will attend to it just as soon as you get the chance. Then with your conscience clear and your bothersome thought recorded on paper, you can get back to the business of concentration. After you have finished studying, read over your list and give these concerns your full attention. If you cannot alleviate them yourself, get the help of friends or counselors.

Use the Stop! Technique

What is the Stop! technique?

Of course, not all distractions are worth writing down. Sometimes thoughts that seem to have no other purpose than to throw you off course will flit into your mind. The Stop! technique, suggested by authors Judith Greenbaum and Geraldine Markel in their book *Finding Your Focus*,[24] is a red light for distractions. It's designed to arrest any dark thoughts or daydreams before they have a chance to gain momentum.

How do you use the Stop! technique?

The Stop! technique is a simple and powerful tool that relies on what psychologists call self-talk. Whenever you find that you're heading in the wrong direction because of distractions or you feel you've been spinning your wheels, just tell yourself "Stop!" That's right. Say the word. Do it out loud and with authority if you can. Letting yourself know you're aware that your focus has been drifting and that you don't intend to let it go any further is often enough to set you right back on the road to concentration. Try it.

Minimize Multitasking

What is multitasking?

As we've seen, distractions are unwanted intrusions that vie for your attention and make concentration difficult if not impossible. Now imagine if you deliberately subjected yourself to several distractions at once. Sounds crazy, eh? That may be so, and yet many of us do it all the time. We call it multitasking. Although we might think of each concern as a task, not a distraction, when you're focusing on one task, all the others are distractions. For example, if you're doing research for a term paper, answering e-mail, listening to the radio, and finishing your lunch all at once or in rapid succession, you're almost certainly multitasking. *Multitasking* means working on several tasks simultaneously or rapidly shifting back and forth between them. The term comes from computer operating systems, which are able to keep several applications running at the same time. The difference, of course, is that people are not machines. Sometimes mistakenly held up as a model of efficiency, multitasking is not only less productive than working on one task at a time, it's also a troubling source of stress.[25] Luckily, there are a handful of simple steps you can take to avoid it.

Multitasking Makes You Less Productive

Why is multitasking less productive?

Dividing your brainpower between several tasks at once has a predictable effect. As a study published in the *Journal of Experimental Psychology* concludes, people who

[24]Judith Greenbaum and Geraldine Markel, *Finding Your Focus* (New York: McGraw-Hill, 2006), pp. 36–37.
[25]Christina Tibbits, "Just Throw 'Multitasking' Out Your Window of Work," *Austin Business Journal* (online) (June 10, 2002), http://austin.bizjournals.com/austin/stories/2002/06/10/smallb3.html

multitask are less efficient than people who don't. According to the study's coauthor, Dr. David Meyer, "There's scientific evidence that multitasking is extremely hard for somebody to do, and sometimes impossible."[26]

Of course, in spite of the evidence, thousands of people continue to multitask and would appear to be doing so successfully. "It doesn't mean you can't do several things at the same time," says Dr. Marcel Just, codirector of Carnegie-Mellon University's Center for Cognitive Brain Imaging. "But we're kidding ourselves if we think we can do so without cost."[27] According to studies by Dr. Just, Dr. Meyer, and others, those costs include forgetfulness and difficulties in concentrating.[28]

Forgetfulness   Chronic multitaskers often feel that their memories are failing them when in fact the converse is true: They are failing their memories. A 2006 UCLA study using functional magnetic resonance imaging (fMRI) confirmed this. It showed that attempting to learn while multitasking actually employs a different part of the brain called the *striatum* instead of the hippocampus, which is normally important for retaining facts and concepts. As a result, although the subjects of the study were able to sort index cards while multitasking, their ability to recall information from those cards was markedly reduced.[29]

Difficulty in Concentration   With multitasking, regardless of what you're working on, there's a good chance that at least part of your mind will be elsewhere. Nothing is as concentrated as it was initially when it's been diluted, and that includes the power of your thinking. Or, as Dr. Meyer explains, "No matter how hard you try, you will never be as good multitasking as you are concentrating on one [task]."[30]

Effect on IQ   Perhaps most shocking of all is multitasking's practical effect on your IQ. Results from a University of London study found that constantly e-mailing or texting led to a 5-point drop in IQ for women and a 15-point drop for men![31] According to David Rock, author of *Your Brain at Work***,** "even the brain of a Harvard graduate can be turned into that of an eight-year-old simply by being made to do two things at once."[32]

---

[26]Sue Shellenbarger, "Juggling Too Many Tasks Could Make You Stupid," *Wall Street Journal Online* (February 28, 2003), http://208.144.115.170/columnists/workfamily/20030228-workfamily.html
[27]Ibid.
[28]Melissa Healy, "We're All Multi-tasking, But What's the Cost?," *Los Angeles Times* (July 19, 2004), http://articles.latimes.com/2004/jul/19/health/he-multitasking19
[29]Stewart Wolpert, "Don't Talk to a Friend While Reading This; Multi-Tasking Adversely Affects the Brain's Learning Systems, UCLA Scientists Report," http://newsroom.ucla.edu/portal/ucla/Don-t-Talk-to-a-Friend-While-Reading-7212.aspx
[30]Amanda S. Fox, "Tallying the Cost of Doing Too Much," *CIO Magazine* (March 15, 2000).
[31]Rock, *Your Brain at Work*, p. 36.
[32]Rock, *Your Brain at Work*, p. 4.

Multitasking Increases Stress

Why does multitasking increase stress?

Not surprisingly, the drain on productivity results in an increase in the potential for stress.[33] You are compelled to struggle against the inevitable forgetting that occurs and fight to maintain your concentration in a climate of relentless distractions. Moreover, multitasking forms an unhealthy alliance with two major culprits in stress—procrastination and loss of control—and can sometimes start you on a vicious cycle of insomnia as well. And some multitaskers have been exhibiting symptoms that are similar to those of attention-deficit hyperactivity disorder.

What is the connection between multitasking and procrastination?

Procrastination   Another notorious source of self-imposed stress—procrastination—often works hand in hand with multitasking. (For more on procrastination and stress, see Chapter 3.) After all, one technique that procrastinators frequently use to put off assignments is to shift back and forth between several tasks instead of focusing on a single one. Avoid multitasking and you may succeed in discouraging procrastination in the same stroke.

Why does multitasking sometimes lead to a loss of control?

Loss of Control   As we'll learn in Chapter 3, your sense of control can have a dramatic effect on your level of stress. Students, even overworked students, feel less stress when they are able to maintain a sense of control over what they are doing. Multitasking robs you of that control. All your activities and obligations are moving targets, and thus maintaining equilibrium becomes difficult for most and impossible for some.

Why does multitasking sometimes cause insomnia?

Insomnia   People who multitask—or attempt to—are often compelled to shift into a kind of mental overdrive that doesn't necessarily downshift when the day's work is done.[34] A troubling side effect of multitasking, according to Drs. Larry Rosen and Michelle Weil, coauthors of the book *Technostress*, "is an inability to sustain a peaceful night's sleep or to enjoy what used to be calming, recreational times."[35] As we'll see in Chapter 3, sleep loss not only results from stress, but can in turn be the source of *more* stress.

Multitasking Can Be Minimized

What can you do to minimize multitasking?

Obviously, some multitasking is arguably beyond your control. If you're in the middle of an assignment and the phone rings or someone comes to your door, it's natural to want to answer. But most factors that lead to multitasking are well within the realm of your control. You can reduce the risk that multitasking will break your concentration by slowing down and planning your day carefully, by making a point to finish one task before beginning another, and by keeping a pad handy to deal with the distractions that may lead to multitasking in the first place.

---

[33]Larry Rosen and Michelle Weil, "Multitasking Madness," *Context* (Fall 1998), http://www.contextmag.com/archives/199809/InnerGameOfWork.asp
[34]Ibid.
[35]Ibid.

How does slowing down help if you're feeling overloaded?

Given that many people multitask because they feel pressed for time, it might seem strange to suggest that slowing down can actually help improve both your attention and your productivity. But it can. If you move too quickly, you're apt to grow flustered and confused. If your executive functions get overloaded and succumb to your stone-age side, you're unlikely to get any quality studying done. On the other hand, if you take the time to figure out what's what, to listen carefully, ask questions, and think deeply, your tension should diminish and your attention should increase. You may be moving more deliberately, but you'll also be working more productively.

Why does a plan discourage multitasking?

Plan Your Day   Use the time-based scheduling outlined in Chapter 2 to outsource your plans and inoculate yourself against multitasking. For many people, multitasking provides a way of getting to work without ever having to decide which task is the most urgent or the most interesting or the most important. If each block of time has a specific task associated with it, you're less likely to bounce back and forth between several tasks.[36]

What can you do to make sure you work to completion?

Work to Completion   Don't start a new task until you've finished the old one.[37] This may be difficult with long-term tasks. But with short-term tasks, it should be achievable. If you do have a task that is stretched out over a longer period of time, try to create subtasks that you can tackle and complete before moving on.

What does a nearby pad do to prevent multitasking?

Keep a Pad Handy   The worry pad (p. 26) is an excellent antidote to multitasking. It is designed to serve as a temporary holding area for pending ideas and concerns and can also be used to arrest early impulses to multitask. It's common to "task-shift" when there's a concern that "if I don't take care of it now, I never will." That's an understandable worry with a simple solution. Write it down, and get back to the task at hand. When you've finished the first job, you'll have the pad to remind you of what to do next.

● Put Theory into Practice   SELF-DIRECTION — PLANNING

How can you use your understanding of goal, plan, and action?

Now that you have a clearer understanding of the role of a goal and the way in which a plan and action can turn a dream into reality, you are ready to put theory into practice by writing out your own goal or goals. The following steps are designed to aid you in this process.

> **Step 1: Brainstorm possible goals.** On a clean sheet of paper, do some brainstorming about your goals. Jot down possible goals or words about them that come to

[36]Ibid.
[37]Ibid.

mind, and do so quickly and freely. Don't stop to correct your spelling, polish a phrase, reorganize your notes, or analyze a thought. Just keep going until you've jotted down all that you can think of about your possible goals. Next, look over what you've written and group similar items together. Formulate each group into a goal by writing a sentence that summarizes its main idea. Strive to make each goal specific and challenging but still achievable.

Step 2: Visualize both your destination and your starting point. Focus in on one of the goals you've just written down and use it as a heading on another clean sheet of paper. Use the technique of mental contrasting, first to vividly visualize achieving your goal and then to arrive at an equally vivid but realistic assessment of your present situation in relation to that goal.

Step 3: List your obstacles. On another sheet, using your mental contrasting as a starting point, jot down the obstacles that stand between you and your chosen goal. They may include classes you have yet to take, skills you need to strengthen or develop, resources (including money) and qualifications you may not yet have, and even habits you need to break.

Step 4: Map out a plan. Select one of the obstacles and arrive at a plan for overcoming it. If you need a specific class to reach your goal, when is your best opportunity for taking it? What prerequisites (if any) will you need? If you lack certain resources for achieving your goal, what are your options for acquiring them? If a bad habit such as procrastination, poor organization, or problems with punctuality is coming between you and your goal, what can you do to eliminate it? See if you can't come up with a step-by-step plan for overcoming this particular obstacle.

Step 5: Automate or outsource your plan. Depending on your plan, you may be able to use an implementation intention to create an instant habit that helps you to accomplish it without having to rely too heavily on willpower. Think of a cue that can serve as an automatic trigger for implementing the plan, such as "Each night when I finish my homework, I will spend an additional 25 minutes studying my Spanish vocabulary cards." Instead of automating your plan, you may choose to outsource it by adding it to your schedule or your daily to-do list. Then use an implementation intention, such as "When I finish an assignment, I will consult my schedule to see what I need to do next" to develop the habit of following your schedule or reading over your list.

Step 6: Repeat steps 4 and 5. Systematically target any obstacles that remain by mapping out a plan and automating or outsourcing it in order to spur you to action. In the end you will have devised a comprehensive strategy for achieving your goal.

What should you do after you've completed the steps?

Don't be surprised if you feel a great sense of relief once you've completed these steps. Even if you're not certain that your goal and your plan are precisely on target, at last you have something concrete that you can adjust and refine. You also have an excellent starting point for guidance and advice. Talk with your academic adviser or with a counselor in your school's career center. Don't underestimate the value of discussing your goals and your plans for achieving them. Get as much feedback as you can. Then, if necessary, modify your goals and plans into realistic, attainable maps for your future. By getting into the goal-setting mode, you can put yourself in control not only of your academic life but also of your life after college.

FINAL WORDS

What should you do if you're worried that your goals are going to change?

Goals can change. There's no rule that you can't rethink your objectives after you've defined them. One student seemed genuinely irked that she had to check in with an academic adviser before registering for her first semester of classes. She knew without a doubt that she wanted to go into dentistry and didn't feel that she needed advice from anyone. But the adviser pointed out something she had overlooked. She needed to take an English course in order to meet the college's distribution requirement. That course was a revelation. She fell in love with literature and shifted sharply toward a career in publishing, a goal she pursued with the same passion, determination, and planning that she had originally devoted to dentistry. Yes, goals can change. But that's no excuse to settle for murky, ill-defined objectives. The skills you develop and the lessons you learn in defining your goals will serve you well, no matter where they wind up taking you.

CHAPTER CHECKUP

SENTENCE COMPLETION

Complete the following sentences with one of the three words or phrases listed below each sentence.

1. Based on many of our common expressions, it seems that a goal is considered a _____.

   promise   **destination**   **liability**

2. Goals and plans won't do you any good without _____.

   action   **education**   **discussion**

3. Concentration is focused _____.

   light   **thinking**   **intensity**

MATCHING

In each blank space in the left column, write the letter preceding the phrase in the right column that matches the left item best.

_____ 1. Frankl   a. Said implementation intentions create "instant habits"

_____ 2. Gollwitzer   b. Self-talk technique that discourages distractions

_____ 3. Thoreau   c. Defined a clear goal of putting Americans on the moon and returning them safely to Earth

_____ 4. Stop!   d. Involves working on several things at once

_____ 5. Kennedy   e. Advocated vividly picturing a desired goal or objective in your conscious mind

_____ 6. Multitasking   f. Helps you keep track of breaks in your concentration

_____ 7. Check mark   g. Suggested that those who seem out of step may just hear a different drummer

_____ 8. Peale   h. Reported that 85 percent of students who attempted suicide said that "life was meaningless"

TRUE-FALSE

Circle T *beside the* true *statements and* F *beside the* false *statements.*

1. T F The purpose of a goal is to give you an idea of where you are headed.
2. T F Mental contrasting involves comparing your goal to the goals of friends and family members.
3. T F Health, happiness, and security are all excellent career goals.
4. T F Anything that stimulates the senses is a potential external distraction.
5. T F Multitasking generally makes you more productive.

www.cengage.com/success/Pauk/HowToStudy11e

MULTIPLE CHOICE

Choose the word or phrase that completes each sentence most accurately, and circle the letter that precedes it.

1. Your goal should be
   a. specific.
   b. achievable.
   c. challenging.
   d. all of the above.

2. Coming up with a plan is like
   a. running a race.
   b. building a fire.
   c. charting a course.
   d. none of the above.

3. Trouble concentrating is due primarily to
   a. internal and external distractions.
   b. boredom.
   c. anxiety.
   d. poor eyesight.

4. The face-goblet image in Figure 1.3 illustrates our natural tendency to
   a. forget faces.
   b. divide attention.
   c. recognize people.
   d. focus thoughts.

5. Multitasking can interfere with
   a. sound sleep.
   b. concentration.
   c. consolidation.
   d. all of the above.

REFLECTION

Think about the ideas outlined in this chapter and then draw upon your own opinions and experiences to answer each question fully.

1. Most of us think of ourselves both as individuals and as members of at least one larger group. In what ways do you follow Thoreau's advice to march to the beat of a different drummer? In what ways do you adhere to Le Bon's observations about crowds?

2. Specify some subgoals and then come up with some implementation intentions that will enable you to achieve them without having to rely on willpower.
3. Of all the techniques mentioned in this chapter for encouraging concentration, which seems as though it will be most useful for you personally. Why?

IT'S YOUR Q

The Q System uses marginal questions to encourage active reading. You'll notice that most but not all paragraphs in this chapter are accompanied by marginal questions. Now it's your Q. Scan the chapter for any paragraph that is missing a question, reread the paragraph, establish the main idea, and then arrive at a question that elicits it. Use the questions in the surrounding paragraphs as models for your own marginal questions.

VOCABULARY IN ACTION

The English language is alive. It is constantly growing and changing. The same can be said for your own personal vocabulary. To expand the horizons of your understanding and to refine the precision of your thought, it is vital to continually grow, strengthen, and maintain your own vocabulary. The three exercises that follow are designed to help you with this fascinating, lifelong pursuit.

SAY WHAT?

To gain lasting insight from a quotation, you need a precise understanding of the words it comprises. From the three choices beside each numbered item, select the one that most nearly expresses the meaning of the italicized word in the quote. Make a light check mark (√) next to your choice.

A good head and a good heart are always a *formidable* combination.

—Nelson Mandela (1918–), former president of South Africa

| 1. *formidable* | impressive | frightening | polite |

Truly successful decision making relies on a balance between *deliberate* and *instinctive* thinking.

—Malcolm Gladwell (1963–), British-born Canadian journalist and author

| 2. *deliberate* | educated | intentional | methodical |
| 3. *instinctive* | habitual | impulsive | primitive |

If you do good, people will accuse you of selfish *ulterior motives*. Do good anyway.

—Dr. Robert Schuller (1926–), American evangelist

| 4. *ulterior* | monetary | hidden | self-serving |
| 5. *motives* | advantages | profits | reasons |

VOCAB-U-LADDER

Seemingly unrelated words in our language often share numerous connections. Use your knowledge of word synonyms, prefixes, and roots to connect the word at the top rung to the word at the bottom rung, using the words listed below.

finish
pecuniary
eccentric
conclusion
peculiar
financial

concentrate

share root "centrum," "center"

synonyms for "irregular"

share root "pecu," "cattle, flock"

synonyms for "monetary"

share root "finis," "boundary, end"

synonyms for "completion"

share root "claudere," "to shut"

preclude

Here's the story behind a word that figures prominently in the chapter you've just read.

Focus The warm fire behind our word for concentration

focus *fō'-kəs n.* 1. A point in which the rays of light meet, after being reflected or refracted, and at which the image is formed. 2. A point so related to a conic section and certain straight line called the directrix that the ratio of the distance between any point of the curve and the focus to the distance of the same point from the directrix is constant. 3. A central point; a point of concentration.*

Four hundred years ago, "maintaining your focus" meant throwing another log on the fire. It's puzzling even for some lexicographers to realize that our modern word *focus* came from a Latin word for hearth or fireplace. Even now, the transition is a bit of a mystery, although most experts acknowledge that it was German astronomer Johannes Kepler (1571–1630) who started the word *focus* on its modern path. Because he devoted his life—or you might say, his focus—to understanding the stars and the planets, Kepler was also interested in lenses and light, publishing a book called *The Optical Part of Astronomy* in 1604. It was in this book—now recognized as ushering in the modern study of optics—that Kepler first used the word *focus* to describe the point on a lens where light waves converge. Why did he give it that name? No one knows for certain, but as anyone who's ever used the sun and a magnifying glass to burn a dry leaf knows, if you can bring together the strength of the sun's rays at a single point, you can start a fire. According to the *Oxford English Dictionary*, it took almost another 200 years for this term that dealt with light and waves to finally acquire its figurative meaning of "the center of activity, or area of greatest energy." And that's what we mean today when we use focus as a synonym for concentration.**

*Adapted from "focus." *The American Heritage Dictionary of the English Language*, 4th ed. (Boston: Houghton Mifflin, 2000).
**Based on information from "focus." *The American Heritage Dictionary of the English Language*, 4th ed. (Boston: Houghton Mifflin, 2000); "focus." *Online Etymology Dictionary*. Douglas Harper, Historian, http://www.etymonline.com/index.php?search=focus (accessed May 1, 2009); "focus, *n.*" *Oxford English Dictionary*, 2nd ed. 20 vols. (Oxford: Oxford University Press, 1989).

Use Your Time and Space Effectively

Time flies, but that's no reason for you to go through each day simply "winging it." Through conscientious use of time and commonsense planning, you can make the most of your day. This chapter ticks off the important elements of effectively managing your time and organizing your space, including how to

- **Reclaim Lost Time**
- **Stick to a Schedule**
- **Organize All Your "Stuff"**

In this chapter

How important is time management to your academic success?

Time is a precious and irreplaceable commodity. As she lay on her deathbed, Queen Elizabeth I of England (1533–1603) reportedly said, "All my possessions for a moment of time." How you use time can determine your success or failure in college. If you use time wisely, you'll prosper. If you use it poorly, you'll fail in the job you came to do. That's why the management of time is the number-one skill to master in college.

How can you gain extra time?

Although many people waste time needlessly and habitually, you needn't put yourself in the same position. You can gain extra time by reclaiming lost time, by taking control of your schedule, and by organizing all your "stuff," which will help you use your time more efficiently.

Reclaim Lost Time

How can you put your time to better use?

All of us have claimed that we don't have enough time to accomplish what we need to do. But the fact is that everyone is allotted the same amount of time: 24 hours a day. Many of us allow a lot of this time to go to waste by failing to realize it is available in the first place. In addition, it's often our day-to-day habits—activities we no longer notice—that save time or waste it. You can put your time to better use by pinpointing areas of "hidden" time and cultivating time-saving habits.

Find "Hidden" Time

SELF-DIRECTION

What is "hidden" time?

There's a lot of valuable time in your day that is being overlooked simply because you didn't realize it was time you could use. For those who flush tiny slivers of soap down the drain or toss small scraps of cloth into the wastebasket, there are others who combine those slippery bits and pieces into a whole new bar of soap or stitch discarded shreds into a comfortable quilt. Think of all the time you spend standing in line or even waiting for a traffic light to change. If you could find ways to make use of this "hidden" time, you could almost certainly add hours to each week.

How does pocket work use hidden time?

Carry Pocket Work Many situations may leave you with a few moments of unexpected free time—a long line at the bank or supermarket, a delayed bus or train, a wait at the doctor's office, a lunch date who arrives late. If you make a point to bring along a book, a photocopied article, index cards on which you've written key concepts, vocabulary words, or formulas, you'll be able to take advantage of otherwise frustrating experiences.

When is your mind free for studying?

Use Your Mind When It's Free Some activities may afford an overlooked opportunity for studying if you're prepared. For example, if you're shaving, combing your hair, or washing dishes, there's no reason you can't be studying at the same time. Because many of us tend to "zone out" in such situations, they are excellent opportunities to use time that might otherwise be squandered. Attach small metal or plastic clips near mirrors and on walls at eye level. Place a note card in each clip. Do a math problem or two, or master some new vocabulary words as you eat a sandwich at work.

How can recording information use hidden time?

Record Study Information   Another way of using hidden time is by listening to information you've recorded on MP3 files or burned onto CDs. Recorded information enables you to keep studying in situations where you're moving about or your eyes are otherwise occupied, such as when you're getting dressed or driving. In addition, recorded information can provide a refreshing change from written material.

What is spare-time thinking?

Employ Spare-Time Thinking   You can make the most of the moments immediately before or after class by recalling the main points from the last lecture as you're heading to class or by quickly recalling the points of a just-completed lecture as you're leaving class.

IT'S YOUR Q

Use Your Subconscious   At one point or another, you have awakened during the night with a bright idea or a solution to a problem that you had been thinking about before bedtime. Your subconscious works while your conscious mind is resting. If you want to capture the ideas or solutions produced by your subconscious, write them down as soon as you wake up; otherwise, they'll be lost. Many creative people know this and keep a pad and pencil near their beds. For example, Nobel Prize winner Albert Szent-Györgyi said, "I go to sleep thinking about my problems all the time, and my brain must continue to think about them when I sleep because I wake up, sometimes in the middle of the night, with answers to questions that have been eluding me all day."[1]

Change Your Time Habits

SELF-DIRECTION — REFRAMING

What's a good way to begin saving time?

As we learned in Chapter 1, habits, by their very nature, are things we do routinely without even thinking. Most of us are unaware of our habits unless someone or something draws attention to them. A good way to take inventory of your time habits is by keeping a daily activities log. From the time you wake up to the time you go to sleep, note all your major activities, the time you started and finished each, and the time each activity consumed. With your day itemized on paper, you can gain a clearer picture of where your time is being spent and where it's being wasted. The activities log in Figure 2.1 shows one student's daily routine and how he decided to put his time to better use.

[1]Originally published in *Some Watch While Some Must Sleep*, by William C. Dement, as a volume in The Portable Stanford series published by the Stanford Alumni Association. Copyright © 1972. Reprinted by permission of the author.

Figure 2.1
Record of One Day's Activities and Suggestions for Making Better Use of Time

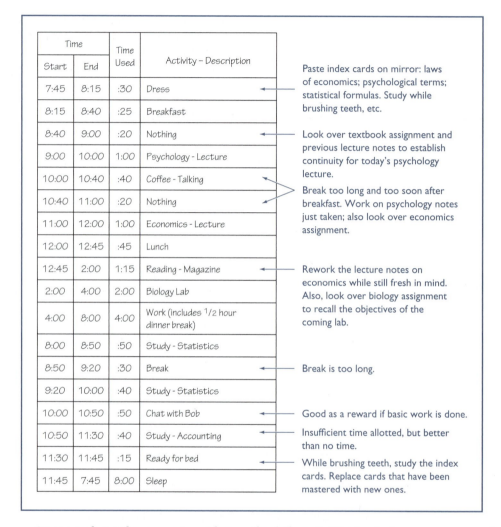

Time		Time Used	Activity – Description
Start	End		
7:45	8:15	:30	Dress
8:15	8:40	:25	Breakfast
8:40	9:00	:20	Nothing
9:00	10:00	1:00	Psychology - Lecture
10:00	10:40	:40	Coffee - Talking
10:40	11:00	:20	Nothing
11:00	12:00	1:00	Economics - Lecture
12:00	12:45	:45	Lunch
12:45	2:00	1:15	Reading - Magazine
2:00	4:00	2:00	Biology Lab
4:00	8:00	4:00	Work (includes 1/2 hour dinner break)
8:00	8:50	:50	Study - Statistics
8:50	9:20	:30	Break
9:20	10:00	:40	Study - Statistics
10:00	10:50	:50	Chat with Bob
10:50	11:30	:40	Study - Accounting
11:30	11:45	:15	Ready for bed
11:45	7:45	8:00	Sleep

Paste index cards on mirror: laws of economics; psychological terms; statistical formulas. Study while brushing teeth, etc.

Look over textbook assignment and previous lecture notes to establish continuity for today's psychology lecture.

Break too long and too soon after breakfast. Work on psychology notes just taken; also look over economics assignment.

Rework the lecture notes on economics while still fresh in mind. Also, look over biology assignment to recall the objectives of the coming lab.

Break is too long.

Good as a reward if basic work is done.

Insufficient time allotted, but better than no time.

While brushing teeth, study the index cards. Replace cards that have been mastered with new ones.

Once you have the concrete evidence of a daily activities log before you, you can begin to eliminate your time-wasting habits and develop or reinforce the time-saving ones.

What can you learn from Parkinson's law?

Defy Parkinson's Law Parkinson's law says that work expands to fit the time allotted.[2] To avoid running out of time, work Parkinson's law in reverse: For each task, set a deadline that will be a challenge to meet, and strive to meet that deadline. Neuroscientists have found that introducing a modest amount of "good stress" to a task helps you to increase

[2]C. Parkinson, *Parkinson, the Law* (Boston: Houghton Mifflin, 1980).

your focus and adds to your sense of well-being once that task is completed. Each time you achieve your goal, reward yourself with some small but pleasant activity. Take a break. Chat with a friend. Stroll around the room. Have a special snack you've saved just for the occasion. If you fail to meet a deadline, don't punish yourself. Just hold back your reward and set another goal. Positive reinforcement is powerful in effecting a change in behavior.

Why is it so important to obey your alarm?

Obey Your Alarm Clock How many times do you hit the snooze button on your alarm clock before you finally get out of bed? Even one time is too many. Set your alarm for the time you want to get up, not for the time you want to *start* getting up. If you can't obey your alarm, you'll have a hard time sticking to your time schedule. After all, it doesn't even buzz.

IT'S YOUR Q

Manage Texting, E-mail, and Internet Time As marvelous as they can be, text messages, e-mail, as well as the Internet in general can all be tremendous "time sinks," swallowing up hours in a typical day. Rather than checking it constantly, designate specific times during the day when you read and send e-mail or cell phone text messages. It's obvious that e-mail and texting have sped up communication, but it's a rare message that can't wait a while before being read or sent. The same applies to any Web surfing you may do. Time has a tendency to fly by as you click from one link to the next. You can help keep things under control by setting a timer when you surf and returning to your studies when the timer goes off.

What is the value of taking time out?

Take "Time Out" Reward yourself with regular short breaks as you work. Learning in several small sessions, rather than in one continuous stretch, increases comprehension. In one study, students who practiced French vocabulary in three discrete sessions did 35 percent better on an exam than those who tried to learn the words in one sitting.[3] So take a breather for ten minutes every hour or rest for five minutes every half-hour. Whichever method you choose, try to keep your breaks consistent. This way, you'll study with more energy and look forward to your regular rests. When you return to your desk, you'll find that you feel more refreshed.

How can understanding circadian rhythms affect your scheduling?

Listen to Your Body All of us are subject to circadian rhythms. That is, we have periods when we're most wide awake and alert and other periods when we're sluggish or drowsy. In general, we're sleepiest a few hours before dawn and 12 hours later, in mid-afternoon. In keeping with these natural cycles, we're widest awake about every 12 hours, usually at mid-morning and again in mid-evening. Knowing this can help you plan the day's activities more strategically.

---

[3]Kristine C. Bloom et al., "Effects of Massed and Distributed Practice on the Learning and Retention of Second-Language Vocabulary," *Journal of Educational Research* 74, no. 4 (March–April 1981): pp. 245–248.

1. *Schedule cerebral tasks for mornings and evenings.* Reading, writing, problem solving, and other "thinking tasks" should be done when you're likely to be most alert.
2. *Save active behavior for mid-afternoon.* Fieldwork, lab work, exercise, and errand running are best done at this time of day, when more sedentary activities may make you feel drowsy. If you're not a heavy coffee drinker, a cup of coffee might get you through the afternoon slump.
3. *Resist the temptation to sleep in on the weekends.* Changing your sleep schedule on the weekends can have a chain reaction effect on the following week. You may find yourself feeling jet-lagged on Monday or Tuesday if you sleep in on Saturday or Sunday.
4. *Read in the morning; review in the afternoon.* Scientists have discovered that short-term memory peaks at about nine o'clock in the morning and that long-term memory is strongest at about three o'clock in the afternoon.

Stick to a Schedule

What is the function of a time schedule?

A time schedule is a game plan, a written strategy that spells out exactly what you hope to accomplish—during a day, a week, or even the entire term—and how you plan to do it. Committing yourself to planning and keeping to a schedule can seem a bit frightening at first, but following a schedule soon becomes a source of strength and a boon to your life. There are several benefits to a schedule.

How will a schedule provide greater control?

A schedule provides greater control. A thoughtfully constructed time schedule can increase your sense of control in four ways. First, because your schedule is tangible, your plans seem more manageable. You can start working without delay. Second, you know you'll study all your subjects—even those you dislike—because you've allotted time for them in your schedule. There's less of a temptation to skip disliked subjects when study time has already been set aside for them. Third, a schedule discourages laziness. You've got a plan right in front of you, and that plan says, "Let's get down to business!" Fourth, you can schedule review sessions right from the start and avoid last-minute cramming for tests.

How does a schedule encourage relaxation?

A schedule encourages relaxation. At the same time, because your plan is on-screen or on paper instead of floating around in your head, your mind is freed for other things. There's no time wasted worrying about what to do next. It's all there in front of you. There's no guilt either. Both work and play are incorporated into your schedule. This means that when you take a break, you know you deserve it.

Why are some students reluctant to use time schedules?

Despite these benefits, many students are reluctant to start using time schedules. They feel not only that a schedule will do them little good but also that keeping track of time will turn them into nervous wrecks. Neither worry is warranted.

How does a schedule save you time?

A schedule saves time. Yes, it takes time to devise a schedule, but that time is rewarded. You will be able to shift smoothly from one activity to another, without wondering what to do next.

How does a schedule provide freedom?

A schedule provides freedom. Scheduling frees you from time's control. The people you see dashing from class to library to gym, or eating lunch on the run, are slaves to time. The students who schedule time, who decide how time will be used, are the masters of time.

In what way does scheduling increase flexibility?

A schedule increases flexibility. Disorganized people often waste so much time that there's no room for flexibility. People who use schedules free their time for a variety of activities and are therefore more flexible.

Which schedule type is best: time-based or task-based?

If you are a full-time student or have considerable control over the hours in your day, your best bet is to rely on traditional schedules that divide your time into manageable blocks. If, however, you are juggling your academic life with the responsibilities of a job or the demands of raising a family, you're probably better off using schedules that focus on tasks instead of on time. Each approach has advantages, but both provide an opportunity to tackle tasks with a genuine game plan instead of flailing at them haphazardly. Regardless of the approach you take, it's important to use your scheduling system not simply as a tool for efficiently filling up your days but as an instrument to help you get your priorities straight.

Divide Your Time into Blocks

FOCUSING

What does the story of the sticks illustrate about time?

A father once tied a bundle of small, thin sticks together with a strand of twine, handed the bundle to his youngest son, and said, "Son, break these sticks in half." The boy used his hands and knees but could not break the bundle. Sadly, he handed it back to his father. Without a word, the father untied the twine, and using only his fingers, snapped each stick one by one.

What is the advantage of dividing your time into blocks?

When the sum total of your obligations and academic assignments seems overwhelming, it helps immensely to split them up into small, manageable units. By dividing each day into blocks, time schedules break up your responsibilities and allow you to deal with them one by one. Assigning a block of time to each activity ensures that you will work at peak efficiency. Completing each activity perpetuates a steady sense of accomplishment throughout your day.

What are the components of the three-part scheduling system?

Using time blocks, you can create a three-part scheduling system consisting of (1) a master schedule, (2) a weekly schedule, and (3) a daily schedule. Each plays an integral role in managing your time. The master schedule serves as a basic structure for organizing your activities, the weekly schedule adds specific details to the master schedule, and the daily schedule puts the weekly schedule into a portable form. Although each schedule performs a different function, all three follow the same basic scheduling guidelines.

www.cengage.com/success/Pauk/HowToStudy11e

What is the best way to use big blocks of time?

1. *Don't waste big blocks.* If you have a big block of time, use it for a big assignment. There's a strong tendency to say, "I'm going to get these smaller assignments out of the way before I tackle the big assignment." This is a poor decision. Instead, use the large block of time for a large and time-intensive assignment, and save your small assignments for the little slivers of time.

When it comes to studying, what is prime time?

2. *Study during prime time.* For most of us, prime time is daytime. In fact, research has shown that each hour used for study during the day is equal to an hour and a half at night. Even so, you may find that you have dead hours during the day when you are less productive than you'd like to be. Schedule less-demanding tasks for these hours.

How does the type of class influence when you should study for it?

3. *Study before recitation classes and after lecture classes.* A study session before a recitation or discussion class (e.g., a foreign language course or a psychology seminar) helps warm you up. When you walk into class, the material is fresh in your mind. For lecture classes, use the time immediately after class to fill in any gaps in your notes and to review the information you've just learned.

Why should you shy away from making your schedule too detailed?

4. *Don't let details tie your hands.* Account for all your time, but don't be overly detailed. The time you'd take to make an overly meticulous schedule can be better used in studying a subject directly, and the chances of your following such a strict plan are slim.

What sorts of nonacademic activities belong in your schedule?

5. *Include nonacademic activities.* Always set aside time for food, sleep, and recreation as well as the other activities of your life. Cheating yourself out of a meal, a good night's sleep, a swim, a family get-together, or a meeting with friends won't save you time in the long run. In fact, it may cost you time because all these activities are necessary for your overall mental and physical well-being. Make your plan for living, not just for studying.

Lay a Foundation with a Master Schedule

What is the purpose of the master schedule?

A master schedule provides an agenda of fixed activities around which your varying activities are arranged. Unless changes occur in your basic program, you need to draw up a master schedule only once per term.

What does a master schedule look like?

A master schedule grid lists the days of the week at the top and the hours of the day down the left side. The boxes in the grid are filled in with all your required activities: sleep, meals, job, regular meetings, community activities, sports, and, of course, classes. The empty boxes that remain represent your free time. Figure 2.2 provides an example of a typical master schedule.

How does a master schedule help?

A master schedule, whether it's written on a five-by-eight-inch card taped over your desk or carried in your notebook or entered into your regular calendar application, will help to unclutter your mind. More important, it enables you to visualize actual blocks of time into which you can fit necessary activities.

Account for Changing Details with a Weekly Schedule

What is the purpose of a weekly schedule?

The weekly schedule is built on the foundation of the master schedule. To construct it, photocopy or print out another copy of your master schedule and fill in the empty

Figure 2.2
A Master Schedule with Work

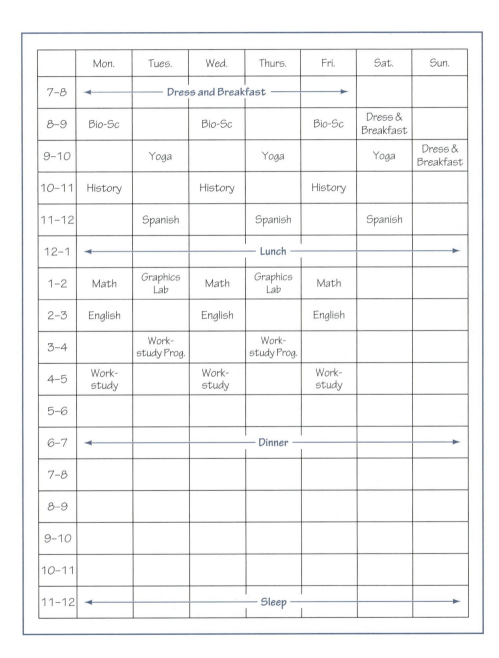

	Mon.	Tues.	Wed.	Thurs.	Fri.	Sat.	Sun.
7–8	Dress and Breakfast						
8–9	Bio-Sc		Bio-Sc		Bio-Sc	Dress & Breakfast	
9–10		Yoga		Yoga		Yoga	Dress & Breakfast
10–11	History		History		History		
11–12		Spanish		Spanish		Spanish	
12–1	Lunch						
1–2	Math	Graphics Lab	Math	Graphics Lab	Math		
2–3	English		English		English		
3–4		Work-study Prog.		Work-study Prog.			
4–5	Work-study		Work-study		Work-study		
5–6							
6–7	Dinner						
7–8							
8–9							
9–10							
10–11							
11–12	Sleep						

blocks with the activities you have planned for the week. (If you are using a calendar application, fill in open time slots with activities specific to the upcoming week.) For example, if you have a math test on Friday, you will need to schedule a little extra study time for math. Next week you may be assigned a research paper. If so, you'll probably want to leave space in your schedule for library or Internet research. The weekly schedule helps you adapt your time to your changing priorities. Keep it posted by your desk, pasted on the inside cover of your notebook, or easily accessible on a screen.

A sample weekly schedule is shown in Figure 2.3. The lists that follow show how the guidelines for scheduling were used to set it up.

Monday Through Friday/Saturday

7–8 A.M.	Avoid the frantic dash and the gobbled (or skipped) breakfast by getting up on time.
12–1 P.M.	Take a full, leisurely hour for lunch.
5–6	Relax before dinner—your reward for a day of conscientious work.
7–9	Keep up with current notes and assignments through systematic studying.
9–10	To forestall cramming at quiz and examination times, give some time every day to a review of previous assignments and ground covered to date.
10	A cease-study time of 10 P.M. provides an incentive for working hard during the day and early evening.
10–12	Devote some time every day to reading books that truly interest you. Recreational reading and conversation help you unwind for a good night's sleep.

Tuesday/Thursday/Saturday

8–9 A.M.	Because chemistry (10–11) is your hardest subject, build your morning study program around it. An hour's study before class will make the class period more meaningful.
11–12 P.M.	Another hour's study immediately after chemistry class will help you remember the work covered in class and move more readily to the next assignment.

Special

Tuesday	2–5 P.M. Library: paper
Sunday	7–9 P.M. English paper
	For some assignments you will need to schedule blocks of time to do research or to develop and follow up on ideas.
Saturday	From noon on, Saturday is left unscheduled—for recreation, for special projects to which you must devote a concentrated period of time, for extra work on difficult subjects, for thorough review.
Sunday	This is your day until evening. Study history before you go to bed because it is the first class you'll have on Monday morning.

Figure 2.3
A Detailed Weekly Schedule Based on a Master Schedule

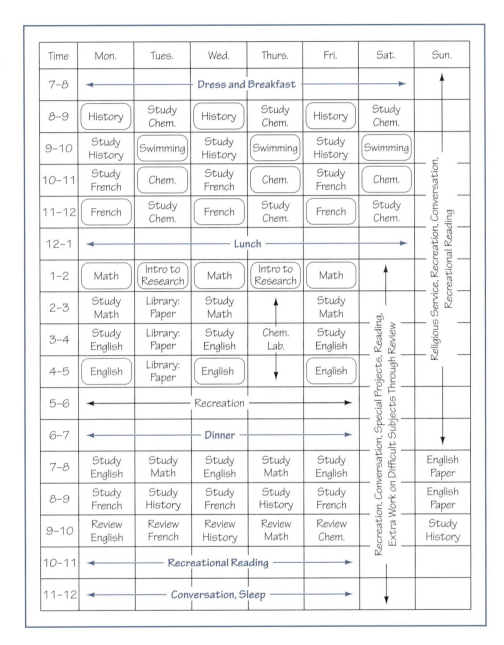

Time	Mon.	Tues.	Wed.	Thurs.	Fri.	Sat.	Sun.
7–8	Dress and Breakfast						
8–9	History	Study Chem.	History	Study Chem.	History	Study Chem.	
9–10	Study History	Swimming	Study History	Swimming	Study History	Swimming	Religious Service, Recreation, Conversation, Recreational Reading
10–11	Study French	Chem.	Study French	Chem.	Study French	Chem.	
11–12	French	Study Chem.	French	Study Chem.	French	Study Chem.	
12–1	Lunch						
1–2	Math	Intro to Research	Math	Intro to Research	Math		
2–3	Study Math	Library: Paper	Study Math		Study Math		
3–4	Study English	Library: Paper	Study English	Chem. Lab.	Study English	Recreation, Conversation, Special Projects, Reading, Extra Work on Difficult Subjects Through Review	
4–5	English	Library: Paper	English		English		
5–6	Recreation						
6–7	Dinner						
7–8	Study English	Study Math	Study English	Study Math	Study English		English Paper
8–9	Study French	Study History	Study French	Study History	Study French		English Paper
9–10	Review English	Review French	Review History	Review Math	Review Chem.		Study History
10–11	Recreational Reading						
11–12	Conversation, Sleep						

Provide a Portable Game Plan with a Daily Schedule

What goes into a daily schedule?

A daily schedule is a brief yet specific list of the day's tasks and the time blocks you plan to accomplish them in. You should be able to fit all this information on an index card that you can carry around with you all day. Make up your daily schedule each night before you go to bed. Once you have put your worries and concerns on paper, your mind will be free for sleep. You will also have thought through your day and will be better prepared when the morning comes. Figure 2.4 shows one student's daily schedule and explains why it is effective.

Figure 2.4
A Daily Schedule

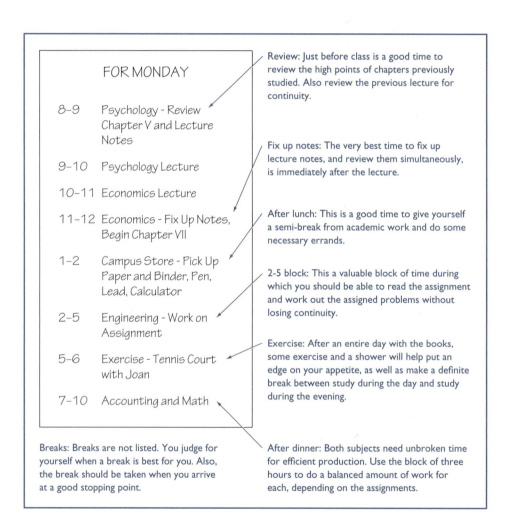

FOR MONDAY

8–9	Psychology - Review Chapter V and Lecture Notes
9–10	Psychology Lecture
10–11	Economics Lecture
11–12	Economics - Fix Up Notes, Begin Chapter VII
1–2	Campus Store - Pick Up Paper and Binder, Pen, Lead, Calculator
2–5	Engineering - Work on Assignment
5–6	Exercise - Tennis Court with Joan
7–10	Accounting and Math

Review: Just before class is a good time to review the high points of chapters previously studied. Also review the previous lecture for continuity.

Fix up notes: The very best time to fix up lecture notes, and review them simultaneously, is immediately after the lecture.

After lunch: This is a good time to give yourself a semi-break from academic work and do some necessary errands.

2-5 block: This a valuable block of time during which you should be able to read the assignment and work out the assigned problems without losing continuity.

Exercise: After an entire day with the books, some exercise and a shower will help put an edge on your appetite, as well as make a definite break between study during the day and study during the evening.

Breaks: Breaks are not listed. You judge for yourself when a break is best for you. Also, the break should be taken when you arrive at a good stopping point.

After dinner: Both subjects need unbroken time for efficient production. Use the block of three hours to do a balanced amount of work for each, depending on the assignments.

Use Scheduling Tools If You Feel Comfortable with Them

What are the pros and cons of special scheduling tools?

These days, you can choose from a growing variety of tools and utilities, from computer software to personal digital assistants to Internet applications to hefty loose-leaf notebooks, all designed to make scheduling your time both easier and more intelligent. These tools may provide the breakthrough that some students need to finally begin to appreciate the importance of keeping a schedule. For other students, they are an elaborate, costly, time-intensive distraction that does little to control or organize time. Index cards and blank sheets of paper may not be all that sophisticated, but they are extremely inexpensive, refreshingly flexible, and breathtakingly simple, and they can usually provide all you need to get a firm grasp on your available time. If you swear by your calendar application or your store-bought appointment book, that's fine. As long as you keep in mind that your goal is managing time, you can make just about any system work. The essential component is not the tool, but rather the person who is using it.

Think in Terms of Tasks

FOCUSING

When is it preferable to use task-based scheduling?

Because of the way a schedule based on time blocks divides the day into manageable bite-sized segments, it is often preferable for most students. But some of us don't have the luxury of predictably structuring our days from top to bottom. If your days are largely unpredictable or your free time is fluid, you may need schedules that emphasize tasks instead of blocks of time. In addition, long-term assignments, which can't always be squeezed into time blocks, may require a task-based approach.

How did Ivy Lee demonstrate the value of tasks?

Anyone who's ever had the satisfaction of systematically crossing items off a lengthy to-do list has at least an inkling of the effectiveness of a task-based approach. During the first half of the twentieth century, legendary management consultant Ivy Lee demonstrated just how effective—and lucrative—it could be to view things in terms of tasks.

Charles Schwab, then chairman of the Bethlehem Steel Company, challenged Lee: "Show me a way to get more things done with my time, and I'll pay you any fee within reason." Lee thought for a while, then said,

- Every *evening* write down the six most important tasks for the next day in order of priority.
- Every *morning* start working on task #1 and continue until you finish it; then start on task #2, and so on. Do this until quitting time and don't be concerned if you have finished only one or two tasks.
- At the end of each day, tear up the list and start over.

When Schwab asked how much he owed for this advice, Ivy Lee told him to use the plan for a few weeks, then send in a check for whatever he thought it was worth.[4] Three weeks later, Lee received a check for $25,000, which is worth more than ten times that amount in today's dollars!

[4]T. W. Engstrom and R. A. Mackensie, *Managing Your Time* (Grand Rapids, MI: Zondervan, 1967).

www.cengage.com/success/Pauk/HowToStudy11e

What sort of schedules do you need for a task-based approach?

Of course, just as a daily schedule would provide only a limited view of your tasks, a single to-do list is not sufficient for a task-based approach to help you through the entire semester. Whether it hinges on time blocks or tasks, a three-part scheduling system still makes sense. If you're focusing on tasks, you'll need (1) a task-based master schedule and (2) a weekly assignment-oriented schedule in addition to (3) a daily to-do list.

Figure 2.5
A Task-Based Master Schedule

	Psychology Research Paper April 21	Train for Amateur Triathlon May 1	Self-Paced Data Mgmt Course
Feb. 7	Select Three Topic Ideas	Up Minimum to 60 Laps	Complete Ch. 1–3
Feb. 10	Do Preliminary Research	Try Ride Up Satyr Hill	
Feb. 14	Make Final Topic Choice	Run 30 Miles Per Week	Complete Ch. 4–6
Feb. 18	Complete Bibliography		
March 15	Finish First Draft		Mid-term Exam
March 18	Begin Rewriting		
April 21	Paper Due		Final

Develop a Task-Based Master Schedule

How does a task-based master schedule differ from a standard master schedule?

A task-based master schedule enables you to keep track of one or more assignments or goals over an extended period of time. Figure 2.5 provides an example of a task-based schedule. Across the top of the schedule, instead of listing the days of the week, write out the major goals you hope to accomplish or the assignments you plan to complete. Deadlines for subgoals may be written down the left side, where the hours of the day would normally be written in a standard master schedule.

How do you divide your goals into subgoals?

Now divide each goal or long-term assignment into manageable subgoals. List them in a column beneath the task they refer to. For example, if you've been assigned a research paper, you may arrive at the following subgoals: do preliminary research, choose topic, plan outline, conduct research, complete first draft, and revise first draft. As you reach each milestone on the way to completing your assignment, cross it off your schedule. As you do, you provide yourself with visual evidence of and positive feedback for the progress you've made.

Make Your Weekly Schedule Assignment-Oriented

When should you use an assignment-oriented weekly schedule?

If the span of your goal or assignment is a week or less, you can use an assignment-oriented weekly schedule as a supplement to your master schedule. Figure 2.6 shows such a schedule. The format is simple. Divide your page or document in half horizontally. In the top half, list your subjects, assignments, estimated study times, and due dates. Then, with the due dates and estimated times as control factors, check your master schedule for available time. Allocate enough hours to do the job, and add them to the appropriate line on the bottom half of the document. Stick to your schedule. As long as you give study hours top priority, your remaining hours will be truly free.

Turn Your Daily Schedule into a To-Do List

How should you adjust your daily schedule when your time is unpredictable?

Your daily study schedule should simply be a list of things to do arranged in order of priority on an index card. In this case, assigning specific times is likely to lead to frustration.

Figure 2.7 shows a typical daily list. To be successful, you need to develop a habit of referring to your list continually throughout the day. Cross off the tasks as you complete them.

Get Your Priorities Straight

FOCUSING — REFRAMING

Even the best schedules can create a false sense of security and accomplishment if they're filled with tasks that may take time but aren't top priorities.

How do efficient and effective time management differ?

Efficient time management is often mistaken for effective time management. Although it's admirable to work efficiently, that is, to accomplish as much as possible in the time allotted, your efficiency will be wasted if you are focusing on the wrong tasks. As Tom Connellan, an author and consultant, put it, "There's no point in doing well

Figure 2.6
A Weekly Schedule
Based on
Assignments

Subject	Assignment	Estimated Time	Date Due	Time Due
Electronics	Chapter V - 32 pp. - Read	2 hr.	Mon. 13th	8:00
English	Paper to Write	18 hr.	Mon. 20th	9:00
Math	Problems on pp. 110–111	3 hr.	Tues. 14th	10:00
Industrial Safety	Make Shop Layouts	8 hr.	Fri. 17th	11:00
Web Development	Generate Website Prototype (6-10 pages)	6 hr.	Fri. 17th	1:00
Electronics	Chapter VI - 40 pp. - Read	2 1/2 hr.	Weds. 22nd	8:00

Day	Assignment	Morning	Afternoon	Evening
Sun.	Electronics - Read Chap V English - Find a Topic			7:30-9:30 9:30-10:30
Mon.	English - Gather Notes Math - Problems		2:00-6:00	7:00-10:00
Tues.	English - Gather Notes Industrial Safety	8:00-10:00	3:00-6:00	7:00-10:00
Wed.	English - First Draft Web Development		2:00-6:00	7:00-10:00
Thurs.	Industrial Safety English - Paper Web Development	8:00-10:00	3:00-6:00	7:00-10:00
Fri.	English - Final Copy Electronics		2:00-6:00	7:00-9:30
Sat.				

what you should not be doing at all."[5] To manage time effectively, you need to allocate your energy and attention to those tasks that are most important.

What is the purpose of the urgency-importance matrix?

Well-known author, consultant, and time-management expert Dr. Stephen Covey devised a simple, much-imitated matrix to help you to gain a better understanding of the relative values of the tasks you're faced with on a regular basis. The matrix has "urgency" on the vertical axis and "importance" on the horizontal one (see Figure 2.8).

[5]Dorothy Lehmkuhl and Dolores Cotter Lamping, *Organizing for the Creative Person* (New York: Crown, 1993), p. 46.

Tasks that are urgent demand your immediate attention. Important tasks are tasks that will help you to achieve your goal.[6]

The real time wasters are tasks that are neither urgent nor important. They can be easily ignored and do little or nothing to help you achieve either your short-term or long-term

Figure 2.7
A Things-to-Do List

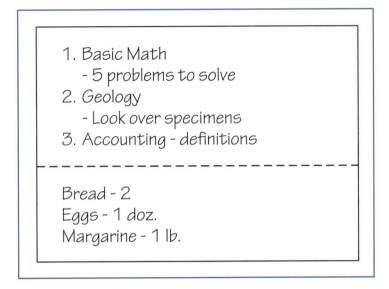

1. Basic Math
   - 5 problems to solve
2. Geology
   - Look over specimens
3. Accounting - definitions
- - - - - - - - - - - - - - - - - - -
Bread - 2
Eggs - 1 doz.
Margarine - 1 lb.

Figure 2.8
An Urgency-Importance Matrix
Source: From *Organizing for the Creative Person* by Dorothy Lehmkuhl and Dolores Cotter Lamping. Copyright © 1993 by Dorothy Lehmkuhl and Dolores Cotter Lamping. Reprinted by permission of Random House, Inc.

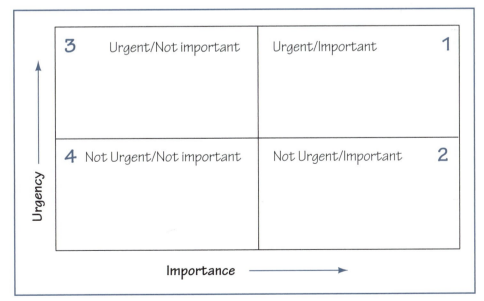

3 Urgent/Not important	Urgent/Important **1**
4 Not Urgent/Not important	Not Urgent/Important **2**

Urgency

Importance

[6]Ibid., pp. 44–45.

goals. These are the sorts of things we often refer to as busywork. If, for example, you are working on the computer but you still take time out to sharpen all your pencils, you're focusing on a task that isn't urgent or important. This is clearly the sort of thing that can wait.

Common interruptions—such as a phone call, a text message, or a friend who drops by unexpectedly while you're studying—tend to fall into the urgent but unimportant category. These things rarely relate to your goals, but they're hard to ignore. If you need to get work done, it's generally a good idea to put yourself in a position in which you are less susceptible to these sorts of interruptions. (See Chapter 1.)

Urgent and important items are tasks you can't ignore and shouldn't ignore. They include things such as scheduled classes or looming deadlines, as well as more spectacular unscheduled tasks, such as dodging projectiles or escaping burning buildings. If you have a class that starts in five minutes, then that's urgent and important. You need to attend the course, and you can't be late. If your assignment is due tomorrow, and you've hardly started, then you've really got no choice but to work until you finish it. All items in this category should get top priority on your task list.

The most valuable quadrant in the entire matrix in Figure 2.8 is the one for tasks that are important but not urgent. This is where your long-range planning occurs. The more you accomplish in this area, the more successful and organized you're likely to be. What are some examples of important but not-yet-urgent tasks? Mastering the notes for a recent textbook reading assignment is one. Beginning research on a paper that isn't due for another month is another. Mastering your notes will put you in a good position the next time a test or quiz is announced (or sprung upon you by surprise). Getting a head start on your paper will prevent you from having to compete with fellow students for limited resources at the library or from having to put in an all-nighter before the paper is due. Some urgent and important tasks (like attending class or leaving the building when a fire alarm sounds) are unavoidable, but, in general, the more time you devote to important but not urgent tasks, the more likely you'll be able to avoid the tasks that increase your stress, force you to cram, or make you skip sleep.

When planning out your time, tackle the tasks in quadrant 1 first, but see if you can keep them to a minimum, and spend the bulk of your time on tasks in quadrant 2. Avoid adding tasks from quadrant 3 or 4 to your task list. The former are typically going to be unexpected interruptions. Try to establish a study environment where you are less likely to encounter these. And as for the items in quadrant 4, they really don't belong on any task list. If you find you're spending time on tasks that are neither urgent nor important, make a point to avoid doing so in the future. Adding such items to your schedule or task list is likely to give you a false sense of accomplishment and distract you from completing truly important tasks.

Once you've figured out the urgency and importance of each task you plan to accomplish, you can use this information in a number of ways.

1. Go back to a task list you may have already created and number each item depending on whether it's urgent and important, important but not urgent, and so on.

Where do common interruptions fall in the matrix?

How should you handle tasks that are both urgent and important?

IT'S YOUR Q

How should the urgency-importance matrix affect the way you plan out your time?

How can you put the matrix to practical use with task-oriented schedules?

2. Use the urgency-importance matrix as your actual task list. Looking at which quadrant has more crossed off items will provide a snapshot of how truly productive your day has been.
3. Position your tasks in the matrix first and then create a standard task list, ordering the items by priority based on where you placed them in the matrix.

How can you put the matrix to practical use with a traditional three-part schedule?

If you are using a traditional schedule, the matrix can help you budget your available time blocks. Begin by using the master schedule as your template, just as you normally would, adding in any tasks or events for the week that already have specific time frames. Then use your matrix to help you decide how to fill in the remaining blocks in your schedule. The weekly view provides excellent reinforcement for those important but not urgent tasks that call for long-term planning.

Organize All Your "Stuff"

What does organizing your stuff have to do with managing time?

Of course, the effort you devote to finding "hidden" time, changing your time habits, and sticking to a schedule will be squandered if the tools you use to tackle your tasks are in a state of disarray. A huge part of being a successful student has to do with being able to find exactly what you need as quickly and efficiently as possible. After all, what good is a carefully planned schedule if you spend the first 20 minutes of the hour you planned to use for mastering your notes, searching for those very notes under a pile of papers or in a maze of nested computer directories? To stay organized and thereby make the best use of that time you've so carefully plotted, you need to devise a system, keep it flexible, and cut down on clutter.

Devise a System

CLUSTERING — PLANNING

What sort of organizational system do you need to devise?

Like so many successful study techniques, organizing your work area depends on a system. To a great extent, the kind of system you use doesn't matter just as long as you have one and it works for you. But in general, it pays to follow the old saying "A place for everything and everything in its place" by designating a logical home base for all the materials you are likely to encounter in your work area. In addition, it makes sense to organize things intelligently, so the materials you need most often are easiest to reach and those you need least are well out of your way. And finally, it helps to logically label items so you can tell at a glance what they contain and where they belong.

Find a Place for Everything

Why is it important to find a place for everything?

There are several reasons why your school materials may be obstructing your workspace and even littering your floor, but one of those reasons is so painfully obvious that it's amazing that it doesn't occur to those students who have to wade through a sea of supplies each time they try to do some work: *You never found a place for them.* Although some people may be too tired or lazy to put things away, more people leave things lying about simply because they never figured out where to put them in the first place.

How can you
gradually find places
for your possessions?

If the prospect of designating a place for everything you own seems complicated and scary, start gradually by designating broad areas for things: bookshelf for your books, drawer for your notebooks, file box for your papers, basket for your mail, jar for your pencils and pens, and so on. Using that as a starting point, start to subdivide your broader areas by, for example, putting this semester's books on the easiest-to-reach shelf and last semester's books on another or by putting science and math books on the first shelf, history and English books on the second. As you refine your system, you'll find it easier to go directly to what you need.

Organize Things Intelligently

How do you organize
things intelligently?

Have you ever reached into the refrigerator at breakfast and found that a ketchup bottle, a covered casserole dish, and a slice of apple pie are all blocking your access to the carton of milk? Some people have a workspace that is similarly arranged, where the materials they don't need are right there in front of them, and the supplies they do need take some effort to reach. The ketchup, the casserole, and the apple pie are all things you can use at some point. You just don't need them now. It makes sense to arrange things so they're where you need them when you need them.

How does the
CIA system help
you arrange your
materials?

Just as you arrange your tasks in order of their priority, you should arrange your supplies in a similar fashion. CIA creates a mnemonic to remind you how to arrange things intelligently; that is, according to whether they are current, imminent, or archived.

- *Current.* Current items are the notes and materials you're using right now. They usually belong on your desktop or somewhere close by. They should all be within easy reach. And there's another implied message in this routine: Before you settle down to study, not only should you have the things you need at your fingertips, but also you should get those things you don't need *out of your way.*
- *Imminent.* Imminent items are those you aren't using right now, but plan on using shortly. These are typically the notes and materials from your other classes this semester. In addition, imminent items may include textbooks or materials from previous semesters if they provide background, support, or context for your current semester's work. Imminent items typically sit on a nearby shelf or in a desk drawer.
- *Archived.* Archived items are those you've used in past semesters that may help you this semester or in some future semester but that aren't necessary for your day-to-day work. This would include your notes from previous classes as well as any textbooks from those classes that you've held onto. Because these items don't have to be easy to reach, you can place them on a less accessible shelf in your bookcase, in a file cabinet, or in banker's boxes. If you do put these items in boxes, be very specific in the way you label them so that you can still find the right book or set of notes if it turns out that you need them.

Choose Logical Labels

What good are labels?

Imagine how difficult it would be to pick out the right book from a shelf if all the books were shelved backward. Although we depend on labeling, we frequently take it for granted. Labels are designed to make it easier to recognize and find what you need and to organize things systematically, whether by alphabetizing or by some other system.

What should you label?

Label notebooks, individual note pages, and computer files. If you're putting things in a file cabinet, label those folders as well. If you're burning files onto CDs, be sure to label the CDs so that you can quickly differentiate one disk from another. Anything you're likely to sort through, organize, or search for should be labeled. It just takes a second, and it can save you a lot of time. There are lots of good reasons to label your materials and few if any not to do so.

What should the labels say?

How you choose to label your materials is basically up to you as long as you label things consistently. The idea is to be able to find what you need as quickly as possible. That said, here are some suggestions you may want to adopt:

How do you label folders or computer directories for a course?

Label folders or directories according to the course identifier. Rather than labeling a folder or directories with the title of your course (e.g., "Introduction to Macroeconomics"), it's usually better to start with the course identifier (e.g., "ECON102"), which should be easier to locate when you are rifling through a notebook or cabinet or searching through a computer directory. Also, it will mean that all folders from the same subject when alphabetized will wind up in the same basic location.

How should you organize different materials for each course?

Use separate labeled folders or dividers for different parts of a class. Keep class notes, lab notes, textbook notes, handouts, and any other course materials in separate labeled sections of your notebook or in their own subfolders in your file cabinet or computer directory.

What sorts of labels do your notes need?

Add enough information to each note page or file so that it can stand alone. It's almost inevitable that your notes will get shuffled at some point. In fact, there are some situations in which you may deliberately want to shuffle them (see Chapter 11). To ensure that your notes don't get easily mixed up, label each note sheet with a course identifier (e.g., "BIO203" or "Biology 203"), the date you took the notes, and the page number. Put the information on an outside corner, so it's easy to flip through and find what you need. With the Cornell System (see Chapter 10), the outside upper corner is probably best because the label is less likely to get in the way of your summary area jottings or marginal cues. To make any notes you've taken on your computer easier to find, name the file after the date (expressed numerically by year, month, and day) and the course identifier. So, for notes you took on February 12, 2013, for a reading in your Biology 203 class, the file name might be 20130212-bio203. If this type of label seems complicated or a little unfriendly to you now, you'll soon get used to it. And you'll discover how much easier it is to quickly find the notes you need.

How can you keep file folders better organized?

Provide an index for any file folders. If you're keeping materials in a file cabinet, create an alphabetical list of all the folder names and attach it to the cabinet door. That way you'll be able to search for the right folder before you even open the drawer. Also, it should make it easier to tell if you accidentally have two folders serving the same purpose (such as "Lecture Notes" and "Class Notes").

www.cengage.com/success/Pauk/HowToStudy11e

Keep Things Flexible

REFRAMING — CLUSTERING

Why should you keep your organization system flexible?

Perhaps somewhere there's a gigantic landfill devoted to obsolete organizers, to partially completed plans, to filing systems gone awry, and to calendars that were abandoned or ignored. Why do so many of these systems wind up on the trash heap? It's true that in many cases people simply lose interest, but it's just as likely that the systems were far too rigid and demanding. Ultimately, a simple, bare-bones system that works is more powerful than a complex, powerful one that fails. You can keep your organization system going for the long haul if you keep things flexible, by doing things like using loose-leaf paper instead of spiral notebooks and by keeping each class in a separate binder instead of combining them all into one.

Use Loose-Leaf Paper

Why is loose-leaf paper your best option for taking notes?

You want any notes you take to be as flexible as possible. Spiral-bound notebooks may seem appealing, but they put your notes into sort of a straitjacket, limiting the things you can readily do with your notes once you've taken them. If you prefer to take notes on lined-paper tablets, buy the three-hole kind and then carefully tear off the pages of notes once you've taken them and store them in a loose-leaf binder. This will give you the freedom to shuffle their order. As you'll discover in Chapter 11, being able to separate your notes into individual sheets instead of keeping them as part of a notebook or pad will prove to be a real advantage when it is time to prepare for a test or quiz. Despite impressive innovations in productivity software, loose-leaf paper remains your most versatile, flexible, and affordable note-taking tool.

Limit Each Notebook to One Class

IT'S YOUR Q

Standard loose-leaf notebooks can be large and unwieldy, not to mention kind of expensive. Luckily, you don't really require anything so elaborate for your class. All you really need are three rings and a cover. Full-sized, soft-sided notebooks still hold standard-sized paper. But these are thinner and less expensive and enable you to use a different notebook for each class instead of putting the materials from several, often unrelated classes in a single binder. Then you can take only what you need when you head to class. Why do you need your economics notes when you're in class taking notes for sociology? Besides, most of the loose-leaf additions that improve the organization of a large notebook—pockets, dividers, graph paper, and so on—work just as well in a thinner, more flexible notebook. In fact, thinner notebooks often come with a pocket on the inside of the front and back covers. Also, you can buy a notebook of a different color for each class, making it easy to distinguish one from another.

Cut Down on Clutter

CLUSTERING — FOCUSING

What causes clutter and how can you reduce it?

Although getting organized involves far more than just minimizing clutter, clutter is generally what most people think of when they imagine disorganization. The cause of clutter is pretty straightforward. It usually results when too many things are out of place. If you reduce your level of "stuff" and make a routine of putting the things that remain back in their place, you should go a long way to reducing clutter.

Use the OHIO Rule for Papers and E-mail

What does the OHIO rule suggest?

The acronym OHIO stands for "Only Handle It Once."[7] When you get a new piece of paper, do something with it right away. Read it and then throw it out, file it, or if it's something that requires your immediate attention, act on it. Many people needlessly pick up the same sheets of paper again and again without doing anything decisive. That wastes time and it usually leads to clutter. By the way, the same advice applies to e-mail. If your inbox is filled with e-mail messages, you're creating electronic clutter. Delete the message, file it in a directory, or act on it right away if it's urgent. But don't leave it sitting in your inbox, to be scrolled past day in and day out or repeatedly opened and closed. The negative effects of slogging through clutter, whether paper-based or electronic, can be subtle but cumulative, leading to a growing, and almost completely unnecessary sense of crushing information overload.

Allow Time for Cleanup and Setup

What's the last thing you should do at the end of the study day?

When you reach the end of your study day, instead of abruptly getting up from your chair and moving on to something else, take just a few minutes to stow away the things you've been working on in their proper places and to set out the things you plan to be working on the next time you sit down.

Why is straightening your work area worth the time and effort?

Anything you leave lying around from the previous day is likely to interfere with the work you do the following day. Also, things you leave out have a tendency to pile up. After all, no one plans to have a messy desk or work area. It tends to happen over time. Most cluttered surfaces are covered with items that were left there just "temporarily." Take a few minutes to put books, notebooks, and other supplies back in their places. The few minutes you devote to this end-of-study ritual will ensure that your well-organized work area remains organized.

What if your desktop is a computer desktop?

The practice of straightening your desktop is still helpful, even if that desktop is a computer desktop. In fact, it's usually a lot easier to straighten your computer desktop. The process of moving, storing, and deleting files is much faster when those files are computer files.

What's the advantage of setting out your materials in advance?

If you gather together materials that you plan to use the next day, you'll have an important head start. If you have a class the first thing in the morning and there's a risk that you may have to head out the door a little faster than you'd like, the few minutes you spent the night before, calmly getting everything together, should minimize the risk that you will forget something if you're in a hurry. Also, setting out the next day's materials has an important psychological effect. It gets you to think about the following day's activities and helps to put you in the proper mindset. Finally, assembling tomorrow's materials in advance helps to counteract inertia and discourage procrastination. When

[7]Edward M. Hallowell, "Overloaded Circuits: Why Smart People Underperform," *Harvard Business Review* (January 2005): p. 60.

www.cengage.com/success/Pauk/HowToStudy11e

you wake up the next day and find that everything you need is there waiting for you, you should find it easier to hit the ground running instead of just spinning your wheels.

FINAL WORDS

Let's face it. Most people understand the supreme importance of time and the value of sticking to a schedule, yet many of us continue to waste time needlessly. Why? Perhaps it is because we are human beings, not machines. Learning to use time wisely after years of wasting it doesn't happen by simply flipping a switch. Controlling your time is ultimately a matter of developing the right mindset. If the dying words of Queen Elizabeth and the compelling evidence of this chapter haven't been enough to convince you to change your time-wasting ways, perhaps the following tidbits about time will finally make things click.

Seven Valuable Tidbits About Time

1. One of America's greatest composers, jazz giant Duke Ellington, still wasn't ashamed to admit, "Without a deadline, I can't finish nothin'."
2. Be a contrarian. Go to the library when almost nobody is there. Get into the dining-hall line before the crowd. Get the reserved books before the line forms. The time you save will add up quickly.
3. Make decisions wisely by asking, "What are the alternatives?" Make a list of the alternatives, and then put pluses and minuses alongside them. Learn this process. It will save lots of time.
4. Don't spread yourself thin by attempting to become an "information junkie." This scattershot approach takes up a great deal of time and can still leave you feeling stressed and dissatisfied. Just make sure that you gain a firm grip on your own field.
5. When you're really through studying, spend an extra 15 minutes studying just a little bit more.
6. If the thought of saving time sounds sensible but uninspiring, ask yourself this simple question: What do I want to save time for? Suddenly, the efficient use of time may take on a significance that it never had before.
7. A Sanskrit proverb puts everything in proper perspective:

   Today well lived
   Makes every yesterday a dream of happiness
   And every tomorrow a vision of hope
   Look well therefore to this day.

CHAPTER CHECKUP

SENTENCE COMPLETION

Complete the following sentences with one of the three words listed below each sentence.

1. A time schedule functions as a _____.

   reward   **game plan**   **punishment**

2. When it comes to studying, "prime time" is usually _____.

   daytime   **mid-afternoon**   **flexible**

3. A master schedule should normally be drawn up once a _____.

   day   **week**   **term**

MATCHING

In each blank space in the left column, write the letter preceding the phrase in the right column that matches the left item best.

_____ 1. Pocket work   a. Work expands to fit the time allotted

_____ 2. E-mail   b. Method for minimizing paper clutter

_____ 3. Master schedule   c. Nobel Prize winner who used sleep time to solve problems

_____ 4. OHIO   d. Provides a basic structure for organizing the term's activities

_____ 5. CIA   e. Rhythms that influence your body's cycle of sleeping and waking

_____ 6. Szent-Györgyi   f. Productivity boon that can sometimes be a "time sink"

_____ 7. Parkinson's law   g. Supplies study material for unexpected free time

_____ 8. Circadian   h. Method for arranging your study materials

TRUE-FALSE

Circle T beside the true statements and F beside the false statements.

1. T F Taking breaks has a detrimental effect on comprehension.
2. T F Schedules don't have to be effective as long as they're efficient.
3. T F Using a time schedule can make you a slave to time.
4. T F Scheduling saves time that might otherwise be wasted.
5. T F An hour of daytime work is usually more productive than an hour at night.

Choose the word or phrase that completes each sentence most accurately, and circle the letter that precedes it.

1. When your obligations and assignments begin to seem overwhelming, it helps to
   a. take a nap.
   b. divide your time into blocks.
   c. use Parkinson's law.
   d. all of the above.

2. "Hidden" time is time that you
   a. aren't allowed to use.
   b. managed to overlook.
   c. reserve for recreation.
   d. leave off your schedule.

3. The most *valuable* quadrant of the urgency-importance matrix is
   a. urgent but not important.
   b. important but not urgent.
   c. not urgent and not important.
   d. none of the above.

4. The master schedule provides
   a. an alternative to a weekly schedule.
   b. an excuse for increased recreation.
   c. a basic structure for organizing your activities.
   d. a solution to the problem of hidden time.

5. A task-based schedule may be your best bet if
   a. your days are unpredictable.
   b. your free time is fluid.
   c. you have a full-time job.
   d. all of the above.

Think about the ideas outlined in this chapter and then draw upon your own opinions and experiences to answer each question fully.

1. Identify at least two instances of "hidden" time in your typical week and suggest some ideas you've arrived at after reading this chapter for putting that time to better use.
2. Explain which type of schedule you think will be the most effective for your particular needs and why.

3. Use the urgency-importance matrix (see Figure 2.8) to arrange your own tasks in the four quadrants. Which of your quadrants contains the most tasks? Which has the fewest? Were you surprised by the results? If so, why? If not, why not?

IT'S YOUR Q

The Q System uses marginal questions to encourage active reading. You'll notice that most but not all paragraphs in this chapter are accompanied by marginal questions. Now it's your Q. Scan the chapter for any paragraph that is missing a question, reread the paragraph, establish the main idea, and then arrive at a question that elicits it. Use the questions in the surrounding paragraphs as models for your own marginal questions.

VOCABULARY IN ACTION

To expand the horizons of your understanding and to refine the precision of your thought, the three exercises that follow are designed to help you grow, strengthen, and maintain your own vocabulary.

SAY WHAT?

From the three choices beside each numbered item, select the one that most nearly expresses the meaning of the italicized word in the quote. Make a light check mark (√) next to your choice.

The most *erroneous* stories are those we think we know best—and therefore never *scrutinize* or question.

—Stephen Jay Gould (1941–2002), American paleontologist and evolutionary biologist

1. *erroneous*	misguided	inaccurate	misleading
2. *scrutinize*	inspect	see	criticize

Any good piece of material like Shakespeare ought to be open to *reinterpretation*.

—Denzel Washington (1954–), American actor and director

3. *reinterpretation*	translation	rethinking	duplication

Gentility is what is left over from rich ancestors after the money is gone.

—John Ciardi (1916–1986), American poet and critic

4. *gentility*	refinement	large debts	large family

Those who make the worst use of their time are the first to complain of its *brevity*.

—Jean de La Bruyère (1645–1696), French writer and moralist

5. *brevity*	briefness	dullness	wastefulness

www.cengage.com/success/Pauk/HowToStudy11e

VOCAB-U-LADDER

Use your knowledge of word synonyms and roots to connect the word at the top rung to the word at the bottom rung, using the words listed below.

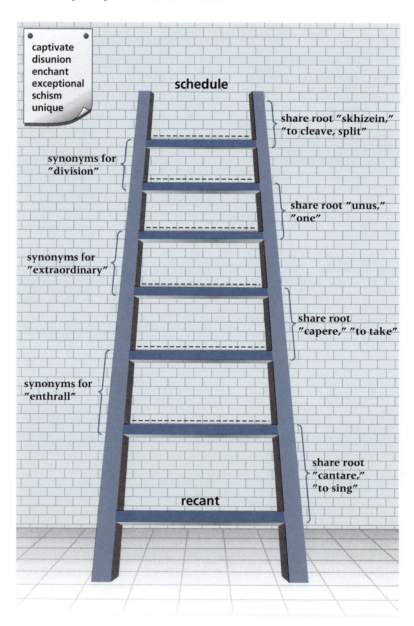

captivate
disunion
enchant
exceptional
schism
unique

schedule

share root "skhizein," "to cleave, split"

synonyms for "division"

share root "unus," "one"

synonyms for "extraordinary"

share root "capere," "to take"

synonyms for "enthrall"

share root "cantare," "to sing"

recant

backstory.

Here's the story behind a word that figures prominently in the chapter you've just read.

Deadline **Facing a deadline can still be stressful. But once it meant risking your life.**

deadline dĕd' līn' *n.* 1. A time limit, as for payment of a debt or completion of an assignment. 2. A boundary line in a prison that prisoners can cross only at the risk of being shot.*

These days we typically think of a deadline as a due date. In fact, that's been the word's predominant meaning since journalists adopted it in the early twentieth century. But where did the newspapers find the term in the first place? In prison. During the American Civil War, one of the most notorious prisons was Andersonville, a stockade in Sumter County, Georgia, where captured Union soldiers were detained under appalling conditions. The stockade itself was little more than a large plot of land, open to the elements but surrounded by a 15-foot wooden wall. Because Confederate guards feared their Union prisoners would try to vault the wall, they erected a second, smaller fence, roughly four feet tall and about three feet inside the stockade's main wall. This fence was known as the "dead-line." Any prisoner caught trying to cross it would be shot dead. Thanks to the country's vibrant newspaper business, which covered the Civil War extensively, Andersonville and its "dead-line" were soon infamous. Dead-line traveled from prison to printing press, where it was used to describe the border that each page of type had to fit within in order to be printed properly. If your type crossed the dead-line, those words wouldn't show up on the page. In time, the word went upstairs to the newsroom where editors turned "dead-line" into "deadline" and began to use it as a colorful term to describe a time limit that shouldn't be crossed by their reporters.**

*Adapted from "deadline." *The American Heritage Dictionary of the English Language*, 4th ed. (Boston: Houghton Mifflin, 2000), http://dictionary.reference.com/browse/deadline (accessed May 2, 2009).
**Based on information from "deadline." *The American Heritage Dictionary of the English Language*, 4th ed. (Boston: Houghton Mifflin, 2000); "deadline." *Online Etymology Dictionary*. Douglas Harper, Historian, http://www.etymonline.com/index.php?search=deadline (accessed May 2, 2009); "dead-line, *n.*" *Oxford English Dictionary*, 2nd ed. 20 vols. (Oxford: Oxford University Press, 1989); "Andersonville Prison, Georgia, August 17, 1864 – Southwest View of Stockade Showing the Dead-Line," *Old Pictures* (2006–2008), http://www.old-picture.com/civil-war/Andersonville-Southwest-deadline-stockade.htm (accessed May 2, 2009).

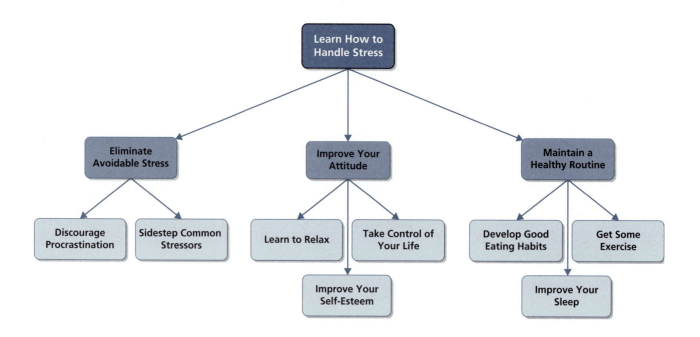

Learn How to Handle Stress

Stress, writes Dr. Hans Selye, a pioneer in its study, is "the spice of life or the kiss of death—depending on how we cope with it."[1] Unfortunately, most of us cope with it poorly. We worry too much, criticize too much, get angry too often, and become too tense. But if you can deflect the stress that comes your way, if you can learn how to handle the pressure that seems to be an inescapable part of academic life, you can thrive both as a student and as a human being. This chapter helps by telling you how to

- **Eliminate Avoidable Stress**
- **Improve Your Attitude**
- **Maintain a Healthy Routine**

In this chapter

▶ How the Marx Brothers helped to rescue one man from the brink of death. (p. 78)

▶ Your harshest critic may be the person you know best. (p. 77)

▶ The surprising natural substitute for antidepressants. (p. 89)

[1]Hans Selye, "How to Master Stress," *Parents* 52 (November 1977): p. 25.

When can stress be a good thing?

Mere mention of the word *stress* is enough to make most people anxious. It brings to mind images of frayed nerves, shortened tempers, and rising blood pressure. But being under stress isn't always a bad thing. In fact, stress can prompt us to respond effectively to a tough situation, to rise to the occasion when a paper comes due or a test is handed out. According to Marilyn Gist, a professor at the School of Business Administration of the University of Washington, "A certain amount of stress is healthy and beneficial; it stimulates some to perform, makes them excited and enthusiastic."[2]

"Stress," according to Dr. Hans Selye, "is the nonspecific response of the body to any demand made upon it."[3] In other words, it is the body's attempt to adjust to a demand, regardless of what the demand may be. You undergo stress when you run or walk at a brisk pace. Your body responds to the demand for more oxygen by increasing your breathing and causing your heart to beat faster. Yet most people view exercise not as a source of stress, but as a means of stress relief. Likewise, watching a quiz show or doing a crossword puzzle is technically stressful. In each case, the brain responds with increased mental activity. Yet most people undertake these activities specifically for relaxation.

What makes stress a problem?

The problem is that we don't always respond to the sources of stress (known as *stressors*) in a positive fashion. If instead of running for exercise, you're racing to catch a bus, or instead of solving a crossword puzzle, you're struggling with a math test that you didn't study for, your reaction is apt to be quite different. Rather than experiencing the exhilaration of exercising or the stimulation of solving a puzzle, you may wind up feeling exhausted or intimidated.

How can we better manage stress?

That's the two-sided potential of stress. Instead of compelling us to rise to the occasion, stress can sometimes plunge us into a sea of anxiety, worry, hostility, or despair. The way we respond to stress, whether we use it as a boon or a burden, depends on two major factors: our overall approach to life, and the number of stressors we face at any one time. To better manage the stress in your life, it helps to eliminate the avoidable sources of stress, improve your overall attitude, and maintain a healthy routine.

Eliminate Avoidable Stress

What can you do to eliminate avoidable stress?

Not all stress is unavoidable, of course. But a lot of it is. You can work to eliminate needless stress by discouraging procrastination and by sidestepping some of the other common sources of stress.

---

[2]Quoted in Pam Miller Withers, "Good Stress/Bad Stress: How to Use One, Lose the Other," *Working Woman* (September 1989): p. 124.
[3]Hans Selye, *Stress Without Distress* (New York: J. B. Lippincott, 1974), p. 27.

PEANUTS reprinted by permission of United Features Syndicate, Inc.

Discourage Procrastination

SELF-DIRECTION — PLANNING

How can you avoid procrastination?

"Nothing [is] so fatiguing as the eternal hanging on of an uncompleted task."[4] These words of William James, distinguished American psychologist, strike at the hearts of us all. Everyone has had bouts with procrastination. The best way to avoid future ones is to learn why people procrastinate and what you can do to prevent procrastination.

Learn Why You Procrastinate

What are the common sources of procrastination?

There's no single explanation for why people procrastinate. Nevertheless, many of the stressors that are discussed in this chapter can trigger procrastination. Here's a list of common sources:

How does fear of failure prompt procrastination?

Fear of failure. Many students hesitate to begin a task because they're afraid they won't be able to complete it successfully. Have some faith in yourself. Think back to past successes, and realize that if you've achieved success before, you can achieve it again. If you've failed in similar situations in the past, think of times when you've succeeded in other areas and apply the confidence you gained then to face the present challenge.

Why would fear of success make you put things off?

Fear of success. Some students put tasks off because they are afraid of succeeding. A person might be afraid of success for at least two reasons. First, successful people are a minority. There is a kind of loneliness in success. Some students unconsciously procrastinate because they don't want to be resented by people who aren't as successful. Second, success brings responsibility and choices. When a person succeeds, doors suddenly open. That should be good news, but some students view these opportunities as threats and burdens instead of challenges and choices. The solution involves a shift in attitude—to embrace success instead of fleeing from it.

What's at the heart of the problem of lack of time as a cause of procrastination?

Lack of time. If you used all the time you've been spending worrying about the time you don't have, you'd be well on your way to completing the task you've been putting off.

[4]Criswell Freeman, ed. *Wisdom Made in America* (Nashville, TN: Walnut Grove Press, 1995), p. 97.

www.cengage.com/success/Pauk/HowToStudy11e

This is a problem of control. Realize that how you budget your time is up to you (see Chapter 2). If you feel in control, you'll find it easier to complete the jobs that need to be done.

Why does poor organization sometimes lead to procrastination?

Poor organization. Perhaps you begin each day determined to get started on that task you've been putting off. But when nighttime comes, you find that despite your best intentions, you didn't get around to it. If that's your trouble, the cause may be a lack of priorities and/or poor organization. Draw up a to-do list and use the urgency-importance matrix (explained in Chapter 2) to help you put your priorities in perspective.

Devise Ways to Prevent Procrastination

How can you prevent procrastination?

Although the roots of procrastination are varied, the following methods of preventing procrastination should work regardless of the cause:

How does publicizing your plans discourage procrastination?

Make your plans a part of the public record. When you have a job that has to be completed or a goal that you want to reach, write it down. Or announce your intentions to close friends or family members. For example, "I plan to finish the bibliography for my research paper this weekend." Once you've made your intentions official, you're less likely to put them off. Procrastinators commonly fall into the habit of deceiving themselves, but they are less likely to deceive the people around them.

How do progress checks keep procrastination from getting out of hand?

Step back and check your progress from time to time. One way many people procrastinate is by getting needlessly entangled in the details of their work. If, as you're working, you periodically step back and measure your progress, it will be easier to tell if you've gotten unnecessarily bogged down. If you discover that you have, you should be able to pick up your pace so you can reach your goal in the allotted time.

What is the five-minute plan?

Use the five-minute plan. William J. Knaus, author of *Do It Now: How to Stop Procrastinating*, recommends what he calls the "five-minute plan."[5] Tackle a long-neglected task by agreeing to work on it for only five minutes. When the five minutes are up, decide whether you want to keep going. You usually will. The hardest part of almost any job is just getting started. The five-minute plan takes the sting out of that painful first step.

How can you use momentum to halt the progress of procrastination?

Let your momentum work for you. If you've successfully completed a task that you were eager to finish, let your momentum carry over to an activity that you aren't as enthused about. Your extra energy can help you get started on the dreaded task, and once you've begun (the hardest part), completion will become much easier.

[5]Quoted in Emrika Padus, *The Complete Guide to Your Emotions and Your Health* (Emmaus, PA: Rodale Press, 1986), p. 393.

Why is a timer more
effective than a
watch for beating
procrastination?

Use a timer instead of a watch. Clock-watching is a time-honored technique of perpetual procrastinators. If you want to keep to a schedule but avoid disrupting your concentration by constantly checking your watch or clock, use a timer instead. Many watches come with them. If your watch doesn't have one, an ordinary kitchen timer should do.

How can being specific
prevent you from
putting things off?

Be specific. A task is almost always more intimidating and stressful when it looms large and undefined. Instead of constantly telling yourself, "I've got to start writing that research paper," zero in on a specific aspect of your paper, such as choosing the topic or compiling a working bibliography. Suddenly your goal becomes more concrete, more doable, and thus much easier to complete. Or as James R. Sherman, author of *Stop Procrastinating*, puts it, "A job well defined is a job half done."[6]

What happens
when you verbalize
your reasons for
procrastination?

Verbalize your excuses. You may think you've got perfectly good reasons for putting off what needs to be done. If you let your excuses see the light of day by writing them out or explaining them to a friend, you'll often find that your reasoning isn't nearly as logical as you'd thought.

How does imagining
success fight
procrastination?

Visualize success or completion. Take a moment to imagine yourself accomplishing a task, passing a test, or achieving a goal. Through visualizing, you chart a course in your mind's eye. That course gives you a tangible game plan. The positive outcome you've imagined provides an incentive to follow that course until you reach the point of completion.

Sidestep Common Stressors

SELF-DIRECTION — PLANNING

IT'S YOUR Q

In addition to procrastination, there are several other sources of stress that can be sidestepped relatively easily. Here are some suggestions for doing so:

Wake up a half-hour earlier. If you find yourself skipping breakfast or taking your last bite just as you race out the door, you're starting your day on a stressful note. Although getting an adequate amount of sleep is crucial, waking up a half-hour earlier than usual won't significantly affect your sleeping habits but can do wonders to ease the pace of your morning preparations.

Allow yourself plenty of travel time. High-strung travelers are easily aggravated by slow drivers or long traffic lights. But slow drivers and long lights are facts of every commute. Factor them into your travel time.

Never wait empty-handed. The stress that comes from standing in line or waiting in traffic stems from boredom and from irritation about wasting time. Both problems have the

[6]James R. Sherman, *Stop Procrastinating* (Los Altos, CA: Crisp Publications, 1989), p. 38.

same easy solution: Bring a book to read or some notes to review the next time you're kept waiting, and the time will fly by. Simply listening to the radio while waiting may be relaxing for some, but in general it won't provide the same sense of accomplishment.

Eat dinner early. If you eat at a college dining hall, it's usually wise to get there early. The trivial but real stress that comes from waiting in line, searching for a seat, or racing to get a second helping before the kitchen closes can be eliminated if you show up soon after the dining hall opens. Whether you eat your meals at home or at school, an early dinner gives you more time before bed to be productive.

Don't take your work to bed with you. Your bed is for relaxation. Don't mix your mind's signals by turning it into an auxiliary workspace. If you establish a clear boundary between where you work and where you sleep, your work will become more productive, and your sleep will be more restful. And both activities will tend to improve your approach to life's stressors.

Stay calm, cool, and in queue. Try this Buddhist "loving kindness" meditation to help maintain a positive attitude while waiting in ticket or baggage lines. Take a few deep breaths and say these words slowly and silently several times: "May I be peaceful. May I be happy. May I be free from harm." Then say this blessing for each person in line one by one: "May you be peaceful," and so on. By the time you've reached the front of the line, you'll likely feel more generous and forgiving.[7]

Improve Your Attitude

What did James, Lange, and Peale suggest about attitude?

You can't turn away disaster simply by keeping a smile on your face, but there are now abundant indications that your overall attitude can have a powerful influence on the outcome of potentially upsetting or stressful situations. The first evidence was offered near the end of the nineteenth century, when American philosopher and psychologist William James and Danish psychologist Carl Lange simultaneously developed a remarkable theory of emotion. You don't cry because you're sad, they suggested. You're sad because you cry. This revolutionary reversal of the apparent cause and effect of emotions briefly sent the scientific community into an uproar. As the twentieth century progressed, the controversial proposal, known as the James–Lange theory, was scoffed at by most members of the mainstream scientific community and was advocated instead by "inspirational" writers and speakers such as Dr. Norman Vincent Peale, who championed the virtues of "positive thinking." Now the James–Lange theory has been vindicated, and Peale's ideas, bolstered by recent scientific evidence, have garnered mainstream defenders.

[7]Andrew Weil, "A Healthier Way to Fly," *Self Healing* (August 2000): p. 4.

How did one study test the effect of facial expressions?

As part of a study conducted by Paul Ekman, Robert W. Levenson, and Wallace V. Friesen from the department of psychiatry at the University of California, San Francisco, subjects were given specific instructions for contracting various facial muscles to imitate six basic emotions: happiness, sadness, disgust, surprise, anger, and fear.[8] Instead of being told, for example, to "look scared," the subject was instructed to "raise your brows and pull them together, now raise your upper eyelids and stretch your lips horizontally, back toward your ears."[9] Expressions were held for ten seconds, while electronic instruments measured the subjects' physiological responses.

What effect did the facial expressions have on the subjects' bodies?

The results were fascinating. Simply imitating an emotional expression was enough to trigger the physiological changes normally associated with that emotion. The most interesting contrast was between expressions for anger and for happiness. The average subject's heart rate and skin temperature increased more with anger than they did with happiness. Yet the subjects weren't truly angry or happy: They were just imitating the expressions associated with the two emotions.

How did facial expressions affect assessment of humor?

In another experiment, two groups of students were asked to look at the same set of cartoons. Members of the first group were instructed to view the cartoons while holding a pencil between their teeth with the eraser pointing to their right and the point to their left, a posture that forced their face into a smile. Members of the second group held the pencil in their mouth with their lips around the eraser and the point extending directly out of their mouths, creating a pursed-lipped frown. Neither group was aware of their artificially created facial expressions. And yet when asked to rate the humor of the cartoons, the "smiling" group found the drawings funnier than the "frowning" group did.[10]

How can you improve your attitude?

We can conclude from these studies that simply putting on a happy face may make you feel happier and that taking a dim or overly pessimistic view can lead to the discouraging outcome you expected. But managing stress shouldn't simply be a fuzzy-headed smile-at-all-your-troubles strategy. Improving your attitude should be done systematically by learning to relax, by improving your self-esteem, and, above all, by *taking control of your life*.

Learn to Relax

SELF-DIRECTION

What does relaxation mean?

The regular use of relaxation techniques, according to studies at the Mind/Body Medical Institute of Harvard Medical School, reduces stress and the prevalence of stress-related illness.[11] But many of us don't consider using such techniques because we misinterpret

---

[8]Paul Ekman, Robert W. Levenson, and Wallace V. Friesen, "Autonomic Nervous System Activity Distinguishes Among Emotions," *Science* 221 (1983): pp. 1208–1210.
[9]Ibid., p. 1208
[10]Daniel Kahneman, *Thinking, Fast and Slow* (New York: Farrar, Straus, and Giroux, 2011), p. 54.
[11]Stephanie Wood, "Relax! You've Earned It," *McCall's* 118 (July 1991): p. 50.

what the word *relaxation* means. Relaxation doesn't necessarily mean that you're about to fall asleep. In fact, some World War II pilots used relaxation techniques not to prepare themselves for sleep or to "take it easy," but to stay alert and avoid fatigue during bombing missions.[12]

What effect does relaxation have on your muscles?

Nor is relaxation a synonym for lethargy. "Relaxation," wrote psychologists Edward A. Charlesworth and Ronald G. Nathan in *Stress Management*, "simply means doing nothing with your muscles."[13] Relaxation is relief from wasted effort or strain, an absence of tension. Indeed, explains author Emrika Padus, "Tenseness wastes energy; tenseness causes anxiety…. The best performances come when the mind and body are *floating*, enjoying the activity just as we did when we were young children, completely absorbed in the experience and unaware of any consequences of the actions. This is true relaxation."[14]

What techniques can you use to encourage relaxation?

There's nothing mystical about relaxation. Two simple techniques—breathing deeply and using progressive relaxation—can help you get the hang of this life-sustaining practice.

Breathe Deeply

What is the connection between breathing and how you feel?
What have experiments shown about the effect of rapid breathing?

There is a strong connection between the way you breathe and the way you feel. When you're relaxed, your breaths are long and deep, originating from your abdomen. When you're anxious, your breathing is often short and shallow, originating from high in your chest.

The link between breathing and emotion operates in both directions. Just as the way you feel affects the way you breathe, the way you breathe affects the way you feel. A handful of experiments have established this connection. Dr. James Loehr found that when relaxed subjects were asked to take short, rapid, and irregular breaths for two minutes—in other words, to pant—nearly everyone interviewed felt worried, threatened, and panicky.[15] Simply by imitating the response of an anxious person, the subjects had made themselves anxious.

How can experiments about rapid breathing promote relaxation?

Luckily, this principle can be used to encourage relaxation as well. By breathing slowly, steadily, and deeply, and by beginning your breaths in your abdomen instead of up in your chest, you can encourage a feeling of relaxation. So just before an exam, an interview, or a dental appointment, when your palms are sweating, your body is tense, and your breath is short and shallow, try the count-of-three method to induce a more relaxed state. Count slowly and calmly through each step:

What are the steps in the count-of-three relaxation method?

1. Inhale slowly through your nose while silently counting to three.
2. Hold your breath for the count of three.

---

[12]Edward A. Charlesworth and Ronald G. Nathan, *Stress Management* (New York: Atheneum, 1984), p. 41.
[13]Ibid., p. 42.
[14]Emrika Padus, *Complete Guide to Your Emotions and Your Health*, p. 490.
[15]James E. Loehr and Peter J. McLaughlin, with Ed Quillen, *Mentally Tough* (New York: M. Evans and Company, 1986), pp. 141–142.

3. Exhale slowly through your nose while silently counting to three.
4. With your breath expelled, count to three.
5. Repeat steps 1 to 4 several times. (Once you have the rhythm, you need not continue counting; but maintain the same timing and the same pauses.)

Use Progressive Muscle Relaxation

When can you use progressive muscle relaxation?

A big advantage of the count-of-three method is that it can be done inconspicuously almost anywhere, including in an exam room. But if you have some time, a quiet place, and a little privacy, you may want to try progressive muscle relaxation (PMR), a method for systematically tensing and relaxing the major muscles in your body.

What is the history of PMR?

PMR was developed almost 90 years ago by Edmund Jacobson, a doctor who saw the connection between tense muscles and a tense mind. PMR is a form of mindfulness. It works by helping you become aware of the difference between how your muscles feel when they're tensed and how they feel when they're relaxed.

What are the steps involved in progressive muscle relaxation?

Start PMR by assuming a comfortable position, either sitting or lying down, and by closing your eyes. Make a tight fist with your right hand, and at the same time tense your right forearm. Hold this position for five seconds, feeling the tension in both your hand and arm, and then slowly release that tension, letting it flow out of you as you unclench your fist. Repeat the procedure with your left hand, noting the difference between how this hand feels tensed compared with your right hand and arm, which are now relaxed. Continue by separately tensing your shoulder muscles, your neck, and the muscles in your face. Then start with your feet and toes, moving up each leg; finish by tensing the muscles in your abdomen and chest. Once you've tensed and released every muscle group in your body, take a moment to savor the overall feeling of relaxation. Then open your eyes and end the exercise.

Improve Your Self-Esteem

SELF-DIRECTION

What is self-esteem?

Self-esteem is your personal assessment of your own value. Unfortunately, many of us are our own toughest critics. We overlook our positive attributes and forget our successes, emphasizing our shortcomings instead and providing ourselves with a silent but constant stream of discouraging dialogue. The stress that results from this inner discouragement is far worse than criticism from a nagging parent, an insulting instructor, or an overly demanding boss.

What can you do to improve your self-esteem?

A healthy level of self-esteem is crucial to keeping stress at bay. If your self-esteem needs improvement, rewrite the potentially destructive inner dialogue that haunts you throughout the day and take some time to dwell on your successes.

Rewrite Your Inner Dialogue

What's the first step in rewriting your inner dialogue?

You can't rewrite your inner dialogue unless you've seen the script. So, the first step in eliminating the destructive thoughts that undermine your self-esteem is to become aware of them.

www.cengage.com/success/Pauk/HowToStudy11e

What can you do to answer your self-talk?

Most of us talk silently to ourselves almost continually. Psychologists commonly refer to this inner conversation as *self-talk*. Although you may have learned to ignore the sound of your self-talk, the effect it has on your overall attitude can still be damaging. In other words, you may not hear it but you're probably still listening. So when you enter a new situation or are faced with a difficult challenge, take a moment to express your apprehensions to yourself. Then listen to your self-talk. Whenever you have a negative thought, counteract it with a positive one. Remember that the thoughts you have are your own and are under your control. You can open the door of your mind to whatever thoughts you want. Admit only the positive ones, and leave the negative ones out in the cold.

Build on Your Success

How do you build on your past success?

All of us have experienced success at one time or another. When you feel your self-esteem slipping, use what psychologists call *self-efficacy*. Remember when you did a job you were proud of, when you overcame an obstacle in spite of the odds, or when everything seemed to go smoothly. Reminding yourself of past success should help to put you in an achieving frame of mind so that you can achieve success again.

Take Control of Your Life

SELF-DIRECTION

How does self-esteem relate to your sense of control?

One of the results of increased self-esteem is an increased sense of control, a quality that both medical doctors and psychologists are finding can have a measurable effect on your physical well-being and state of mind. According to the *Wellness Letter* from the University of California, Berkeley, "A sense of control may, in fact, be a critical factor in maintaining health."[16] When you're in control, you act; you set your own agenda instead of reacting to the wishes or whims of others or resigning yourself to what we often call "fate."

Appreciate the Significance of Control

How did Norman Cousins use control to change his life?

In the early 1960s, writer and magazine editor Norman Cousins was stricken with a painful life-threatening illness. Determined not to let the illness control his life and sentence him to death, Cousins fought back. He watched movie comedies, including a couple of classics from the Marx Brothers, one after another. The laughter the films elicited made the sleep that had eluded him come more easily and ultimately reversed the crippling illness.[17] In fact, the results so impressed the medical community that Cousins, who had no medical background, was awarded an honorary degree in medicine by the

---

[16]"Healthy Lives: A New View of Stress," University of California, Berkeley, *Wellness Letter* 6, no. 9 (June 1990): p. 4.

[17]*Managing Stress—From Morning to Night* (Alexandria, VA: Time-Life Books, 1987), p. 21.

Yale University School of Medicine and was appointed adjunct professor in the School of Medicine at the University of California, Los Angeles.

What quality do many survivors of stress share?

Norman Cousins is not the only person who has demonstrated the importance of a sense of control. Author Richard Logan investigated the lives of people who were able to survive extreme stress—such as imprisonment in a concentration camp—and found that they all had at least one quality in common: a belief that their destiny was in their own hands. In other words, they had a sense of control.[18]

What did one experiment show about the relationship between control and the hormone cortisone?

The importance of control was reinforced in a study that provided a physiological insight into the phenomenon. When your body is under stress, your adrenal glands release *cortisone*, a hormone that in small doses can fight allergies and disease but that in larger amounts can impair the body's ability to fight back. When the two groups of employees who made up the study worked almost to the point of exhaustion, only one group experienced a significant increase in cortisone production. Those employees with high levels of cortisone had jobs that allowed them very little control. Employees who experienced no increase in cortisone held positions with a high level of control.[19]

What are the long-term effects of lack of control?

Lack of control can result in a sense of helplessness almost guaranteed to bring about the frayed nerves, tense muscles, and overall feeling of panic normally associated with short-term stress. If these conditions persist, they can have an adverse effect on your body's immune system, making you more susceptible to illness. Robbed of your sense of control, you not only react instead of acting, but also overreact. Turned outward, this overreaction may surface as anger. Turned inward, it can lead to fear, anxiety, and general depression.

How did a button affect the stress level of office workers?

In *The Joy of Stress*, Dr. Peter Hanson described an experiment in which two groups of office workers were exposed to a series of loud and distracting background noises. One group had desks equipped with a button that could be pushed at any time to shut out the annoying sounds. The other group had no such button. Not surprisingly, workers with the button were far more productive than those without. But what's remarkable is that no one in the button group actually *pushed* the button. Apparently, the knowledge that they could shut out the noise whenever they wanted was enough to enable them to work productively in spite of the distractions. Their sense of control resulted in a reduction in stress and an increase in productivity.[20]

Understand How Attitude Affects Control

How can you gain a better sense of control?

Dr. Hanson's story of the control button underscores an important element of control: Taking control is primarily a matter of adjusting your attitude. Even in unavoidable or unpredictable situations, you can still exercise some degree of influence. According to psychologist Mihaly Csikszentmihalyi, "Of all the virtues we can learn, no trait is more

[18]Mihaly Csikszentmihalyi, *Flow: The Psychology of Optimal Experience* (New York: Harper & Row, 1990), p. 203.
[19]Robert M. Bramson, *Coping with the Fast Track Blues* (New York: Doubleday, 1990), p. 217.
[20]Peter Hanson, *The Joy of Stress* (New York: McMeel & Parker, 1985), pp. 15–16.

useful, more essential for survival and more likely to improve the quality of life than the ability to transform adversity into an enjoyable challenge."[21] When academic life—or life in general—leaves you feeling especially helpless and frazzled, strive to change your attitude and reassert a sense of control by labeling the source of your stress or by reframing the situation in a way that makes it seem less threatening.

Label the Source of Your Stress

What is the benefit of labeling the source of your stress?

Labeling the source of your stress isn't a matter of finger pointing. It's a strategy that allows you to tell your brain you know what it's up to. Merely taking a moment to think about your thinking (psychologists call this *metacognition*) will often be all you need to regain control of your thoughts from the more primitive parts of your brain.[22]

How do you label the source of your stress?

When you feel yourself experiencing stress, stop and quickly attempt to determine the source of that stress. If you're taking a test or scrambling to finish a research paper before its looming deadline, the answers may seem obvious. But the sources of stress in these cases aren't quite what you think. After all, there's nothing inherently stressful about a test or a research paper. Students who experience stress in the face of tests and papers are feeling this way for other reasons. In the case of a test, for example, your uncertainty about what topics the test will be covering may account for your dry mouth and your sweaty palms. For the research paper, you may feel your writing ability is not as strong as that of your classmates or worried that you will be embarrassed by a bad grade if you fail to turn in an acceptable paper.

What happens when you label the source of your stress?

When you take a moment to label the source of your stress something miraculous happens: The brain is forced to shift away from the source of its fight-or-flight caveman response and focus instead on the so-called "executive functions," the area where more methodical, reasoned reactions are based. The rapid move from your amygdala (where the former occurs) to your prefrontal cortex (PFC; the home of the latter) is like a gust of wind, blowing out a stressful fire that's just getting started. Although that fire may still be rekindled, labeling has at least dealt it a significant setback.[23]

Reframe Your Reaction to Stress

IT'S YOUR Q

Reframing your reaction to stress follows the philosophy of that old adage "When life gives you lemons, make lemonade" or the idea of viewing a glass as half full instead of half empty. It simply involves taking a stimulus that may seem negative or stressful and reinterpreting it as something positive.[24] Tests and papers are two notorious sources of college stress that are ripe for reframing. Successful students often do this as a matter of course. Unlike many of their colleagues, they may relish the opportunity to take a

---

[21]Csikszentmihalyi, *Flow*, p. 200.
[22]David Rock, *Your Brain at Work* (New York: Harper Business, 2009), pp. 113–115.
[23]Ibid.
[24]Ibid., pp. 126–127.

test because it gives them a chance to show what they know. They may delight in the experience of writing a paper because they are able to immerse themselves in a topic of their choice and earn college credit for doing so! Students with these approaches to notorious academic nightmares may elicit rolled-eye responses from some of their classmates, but when the semester comes to a close, they are often the ones who earn the highest grades and have the best time doing it.

What happens when you reframe your reaction to stress?

Although the philosophy may be old, the cognitive neuroscience that supports the value of reframing is relatively new. A breakthrough in cognitive science has been the introduction of functional magnetic resonance imaging (fMRI), which allows scientists to track brain activity in real time. In one experiment, Columbia University psychologist Kevin Ochsner showed subjects a photograph of a woman crying outside a church. The subjects' reactions were predictable. They felt sad. But when Ochsner told them to imagine that the woman outside the church had been attending a wedding and was actually crying tears of joy, their emotional responses changed markedly even though they were still looking at the same photograph.[25] Ochsner summed things up succinctly: "Our emotional responses ultimately flow out of our appraisals of the world, and if we can shift those appraisals, we shift our emotional responses."[26] If you can train yourself to reframe your reaction to traditionally stressful elements of academic life, you should be able to not only defuse incidents of stress, but also increase your level of motivation, satisfaction, and performance!

Maintain a Healthy Routine

What can you do to your physical self to minimize the effects of stress?

Stress isn't all in your head. It has a noticeable effect on your body and can often be avoided through changes in your physical routine. If you make a concerted effort to develop good eating habits, improve your sleep, and get some exercise, you'll make yourself more stress-resistant and decrease your chances of being subjected to stress in the first place.

Develop Good Eating Habits

SELF-DIRECTION

How are stress and eating interconnected?

Stress may harm your immune system, and eating well can restore it. But that connection doesn't stop there. There is a destructive, cyclical nature involving stress and eating that you want to work hard to avoid. If you develop poor eating habits, the negative effect on your body may make you more susceptible to stress. And there's ample evidence that a by-product of stress is poor eating habits. Because

[25]G. M. Bebko, S. L. Franconeri, K. N. Ochsner, and J. Y. Chiao, "Look Before You Regulate: Differential Perceptual Strategies Underlying Expressive Suppression and Cognitive Reappraisal." *Emotion* 11, no. 4 (2011): pp. 732–742.
[26]Quoted in Rock, *Your Brain at Work,* p. 127.

stress is so demanding, your body needs extra energy to address it. According to Dr. Robert Sapolsky, we expend between 10 and 23 percent of our energy on digestion.[27] It's not surprising, then, that when your body undergoes stress, it often robs energy from the digestive process. In response to stress, corticotropin releasing factor (CRF) shuts down your digestion. This accounts not only for the lack of appetite, but also for the dry mouth that many of us experience in a stressful situation. But stress also triggers glucocorticoids, which enter your bloodstream at a slower pace. Whereas CRF depresses your appetite, glucocorticoids actually stimulate it and, according to Sapolsky, serve as the means for recovering from the stress response.[28]

"Thus, lots of short stressful events should lead to overeating," Dr. Sapolsky explains, "while one long, continuous stressor should lead to appetite loss."[29]

How can you break the cycle of stress and bad eating habits?

If you're overfed or undernourished, you may be putting an extra strain on your body that could be resulting in stress. And with that, the cycle continues. The way to break this vicious cycle is by taking time out for meals, rather than letting stress dictate whether you eat, and by eating in a way that counteracts stress instead of contributing to it.

Take Time Out for Meals

How do erratic meal schedules affect stress?

Stress can diminish or deplete certain vitamin and mineral supplies. An erratic meal schedule can aggravate this problem. According to nutritionist Jane Brody:

> Millions of Americans have fallen into a pattern of too-late-for-breakfast, grab-something-for-lunch, eat-a-big-dinner, and nibble-nonstop-until-bedtime. They starve their bodies when they most need fuel and stuff them when they'll be doing nothing more strenuous than channel-surfing or flipping through pages of a magazine. When you think about it, the pattern makes no biological sense.[30]

What's the best way to restore a sensible eating routine?

The simplest way to put some sense back into your eating routine is by beginning each day with breakfast. Breakfast stokes your body's furnace so you have energy to burn for the rest of the day. Lunch and dinner simply throw a few coals on the fire; breakfast gets that fire burning.

What are some other benefits of meals?

Meals not only provide needed nutrients; they also supply you with a necessary break from the stresses of school or work. Here are some stress-relieving suggestions for mealtime:

Why is it a bad idea to work while you eat?

Don't work as you eat. Time will have been wasted, and you won't have gained the break you deserved when you sat down to eat. As a result, you'll probably feel more stressed than you were before you ate.

What is the difference between eating quickly and rushing your meal?

Eat quickly, but don't rush. There's a difference. If you have a lot of work to do, you won't have time for a leisurely lunch. But if you keep one eye on your sandwich and the

[27]Robert M. Sapolsky, *Why Zebras Don't Get Ulcers* (New York: W. H. Freeman, 1998), p. 64.
[28]Ibid., p. 78.
[29]Ibid., p. 79.
[30]Jane E. Brody, *Jane Brody's Good Food Book* (New York: W. W. Norton, 1985), p. 187.

other on the clock, you'll increase your chances of getting indigestion and stress without significantly speeding up your meal.

Eat the Right Foods

What are the drawbacks of the USDA's nutritional guidelines?

Although nutritional guidelines from the United States Department of Agriculture (USDA) have improved over time, well-meaning efforts to make those guidelines easy to follow continue to create confusion. More than 20 years ago, the USDA unveiled the Food Guide Pyramid, which universally appeared to discourage fat consumption and endorse consumption of complex carbohydrates when the nutritional story on both of these components was actually far more complex. In 2005, a revamped version of the pyramid called MyPyramid corrected some of the flaws of its predecessor but still lacked the specifics that many consumers required to make sensible food choices. Finally, in 2011, the USDA scrapped the pyramid motif altogether and introduced MyPlate, a brightly colored illustration of a dinner plate divided up much like a pie chart in order to convey the recommended components of a healthy diet. Unfortunately, in its efforts to simplify, MyPlate places a disproportionate emphasis on dairy products and fails to distinguish between whole and refined grains and between meat and plant-based sources of protein.

What was the purpose of Willett and Stampfer's guidelines?

Between the demise of the Food Guide Pyramid and the arrival of MyPyramid, two professors at the prestigious Harvard Medical School, Walter C. Willett and Meir J. Stampfer set out to clarify and refine the USDA recommendations. Despite the arrival of MyPlate, Willett and Stampfer's guidelines remain the most complete, clear-cut, and authoritative research-based recommendations currently available.[31]

Curb Your Consumption of Calories

What is the simple math behind calorie consumption?

Strictly speaking, fat doesn't make you fat. Calories do. The confusion lies in the fact that there are more calories in a gram of fat than in the same amount of protein or carbohydrate. Thus, some people overcompensate by avoiding fats and piling up calories from proteins and carbohydrates instead. Ultimately, it's a matter of simple math. If you consume more calories than you use up, you will gain weight. If you burn up more than you consume, you will have a "caloric deficit" and will lose weight as a result. Over the past few decades there has been an alarming rise in the incidence of obesity in the United States. Not everyone is destined to be as skinny as a rail. Nor should they be. But if you're above or below your natural weight, you may be putting extra stress on your body. The way to control that weight is by watching your calories.[32]

Avoid Butter, Red Meat, and Refined Carbohydrates

What are the drawbacks of butter, red meat, and refined carbohydrates?

Just because fats can't be entirely blamed for obesity doesn't mean that some of them don't have faults. In order to discourage people from eating those that are bad, MyPlate has removed fats from the picture completely. The "bad fats" are saturated fats, most

---

[31]Walter C. Willett and Meir J. Stampfer, "Rebuilding the Food Pyramid," *Scientific American* (January 2003).
[32]Ibid.

commonly found in butter and red meat. It's their content, not their calories, that causes trouble. Saturated fats are high in low-density lipoprotein (LDL), also known as "bad cholesterol" and associated with an increased risk of heart disease. Refined carbohydrates, such as white rice, white bread, sugar, and even potatoes, have an indirect link to cholesterol that is potentially troubling. Because these carbohydrates break down so quickly, they can spark a rapid rise in both glucose (blood sugar) and insulin, the hormone designed to keep glucose in check.[33] According to Willett and Stampfer, "High levels of glucose and insulin can have negative effects on cardiovascular health."[34] In addition, there's evidence that the sudden drop in glucose that results when insulin washes it away can make you feel hungrier faster, thus prompting you to eat more than you need.[35]

Emphasize Healthy Fats and Whole-Grain Foods

IT'S YOUR Q

Although eliminating a place for fats on MyPlate may correctly discourage Americans from consuming saturated fats, unsaturated fats have been swept up in the "fat is bad" barrage. As it turns out, polyunsaturated fats (found in flax seeds and some fish) and monounsaturated fats (found in nuts, olive oil, and other vegetable oils) are actually quite good for you. Unlike eating their saturated siblings, consuming these fats can result in a reduced risk of heart disease.[36] Similarly, although the MyPlate diagram only stipulates "Grains," the whole grains you find in brown rice, whole-wheat flours, and a handful of other whole foods are far superior to the stripped-down, fast-acting refined version of these same foods. For one, they take longer to metabolize and thus do not trigger potentially damaging glucose and insulin spikes. In addition, they hold on to the valuable vitamins and nutrients that are normally removed when carbohydrates are refined.

Eat Lots of Fruits and Vegetables

What are the advantages of fruits and vegetables?

Despite the heated disagreements between nutritionists on a wide variety of topics, very few have anything bad to say about fruits and vegetables. High in fiber, high in vitamins, and low in the sort of "gotchas" that seem to dog almost every other type of food, fruits and vegetables may well be the most beneficial foods to eat in abundance.

Drink Plenty of Water

What is so important about water?

Our world and our bodies are primarily made up of water. Second only to air as the source of our survival, water is the medium for every bodily process and the primary means by which toxins are expelled. It is absolutely essential to remain properly hydrated. Depending on your size, age, and body weight, doctors generally recommend consuming at least six to eight 8-ounce glasses of water per day.[37]

[33]Ibid.
[34]Ibid.
[35]Ibid.
[36]Ibid.
[37]Dr. Fereydoon Batmanghelidj, *Global Health Discoveries* 5, no. 1: p. 4.

Why can't other beverages be used as a substitute for water?

Don't mistakenly assume that you are meeting your body's need for fluids by consuming liquids other than water, such as coffee, tea, alcohol, or soft drinks. Many of these beverages contain harmful ingredients that offset or undermine plain water's beneficial effect. Among these, the worst offenders are soft drinks, which have become the drink of choice in the United States. In 2001, Americans consumed more than 50 gallons of soft drinks per person per year and only 40 gallons of water.[38] What's more, a typical 12-ounce can or bottle of soda is sweetened by a whopping ten teaspoonfuls of sugar,[39] empty calories that are almost certainly contributing to the epidemic of obesity in this country. Making matters worse, tests done in 2006 on soft drinks in Britain and France found that they contained dangerous levels of benzene, a compound known to cause cancer.[40] If you're congratulating yourself for drinking diet soda instead, not so fast. Common artificial sweeteners can actually increase your appetite for sugar and carbohydrates and may be metabolizing into dangerous carcinogens![41] All these ominous findings reaffirm that clean, cool, fresh water is best.

Improve Your Sleep

SELF-DIRECTION

How does the sleep we typically get compare to the sleep we actually need?

If your morning starts with the sound of an alarm clock, you're probably not getting the sleep you need. According to Dr. Wilse Webb, a psychologist at the University of Florida, Gainesville, "If that's how you wake up every day, you're shortening your natural sleep pattern."[42] And yet an alarm clock is a part of most people's lives. Does that mean all of us are cheating ourselves on sleep? Perhaps not all, but most Americans are getting less sleep than they need. In fact, according to an article in the *New York Times*, "Sleep scientists insist that there is virtually an epidemic of sleepiness in the nation."[43]

What are the dangers of sleep loss?

The image of a nation filled with semiconscious citizens may seem comical, but in reality the effects of widespread sleep deprivation are seldom humorous and sometimes deadly. The U.S. Department of Transportation estimates that up to 200,000 traffic accidents each year are sleep related.[44] Furthermore, the worst nuclear power emergency in this country's history, at Three Mile Island, occurred at night, when workers were most susceptible to the effects of insufficient sleep.[45]

---

[38]Wine Institute, *Wine and Other Beverage Consumption in America*, http://www.beekmanwine.com/prevtopat.htm.

[39]Donald S. McAlvany, *The McAlvany Health Alert* 2, no. 4 (April 2002).

[40]Rajeev Syal, "Soft Drinks Found to Have High Levels of Cancer Chemical," *London Times* (March 2, 2006), http://www.timesonline.co.uk/article/0,,8122-2065539,00.html

[41]Dr. William Campbell Douglass, "NutraSweet Is Not So Sweet," *Second Opinion* 7, no. 3 (July 1997): pp. 1–4.

[42]Quoted in Natalie Angier, "Cheating on Sleep: Modern Life Turns America into the Land of the Drowsy," *New York Times* (May 15, 1990), pp. C1, C8.

[43]Ibid., p. C1.

[44]Anastasia Toulexis, "Drowsy America," *Time* (December 17, 1990), p. 80.

[45]Angier, "Cheating on Sleep," p. C8.

How does sleep loss
affect learning?

Of course, sleep loss isn't usually deadly for students, but it can be damaging. Dr. Charles Czeisler, director of circadian and sleep disorders medicine at Brigham and Women's Hospital in Boston, outlined some of the penalties that people pay when they get too little sleep: "Short term memory is impaired, the ability to make decisions is impaired, the ability to concentrate is impaired."[46] Clearly, a student who can't remember, can't make decisions, and has trouble concentrating will have a tough time surviving in an academic setting. Furthermore, the struggle to overcome the disabilities that sleep loss creates frequently leads to an even more pervasive problem: stress.

IT'S YOUR Q

"Weariness corrodes civility and erases humor," reads an article in *Time* magazine. "Without sufficient sleep, tempers flare faster and hotter at the slightest offense."[47] The day-to-day challenges and inconveniences of going to school and of living in the modern world are potentially stress inducing. Add habitual sleep loss, and you turn a chronic problem into an acute one. Dr. Ernest Hartmann's study of "variable sleepers" (patients whose sleep and wake-up times are not consistent) revealed that people under stress tend to need more sleep than do those who lead lives relatively free of anxiety and change. Yet stress often triggers insomnia, which leads to less sleep and the possibility of even more stress.[48] The result can be a vicious circle of stress and sleeplessness.

How do you break
the circle of stress and
sleeplessness?

How can you
determine if you are
getting enough sleep?

You can work to break this circle by getting the right amount of sleep, by following a regular sleep schedule, by avoiding naps, and by taking steps to improve the quality of your sleep.

Get the Right Amount of Sleep

Are you getting enough sleep? In general, your overall alertness provides a pretty good indicator. If you are getting the right amount of sleep, you should be able to stay awake through 20 minutes of darkness at midday. Students in art history and film courses, where slides or movies are commonly shown, often complain that a darkened auditorium or classroom makes them sleepy. These situations don't create sleepiness. They simply reveal a problem of insufficient sleep and should serve as a warning to get more rest. Sleep behavior experts tell us that, on average, most people fall short of their needed amount of sleep by 60–90 minutes each night.[49] Aggravating this daily deficit is the fact that sleep loss is cumulative; it adds up. If you feel tired on Monday morning, you're apt to feel even more so when Friday rolls around.[50]

What is the impact of
"sleeping in" on the
weekend?

Although sleep loss adds up, sleep does not. You can't stash away extra hours of sleep like money in the bank. You need to get sufficient sleep seven nights a week. Just as so-called weekend athletes engage in strenuous exercise only on Saturday and Sunday and thereby jeopardize their hearts and their overall health in their effort to "stay fit," people

[46]Quoted in Angier, "Cheating on Sleep."
[47]Toulexis, "Drowsy America," p. 80.
[48]Lynne Lamberg, *The American Medical Association (Straight-Talk, No-Nonsense) Guide to Better Sleep*, rev. ed. (New York: Random House, 1984), p. 35.
[49]Angier, "Cheating on Sleep," p. C1.
[50]Ibid., p. C8.

who "sleep in" on weekends don't eliminate the effects of a week of sleep deprivation. In fact, they complicate the problem by disturbing their rhythm of sleeping and waking.

Keep to a Schedule

What effect do circadian rhythms have on sleep?

Achieving full alertness isn't simply a matter of getting enough sleep. It's equally important to do your sleeping at the right time of day. Thanks to *circadian rhythms*, the body's natural pattern of wakefulness and sleep, when morning arrives you instinctively become more alert in anticipation of the day that lies ahead. With the advent of evening, signals in your brain begin preparing you for needed sleep. You go to sleep, and when you wake up the process is repeated.

How can you take advantage of circadian rhythms?

The way to make the most of these circadian rhythms is to maintain a regular sleep/wake schedule. Sleeping late on the weekends or going to bed at widely varying times throws your circadian rhythms out of whack. You find yourself feeling drowsy when you should be alert and wide awake when you should be fast asleep.[51] If you consistently rise at the same time regardless of when you went to bed, you'll keep your circadian rhythms in tempo.[52] Furthermore, an unwavering wake-up time should help discourage you from staying up too late.

Recognize the Truth About Naps

What are the drawbacks of taking naps?

Students and others who have flexible schedules often see naps as the solution to sleep deprivation. Unfortunately, naps fall far short of their reputation and actually create a number of problems: They're impractical; they adversely affect learning; they harm both sound sleep and the sleep cycle; and they act as a convenient excuse for chronic procrastinators.

What do you lose by taking a nap?

In addition, naps generally deprive you of two of sleep's more important components: dream, or rapid eye movement (REM), sleep, the period in which all our dreaming occurs; and deep sleep (also called *delta sleep*), which many sleep experts believe recharges our batteries and increases our overall alertness.[53] Therefore, if you take a nap, you may be adding to the quantity of your sleep but you'll probably be lacking the dream and deep sleep your body requires. According to Dr. William Douglass, "There is no doubt that this deep sleep is essential to health. Muramyl peptides, which are vital to tissue renewal and immune enhancement, are only released during deep, slow-wave sleep."[54]

How do naps affect your sleep/wake cycle?

As you might expect, naps also interfere with your sleep/wake cycle. Unless you take a nap every day at the same time and for the same duration, you'll probably wind up with stay-at-home jet lag and have difficulty falling asleep at night.

What is the connection between naps and procrastination?

Finally, the temptation to misuse naps can be great. Many students give in to the urge to sleep, rationalizing that when they awaken they will feel refreshed and perform more productively. Unfortunately, few students report this happy result. The harsh reality is that if you try to escape a mountain of work by taking a nap, you will wake up to face

[51]Richard M. Coleman, *Wide Awake at 3:00 a.m.* (New York: W. H. Freeman, 1986), p. 149.
[52]Robert K. Cooper, *The Performance Edge* (Boston: Houghton Mifflin, 1991), p. 222.
[53]Dianne Hales, *The Complete Book of Sleep* (Menlo Park, CA: Addison-Wesley, 1981), p. 18.
[54]William Campbell Douglass, M.D., *Second Opinion* 4, no. 12 (December 1994): p. 7.

www.cengage.com/success/Pauk/HowToStudy11e

the same amount of work, and you'll have less time in which to do it. It is far better to combat the desire to sleep, get the work done, and go to bed at your usual time with a clear conscience. You'll get the sleep you need; you'll minimize disruptions to your body's circadian rhythms; you'll feel healthier and more alert; and you'll be less susceptible to the potentially corrosive effects of stress.

Take Solid Steps for Better Sleeping

What are the advantages of optimal sleep?

IT'S YOUR Q

What other steps can you take to improve sleep?

"A good night's sleep," says Dr. Edward Hallowell, "is like pushing the reset button in your brain."[55] Optimal sleep promotes not only a more alert, energetic, zestful life, but also, according to some studies, a longer life. If you're not concentrating, if you're dozing off in class and at your desk, or if you're feeling dragged out, take steps to put yourself on the right track.

The right track means deep sleep in a dark room, which activates secretion of melatonin by the pineal gland. According to Dr. Alexander Grant's *Health Gazette*, "Melatonin not only helps us to sleep, but also may help to prevent tumors since it stimulates our tissues to destroy oxidants, chemical pollutants that produce cancer."[56] Also, under these favorable conditions, the pituitary gland releases large quantities of growth hormone into the blood. The hormone travels throughout the body to restore and rebuild body tissue. When you don't give the rebuilding process enough time, you upset the body's processes. For example, in a sleep-deprived state, the rate that the brain metabolizes glucose slows down; thus thinking slows down. Researchers calculate that a sleep-deprived person takes about 1 hour to do the work that could be done in 45 minutes during the feeling-good stage.

You can incorporate a few simple practices into your daily life to optimize the quality of your sleep:

Don't use caffeine after 4 p.m. Caffeine can often result in insomnia and thus throw your sleep/wake schedule off.[57] In addition, laboratory studies show that from 200 to 500 milligrams of caffeine per day may produce headaches, nervousness, and gastrointestinal disturbances, symptoms that can trigger or exacerbate stress. Keep in mind that coffee is not the only substance that contains caffeine. There's also caffeine in tea, some soft drinks, chocolate, and some nonprescription drugs.

Don't drink alcohol after 8 p.m. Although it has a reputation for making you drowsy, alcohol actually upsets your body's sleep pattern, first by reducing your REM sleep and then by triggering a "REM rebound," which can result in excessive dreaming and/or nightmares.[58]

[55]Quoted in "Fuzzy Brain? Improve Your Attention Span," *CNN Health* (November 14, 2008), http://articles.cnn.com/2008-11-14/health/rs.increase.your.attention.span_1_dopamine-prefrontal-cortex-concentration (accessed May 30, 2012).
[56]*Dr. Alexander Grant's Health Gazette* 18, no. 2 (February 1995).
[57]Milton K. Erman and Merrill M. Mitler, *How to Get a Good Night's Sleep* (Washington, DC: Phillips Publishing, 1990).
[58]Coleman, *Wide Awake at 3:00 a.m.*, p. 124.

Reserve your bed for sleeping. Eating, doing coursework, and even worrying in bed can scramble your body's contextual cues. If your bed becomes a multipurpose area, you may find it more difficult to fall asleep when the time comes.

Exercise! In addition to the benefits it provides to your heart, muscles, and self-esteem, exercise also enhances both the waking and sleeping phases of your circadian rhythms. Twenty minutes or more of vigorous aerobic exercise will boost your alertness in the daytime and improve the quality of your sleep at night. People who exercise regularly have been found to enjoy more deep sleep than people who don't.[59]

Get Some Exercise

SELF-DIRECTION

What does research show about the relationship between exercise and stress?

According to respected American cardiologist Dr. Paul Dudley White, "Vigorous ... exercise is the best antidote for nervous and emotional stress that we possess."[60] In study after study, experts are corroborating the finding that exercise decreases stress and anxiety. Many other researchers report that regular exercise raises self-esteem and well-being and decreases depression. A study of 48 students who had been suffering from test anxiety found that their anxiety was reduced after meditative relaxation and exercise.[61] In another study, both prisoners and prison guards took part in a carefully monitored exercise program. After a regimen of aerobic exercise, participants on both sides of the law found that they were able to sleep better, that their sense of well-being and self-esteem often improved, and that they experienced less tension and depression.[62]

What effect does exercise have on depression?

The effect of exercise on depression, one of the most damaging emotional outgrowths of prolonged stress, led psychologist William Morgan, past president of the American Psychological Association's Division of Exercise and Sport Psychology, to suggest "that running should be viewed as a wonder drug, analogous to penicillin, morphine and the tricyclics [drugs used to treat depression]. It has a profound potential in preventing mental and physical disease and in rehabilitation after various diseases have occurred."[63] And the most effective exercise is that done regularly and aerobically.

Exercise Regularly

What are the advantages of exercising regularly?

You don't have to be an Olympic athlete to reap the benefits of exercise. Exercising three or more times per week is usually enough to improve your overall conditioning, although many students who follow an exercise routine look forward to the time away

---

[59]Ibid., p. 146.
[60]Quoted in Robert K. Cooper, *Health and Fitness Excellence* (Boston: Houghton Mifflin, 1989), p. 100.
[61]Kenneth H. Cooper, *The Aerobics Program for Total Well-Being* (New York: Bantam Books, 1982), p. 186.
[62]Ibid.
[63]Quoted in Keith W. Johnsgård, "Peace of Mind," *Runner's World* 25, no. 4 (April 1990): p. 81

Caffeine: A Poor Substitute for Sleep

Caffeine is the most widely used drug in the United States. Many people drink a cup of coffee or a can of caffeinated soda to produce the feeling of alertness normally associated with sound sleep. Ironically, though, caffeine can actually lead to sleepiness.

- Although morning coffee can mean morning alertness, afternoon coffee may cause afternoon blahs.
- Regular use of caffeine reduces its ability to stimulate alertness.
- Large quantities of caffeine can induce behavioral depression, which results in sleepiness and decreased performance.
- Caffeine burns calories (energy) as it stimulates insulin production, leading to a sudden drop in blood sugar and feeling of lethargy.
- Drinking only 250 mg of caffeine can produce symptoms associated with clinical anxiety.

Sources: Richard M. Coleman, *Wide Awake at 3 a.m.* (New York: W. H. Freeman & Co., 1986); Susan Perry and Jim Dawson, *The Secret Our Body Clocks Reveal* (New York: Rawson Associates, 1988); Jere E. Yates, *Managing Stress* (New York: AMACOM, 1979).

from their desks and exercise between five and seven times per week. Aside from its well-documented benefits, one of the reasons that exercise is so effective in reducing stress is a simple one. Like eating, sleeping, or any other type of recreation, it provides a welcome break from studying and recharges your mental and physical batteries.

Exercise Aerobically

Why is aerobic exercise especially important?

Although all exercise can provide relief from stress, only aerobic exercise can actually prevent the harmful effects of negative stress. Aerobic exercise is any activity that causes a steady, prolonged increase in your breathing and heart rate. A quick sprint across a football field or a dash from home plate to first base is certainly exercise, but it isn't aerobic exercise. You are inhaling lots of oxygen and speeding up your heart, but you are doing so for only a few seconds, probably not at a steady rate, and definitely not for a prolonged period of time. If, however, you swim 25 laps or so, pedal your bike steadily for several miles, or take a brisk 30-minute walk, you are getting aerobic exercise.

What is the greatest benefit of aerobic exercise?

Perhaps the greatest benefit of aerobic exercise is that it lowers your heart rate. Once your heart muscle has been strengthened through exercise, it acts more efficiently, beating fewer times to circulate the same amount of blood. And if anxiety should strike, the increase in the heart rate of an aerobically fit person is not as drastic or potentially dangerous as it is in someone who gets little or no aerobic exercise.[64] If your heart rate remains comparatively low when subjected to stress, you are less likely to overreact physically or emotionally.

How does exercise provide "good stress"?

Exercise provides a perfect example of good stress. It works as a stimulant to release the hormone *norepinephrine*, which promotes enhanced awareness, and *endorphins*, morphinelike hormones that provide the euphoric feeling commonly referred to as "runner's high." According to Dr. Kenneth Cooper, if you exercise at the end of the day when stress levels are traditionally highest, "you can continue to work or play much later into the evening than might be possible otherwise."[65] Exercise leaves you feeling simultaneously alert and relaxed, a nearly ideal state for efficient, prolonged, and stress-free study.

FINAL WORDS

Why are the stress habits you develop in college so important?

Many students are tempted to write off their college days as a time when anything goes. They eat too much (or too little), drink too much, rob themselves of sleep, and subject their bodies to an extraordinary amount of stress. As removed as college may seem to be from the "real world," the habits you develop in school may well set the tone for the rest of your life. Health doesn't take a holiday simply because you're at school. By all means, work hard and enjoy yourself. But do so in a healthy and sensible way. Keep in mind that you are gaining more than academic expertise while you're in school. You're also learning how to live your life. And in the grand scheme of things, that is the grade that truly matters.

[64]Cooper, *The Aerobics Program for Total Well-Being*, p. 189.
[65]Ibid., p. 191.

CHAPTER CHECKUP

SENTENCE COMPLETION

Complete the following sentences with one of the three words listed below each sentence.

1. Sources of stress are called _____

   lesions   **endorphins**   **stressors**

2. Self-esteem is your personal assessment of your own _____

   intelligence   **value**   **finances**

3. The "bad fats" are _____

   polyunsaturated   **saturated**   **monounsaturated**

MATCHING

In each blank space in the left column, write the letter preceding the phrase in the right column that matches the left item best.

_____ 1. Timer   a. Has a silent effect on self-esteem
_____ 2. Panting   b. Developed progressive muscle relaxation
_____ 3. Jacobson   c. Illustrates the U.S. government's nutritional guidelines
_____ 4. Cortisone   d. Defined as "doing nothing with your muscles"
_____ 5. Self-talk   e. Released when body undergoes stress
_____ 6. Reframing   f. Tool to counteract clock-watching
_____ 7. Relaxation   g. Has been shown to cause feelings of panic
_____ 8. MyPlate   h. Reinterprets a stressful situation into something positive

TRUE-FALSE

Circle T beside the true statements and F beside the false statements.

1. T F You can undergo stress when you run or walk at a brisk pace.
2. T F Caffeine is the most widely used drug in the United States.
3. T F Fear of success is one cause of procrastination.
4. T F Some artificial sweeteners may actually increase your appetite for sugar.
5. T F "Sleeping in" should eliminate the effects of sleep deprivation.

MULTIPLE CHOICE

Choose the word or phrase that completes each sentence most accurately, and circle the letter that precedes it.

1. Stress is the body's attempt to adjust to a
   a. crisis.
   b. test.
   c. demand.
   d. situation.

2. One way to counteract procrastination is by
   a. taking a cat nap.
   b. eating complex carbohydrates.
   c. using the five-minute plan.
   d. all of the above.

3. The simplest way to put some sense back into your eating routine is by
   a. avoiding fats.
   b. eating breakfast.
   c. drinking water.
   d. taking vitamins.

4. A typical 12-ounce can of soda contains
   a. a generous supply of nutrients.
   b. five grams of fat.
   c. ten teaspoons of sugar.
   d. all of the above.

5. Exercise has been shown to
   a. improve self-esteem.
   b. increase well-being.
   c. reduce depression.
   d. all of the above.

REFLECTION

Think about the ideas outlined in this chapter and then draw upon your own opinions and experiences to answer each question fully.

1. Is procrastination a problem for you? If so, which of the four common sources (see p. 73) lies at the heart of your procrastination? If you don't procrastinate often, explain the techniques you use to avoid this common pitfall.

www.cengage.com/success/Pauk/HowToStudy11e

2. Do you use relaxation techniques such as exercise, yoga, or the methods outlined in this chapter? If so, explain which technique you use and its effect on your level of stress. If not, explain which relaxation technique seems to be the most practical for your purposes.

3. This chapter contains a great deal of information about eating, sleeping, and exercise. Cite a specific fact or technique you read in this chapter that you think will be the most useful in your own efforts at managing stress and explain why.

IT'S YOUR Q

The Q System uses marginal questions to encourage active reading. You'll notice that most but not all paragraphs in this chapter are accompanied by marginal questions. Now it's your Q. Scan the chapter for any paragraph that is missing a question, reread the paragraph, establish the main idea, and then arrive at a question that elicits it. Use the questions in the surrounding paragraphs as models for your own marginal questions.

VOCABULARY IN ACTION

To expand the horizons of your understanding and to refine the precision of your thought, the three exercises that follow are designed to help you grow, strengthen, and maintain your own vocabulary.

SAY WHAT?

From the three choices beside each numbered item, select the one that most nearly expresses the meaning of the italicized word in the quote. Make a light check mark (√) next to your choice.

I'm a perfectionist. I'm pretty much *insatiable*. I feel there's so many things I can improve on.
—Serena Williams (1981–), American tennis player

1. *insatiable*   always hungry   never satisfied   impatient

The ideals which have lighted my way, and time after time have given me new courage to face life cheerfully, have been Kindness, Beauty, and Truth. The *trite* subjects of human efforts—possessions, outward success, luxury—have always seemed to me *contemptible*.
—Albert Einstein (1879–1955), German-born American theoretical physicist

2. *trite*   concise   precise   stale

3. *contemptible*   temporary   despicable   probable

Insult: a *callous* or *contemptuous* statement or action; a verbal attack upon another person.
—dictionary definition

4. *callous*   thoughtless   unfeeling   careless

5. *contemptuous*   disdainful   inconsiderate   impolite

VOCAB-U-LADDER

Use your knowledge of word synonyms and roots to connect the word at the top rung to the word at the bottom rung, using the words listed below.

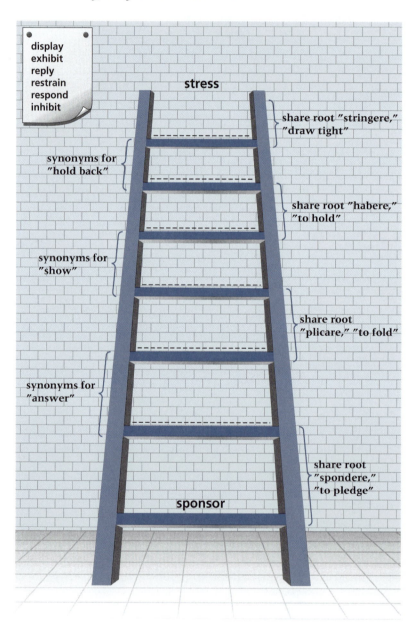

display
exhibit
reply
restrain
respond
inhibit

stress

share root "stringere," "draw tight"

synonyms for "hold back"

share root "habere," "to hold"

synonyms for "show"

share root "plicare," "to fold"

synonyms for "answer"

share root "spondere," "to pledge"

sponsor

Here's the story behind a word that figures prominently in the chapter you've just read.

Circadian rhythm It's not about bugs with drums

circadian rhythm sər-kā′ dē-ən rĭth-əm *n.* A daily rhythmic activity cycle, based on 24-hour intervals, that is exhibited by many organisms.*

The similarity between the words *cicada* and *circadian* can sometimes create confusion, especially since many *cicadas* (such as the erroneously named "17-year locusts") appear and disappear with a predictable rhythm. But the "r" in *circa-* and the "i" in *dian* make all the difference and provide some helpful clues to the meaning of circadian that even the casual word sleuth may be able to uncover. If you know Spanish, for example, then you're already well on your way to understanding *circadian*. The *dian* in *circadian* has the same origin as the dias in *buenas dias* or the dia- in the English word diary. In each case, it means "day." (A diary is a daily record.) And what about *circa?* It shares the same root with circle and in this case means "around or about." (When we say "*circa* 1934" we mean around that particular year.) So *circadian* simply means "about a day." Adding the word *rhythm* from the Greek word rhuthmos for "recurring motion" just makes it clearer that our *circadian* rhythms happen over and over again.**

*Adapted from "circadian rhythm." *The American Heritage Dictionary of the English Language*, 4th ed. (Boston: Houghton Mifflin, 2000), http://dictionary.reference.com/browse/circadian+rhythm (accessed May 26, 2009).
**Based on information from "circadian rhythm." *The American Heritage Dictionary of the English Language*, 4th ed. (Boston: Houghton Mifflin, 2000), http://dictionary.reference.com/browse/circadian+rhythm (accessed May 26, 2009); "circadian, *a.*" *Online Etymology Dictionary*. Douglas Harper, Historian, http://www.etymonline.com/index.php?search=circadian (accessed May 26, 2009); "rhythm." *Online Etymology Dictionary*. Douglas Harper, Historian, http://www.etymonline.com/index.php?search=rhythm (accessed May 26, 2009); "rhythm." *Oxford English Dictionary*, 2nd ed. 20 vols. (Oxford: Oxford University Press, 1989).

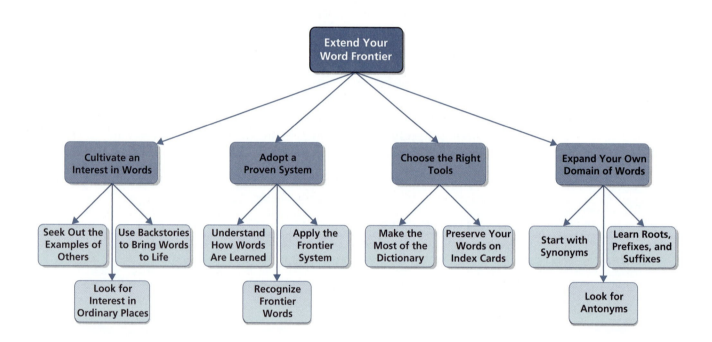

Extend Your Word Frontier

> *One forgets words as one forgets names. One's vocabulary needs constant fertilizing or it will die.*
>
> **Evelyn Waugh** (1903–1966), English writer

Accumulating a large and precise vocabulary can be an adventure. If you're equipped with the right tools and a sense of curiosity, you'll have an exciting journey. The territory may seem strange at first, but in time you'll be living in a community of interrelated words where you'll always be genuinely at home. This chapter tells you how to

- **Cultivate an Interest in Words**
- **Adopt a Proven System**
- **Choose the Right Tools**
- **Expand Your Own Domain of Words**

In this chapter

What is the relationship between thinking and vocabulary?

The quality of our vocabulary can have a direct effect on the quality of our thought. True, some of our thoughts come in images, but we do much of our thinking in words. If we come across a person who is muttering, we're inclined to say, "He's talking to himself," when what we really should be saying is, "He's thinking out loud." Whether spoken or silent, words are the impulses sent over the electrical pathways of the mind. When you're thinking, you're probably talking. It logically follows that the more powerful and precise your vocabulary is, the more powerful and precise your thoughts will be.

How can you improve the quality of your vocabulary?

To improve the quality of your vocabulary and with it the quality of your thoughts, you need to cultivate an interest in words, adopt a proven system, choose the right vocabulary-building tools, and expand your own domain of words.

Cultivate an Interest in Words

What role does interest play in building your vocabulary?

Imagine trying to build something using a power drill and a power saw but without any electricity. It wouldn't work. In the same way, it's difficult to expand your vocabulary without the addition of one indispensable tool: your own interest. Interest provides the electricity that powers all learning. In many cases, that interest comes from a motivation to get better grades, get a better job, or perhaps delight your friends, your family, or yourself with your knowledge. In other cases, it may be activated by a fear of ridicule or failure. When it comes to building your vocabulary, your interest can go much deeper. It can come from a desire to make your life richer and more meaningful. A powerful vocabulary can transform the way you view the world, the way you understand others, and the way in which you form your thoughts and express your ideas.

What should you do if you don't already have an interest in words?

But what if you personally don't have an interest in words? Although all of us use words in one form or another to think and communicate, we aren't all born "word people." If words don't already interest you, don't be discouraged. You can cultivate an interest in words, just as you can cultivate concentration (see Chapter 1) or teach yourself to manage stress (see Chapter 3). To encourage your interest in words, seek out the inspiration and examples of others whose lives have been changed by words, and look to words all around you, even in ordinary places, as potential sparks to activate your own interest.

Seek Out the Examples of Others

SELF-DIRECTION

How can developing an interest in words change your life?

Developing an interest in words can change your life. In the case of Malcolm X, that change was dramatic. In fact, it altered the course of American history. In the case of a Depression-era caddy, although the change wasn't as momentous, it made his life richer, not just in terms of money but in his appreciation for the power and pleasure of language.

The Transformation of Malcolm X

While in a penitentiary, Malcolm X was unable to answer letters from his brother and sister because he could not write a sentence or spell a word. He felt helpless. In his spare time, he listened to lectures by Bimbi, a self-educated black man.

> What fascinated me with him most of all was that he was the first man I had ever seen command total respect with his words.[1]

Other men commanded respect because of their strength or cunning, the number of robberies they had committed, and so forth. But Bimbi was different. Malcolm X developed a strong desire to be like Bimbi—to learn and use words. He reasoned that the best way to learn words was by studying a dictionary. So he borrowed one from the prison school and took it to his cell. He described his first encounter:

> In my slow, painstaking, ragged handwriting, I copied into my tablet everything printed on that first page. I believe it took me a day. Then, aloud, I read back to myself, everything I'd written. Over and over, aloud, to myself, I read my own handwriting. I woke up the next morning thinking about those words.[2]

Either Malcolm X shaped his life around words or the words took over and shaped his life. Either way, he was a winner—he became a "thinking man." He had words with which to think.

Malcolm X went on to become an outstanding leader, preacher, and public speaker. He even lectured to law students at Harvard University. With a wide and exact vocabulary, he was able to express his thoughts and ideas forcefully and intelligently. He earned and commanded respect all over the world. Sadly, his life was cut short by an assassin's bullet in 1965.

The Education of a Caddy

During the Great Depression of the 1930s, jobs were hard to find. Caddying at the nearby golf course provided some income for high school boys growing up in Branford, Connecticut. Among the caddies, one fellow always got bigger tips than the others. When asked by a friend, he reluctantly divulged his secret.

On the golf course as well as on the street, one common topic of conversation is the weather. It often begins like this: The golfer would say, "Do you think it will rain this morning?" Almost all the caddies would answer "Yep!" or "Nope!" That would be the end of the conversation. But this one fellow had a better scenario. He'd say, "I'm

---

[1]Alex Haley and Malcolm X, *The Autobiography of Malcolm X* (New York: Ballantine Books, 1964), p. 428.

[2]Ibid.

optimistic; there's a bit of blue in the sky. It won't rain." If he were to predict rain, he'd say, "I'm pessimistic today. The clouds are gathering. It'll rain." The magic, of course, was in the words *optimistic* and *pessimistic*. These are college-type words, and they made the caddy the mental equal of the golfer. Psychologically, the golfer wouldn't degrade himself in the eyes of the caddy by tipping him the mere minimum. When his friend learned his secret, he tried it out, and it worked. The story sounds mercenary, but there's a more important dimension; that is, using college-type words creates within you a healthy self-concept—yes, self-esteem.

Look for Interest in Ordinary Places

Where can you look for words to ignite your interest?

IT'S YOUR Q

Of course, you certainly don't have to serve time in prison or even work on a golf course in order to develop an interest in words. There are words all around you that have the potential to ignite your own personal interest. You just need to keep your eyes open and your mind engaged.

In print or online, newspapers are a prime and readily accessible source for the clever use of words. Copy editors, who spend much of their time adding punctuation and correcting grammar, have a real flair for words and a genuine love of language. It is in writing headlines that they get a chance to exhibit their superior skills and even have a little fun in the process. When you catch on to what these copy editors are up to, your interest in words is likely to increase, and with it a desire to strengthen your own vocabulary. To illustrate, the following came from a paper in Springfield, Illinois:

Woman Who Wouldn't Wear Pants Wins Suit

A headline in an Atlanta paper dismissed the notion that children pay attention to height when choosing their friends:

Short-Kid Stereotypes Found to Be Tall Tales

There is nothing earthshaking in these headlines—only the personal delight that comes when you see and appreciate what the writer is doing, using words such as "suit" and "tall" that we'd expect to find in an article about clothes and height but then turning our expectations on their heads. Pick up a paper or go online and find some examples for yourself. Once you become aware of these headlines, it's like discovering treasure that's been hidden in plain sight.

Even the writers at the stately *New York Times* seem to enjoy using mind-catching headlines. An article on the popularity of digital cameras was topped off with this ingenious entreaty:

You Ought to Be in Pixels

Here the writer took the old song about Hollywood called "You Ought to Be in Pictures" and puckishly replaced "pictures" with "pixels," which are the tiny dots that make up a digital photograph.

How do you acquire an interest in words?

The question now is how to acquire an interest in words. The creative use of words in newspaper headlines may work for you. Then again, it may not. There is no neat formula. You just need to keep your eyes and ears open. Different people acquire interest in different ways. Within all of us, there is a desire to lift our self-esteem; that is, we want to feel good about ourselves. And a good vocabulary is one excellent way to achieve this.

Use Backstories to Bring Words to Life

SELF-DIRECTION

What are the benefits of learning a word's backstory?

Words are vibrant, dynamic things, each with a history, a story of its own. If you learn the life history of a word, the chances are great that you'll grow to *like* the word, not simply *learn* it. To help you in this endeavor, each chapter in this book ends with an intriguing and often entertaining history of a word that has figured prominently in that chapter. These "backstories" not only provide a definition for each word, they also establish a bond.

For example, the backstories for two common words in a college context—*scholar* and *sophomore*—are entertaining examples of how histories can strengthen your understanding and appreciation of the words around you.

What is the connection between the word scholar and leisure?

Scholar. Although we generally think of a scholar as a hard-working, serious student, the word has a surprisingly different history. *Scholar* comes from the ancient Greek word for leisure. That's because originally the only people who had the luxury of learning were the children of the privileged classes. Everyone else was expected to work. In time, the connection with leisure was lost, and these days most scholars would bristle at any suggestion that they are simply taking it easy.

How does the origin of sophomore convey the status of a second-year student?

Sophomore. The word *sophomore* may be viewed as a rather harmless label for a second-year student, but its derivation provides a fascinating insight into how students partway through their education are viewed. The word originates from the Greek word *sophos* for "wise," but also from *moros*, which means foolish! So, although sophomores may feel as though they know it all, the people who coined the word *sophomore* must have felt these "wise fools" still needed a little humility.

Where can you learn more about the histories of words?

There are dozens of books that relate the often-fascinating histories of words. Here's a list of books both in and out of print that tell the backstories of some well-known words. You should be able to find many of the books in library catalogs. The books still in print should also be available for purchase in stores or online.

Books Still In Print

Almond, Jordan. *Dictionary of Word Origins: A History of the Words, Expressions and Clichés We Use*. Citadel Press, 1995.

American Heritage Dictionary Editors. *Word Mysteries and Histories: From Abracadabra to Zeus*. Houghton Mifflin, 2004.

www.cengage.com/success/Pauk/HowToStudy11e

American Heritage Dictionary Editors and Barry Moser. *Word Mysteries and Histories: From Quiche to Humble Pie*. Houghton Mifflin, 1987.

Ayto, John. *Dictionary of Word Origins*. Arcade, 1993.

Funk, Charles Earle. *Thereby Hangs a Tale: Stories of Curious Word Origins*. Collins, 2002.

Hendrickson, Robert. *The Facts on File Encyclopedia of Word and Phrase Origins*. 4th ed. Checkmark, 2008.

Isil, Olivia A. *When a Loose Cannon Flogs a Dead Horse There's the Devil to Pay: Seafaring Words in Everyday Speech*. International Marine/Ragged Mountain Press, 1996.

Liberman, Anatoly. *Word Origins . . . and How We Know Them: Etymology for Everyone*. Oxford University Press, 2005.

Morris, Evan. *The Word Detective: Solving the Mysteries Behind Those Pesky Words and Phrases*. Plume, 2001.

Quinion, Michael. *Ballyhoo, Buckaroo, and Spuds: Ingenious Tales of Words and Their Origins*. Harper Perennial, 2006.

Rees, Nigel. *Cassell's Dictionary of Word and Phrase Origins*. Cassell Academic, 2002.

Out-of-Print Books

Ernst, Margaret S. *In a Word*. HarperCollins, 1989 (with illustrations by James Thurber).

Picturesque Word Origins. G. & C. Merriam, 1933.

Adopt a Proven System

How can you increase your vocabulary systematically?

The most efficient way to expand your vocabulary is by doing so systematically. Consulting the dictionary whenever you encounter a word you don't know can help increase your vocabulary a word at a time. But it can be an inconsistent and unpredictable process. One highly effective way to increase your vocabulary more systematically is by using the Frontier Vocabulary System developed by Johnson O'Connor.

Understand How Words Are Learned

PLANNING

What principles underlie the Frontier Vocabulary System?

From his analytical research, O'Connor concluded that learning new words is much like learning any other skill. We progress from simple words to more difficult ones in an orderly sequence. The difficulty or ease of learning a word does not depend on the length of the word, its frequency of use, its geographic origin, or its pronunciation—or on teachers, books, or parents. Instead, difficulty in learning a word depends on the complexity of the *idea* that the word stands for. The following findings by O'Connor form the basis of the Frontier Vocabulary System:

1. The easiest words are learned first; then the harder ones are learned.

2. At the forward edge of the mass of all the words that have been mastered is the individual's *frontier*. Only a very few words *beyond the frontier* have already been mastered.
3. The greatest learning takes place in the frontier area, which lies between the zone of known words and the zone of totally unknown words (see Figure 4.1).
4. The most significant characteristic of the words in the frontier area is that they are, to some extent, familiar. The maximum advancement in a person's mastery of words takes place in the frontier area, where hundreds of almost known words need only a slight straightening out to make them familiar.
5. Learning becomes extremely inefficient and may actually break down when a person skips the frontier area and tries to learn totally unknown words.

What is the value of being familiar with words in the frontier area?

Familiarity with a word in the frontier area means that you already know something about the word or its definition. You may, for example, know its general meaning and how to pronounce it. Or you may know one of its several meanings. The important point is this: By singling out a frontier word and learning its specific meaning, or its several definitions, you can master the word with minimal time and effort. By working continually in the frontier area, you can rapidly master words. At the same time, you will continually be discovering new frontier words to conquer. As the process continues, your frontier area will push further into the zone of what were once totally unknown words.

Figure 4.1
The Concept of Frontier Words

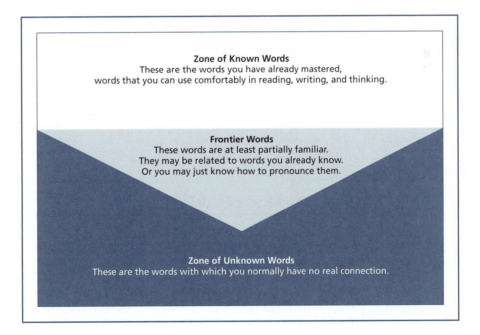

Zone of Known Words
These are the words you have already mastered,
words that you can use comfortably in reading, writing, and thinking.

Frontier Words
These words are at least partially familiar.
They may be related to words you already know.
Or you may just know how to pronounce them.

Zone of Unknown Words
These are the words with which you normally have no real connection.

Recognize Frontier Words

PLANNING

How can you find your own frontier words?

To find your own frontier words, first become aware of your daily speech, and make a list of the unusual words you use. Next, be on the lookout for words that you recognize in reading but do not use in speaking and writing. From this source choose *only* the words that interest you. Listen attentively while other people speak. The chances are great that you will recognize and know the general meaning of all the words you hear. From this stream of speech, choose the words that appeal to you—words that you would like to incorporate into your own speech.

Apply the Frontier System

CLUSTERING — PLANNING

What should you do with your frontier words once you've found them?

After you have selected words from your own frontier, you must set out to master them by strengthening their connection to the words that already make up your working vocabulary. As you master the precise meaning of each frontier word, there will be a corresponding advance in your reading, writing, speaking, and thinking. Because by definition you are already acquainted with your frontier words, your motivation and interest in mastering them should be higher than it would be if you were called upon to learn a list of words with which you had no connection. Now all you need are a few simple tools to add them to your vocabulary.

Choose the Right Tools

What sort of tools do you need to add words to your vocabulary?

One of the great things about building a lasting vocabulary is that it requires so few tools to do so. You don't need to take a class, use computer software, or purchase some other specialized book or device. All you really require is a decent dictionary and a generous stack of index cards.

Make the Most of the Dictionary

SELF-DIRECTION — PLANNING

Aside from interest, what is your best vocabulary-building tool?

Beyond your own sense of interest, the best tool for building your vocabulary is a good dictionary. Keep one close to your elbow or bookmarked in your browser and use it whenever uncertainty arises. Gliding over a word that you don't quite know can be costly. Consider this sentence: "The mayor gave *fulsome* praise to the budget committee." What does *fulsome* mean? If you think it means "full of praise," you're mistaken. Look it up.

What are the limitations of using context to learn new words?

Sometimes, you can get some idea of the meaning of a new word from its context, but sometimes you can't. Lee C. Deighton of Columbia University points out three limitations to context: (1) It provides only the meaning that fits that particular situation. (2) You often end up with a synonym, which is not quite the same as a definition. (3) When you have to infer the meaning of a word, you can be slightly (or greatly) in error.[3] Your safest bet is to avoid all the guesswork and go straight to your dictionary.

What should you do when you come across a word you don't understand?

As you study, consult your dictionary whenever you come to a word that you don't know precisely. Find the exact meaning you need; then go back to your textbook and reread the paragraph, with the meaning substituted for the word. If you become interested in a particular word, write it along with the sentence it occurred in on an index card. Later, go back to the dictionary and investigate the word. But don't break into your studying for a long session with the dictionary; save that for later.

Always Carry a Dictionary with You

What is the value of a portable dictionary?

A portable dictionary is no substitute for a larger desk dictionary, but as a learning tool that you can take with you practically anywhere, it can be worth its weight in gold. Given the wide variety of options, both hard copy and electronic, it would be a pity these days to go anywhere without some sort of portable dictionary. Follow the example of thousands of successful people and get yourself one. Then when you catch yourself reading the print on cereal boxes, gazing at advertising placards on buses and subways, or simply staring into space, you can take out your dictionary and *read* it. It'll make adding to your vocabulary remarkably easy and provide a welcome antidote to wasted time or boredom.

IT'S YOUR Q

From the standpoint of price, you can't beat a paper dictionary. You can usually find a pocket dictionary, such as *Webster's II New Riverside Pocket Dictionary*, for just a few dollars. Of course, electronic dictionaries can be equally inexpensive—sometimes they're even free—but they require the initial and not insignificant cost of some sort of handheld device. If you already have an iPhone, Android, or something similar, an electronic dictionary is a viable option. If you don't have a handheld device, a paperback pocket dictionary should serve you well. Paperbacks not only are cheaper, but they can also be dropped, stepped on, or hurriedly crammed into a backpack or purse without undue concern about costly damage.

How do you read a paperback dictionary?

Reading Your Paperback Dictionary   If the idea of simply reading a dictionary sounds boring or difficult, it's neither. Although the ways in which you read a paperback dictionary and an electronic one are different, both can light the spark that fires a lifelong interest in words. To illustrate how a paper dictionary is read, let's study Figure 4.2,

---

[3]Lee C. Deighton, *Vocabulary Development in the Classroom* (New York: Teachers College Press, 1959), pp. 2–3.

Figure 4.2
How to Read a Dictionary
Source: Copyright © 1991 by Houghton Mifflin Company. Reproduced by permission from *Webster's ll New Riverside Pocket Dictionary,* Revised Edition.

which is a page from a pocket dictionary.[4] When you open to page 1 and your eyes drift down the column of words, an internal conversation takes place: You think about what you already know about the word and you think about the other aspects of the word, such as the syllable that must be accented, the precise definition, and how you could use the word in your writing and speaking. You may turn to a particular page in the dictionary with a specific word in mind and find yourself delighting in the meanings of some of the other neighboring words on that page. Indeed, one of the distinguishing advantages that paperback dictionaries provide is the strong possibility for *serendipity*.

IT'S YOUR Q

Reading an Electronic Dictionary   Because it normally takes you to exactly the word you were seeking, the experience of reading an electronic dictionary is a little different than that of reading a paper-based one. Not necessarily better. Or worse. Different. Gone is the delight that comes from scanning a group of alphabetically related words and discovering a word you'd never even heard of like spotting a sparkling nugget of gold in a pan full of pebbles. But in its place are a number of formidable advantages. Like those in the paperback version, the definitions in an electronic dictionary will frequently include synonyms and antonyms. But unlike its hard-copy cousin, the electronic dictionary allows you to explore the meanings of these related words in an instant, simply by clicking on them. You can start with a word that interests you or that you need to know and suddenly find yourself traveling along a river of related words that soon become part of your vocabulary as well. Another advantage that certain electronic dictionaries provide is the inclusion of sound files. To truly master a word you need to know how to pronounce it. Whereas paper dictionaries always *show* how a word is pronounced, some electronic dictionaries actually give you an opportunity to *hear* it.

Keep an Abridged Dictionary at Your Desk

What advantages does an abridged dictionary provide over a pocket dictionary?

At times when you know that you're going to stay put, a full-sized abridged dictionary is superior to most portable ones. Rather than simply providing pronunciation and bare-bones definitions, good abridged dictionaries tell you far more about the words you are investigating. With an abridged dictionary, you usually get more definitions, more information on a word's derivation, and in some instances information about a word's usage and history. Buy and use the best abridged dictionary that you can afford, but be aware that no word is ever fully defined, even by a good abridged dictionary. Words have multiple shades of meaning that add richness to our language. These various shades will become apparent to you as you keep reading, listening, and trying to use words in a variety of contexts.

[4]*Webster's II New Riverside Pocket Dictionary* (Boston: Houghton Mifflin, 1991), p. 1.

Good abridged desk dictionaries include the following:

The American Heritage Dictionary (Houghton Mifflin)
Webster's New Collegiate Dictionary (Merriam-Webster, Inc.)
Webster's New World College Dictionary, 4th ed. (Webster's New World)

What are some of the features of the *American Heritage Dictionary*?

Of these three, the *American Heritage Dictionary* has some distinct advantages. Unlike most abridged dictionaries, it offers many of the special features—such as usage notes and word histories—that you normally would expect to find only in unabridged dictionaries. (See Figure 4.3.)

What is the purpose of usage notes?

Usage Notes   It's possible to learn a word's definition and still use it incorrectly. For example, a student who learned that the word *incite* means "to stir up" mistakenly wrote: "The cook incited the soup." Usage notes provide clarification that goes beyond standard definitions. Such notes are not only instructive, but frequently interesting. Here is an example:

USAGE NOTE: The verbs *founder* and *flounder* are often confused. *Founder* comes from a Latin word meaning "bottom" (as in *foundation*) and originally referred to knocking enemies down; it is now also used to mean "to fail utterly, collapse." *Flounder* means "to move clumsily, thrash about," and hence "to proceed in confusion." If John is *foundering* in Chemistry 1, he had better drop the course; if he is *floundering*, he may yet pull through.[5]

Usage notes impart information in an easy-to-read, nontechnical, and often entertaining manner.

What is the value of knowing a word's history?

Word History   There are many books devoted to the history and origin of words, but the word history items you can find in the *American Heritage Dictionary* as well as in most unabridged dictionaries can serve as very good substitutes. A plus factor is that these histories are written in an easy-to-read narrative manner. Here's a sample:

Worrying may shorten one's life, but not as quickly as it once did. The ancestor of our word, Old English *wyrgan*, meant "to strangle." Its Middle English descendant, *worien*, kept this sense and developed the new sense "to grasp by the throat with the teeth and lacerate" or "to kill or injure by biting and shaking." This is the way wolves or dogs might attack sheep, for example. In the 16th century *worry* began to be used in the sense "to harass, as by rough treatment or attack," or "to assault verbally," and in the 17th century the word took on the sense "to bother, distress, or persecute." It was a small step from this sense to the main modern senses "to cause to feel anxious or distressed" and "to feel troubled or uneasy," first recorded in the 19th century.[6]

[5]*The American Heritage Dictionary of the English Language*, 4th ed. (Boston: Houghton Mifflin, 2000), p. 564.
[6]Ibid., p. 1983.

Figure 4.3

A Page from *The American Heritage Dictionary*

Source: Copyright © 2010 by Houghton Mifflin Harcourt Publishing Company. Adapted and reproduced by permission from *The American Heritage Dictionary of the English Language,* Fourth Edition.

politician | polonium

pol•i•ti•cian (pŏl′ĭ-tĭsh′ən) *n.* **1a.** One who is actively involved in politics, especially party politics. **b.** One who holds or seeks a political office. **2.** One who seeks personal or partisan gain, often by scheming and maneuvering: *"Mothers may still want their favorite sons to grow up to be President, but . . . they do not want them to become politicians in the process"* (John F. Kennedy). **3.** One who is skilled or experienced in the science or administration of government.

po•lit•i•cize (pə-lĭt′ĭ-sīz′) *v.* **-cized, -ciz•ing, -ciz•es** —*intr.* To engage in or discuss politics. —*tr.* To make political: *"The mayor was given authority to appoint police commissioners and by virtue of that power was able to politicize the department"* (Connie Paige). —**po•lit′i•ci•za′tion** (-sĭ-zā′shən) *n.*

pol•i•tick (pŏl′ĭ-tĭk) *intr.v.* **-ticked, -tick•ing, -ticks** To engage in or discuss politics. [Back-formation from *politicking,* engaging in partisan political activity, from POLITIC.] —**pol′i•tick′er** *n.*

po•lit•i•co (pə-lĭt′ĭ-kō′) *n., pl.* **-cos** A politician. [From Italian or from Spanish *politico,* both from Latin *politicus,* political. See POLITIC.]

pol•i•tics (pŏl′ĭ-tĭks) *n.* **1.** *(used with a sing. verb)* **a.** The art or science of government or governing, especially the governing of a political entity, such as a nation, and the administration and control of its internal and external affairs. **b.** Political science. **2.** *(used with a sing. verb)* **a.** The activities or affairs engaged in by a government, politician, or political party: *"All politics is local"* (Thomas P. O'Neill, Jr.). *"Politics have appealed to me since I was at Oxford because they are exciting morning, noon, and night"* (Jeffrey Archer). **b.** The methods or tactics involved in managing a state or government: *The politics of the former regime were rejected by the new government leadership. If the politics of the conservative government now borders on the repressive, what can be expected when the economy falters?* **3.** *(used with a sing. or pl. verb)* Political life: *studied law with a view to going into politics; felt that politics was a worthwhile career.* **4.** *(used with a sing. or pl. verb)* Intrigue or maneuvering within a political unit or group in order to gain control or power: *Partisan politics is often an obstruction to good government. Office politics are often debilitating and counterproductive.* **5.** *(used with a sing. or pl. verb)* Political attitudes and positions: *His politics on that issue is his own business. Your politics are clearly more liberal than mine.* **6.** *(used with a sing. or pl. verb)* The often internally conflicting interrelationships among people in a society.

Usage Note *Politics,* although plural in form, takes a singular verb when used to mean the art or science of governing or to political science: *Politics has been a concern of philosophers since Plato.* But in its other senses *politics* can take either a singular or plural verb. Many other nouns that end in *–ics* behave similarly, and the user is advised to consult specific entries for precise information.

pol•i•ty (pŏl′ĭ-tē) *n., pl.* **-ties 1.** The form of government of a nation, state, church, or organization. **2.** An organized society, such as a nation, having a specific form of government: *"His alien philosophy found no roots in the American polity"* (New York Times). [Obsolete French *politie,* from Old French, from Late Latin *polītīa,* the Roman government. See POLICE.]

Polk (pōk), **James Knox** 1795–1849. The 11th President of the United States (1845–1849), whose term was marked by the establishment of the 49th parallel as the country's northern border (1846).

pol•ka (pōl′kə, pō′kə) *n.* **1.** A lively dance originating in Bohemia and performed by couples. **2.** Music for this dance, having duple meter. —*intr.* **-kaed, -ka•ing, -kas** To dance the polka. [Czech, probably from Polish, from *Polka,* Polish woman, feminine of *Polak,* Pole. See **pelə-** in Appendix I.]

polka dot *n.* **1.** One of a number of dots or round spots forming a pattern, as on cloth. **2.** A pattern or fabric with such dots.

poll (pōl) *n.* **1.** The casting and registering of votes in an election. **2.** The number of votes cast or recorded. **3.** The place where votes are cast and registered. Often used in the plural with *the.* **4.** A survey of the public or of a sample of public opinion to acquire information. **5.** The head, especially the top of the head where hair grows. **6.** The blunt or broad end of a tool such as a hammer or ax. ❖ *v.* **polled, poll•ing, polls** —*tr.* **1.** To receive (a given number of votes). **2.** To receive or record the votes of: *polling a jury.* **3.** To cast (a vote or ballot). **4.** To question in a survey; canvass. **5.** To cut off or trim (hair, horns, or wool, for example); clip. **6.** To trim or cut off the hair, wool, branches, or horns of: *polled the sheep; polled the trees.* —*intr.* To vote at the polls in an election. [Middle English *pol,* head, from Middle Low German or Middle Dutch.] —**poll′er** *n.*

pol•lack also **pol•lock** (pŏl′ək) *n., pl.* **pollack** or **-lacks** also **pollock** or **-locks** A marine food fish (*Pollachius virens*) of northern Atlantic waters, related to the cod. [Alteration of Scots *podlok.*]

pol•lard (pŏl′ərd) *n.* **1.** A tree whose top branches have been cut back to the trunk so that it may produce a dense growth of new shoots. **2.** An animal, such as an ox, goat, or sheep, that no longer has its horns. ❖ *tr.v.* **-lard•ed, -lard•ing, -lards** To convert or make into a pollard. [From POLL.]

polled (pōld) *adj.* Having no horns; hornless.

pol•len (pŏl′ən) *n.* The fine powderlike material consisting of pollen grains that is produced by the anthers of seed plants. [Latin, fine flour.]

pol•len•ate (pŏl′ə-nāt′) *v.* Variant of **pollinate**.

pollen count *n.* The average number of pollen grains, usually of ragweed, in a cubic foot or other standard volume of air over a 24-hour period at a specified time and place.

pollen grain *n.* A microspore of seed plants, containing a male gametophyte.

pol•len•if•er•ous (pŏl′ə-nĭf′ər-əs) *adj.* Variant of **polliniferous.**

pollen mother cell *n.* The microsporocyte of a seed plant.

pol•len•o•sis (pŏl′ə-nō′sĭs) *n.* Variant of **pollinosis.**

pollen sac *n.* The microsporangium of a seed plant in which pollen is produced.

pollen tube *n.* The slender tube formed by the pollen grain that penetrates an ovule and releases the male gametes.

pol•lex (pŏl′ĕks′) *n., pl.* **pol•li•ces** (pŏl′ĭ-sēz′) See thumb (sense 1). [Latin, thumb, big toe.]

pollin– *pref.* Variant of **pollini–.**

pol•li•nate also **pol•len•ate** (pŏl′ə-nāt′) *tr.v.* **-li•nat•ed, -li•nat•ing, -li•nates** also **-len•at•ed, -len•at•ing, -len•ates** To transfer pollen from an anther to the stigma of (a flower). [New Latin *pollen, pollin-,* pollen (from Latin, fine flour) + -ATE¹.] —**pol′li•na′tion** *n.* —**pol′li•na′tor** *n.*

pollini– *or* **pollin–** *pref.* Pollen: *polliniferous.* [From New Latin *pollen, pollin-,* pollen. See POLLINATE.]

pol•li•nif•er•ous also **pol•len•if•er•ous** (pŏl′ə-nĭf′ər-əs) *adj.* **1.** Producing or yielding pollen. **2.** Adapted for carrying pollen.

pol•lin•i•um (pə-lĭn′ē-əm) *n., pl.* **-i•a** (-ē-ə) A mass of coherent pollen grains, found in the flowers of orchids and milkweeds. [New Latin, from *pollen, pollin-,* pollen. See POLLINATE.]

pol•li•nize (pŏl′ə-nīz′) *tr.v.* **-nized, -niz•ing, -niz•es** To pollinate. —**pol′li•niz•a′tion** (-nĭ-zā′shən) *n.* —**pol′li•niz′er** *n.*

pol•li•no•sis also **pol•len•o•sis** (pŏl′ə-nō′sĭs) *n.* See hay fever.

pol•li•wog also **pol•ly•wog** (pŏl′ē-wôg′, -wŏg′) *n.* See tadpole. [Variant of *polliwig,* from Middle English *polwigle : pol,* head; see POLL + *wiglen,* to wiggle; see WIGGLE.]

pol•lock (pŏl′ək) *n.* Variant of **pollack.**

Pol•lock (pŏl′ək), **Jackson** 1912–1956. American artist. Using his drip technique of painting, he became a leader of abstract expressionism.

poll•ster (pōl′stər) *n.* One that takes public-opinion surveys. Also called *polltaker.*

Word History The suffix *–ster* is nowadays most familiar in words like *pollster, jokester, huckster,* where it forms agent nouns that typically denote males. Originally in Old English, however, the suffix (then spelled *–estre*) was used to form feminine agent nouns. *Hoppestre,* for example, meant "female dancer." It was occasionally applied to men, but mostly to translate Latin masculine nouns denoting occupations that were usually held by women in Anglo-Saxon society. An example is *bæcestre,* "baker," glossing Latin *pistor;* it survives as the Modern English name *Baxter.* In Middle English its use as a masculine suffix became more common in northern England, while in the south it remained limited to feminines. In time the masculine usage became dominant throughout the country, and old feminines in *–ster* were refashioned by adding the newer feminine suffix *–ess* (borrowed from French) to them, such as *seamstress* remade from *seamster.* In Modern English, the only noun ending in *–ster* with a feminine referent is *spinster,* which originally meant "a woman who spins thread."

poll•tak•er (pōl′tā′kər) *n.* See pollster.

poll tax *n.* A tax levied on people rather than on property, often as a requirement for voting.

pol•lut•ant (pə-lōōt′nt) *n.* Something that pollutes, especially a waste material that contaminates air, soil, or water.

pol•lute (pə-lōōt′) *tr.v.* **-lut•ed, -lut•ing, -lutes 1.** To make unfit for or harmful to living things, especially by the addition of waste matter. See synonyms at **contaminate. 2.** To make less suitable for an activity, especially by the introduction of unwanted factors: *The stadium lights polluted the sky around the observatory.* **3.** To render impure or morally harmful; corrupt. **4.** To make ceremonially impure; profane: *"Churches and altars were polluted by atrocious murders"* (Edward Gibbon). [Middle English *polluten,* from Latin *polluere, pollut-.*] —**pol•lut′er** *n.*

pol•lu•tion (pə-lōō′shən) *n.* **1.** The act or process of polluting or the state of being polluted, especially the contamination of soil, water, or the atmosphere by the discharge of harmful substances. **2.** Something that pollutes; a pollutant or a group of pollutants: *Pollution in the air reduced the visibility near the airport.*

Pol•lux (pŏl′əks) *n.* **1.** Greek Mythology **1.** One of the Dioscuri. **2.** A bright star in the constellation Gemini. [Latin *Poll x,* from Greek *Poludeukēs.*]

Pol•ly•an•na (pŏl′ē-ăn′ə) *n.* A person regarded as being foolishly or blindly optimistic. [After the heroine of the novel *Pollyanna,* by Eleanor Hodgman Porter (1868–1920), American writer.]

pol•ly•wog (pŏl′ē-wôg′, -wŏg′) *n.* Variant of **polliwog.**

po•lo (pō′lō) *n.* **1.** A game played by two teams of three or four players on horseback who are equipped with long-handled mallets for driving a small wooden ball through the opponents' goal. **2.** Water polo. [Balti (Tibeto-Burman language of Pakistan), ball.] —**po′lo•ist** *n.*

Po•lo (pō′lō), **Marco** 1254–1324. Venetian traveler who explored Asia from 1271 to 1295. His *Travels of Marco Polo* was the only account of the Far East available to Europeans until the 17th century.

polo coat *n.* A loose-fitting, tailored overcoat made from camel's hair or a similar material.

pol•o•naise (pŏl′ə-nāz′, pō′lə-) *n.* **1.** A stately, marchlike Polish dance, primarily a promenade by couples. **2.** Music for or based on the traditional rhythm of this dance, having triple meter. **3.** A woman's dress of the 18th century, having a fitted bodice and draped cutaway skirt, worn over an elaborate underskirt. [French, from feminine of *polonais,* Polish, from Medieval Latin *Polōnia,* Poland.]

po•lo•ni•um (pə-lō′nē-əm) *n. Symbol* **Po** A naturally radioactive metallic element, occurring in minute quantities as a product of radium

ā pat	oi boy
ā pay	ou out
âr care	ŏŏ took
ä father	ōō boot
ĕ pet	ŭ cut
ē be	ûr urge
ĭ pit	th thin
ī pie	th this
îr pier	hw which
ŏ pot	zh vision
ō toe	ə about, item
ô paw	✱ regionalism

Stress marks: ′ (primary); ′ (secondary), as in **dictionary** (dĭk′shə-nĕr′ē)

1359

Dig Deeper with an Unabridged Dictionary

What advantages
do unabridged
dictionaries provide?

Although abridged dictionaries occasionally provide interesting and important details about words, for intensive word study, there is no substitute for an unabridged dictionary. Locate the unabridged dictionaries in your library—usually they are in the reference room—and use them to supplement your abridged desk dictionary. An unabridged dictionary provides more definitions, more about the derivations of words, and more on usage. Good one-volume unabridged dictionaries include *Webster's Third New International Dictionary of the English Language* and the *Random House Dictionary of the English Language*. The *Oxford English Dictionary*, in 20 volumes plus supplements, is indispensable for the historical study of words but is more detailed than you will need for most purposes.

How do definitions
in the two types of
dictionaries differ?

Whereas usage notes and word histories are considered extras in abridged dictionaries, they are standard in most unabridged dictionaries. In addition, for words that have multiple meanings, an unabridged dictionary will include all the definitions instead of just the most common ones.

That fact came in handy when a friend wrote a letter about attending a seminar on Vladimir Nabokov, the Russian-born American writer who was best known for the satirical novel *Lolita*. "All the experts were there," he explained in his letter. "Lots of discussion, but it was too precious for me." Too precious? The sentence was startling. After all, *precious* is commonly used to refer to something valuable. But a quick look at the word's definitions helped clear up the mystery. Here they are:

1. Of high cost or worth; valuable
2. Highly esteemed; cherished
3. Dear; beloved
4. Affectedly dainty or overrefined: *precious mannerisms*[7]

The fourth definition was the one that slid into the context of the letter perfectly. "Overrefined" was the answer. By reading all the definitions of a word, we weave more strands into the background of each word we look up. This will enable us to later use and understand such words with greater correctness and precision.

What makes the *Oxford
English Dictionary*
special?

The Oxford English Dictionary   When it comes to unabridged dictionaries, the *Oxford English Dictionary* (popularly known as the *OED*) is in a class by itself. It presents the words that have formed the English vocabulary from the time of the earliest records to the present day. Five million excerpts from English literature were amassed during preparation of the work, many of them furnished by volunteers; about 1,800,000 quotations were actually printed. Unbeknownst to the editors, one of the dictionary's most valuable and prolific volunteers, W. C. Minor, submitted contributions from his room at a London psychiatric hospital, where he'd been committed after murdering a man!

[7]Ibid, p. 1381.

Work began on the *OED* in 1857, and the last page was delivered to the press on April 19, 1928. On its completion in 1928, it was presented to King George V, and a copy was also officially provided to Calvin Coolidge, the president of the United States.

Here is a brief sample of information gleaned from the *Oxford English Dictionary*. The word is *acre*.

a. The historical spellings of *acre* are: acer, aker, & akre.

b. The historical meanings of *acre*, in order of time, are:

(1) a piece of tilled land.
(2) as much as a yoke of oxen could plow in a day.
(3) consists of 32 furrows of the plow, a furlong in length. [A furlong is about 220 yards.][8]

The ruling king had the power to stipulate weights and measures. For example, under Henry VIII, an acre was 40 poles long and 4 poles wide. The measures, though varied, were somewhat similar throughout history.

Over the years, with each printing, the *OED* has increased in size. The latest edition, printed in 1989, consists of 20 volumes, made up of 22,000 pages. Use this prodigious dictionary with gratitude and respect.

Preserve Your Words on Index Cards

PLANNING

How do you make new words a permanent part of your vocabulary?

Once you find the words you need or that interest you, you'll want to hold onto them. Using the word in a sentence is a common suggestion, and it's good as far as it goes. But if you want to make sure that each new word becomes a permanent part of your vocabulary, you have to go a little further. The only sure way to master words is to *overlearn* them by using the undisputedly best memory-enhancing technique of *recitation*.

Write One Word per Card

What should you write on each vocabulary card?

To get started, all you need is a dictionary and a stack of index cards (see Figure 4.4). On the cards, write the words from your personal frontier as well as any difficult words that you find in your textbooks and hear in the classroom. Here are the steps to make the system work for you:

1. *Consider its context.* When you select a word, write it on the front of an index card. But don't just write it in isolation. To provide a meaningful context, write the complete sentence in which the word occurs and underline the word so that it stands out.

---

[8]*Oxford English Dictionary*, vol. 1, 2nd ed. (Oxford: Clarendon Press, 1989), pp. 117–118.

www.cengage.com/success/Pauk/HowToStudy11e

Figure 4.4
Index Card System

2. *Sound it out.* Look the word up in a dictionary and, on the front of the card, write the word out in syllables, including accent and diacritical marks, so that you can pronounce it correctly. If you can't pronounce it and spell it correctly in the first place, you are less likely to use it later.
3. *Break it down.* On the back of the card, write the prefix and root that make up your word. The prefix and root will help you remember the word by showing you its logical linguistic structure.
4. *Find its meaning.* Still on the back of the card, write several pertinent definitions of the word. You might as well extract the maximum in meanings while you're at it! Then put an asterisk beside the definition that best fits the meaning of your word in its specific context.

How should you handle vocabulary cards for technical terms?

Technical terms can be handled in almost the same way. However, for these words you may want to rely on the definitions in your textbook. Special terms are usually defined in a glossary or when they are first introduced. Even for a special term, record any information you find about its derivation on the reverse side of the card. Often, you'll have to consult an unabridged dictionary.

Master Each Word

How do you master the words you've collected on index cards?

The front and back of this vocabulary card for the word *inferred* demonstrates the format of the index card system. Notice that the front of the card shows the new word underlined in a complete sentence. It also shows how to pronounce the word. The reverse of the card defines prefixes and roots and gives important dictionary definitions of the word. An asterisk is placed beside the definition that most nearly matches the use of the word on the front of the card. Synonyms are also given.

CHAPTER
4

In the above four steps, we covered how to construct cards for the index system. Now, we'll present the steps for using the cards efficiently and effectively. You've put in a lot of work. Get the maximum learning from it. To master the words on the cards, do the following:

1. *Start with the front.* Always look first at the front of the card. Begin by pronouncing the word aloud and correctly. Then read the sentence aloud and think about it momentarily. Next, define the word—not necessarily in a dictionary's language, but in your own words. Read the sentence aloud. All this should be done before you look at the definition on the back. Reading and speaking aloud forces you to think alertly, and hearing the word brings your auditory memory into play. Thus, seeing, saying, hearing, and thinking are all working together for you.

2. *Check your work.* After you have defined the word to the best of your ability, turn the card over to check the accuracy of your definition.

3. *Say it again.* If you are not satisfied with your definition, keep reciting until your definition is correct. For memory's sake, you must, in order to extract it later, enter into your mind a correct, crisp, concise meaning for the word.

4. *Mark the difficult ones.* When you fail to define the word correctly on your first try, place a dot in the upper-right-hand corner of the front of the card. The next time you go through your cards, the dot will remind you that you missed the word on a previous try. When a card has three dots, it is time to give that word extra attention by determining why you keep getting it wrong.

5. *Try another stack.* After you have mastered a small stack of cards, place them in a shoebox and put together another small stack for studying.

6. *Conduct a review.* From time to time, review the words that you have mastered. Reviewing mastered words will take much less time than learning unmastered ones. The erosive power of forgetting is working day and night. A quick periodic review will foil this relentless force.

IT'S YOUR Q

Although you might be tempted to type your new vocabulary words into a computer instead of writing them on index cards, here is a case where the "old-fashioned" method is still superior. The advantage of index cards is that they are convenient to carry around for study at odd moments. At all times, carry a few blank cards on which to record interesting words. Learning words that intrigue you will be immeasurably more valuable than memorizing a list made up by someone else. Finally, as you master the precise meaning of each word, there will be a corresponding advance in your reading, writing, speaking, and thinking. The index card system doesn't exhaust its usefulness when your college education ends. Successful people, including company presidents, frequently carry around a small stack of vocabulary cards.

Expand Your Own Domain of Words

What words are associated with each frontier word?

The noted 16th century English poet John Donne famously wrote, "No man is an island entire of itself; every man is a piece of the continent, a part of the main." The same could be said for words. No word exists in isolation. Each frontier word you learn provides an opportunity to learn a number of words that are associated with it. As the original frontier word becomes a known word, its associates assemble along your frontier, ready to be added to your personal vocabulary as well. Take advantage of this opportunity. When you learn a new word, invest a little extra time to get to know some of its friends, its enemies, and its relatives—that is, its synonyms, antonyms, and words that share its roots. If you do so, you'll be adding words to your vocabulary in clusters instead of just one word at a time.

Start with Synonyms

CLUSTERING

What effect have multiple streams had on the English language?

One of the fascinating things about English is that it represents the confluence of countless streams of language traditions. English words didn't simply show up full-blown one day. Many of them journeyed thousands of miles from far-flung places like India (*pundit*), Iran (*checkmate*), Japan (*tycoon*), West Africa (*jazz*), China (*ketchup*), and South America (*chocolate*) while others that traveled the principal routes from Greece, the Roman Empire, and what is now Germany and the Netherlands underwent steady and sometimes perplexing evolutions over time. (Referring to something as "awful" used to be a compliment while calling someone "nice" was once an insult!) The fact that these streams all fed the same river of language has resulted in inevitable duplication of many words. Consider, for example, how many ways you can express something simple, such as *taking*. Here are just a few: *grabbing, snatching, seizing, snagging*. And if that taking is unlawful (that is, theft), the synonyms multiply to include words such as *stealing, filching, pinching, lifting, swiping, boosting*, and even *appropriating*.

Why does English have so many synonyms?

These are what we commonly refer to as *synonyms*, a word that literally means "same name." Sometimes these words are completely interchangeable, but in most cases there are subtle differences. Think about some of your closest acquaintances: Are they *friends, pals, buddies, chums, cohorts, allies, companions, compatriots,* or *comrades,* or something else entirely? Some of them may be all of the above, others may be none, but it's also just as likely that you'll find a few of those words to be wholly appropriate for a particular person in your inner circle and completely unsuitable if not outright embarrassing to use to refer to another. As author Bill Bryson explains in *The Mother Tongue*, his highly entertaining book about the origins of English, "It had been said that English is unique in possessing a synonym for each level of our culture: popular, literary, and scholarly—so that we can, according to our background and cerebral attainments, rise, mount, or ascend a stairway, shrink in fear, terror, or trepidation, and think, ponder, or cogitate upon a problem."[9]

[9]Bill Bryson, *The Mother Tongue* (New York: William Morrow, 1990), p. 69.

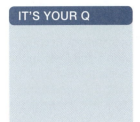

IT'S YOUR Q

What is the best
system for mastering
new words?

How do you find
the synonyms for a
frontier word?

If you had the right level of motivation or interest or both, you could conceivably take a list of synonyms in isolation and master every aspect of them, including their subtle distinctions. But for most of us, attempting to memorize such a free-floating list would be an exercise in futility. Think about the words *inchoate*, *incipient*, and *nascent*, for example, which are all similar in meaning. How many of these words do you use or encounter in your reading or your everyday speech? If you're like most students, the answer is none. Although these words may be valuable to learn (they frequently show up on standardized tests), they lack the connection that is essential to ensure that they will become a permanent part of your vocabulary. A list of words is just that. A list. A list is no more a vocabulary than a pile of bricks is a house. You build a vocabulary by taking words and assembling them to form a stable structure that will often last a lifetime.

If, rather than attempting to learn new words in isolation, you choose words that have a direct connection to words you already know, you will greatly increase your chances of understanding, remembering, and using those new words. That is one of the basic principles of the Frontier Vocabulary System and the reason why learning the synonyms of frontier words can be so powerful.

Finding the synonyms for the word you've just learned is fairly simple. All but the briefest dictionary will usually supply you with one or two along with that word's pronunciation, part of speech, and definitions. Online dictionaries such as dictionary.com (see Figure 4.5) typically include a list of synonyms for each word they define. In addition, the word's original definition will often incorporate a synonym or two, as in the first definition for the word *frontier*:

> 1. *the part of a country that borders another country; boundary; border.*

Figure 4.5
A Page from an Online Dictionary

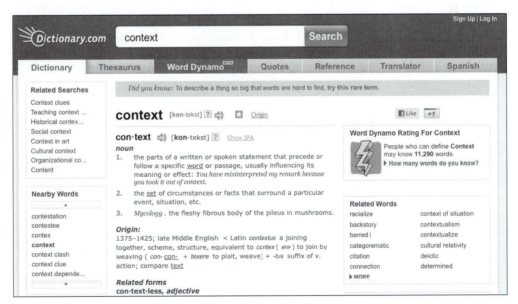

Another option is a thesaurus, which organizes words according to the similarity of their meanings. Because the words found in a thesaurus are handled in groups, the synonyms aren't quite as precise as those you might find listed under specific dictionary entry. Even so, if you return to the dictionary armed with the list of words from the thesaurus and look up the definition for each, you should emerge with a clearer picture of your original word. (By the way, although its name sounds like it could belong to a prehistoric animal, the word thesaurus comes from the Greek *thesauros*, which means "a treasure, treasury, storehouse, chest.")

Look for Antonyms

CLUSTERING

How does a word's antonym help our understanding?

Antonyms are a bit like the diagram of the goblet and the profiles in Chapter 1 (see p. 22), where the picture of the goblet creates the picture of the profiles and vice versa. Learning pairs of contrasting words creates the strong force of spontaneous suggestion—either word suggests the other. For example, you may not know the word *assiduous*, but when you learn that one of its antonyms is *lazy*, you suddenly have a sharper picture of what the word means. Antonyms are not as common or plentiful as synonyms. Not all words have them, and many that do simply take the original word and tack on a prefix, such as non-, un-, in-, dis-, or de-, changes that add no real insight. For example, the fact that the antonym of *compliant* is *noncompliant* doesn't really do anything to clarify the meaning of the original word. On the other hand, learning that an antonym of *cheerful* is *lugubrious* can introduce you to a fascinating new word by establishing a clear connection to a word that you already know.

How do you find the antonyms for a frontier word?

To find out whether your frontier word has an antonym, look it up in a good-sized dictionary or search for it in a dictionary online. Any antonyms will usually be listed at the bottom of the entry. Then, if the word intrigues you, create a frontier card for the antonym and study it along with the original word. The two words will support each other as you work to master them. Another option for finding antonyms is the thesaurus, although once again, any antonyms it provides are not likely to be as precise as those you would find under a specific dictionary entry.

Learn Roots, Prefixes, and Suffixes

CLUSTERING

What is a frontier word's family?

Like all of us, each word is part of a larger family. Every time you learn a new word, you have the opportunity to become acquainted with its relatives as well. The family is the root from which your frontier word has descended; its relatives are the other words in the language that share this root. For example, the root of the word *reduce*—meaning "to bring down or lower"—is *ducere*, which is Latin for "to lead." Because its prefix re- means "back," *reduce* literally means "to lead back." Reduce's relatives include *induce*, *produce*, *deduce*, and even *educate*. Getting to know one word well puts you in a powerful position to meet the rest of the family. (See Figure 4.6.)

How do you learn a word's relatives?

Although mastering the relatives of a frontier word is as straightforward as learning the frontier word itself, actually tracking down its relatives can sometimes be a challenge.

Figure 4.6
A Family of Words from One Root

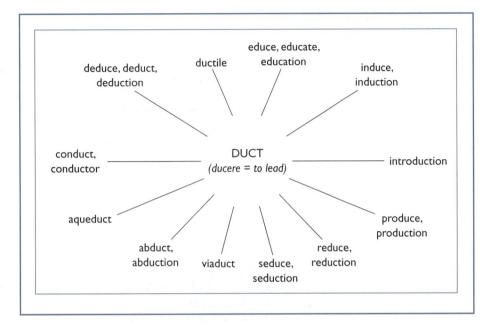

With some words the family resemblance is easy to detect. It's clear, for example, that *omit*, *permit*, and *remit* all come from the same clan (their family is the Latin root *mittere*, meaning "to send") but not quite as obvious with *expect*, *conspicuous*, and *despise*, which share another Latin root, *specere*, meaning "to look at." In cases where a frontier word's relatives aren't readily apparent, a larger reference source, such as the *American Heritage Dictionary of the English Language*, will come in handy. It provides a list of roots and their related words in an appendix. The frontier word's history will usually refer you to the appendix, and the appendix in turn will provide a list of words that are descendants from that particular root. (Table 4.1 provides a list of common roots.)

Where do prefixes and suffixes come in?

Although roots are at the heart, they're only part of an individual word's meaning. A *prefix* is a word beginning that modifies the root. A *suffix* is an element tacked on to the end of a word that alters or refines its meaning. Table 4.2 lists some common word prefixes, and Table 4.3 lists some common suffixes. Whereas changing the prefix can radically alter the meaning of a word—from *competent* to *incompetent*, for example—adding a suffix will sometimes just shift a word's focus or part of speech, such as changing *comfort* to *comfortable* or *elect* to *election*. In other situations, however, suffixes behave almost like prefixes as when *sugar* becomes *sugarfree* or *hope* is changed to *hopeless*.

What's the best way to learn prefixes and suffixes?

Some students conscientiously memorize lists of prefixes and suffixes like the ones provided in this chapter in the hopes of rapidly increasing the size of their vocabulary. Although that's an admirable goal, attempting to master a list of disconnected prefixes can be even more difficult—not to mention considerably more tedious—than mastering a list of disconnected words. In addition, it comes with an unexpected pitfall: The meaning you

Table 4.1
Common Word Roots

Root	Meaning	Example	Definition
agri	field	Agronomy	*Field*—crop production and soil management
anthropo	man	anthropology	The study of *humans*
astro	star	astronaut	One who travels in interplanetary space (*stars*)
bio	life	Biology	The study of *life*
cardio	heart	Cardiac	Pertaining to the *heart*
chromo	color	chromatology	The science of *colors*
demos	people	democracy	Government by the *people*
derma	skin	epidermis	The outer layer of *skin*
dyna	power	dynamic	Characterized by *power* and energy
geo	earth	geology	The study of the *earth*
helio	sun	heliotrope	Any plant that turns toward the *sun*
hydro	water	hydroponics	Growing of plants in *water* reinforced with nutrients
hypno	sleep	hypnosis	A state of *sleep* induced by suggestion
magni	great, big	magnify	To enlarge, to make *bigger*
man(u)	hand	manuscript	Written by *hand*
mono	one	monoplane	Airplane with *one* wing
ortho	straight	orthodox	Right, true, *straight* opinion
pod	foot	pseudopod	False *foot*
psycho	mind	psychology	Study of the *mind* in any of its aspects
pyro	fire	pyrometer	An instrument for measuring high temperatures
terra	earth	Terrace	A raised platform of *earth*
thermo	heat	thermometer	Instrument for measuring *heat*
zoo	animal	zoology	The study of *animals*

remember may not be the one that applies. According to Lee Deighton, "Of the 68 prominent and commonly used prefixes there are only 11 which have a single and fairly invariant meaning."[10] The remaining 57 common prefixes have more than one meaning each. A far better strategy would be to master each new frontier word not strictly for its meaning, but also as the sum of its parts. Connected in this way to actual words that are part of your expanding personal vocabulary, the prefixes and suffixes you learn naturally as an important element in the process of mastery will be easier to remember and reuse than they would be if you attempted to artificially commit them to memory as isolated fragments.

FINAL WORDS

How does
strengthening your
vocabulary relate to
learning career skills?

Thus far in this book, you've seen how words shaped the life of Malcolm X and improved the lot of a golf caddy. Words can shape your life and career as well. It's natural to focus most of your academic energy on preparing for your future career and

[10]Deighton, *Vocabulary Development in the Classroom*, p. 26.

employment. But let the success stories at the beginning of this chapter be a constant reminder of the importance of a lasting vocabulary. Once you are established in your career, professional progress will depend, of course, on your work skills; but your ability to use words—to express yourself clearly and convincingly—may be the real propellant in climbing the ladder. So, let strengthening your vocabulary go hand in hand with building your career skills.

Table 4.2
Common Prefixes

Prefix	Meaning	Example	Definition
ante-	before	antebellum	*Before* the war; especially in the U.S., before the Civil War
anti-	against	antifreeze	Liquid used to guard *against* freezing
auto-	self	automatic	*Self*-acting or *self*-regulating
bene-	good	benefit	An act of *kindness*; a gift
circum-	around	circumscribe	To draw a line *around*; to encircle
contra-	against	contradict	To speak *against*
de-	reverse,	defoliate	*Remove* the leaves from a tree remove
ecto-	outside	ectoparasite	Parasite living on the *exterior* of animals
endo-	within	endogamy	Marriage *within* the tribe
hyper-	over	hypertension	*High* blood pressure
hypo-	under	hypotension	*Low* blood pressure
inter-	between	intervene	Come *between*
intra-	within	intramural	*Within* bounds of a school
intro-	in, into	introspect	To look *within*, as one's own mind
macro-	large	macroscopic	*Large* enough to be observed by the naked eye
mal-	bad	maladjusted	*Badly* adjusted
micro-	small	microscopic	So *small* that one needs a microscope to observe
multi-	many	multimillionaire	One having *two* or *more* million dollars
neo-	new	neolithic	*New* stone age
non-	not	nonconformist	One who does *not* conform
pan-	all	pantheon	A temple dedicated to *all* gods
poly-	many	polygonal	Having *many* sides
post-	after	postgraduate	*After* graduating
pre-	before	precede	To go *before*
proto-	first	prototype	*First* or original model
pseudo-	false	pseudonym	*False* name; esp., an author's pen-name
retro-	backward	retrospect	A looking *back* on things
semi-	half	semicircle	*Half* a circle
sub-	under	submerge	To put *under* water
super-	above	superfine	*Extra* fine
tele-	far	telescope	Seeing or viewing *afar*
trans-	across	transalpine	*Across* the Alps

Table 4.3
Common Suffixes

Nouns		
Suffix	**Meaning**	**Examples**
-acy	quality, state, office	piracy, legacy
-age	total	acreage, mileage
-agogue	leader, bringer	demagogue, pedagogue
-al	of a kind of, pertaining to	logical, natural
-ance	action, condition, or quality	resemblance, hindrance
-ant	one who does or makes something	descendant, informant
-ation	act or result of	generation, imagination
-cide	killing of	homicide, insecticide
-dom	domain, collection, rank, or condition	freedom, kingdom, martyrdom
-eer	one who does or makes something	engineer, volunteer
-ence	action, condition, or quality	difference, persistence
-ent	one who does or makes something	agent, resident
-er	one who does or makes something	baker, programmer
-hood	body of persons of a particular character or class	motherhood, neighborhood
-ian	one who does or makes something	comedian, historian
-ier	one who does or makes something	cashier, financier
-ism	belief in, practice, doctrine	fascism, monotheism
-ist	one who practices or is concerned with something	artist, optometrist, socialist
-ition	act or result of	coalition, expedition
-ity	state or condition	humanity, modernity
-ment	action, state, product, or means	fragment, judgment
-ness	quality, state	darkness, kindness
-or	agent for an action	proprietor, tractor
-phobia	dread of, aversion toward	agoraphobia, claustrophobia
-ship	state, condition of being	leadership, readership

Verbs		
Suffix	**Meaning**	**Examples**
-ate	to become, produce, treat	detonate, replicate
-en	to make, cause to be	broaden, frighten
-fy	to make	magnify, pacify
-ize	to cause or make	apologize, colonize

Adjectives		
Suffix	**Meaning**	**Examples**
-able	able, capable of	manageable, portable
-al	pertaining to, having the form or character of	autumnal, regional
-ible	able, capable of	reducible, visible
-ic	having some characteristics of	dramatic, ironic

CHAPTER CHECKUP

SENTENCE COMPLETION

Complete the following sentences with one of the three words listed below each sentence.

1. Building your vocabulary can increase your _____.

    self-esteem   **self-consciousness**   **self-promotion**

2. A chief advantage of vocabulary cards is their _____.

    completeness   **convenience**   **complexity**

3. The most significant characteristic of a frontier word is its _____.

    difficulty   **familiarity**   **pronunciation**

MATCHING

In each blank space in the left column, write the letter preceding the phrase in the right column that matches the left item best.

_____ 1. Interest   a. Has limitations as a means of learning new words

_____ 2. 57   b. Provides clarification that goes beyond a word's definition

_____ 3. Relatives   c. Number of common prefixes that have more than one meaning

_____ 4. 20   d. Can be a powerful motivator for strengthening vocabulary

_____ 5. Context   e. Greatest learning takes place here

_____ 6. Usage   f. Number of volumes in the current *Oxford English Dictionary*

_____ 7. Serendipity   g. A group of words that share a common root

_____ 8. Frontier area   h. Can be lost when you use an electronic dictionary

TRUE-FALSE

Circle T *beside the true statements and* F *beside the false statements.*

1. T   F   Quality of vocabulary can have a direct effect on quality of thought.
2. T   F   The creative use of words can generate interest in an audience.
3. T   F   Electronic dictionaries enable you to explore related words almost instantaneously.
4. T   F   Words are not always fully defined in an abridged dictionary.
5. T   F   Unabridged dictionaries normally include only the most common definition for each word.

www.cengage.com/success/Pauk/HowToStudy11e

MULTIPLE CHOICE

Choose the word or phrase that completes each sentence most accurately, and circle the letter that precedes it.

1. After he left prison, Malcolm X went on to become an outstanding
   a. leader.
   b. preacher.
   c. public speaker.
   d. all of the above.

2. Frontier words are
   a. inexhaustible in their supply.
   b. the easiest words to master.
   c. familiar in one way or another.
   d. all of the above.

3. From his analytical research, Johnson O'Connor determined that learning new words
   a. requires an above-average memory.
   b. is much like learning any other skill.
   c. interferes with your ability to concentrate.
   d. enables you to clarify your career goals.

4. With some electronic dictionaries, a word's pronunciation can actually be
   a. incorrect.
   b. heard.
   c. abridged.
   d. none of the above.

5. Three dots on a vocabulary card indicate that the word
   a. has three different definitions.
   b. may require extra attention.
   c. has been properly mastered.
   d. consists of a common prefix and root.

REFLECTION

Think about the ideas outlined in this chapter and then draw upon your own opinions and experiences to answer each question fully.

1. Where do you typically acquire most of your new words? Why do you think this is so?

2. Do you normally use a hard-copy dictionary or an online one? Why do you prefer one over the other?

3. What aspect of learning a new word do you usually find the most difficult? Its spelling? Its pronunciation? Its definition? Its context? What ideas do you have for making this part of learning a new word a little easier for you in the future?

IT'S YOUR Q

The Q System uses marginal questions to encourage active reading. You'll notice that most but not all paragraphs in this chapter are accompanied by marginal questions. Now it's your Q. Scan the chapter for any paragraph that is missing a question, reread the paragraph, establish the main idea, and then arrive at a question that elicits it. Use the questions in the surrounding paragraphs as models for your own marginal questions.

VOCABULARY IN ACTION

To expand the horizons of your understanding and to refine the precision of your thought, the three exercises that follow are designed to help you grow, strengthen, and maintain your own vocabulary.

SAY WHAT?

From the three choices beside each numbered item, select the one that most nearly expresses the meaning of the italicized word in the quote. Make a light check mark (√) next to your choice.

Idealism is fine, but as it approaches reality, the costs become *prohibitive*.
—William F. Buckley, Jr. (1925–2008), American author and commentator

1. *idealism*	high-mindedness	creativity	paganism
2. *prohibitive*	illegal	burdensome	formidable

I have a *holistic* need to work and to have huge ties of love in my life. I can't imagine *eschewing* one for the other.
—Meryl Streep (1949–), American actress

3. *holistic*	holy	deep	unified
4. *eschewing*	avoiding	digesting	discarding

Advertising has *annihilated* the power of the most powerful adjectives.
—Paul Valéry (1871–1943), French poet and philosopher

5. *annihilated*	exploited	enhanced	nullified

www.cengage.com/success/Pauk/HowToStudy11e

VOCAB-U-LADDER

Use your knowledge of word synonyms and roots to connect the word at the top rung to the word at the bottom rung, using the words listed below.

decision
truncate
verdict
incisive
curtail
trenchant

dictionary

share root "dicere,"
"speak, tell, say"

synonyms for
"ruling"

share root
"caedere," "to cut"

synonyms for
"cutting"

share root
"truncus,"
"mutilated, cut off"

synonyms for
"abbreviate"

share root
"curtus,"
"short"

curt

Here's the story behind a word that figures prominently in the chapter you've just read.

Vocabulary **A place for things you call or name**

vocabulary vō-kă b′ yə-lĕr′ē *n.* 1. All the words of a language. 2. The sum of words used by, understood by, or at the command of a particular person or group. 3. A list of words and often phrases, usually arranged alphabetically and defined or translated; a lexicon or glossary. 4. A supply of expressive means; a repertoire of communication.*

Grain goes in a *granary,* and birds are kept in an *aviary.* So where would you store *vocables?* In a *vocabulary,* of course! But wait a minute. What are *vocables? Vocable* comes from the Latin word *vocabulum,* which grew out of the Latin verb *vocare,* meaning "to call or to name." Sound familiar? It should. *Vocal, voice, vocation* (your "calling"), and yes, *vocable,* all come from the same family. In fact, there are probably a dozen words you know that all share the same *vocare* root, including *provoke* ("call forth"), *revoke* ("call back"), and *convocation* ("a calling together") just to name a few. What's a word by any other name? *A vocable,* that's what! Although no one really uses *vocable* anymore to describe a word or term, that's what it meant. And so when you think about it—and now that you know that the *-ary* ending describes a kind of container—it makes sense that a place for storing *vocables* would be called a *vocabulary.* And that's why we still use the word today.**

*Adapted from "vocabulary." *The American Heritage Dictionary of the English Language,* 4th ed. (Boston: Houghton Mifflin, 2000), http://dictionary.reference.com/browse/vocabulary (accessed May 3, 2009).
**Based on information from "vocabulary." *The American Heritage Dictionary of the English Language,* 4th ed. (Boston: Houghton Mifflin, 2000), http://dictionary.reference.com/browse/vocabulary (accessed May 3, 2009); "vocabulary." *Online Etymology Dictionary.* Douglas Harper, Historian, http://www.etymonline.com/index.php?search=vocabulary (accessed May 3, 2009); "vocabulary, *n.*" *Oxford English Dictionary,* 2nd ed. 20 vols. (Oxford: Oxford University Press, 1989).

Gaining Information

You can't hold onto something if you don't have it to begin with. Before you can retain and explain information, you need to *gain* it. That means ferreting out and understanding the most valuable facts, ideas, and concepts that you encounter in lectures and texts, on websites, in discussions, and even in images and firsthand observations. This part helps you to

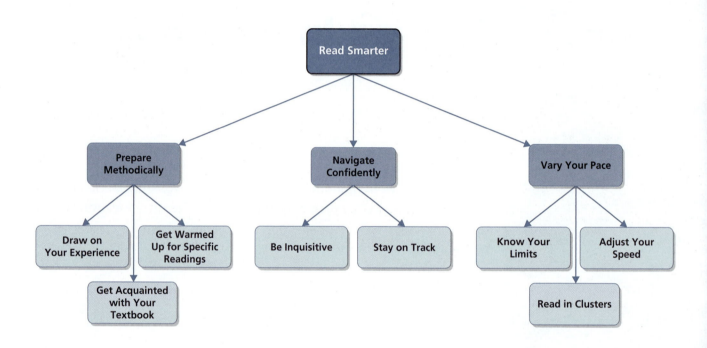

CHAPTER

5

Read Smarter

At this point in your life, a chapter about reading might seem as helpful as a chapter about tying your shoes. After all, you've been reading for most of your life. What else could you possibly need to know? Actually, you may be surprised. This chapter explains how to

- **Prepare Methodically**
- **Navigate Confidently**
- **Vary Your Pace**

In this chapter

How can you improve your reading?

The simple question "How can I improve my reading?" does not have a simple answer. There are many different purposes in reading, many different reading techniques that can be used, and many ways in which reading can be "improved." However, when students ask this question, it usually means "How can I speed up my reading so I can finish my homework in half the time with high comprehension and almost complete retention?" There is no easy way to do so, despite the numerous brochures, newspaper and magazine articles, and television programs that extol the marvels of "speed-reading." Reading smarter isn't simply reading faster. It is a matter of preparation, navigation, and pace. To truly improve your reading, you need to prepare properly, navigate confidently, and learn how to strategically vary your pace.

Prepare Methodically

Comprehension is all about connections. The rules for vocabulary building apply to reading as well. If you can take what you learn and fit it into the framework of what you already know, you have an excellent chance of retaining that information over the long haul. Establishing this framework takes methodical preparation. You can prepare for readings by drawing on your experience, by taking the time to get acquainted with your textbook, and by briefly but systematically warming up for each chapter or article before you begin reading.

Draw On Your Experience

CLUSTERING

How would lack of experience affect your reading rate?

Think how long it would take to read a chapter if you had to look up every word in the dictionary. Not just multisyllabic 50-cent words. Every single word. Or what if a casual reference to "freedom of speech" or "Pearl Harbor" or "1984" or "Judas" sent you rushing off to the library in search of an explanation? At that rate, a single assignment might take days to read and complete.

How does your experience come into play as you read?

Luckily, even difficult assignments don't normally take days to read. That's because you can count on a certain level of experience each time you begin reading. The definitions of words you might have struggled with in elementary school have long since become hardwired in your brain. You added more in high school and will continue to add words as you go through college. You read them, unconsciously look them up in your mind's internal dictionary, and keep moving. A maneuver that might have taken minutes if you actually had to flip through the pages of a hard-copy dictionary or surf through the screens of an online one takes a fraction of a second instead.

What do authors assume?

The same applies to historical or cultural references. Many of them have become part of your personal body of knowledge. Authors know this and can use these references as a kind of shorthand to efficiently express complicated ideas in just a word or two.

How can you increase your experience?

It follows that you can improve both comprehension and speed by minimizing your "lookup time" when you read. The way to do that is by drawing on your experience. And the way to increase that experience is to build on your background and to boost your vocabulary.

Bolster Your Background

Why will reading good books improve your reading?

The best tool for strengthening reading is reading! Reading avidly does more than just provide you with practice. It builds up a stock of concepts, ideas, events, and names that will lend meaning to your later reading. Start with books that both interest and challenge you. Once you begin reading, your interests should widen naturally. The more good books you read, the easier reading becomes, because with an expanded background, you can more readily and rapidly understand the ideas and facts in other books.

What does Ausubel point to as the most important prerequisite for learning?

Psychologist David P. Ausubel says that the most crucial prerequisite for learning is your already established background of knowledge.[1] Ausubel means that to understand what you read, you must interpret it in the light of knowledge (background) you already have. A background is not something you are born with. You accumulate one through both direct and vicarious experiences. The vicarious experiences, of course, are those you acquire by listening, seeing films, and reading books. Always keep in mind what Mark Twain once said: "The man who doesn't read good books has no advantage over the man who can't read them."

Beef Up Your Vocabulary

What is the relationship between vocabulary and reading speed?

According to Anne Cunningham, a professor of education at the University of California at Berkeley, the fastest readers have excellent "recognition vocabularies." They not only see words faster; they understand them more quickly.[2] In a precise vocabulary, every word is learned as a concept. You know its ancestry, its principal definition as well as several secondary definitions, its synonyms and the subtle differences among them, and its antonyms. Then, when you encounter the word in your reading, this vast store of knowledge flashes before you, illuminating the sentence, the paragraph, and the idea the author is trying to convey. This transfer from word to concept to understanding is quick, automatic, and powerful. Maryanne Wolf, the director of Tufts University's Center for Reading and Language Research, put it simply: "The more you know about a word, the faster you can read it."[3]

[1]D. R. Ausubel, J. D. Novak, and H. Hanesian, *Educational Psychology: A Cognitive View*, 2nd ed. (New York: Holt, Rinehart & Winston, 1978).

[2]Quoted in Blair Anthony Robertson, "Speed-Reading Between the Lines," *Sacramento Bee* (October 21, 1999), p. A1.

[3]"Best Practices: Teaching Fluency with Maryanne Wolf," http://teacher.scholastic.com/reading/bestpractices/fluency/understand.htm

Get Acquainted with Your Textbook

IT'S YOUR Q

Textbooks aren't mystery novels. There's nothing to be gained by keeping yourself in the dark. In fact, the more you know about them in advance, the better off you'll be. Give yourself enough time to understand how each of your textbooks works by buying them as soon as you've registered for your classes. Get a head start by reading the prefatory material and the introduction and by previewing the rest of the text from front to back. Underline important words and sentences, and make notes in the margins. Look at the pictures, tables, and diagrams; read the captions. Read chapter titles, headings, and sub-headings that interest you. This will give you a good idea of what the book is like and where you will be going during the semester. Later, you'll be glad you did, for you'll be able to see how the various parts of the course fit together.

Read the Prefatory Material

How does a book's prefatory material differ from the rest of its pages?

Whether it's called "Preface" or "To the Student," or something similar, a book's prefatory material is often the most personable part of the entire text. Unlike the rest of the book, which is usually written in a serious, scholarly tone, the prefatory material's more informal approach provides a unique opportunity to meet the authors as people and to get comfortable with them. Once you do, you'll find that you can converse and even argue with them as you read the text. Now and then, you'll find yourself saying, "No, I don't agree with that statement," or "What do you mean by that?"

What sort of valuable information does a preface typically contain?

The prefatory material often provides essential information about the concepts and content of the book. For instance, if you began this book by reading the "To the Student" section, you know the purpose and use of the questions that appear in the margins of every chapter. If, on the other hand, you skipped over this part, you may have squandered a valuable component of the book. Through the preface, you'll often learn things such as (1) what the author's objective is and is not, (2) the organizational plan of the book, (3) how and why the book is different from other books about the same subject, (4) the author's qualifications for writing the book, and often (5) an explanation of any supplementary learning aids.

How does learning the author's objective help?

The Author's Objective   Learning the author's objective—the purpose or goal he or she meant to achieve—enables you to read and interpret the text appropriately. For instance, the authors of *American Government: Student Choice Edition* state their objective succinctly:

> Everything in this textbook—from its structure and organization to its learning system, design, packaging and marketing—has been orchestrated to meet the teaching and studying requirements of today's instructors and students.[4]

In a single sentence, they tell you straight off what to expect and what particular philosophy they will be following.

[4]Alan R. Gitelson, Robert L. Dudley, and Melvin J. Dubnick, *American Government: Student Choice Edition*, 9th ed. (Belmont, CA: Wadsworth, Cengage Learning, 2009), p. xv.

Why is it helpful to know a book's organizational plan?

The Organizational Plan of the Book Knowing the book's organizational plan provides you with a road map. You know not only what the authors are doing but also where they are going. In the following example, you learn the total number of chapters in the book as well as the topics of the five parts under which they are categorized:

> We have carefully constructed the ninth edition to address instructors' concerns about getting through all the necessary material for this course. The new, streamlined table of contents consists of 18 chapters total broken into 5 Parts: Financial Planning, Money Management, Income and Asset Production, Investments, and Retirement and Estate Planning. A new chapter on Career Planning provides students with the steps they need for successful career planning.[5]

Why does it help to know how a book is different?

How and Why the Book Is Different Recognizing what makes the textbook unique enables you to read with greater awareness and comprehension and to avoid the trap of thinking the book is "more of the same old stuff."

Why are the author's qualifications important?

The Author's Qualifications Writers usually try in some subtle way to let the reader know that their book is written by an expert on the subject and that therefore the information is trustworthy and credible.

What does the prefatory material tell you about learning aids?

Supplementary Learning Aids Textbooks are often just one component of a larger package of learning aids that frequently include study guides, practice tests, and websites. The prefatory material generally names these aids and explains how they'll benefit you.

Read the Introduction

What is the role of a book's introduction?

While the prefatory material often supplies a glimpse of the author's personality, the introduction provides a preview of the book itself. The introduction is the book's showcase. Authors and publishers both know that this is the place prospective customers often go to decide whether a book is worth reading and worth buying. As a result, the introduction is often especially well written and inviting.

Figure 5.1 is a densely packed introduction containing information of great and immediate value for the sharper reading of textbooks. It is from a book titled *Six-Way Paragraphs*.[6] The book's sole purpose is to teach students how to spot main ideas. One hundred paragraphs are provided for practice. To prepare students for such practice, the introduction strives to explain the ins and outs of the paragraphs found in textbooks. As you read it, be aware not only of *what* the writer says but also of *how* he says it and his *purpose* for saying it.

---

[5]E. Thomas Garman and Raymond E. Forgue, *Personal Finance*, 9th ed. (Boston: Houghton Mifflin, 2008), p. xvii.

[6]Walter Pauk, *Six-Way Paragraphs* (Providence, RI: Jamestown Publishers, 1974).

www.cengage.com/success/Pauk/HowToStudy11e

Figure 5.1
The Content of an Introduction
Source: Walter Pauk, Six-Way Paragraphs (Providence, RI: Jamestown Publishers, 1974), pp. 7–8. Reprinted by permission.

what: wants you to focus on the paragraph – unit

how: brings you and the writer together

purpose: wants you to look at the paragraph through the eyes of the writer

The paragraph! That's the working-unit of both writer and reader. The writer works hard to put meaning into the paragraph; the reader works hard to take meaning out of it. Though they work at opposite tasks, the work of each is closely related. Actually, to understand better the job of the reader, one must first understand better the job of the writer. So, let us look briefly at the writer's job.

what: each paragraph has but one main idea

how: shows you how a writer thinks

purpose: to convince you to look for only one idea per paragraph because writers follow this rule

To make his meaning clear, a writer knows that he must follow certain basic principles. First, he knows that he must develop only one main idea per paragraph. This principle is so important that he knows it backward, too. He knows that he must not try to develop two main ideas in the same, single paragraph.

what: the topic of the main idea is in the topic sentence, which is usually the first one

how: the writer needs to state a topic sentence to keep his own writing clear and under control

purpose: to instill confidence in you that the topic sentence is an important tool in a writer's kit and convince you it is there, so, look for it!

The next important principle he knows is that the topic of each main idea must be stated in a topic sentence and that such a sentence best serves its function by coming at or near the beginning of its paragraph. He knows, too, that the more clearly he can state the topic of his paragraph in an opening sentence, the more effective he will be in developing a meaningful, well-organized paragraph.

what: developing main ideas through supporting material

how: "more to a writer's job," still keeps you in the writer's shoes

purpose: to announce and advance the new step of supporting materials

Now, there is more to a writer's job than just writing paragraphs consisting of only bare topic sentences and main ideas. The balance of his job deals with *developing* each main idea through the use of supporting material that amplifies and clarifies the main idea and many times makes it more vivid and memorable.

Figure 5.1
(Continued)

what: (a) main ideas are often
          supported by examples,
          (b) other supporting
          devices listed

how: still through the
          writer's eyes

purpose: to develop the new idea
          of supporting materals

To support his main ideas, a writer may use a variety of forms. One of the most common forms to support a main idea is the *example*. Examples help to illustrate the main idea more vividly. Other supporting materials are anecdotes, incidents, jokes, allusions, comparisons, contrasts, analogies, definitions, exceptions, logic, and so forth.

what: paragraph contains (a)
          topic sentence, (b) main
          idea, and (c) supporting
          material

how: transfer the knowledge
          from the writer to you,
          the reader

purpose: to summarize all the
          three steps

To summarize, the reader should have learned from the writer that a textbook-type paragraph usually contains these three elements: a topic sentence, a main idea, and supporting material. Knowing this, the reader should use the topic sentence to lead him to the main idea. Once he grasps the main idea, then everything else is supporting material used to illustrate, amplify, and qualify the main idea. So, in the final analysis, the reader must be able to separate the main idea from the supporting material yet see the relationship between them.

Preview from Front to Back

What can you learn from a book's table of contents?

After you've read the introductory material, survey the rest of the book. Begin by scanning the table of contents (TOC). It lists the parts, the chapters, and sometimes the major headings within each chapter. Some books, such as this one, actually have two TOCs, an abbreviated one that supplies the part and chapter names and a more detailed TOC that lists the names and page references of sections and subsections in addition to those for the chapters and parts. General or detailed, the TOC is designed to show the overall organization of the book and how the chapter topics fit together. It also indicates

www.cengage.com/success/Pauk/HowToStudy11e

whether the book contains extra material: appendixes, glossaries, bibliographies or references, and indexes.

What sort of valuable information can you glean from a book's extra sections?

Now turn to the back of the book and look at these extra sections. Appendixes contain additional information such as tables and graphs, documents, or details about specific aspects of a subject. Glossaries are specialized dictionaries of terms common to the subject the book discusses. Bibliographies and references list the sources the authors consulted in writing the book and can point you in the direction of further reading. Indexes—alphabetical listings of significant topics, ideas, and names along with page references that appear at the end of texts—give you a sense of the scope of the book and offer direct access to specific information you may be seeking.

What is the general advantage of getting to know your textbook?

By familiarizing yourself with your textbook, you not only bolster your background knowledge about the subject; you also become aware of the features of the book you can use throughout the term. As a result, future assignments will be easier and less time consuming, and you'll have a greater chance to master the material.

Get Warmed Up for Specific Readings

OVERVIEWING — SUMMARIZING

What is the value of surveying a reading assignment?

Moving systematically through your entire textbook is a tremendous way to warm up. It provides a strong context and a solid foundation that you can build on throughout the semester. But this once-a-semester warm-up isn't enough. For specific readings within your text or for separate texts you are assigned throughout the semester, it makes sense to warm up in a shorter but similar fashion.

IT'S YOUR Q

Although it might seem to save time in the short run, it's unwise in the long term to begin reading without investing some effort to warm up first. Beginning to read unprepared will often mean that you have to stop and reread a portion that was unclear, or, worse, that you will overlook or misunderstand crucial information because you weren't properly prepared for it. What does preparing for your reading entail? The bare-bones approach is a quick survey of the assignment. If you want to increase your preparation, try following the example of a navigator, a surgeon, or an investigative reporter in order to survey your assignments with greater depth.

Survey Your Assignment

How will surveying make a difference in your reading?

There are three practical ways that surveying can make a real and immediate difference in your reading: by creating a background, by limbering your mind, and by overcoming inertia.

How does surveying create a background?

1. *Surveying creates a background.* Surveying provides prior knowledge that counteracts tunnel vision and prepares you for reading. According to psychologist David

Ausubel, previewing the general content of a chapter creates *advance organizers*, which help students learn and remember material they later study closely.[7] These advance organizers become familiar landmarks when you go back to read the chapter in earnest. John Livingston Lowes, a professor of literature at Princeton University, described these landmarks as *magnetic centers* around which ideas, facts, and details cluster like iron filings around a magnet.

How does surveying compare to an athlete's pregame warm-up?

2. *Surveying limbers the mind.* For an athlete, a pregame warm-up limbers the muscles as well as the psyche and brain. An athlete knows that success comes from the coordination of smoothly gliding muscles, a positive attitude, and a concentrating mind. The prestudy survey of a textbook achieves for the scholar what the pregame warm-up achieves for the athlete.

How does surveying overcome inertia?

3. *Surveying overcomes mental inertia.* Many students find it difficult to open a textbook and begin to study. If you are one of them, use surveying to ease yourself into studying. Surveying does the job: It gets you started. (Figure 5.2 provides a mnemonic device that makes it that much easier to survey each textbook chapter systematically.)

Figure 5.2
Surveying a Textbook Chapter

How Surveying TIES UP the Elements of a Textbook Chapter

A chapter's information and elements can become more meaningful if you can tie them all together somehow. Surveying the chapter before you begin reading it can help provide a way.

Title: Read the title of the chapter to get a general idea about its subject.

Introduction: Read the introductory paragraph to get a sense of the key ideas that will be covered.

Ending: Read the chapter's ending paragraph for a summary of its key ideas or a sneak preview of its conclusions or lessons.

Subheadings: Scan the major subheadings to build a framework for the chapter that extends from the introduction to the ending.

Unusual elements: Look for any unique or unusual elements that stand out, such as lists and boxes, and boldfaced, italicized, or underlined text.

Pictures: Glance at pictures, charts, illustrations, or any other graphical elements for a succinct summary of some of the chapter's important ideas or a vivid example of some of its concepts.

---

[7]John F. Wakefield, *Educational Psychology* (Boston: Houghton Mifflin, 1996), p. 368.

www.cengage.com/success/Pauk/HowToStudy11e

Read Like a Navigator

What does it mean to read like a navigator?

A good navigator looks at the whole map before plotting a course. In the same way, you should prepare for a reading assignment by conducting a quick overview of your reading "territory." In most cases, that means understanding captions, headings, subheadings, and portions of paragraphs well enough to locate key concepts in the chapter. This kind of overview provides you with the lay of the land. It helps you to pick out landmarks in an assignment, enables you to see the relative importance of each part to the whole, and places you in a powerful position to organize information more readily and rapidly once you begin exploring the reading landscape in earnest.

Read Like a Surgeon

IT'S YOUR Q

Think of the classic operating room scene that you've witnessed in countless movies and TV shows. The surgeon, face covered by a mask, eyes concentrating on the task at hand, has a nearby tray of tools, a carefully arranged array of shiny medical instruments, ready in case she should need them. The great English historian Edward Gibbon (1737–1794), author of *Decline and Fall of the Roman Empire*, took a similar approach that he called "the great recall." Before reading or before beginning to write on any subject, Gibbon would spend hours alone in his study, or he would take a long walk alone to recall everything that he knew about the subject. In a sense, like a surgeon, he was assembling his mental tools, preparing them for his intellectual operation. Gibbon's system was highly successful. His old ideas were brought to the forefront of his mind so they could be used to understand new ideas and new information. Nearly two centuries later, reading research provides scientific support for Gibbon's method. His activation of prior relevant knowledge has been found to enhance comprehension.[8]

Read Like a Reporter

How do you read like a reporter?

Good investigative reporters tackle a story, backed up by research, armed with questions, and looking for answers. Although Daniel Webster (1782–1852) was an American statesman and orator, like a top-notch reporter, he placed a premium on this kind of preparation. After conducting a systematic survey, Webster would make lists of (1) questions that he expected to be answered in his reading, (2) the knowledge he expected to gain, and (3) where the knowledge would take him. The three lists provided a strong prescription for preparation. They guided him through his reading and ensured that his attention and concentration were intense.

Navigate Confidently

How can you reach your destination with a reading assignment?

Every reading assignment is a journey. Your destination should not be the end of the text but rather your *comprehension* of that text. So how do you get there? How can you confidently reach your true reading destination? An inquisitive mindset supplies the engine you need to propel you on your way, and an understanding of how the text is organized will help you stay on track.

[8]P. Carrell, J. Devine, and D. Eskey (eds.), *Interactive Approaches to Second Language Reading* (Cambridge: Cambridge University Press, 1988), p. 4.

Be Inquisitive

QUESTIONING

How do you encourage an inquisitive mindset?

Nothing beats an inquisitive mindset to encourage comprehension and to help bring your reading alive. Instead of approaching a textbook as a passive recipient, build on the relationship you formed with the author or authors when you first surveyed the book and read over its prefatory material by constantly formulating questions as you read, by wondering out loud about issues or aspects that concern you, and by writing out questions that help you pinpoint and remember the most important information. The latter really serves as the foundation for taking notes and mastering them.

What's a good way to start asking questions as you read?

If asking questions as you read doesn't seem to come naturally at first, a good way to start is by reading the headings and subheadings in your assignment and turning them into questions. This is an important icebreaker in a number of textbook reading systems, including the well-known SQ3R system (see Figure 5.3).

What makes turning headings into questions helpful?

It doesn't take much to transform a typical textbook heading or subheading into an attention-getting question. For example, the main heading "Basic Aspects of Memory" could be turned into the question "What are the basic aspects of memory?" The technique is simple, but it works. Questions encourage interaction. Suddenly you'll feel like a full-fledged participant as you find yourself reading with a genuine purpose. And if your question is answered early in the discussion, simply ask another, based on what you have read.

Stay on Track

OVERVIEWING — REFRAMING

What can you do to stay on track as you're reading?

Questions keep you focused and moving forward but they don't always help you to follow where the author is leading. Even if you're reading actively, how can you be sure that you're taking the right route? Luckily, you're not on your own. Authors routinely provide a detailed map as well as plenty of landmarks to prevent you from losing your way. The solution to reading in the right direction is the same as for reaching any new destination: Read the map and follow the signs.

Read the Map

What do authors use to provide you with a map?

Most authors structure their writing according to one of a number of common patterns. These patterns help them to arrange their ideas effectively and help you, the reader, to follow those ideas to their logical conclusion as though you're reading a map. Familiarize yourself with these organizational patterns, and you should find things easier to follow.

What are movement patterns?

Movement Patterns Authors will frequently move you systematically through time, through space, or through a process. Once you catch on, these patterns can be among the easiest to follow.

With the **time** or **chronological pattern**, events are presented in the order in which they occurred. This pattern can be recognized quickly from the author's use of dates and such phrases as *in previous years*, *the next day*, and *two years later*, which denote the passage of time.

Figure 5.3
The SQ3R System
Source: Adaptation
of "Steps in the SQ3R
Method" (pp. 32–33)
from *Effective Study*,
4th Edition, by Francis
P. Robinson. Copyright
1941, 1946 by Harper
& Row Publishers Inc.
Copyright © 1961,
1970 by Francis P.
Robinson. Reprinted
by permission of the
publisher.

THE SQ3R SYSTEM

S   SURVEY

Glance through all the headings in the chapter, and read the final summary paragraph (if the chapter has one). This survey should not take more than a minute, and it will show you the three to six core ideas on which the discussion will be based. This orientation will help you organize the ideas as you read them later.

Q   QUESTION

Now begin to work. Turn the first heading into a question. This will arouse your curiosity and thereby increase comprehension. It will bring to mind information you already know, thus helping you understand that section more quickly. The question also will make important points stand out from explanatory details. You can turn a heading into a question as you read the heading, but it demands conscious effort on your part.

R_1 READ

Read the paragraph or section to answer the question. Read actively.

R_2 RECITE

After you finish reading the paragraph or section, stop, look away from the book, and try to recite the answer to your formed question. If you cannot recite the answer correctly or fully, reread the section and try again.

R_3 REVIEW

When you have finished reading and reciting page after page, go back to the beginning of the chapter, glance at the headings and subheadings, and think briefly about the answers that you have already recited. Work your way in this manner to the end of the chapter. Now you should have ended with an integrated bird's-eye view of the entire chapter.

Items in a **place** or **spatial pattern** are presented or discussed on the basis of their locations or their arrangement relative to one another. For example, an author might use a spatial pattern to describe the geographical features of the United States from the West Coast to the East Coast. This is often called a *geographical pattern*. It is also called a *topical pattern* when it is used to describe the organization of a corporation along the lines of purchasing, manufacturing, sales, and so forth. The progression from item to item is usually orderly and easy to follow: from left to right, from high to low, from north to south, and so on.

Steps or events in a **process pattern** are presented in an orderly sequence that leads to a desired situation or product. A recipe and the instructions for assembling a bicycle are examples of process patterns. They often include words such as *first*, *after this*, *then*, *next*, and *finally*. You'll frequently encounter this pattern in computer courses and the sciences, where the steps in a process are described in the order in which they must occur to put something together, run an application, or blend ingredients.

How are importance patterns organized?

Importance Patterns A common way of organizing facts or information is by arranging them in terms of their relative importance.

In the **increasing importance pattern**, the most important or most dramatic item in a series is placed at the end. Each succeeding item is more important than the previous one, so a crescendo effect is created. Thus, this pattern is also called the *climactic-order pattern*.

In the **decreasing importance pattern**, the most important or most dramatic item in a series is placed at the very beginning. Such an organization grabs your interest immediately, so there is a good chance that you will stay with the writer all the way through. This pattern is commonly used in newspaper articles and is known by journalists as the *inverted pyramid pattern*.

What do causal patterns all share in common?

Causal Patterns One thing leads to another in a number of patterns, most of which are variations on the well-known idea of cause and effect.

In the **problem–effect–solution pattern**, the writer outlines a problem (cause), explains its effect, and then often (though not always) maps out a solution.

The **problem–cause–solution pattern** inverts this approach. A predicament (effect) is introduced, followed by its antecedents (cause), and eventually by remedies. In short, the effect comes first this time, followed by the cause.

Of course, not all cause–effect patterns involve problems. In technical subjects, the generic **cause–effect pattern** is quite common. In this case, variables are defined and their result (effect) is explained. Meanwhile, in the social sciences, you'll often run into the **action–impact pattern**, where some sort of initiative is outlined, such as increased funding for education, followed by a result, such as a higher average income for employees who received a college education.

Regardless of the variation, phrases such as *as a result* or *consequently* will usually alert you to a causal pattern.

When do writers use comparison patterns?

Comparison Patterns Writers compare things, events, or people when they emphasize similarities and contrast them when they emphasize differences. Individual characteristics may be compared or contrasted one at a time, or several characteristics may be discussed as a group. In either case, the pattern can be recognized from the various similarities or differences and from the use of words such as *similarly, likewise, conversely,* and *on the other hand*.

What do logical
patterns have in
common?

Logical Patterns In these patterns, a conclusion is either drawn or stated at the outset and then supported.

With the **inductive pattern**, a number of incidents are cited, and then a conclusion is arrived at. The main point will be something like this: "So, on the basis of all these facts, we come to this overriding principle, which is so-and-so."

With the **deductive pattern**, the reverse is true. Here, the principle or general statement is given first, and then the events or proofs are enumerated.

Follow the Signs

What other elements
tell you which way the
text is headed?

Without a map you may not be able to get a bird's-eye view of where you are going, but if you follow the signs at least you will get there. Changes in type act as landmarks in the text, highlighting important words, phrases, or sentences in a reading, while certain verbal signposts such as *next, thus,* or *finally* can provide valuable clues to the path that the text will be taking.

Changes in Type

IT'S YOUR Q

Open any textbook and you'll quickly discover that the words aren't all printed in the same size or the same style. The format may differ from text to text, but in general each book takes advantage of a variety of type sizes and styles to convey information. By noting these typographical differences, you can pick up on signals for organization and emphasis.

Boldface (thick, dark type) often signals a textbook heading or subheading. It may also be used to draw your attention to a specific principle, definition, or keyword within the text.

Italics (type that slopes to the right) places emphasis on a word or a phrase.

Underlining often performs the same functions as boldface and italics, depending on the format of the particular textbook.

• Bullets (small markers, often circular or square) set off the items in lists.

How can you learn
the meaning of a
book's typographical
intonation?

Size, color, and placement of type often call attention to headings and subheadings. Take special note of words printed in larger type, in color, or on lines by themselves.

You can usually crack a book's particular typographical code by skimming through it before you start reading. In addition, look for an explanation of format—especially if it is unconventional—in the book's introductory material.

Signposts

What should you do
if you can't identify a
precise organizational
pattern?

Although identifying the precise organizational pattern can be extremely helpful, it isn't always easy or even possible. Luckily, the signposts that often tip you off to a particular organizational pattern can still be helpful even if you have a tough time nailing down the overall arrangement. Table 5.1 lists some common signposts and the directions they're likely to point you in.

Table 5.1
Signposts

Categories and Examples	When you come across these words, immediately think...
Example Words specifically to illustrate for example for instance that is	"Here comes an example. Must be double checking to make sure I understood the point just made."
Cause-and-Effect Words consequently therefore as a result if...then accordingly thus, so hence	"There's an effect word. Better check back when I have a chance to make sure I can find the cause now that I know what the effect is."
Enumeration Words the four steps... first, second, third next, finally	That's a lot of steps. I'd better be sure I'm keeping track of all of them and getting them in the right order."
Addition Words furthermore as well as along with in addition moreover also not only...but also	"Seems there's always something else to be added. Must be worth remembering."
Contrast Words on the other hand in contrast conversely although however, despite whereas	"Here comes the other side of the coin. Let's see how it differs from what's been said already."
Comparison Words likewise similarly comparatively identical	"Lots of similar things, it seems."
Swivel Words however nevertheless yet but still	"Looks like there's going to be a little bit of doubt or 'give back' on the point just made. Better pay attention to this qualifying remark."

(continued)

www.cengage.com/success/Pauk/HowToStudy11e

Table 5.1
Signposts
(*Continued*)

Categories and Examples	When you come across these words, immediately think...

Concession Words
    to be sure
    indeed
    though, although
    granted
    of course
	"Okay! Here comes an argument or two from the opposing point of view."

Emphasis Words
    more important
    above all
    remember
    in other words
    finally
	"Looks as though what's coming up is going to be important."

Repeat Words
    in other words
    it simply means
    that is
    briefly
    in essence
    as we've seen
	"Here comes another explanation. Maybe I'll understand this one a little better."

Time Words
    before, after
    formerly, soon
    subsequently
    prior, during
    meanwhile
	"Hmm! A time relationship is being established. Let's see: What came first, what came last, and what came in between?"

Place Words
    above
    below
    beyond
    adjacent to
	"Okay! I'll put these ideas and facts not only in their proper places, but also in their proper relationship."

Summary Words
    for these reasons
    on the whole
    in conclusion
    in a nutshell
    to sum up
    in short
    finally
	"Good. Now I'll get a simple wrap-up of the points that have been made. It's almost sure to be full of key ideas."

Test Words (lectures)
    This is important.
    Remember this.
    You'll see this again.
    Here's a pitfall.
	"Sounds like a potential test item. Better be sure to pay close attention to it."

Vary Your Pace

How can you optimize
your reading pace?

Understanding an assignment's organization and approaching that assignment with an inquisitive mindset should prepare you for the actual reading involved. Although everyone likes to be able to read as quickly as possible, there are certain inescapable physical realities of reading that limit your speed. Besides, your impatience to go faster shouldn't dictate the pace that you set. Instead, it should be based on the nature of the text you are reading and its role in your class. You can optimize your pace by reading in clusters and by strategically speeding up and slowing down depending on a passage's type and importance.

Know Your Limits

SELF-DIRECTION

Why can't you read
at the rates that
the speed-reading
advocates promise?

Many students, as well as the general public, are convinced that speed-reading is an easy-to-learn technique that can be used with any page of print. Unfortunately, speed-reading is virtually useless to anyone who desires to learn from the printed page. It's certainly possible for you to read faster. But slowed down by your eyes, by your vocal cords, and by the necessity to both comprehend and consolidate what you've read, you'll never be able to come close to some of the spectacular claims that the speed-readers make.

Keep an Eye on Your Eyes

What do recent
experiments tell us
about how we read?

State-of-the-art computerized measurement of eye movements during reading confirms what reading researchers have long suggested. Your eyes don't glide along the words in a fluid motion. They jerk their way across the page, alternating fast, forward movements with momentary pauses. These pauses (called *fixations*) are absolutely necessary, for they allow the eyes to focus on the type, to get a clear image of it. When the eyes are in motion (known as *saccades*), they record nothing but a blur on the retinas.

What sort of speeds do
speed-readers claim?

Keep this in mind as you consider the claims of speed-reading courses, some of which boast graduates who read thousands of words per minute, always making the point, "with nearly 100 percent comprehension."

What is the basic
premise of speed-
reading?

The basic premise of speed-reading advocates is this: The eye is able to see a vast number of words in one fixation. Some advocates say the eye can see phrases at a glance; others say entire lines; still others say paragraphs at a time; and a few say the eye can see an entire page at a glance. Get out your calculator and let's look at the facts.

What does eye movement photography demonstrate about reading rate?

Eye movement photography shows that the average college student makes about four eye fixations per second. Good readers take in an average of about six to eight usable letters per fixation: four letters to the left of the center of fixation and five or six letters to the right of the center of fixation.[9] (Figure 5.4 shows the fixations of a typical reader.) There is no evidence, by the way, that anyone's eyes can see a whole line of type "at a glance." So any advice to run your eyes down the middle of a page or column in order to speed-read the page is nonsense. All you'll get is a word or two from each line—a handful of scrambled words.

How fast can a better-than-average reader read?

These facts indicate that only a most unusual person can see 10 words per second (2.5 words per fixation at 4 fixations per second). So, in 60 seconds it is arithmetically possible for the eye to take in 600 words. This calculation does not include the time needed to return the eyes to the beginning of each line and to turn pages. It also doesn't include *regressions,* the regular, imperceptible backtracks the eyes make (10 to 15 percent of the time) to reread a word or phrase. Nor does it allow time for comprehension and consolidation. These factors make some speed-reading claims sound even more absurd, if not outright unethical. In fact, in 1998, the U.S. Federal Trade Commission charged a well-known, heavily advertised speed-reading system with making claims for their products that were false or unsubstantiated.[10]

What is Professor Cunningham's attitude toward speed-reading rates?

Berkeley's Professor Cunningham is not quite as optimistic. She points to tests that put the speed-reading ceiling at closer to 300 words per minute.[11] Then what of the claims of speed-reading entrepreneurs, who trumpet per-minute totals in the thousands or tens of thousands of words? "People who purport to read 10,000 words a minute," Cunningham explains, "are doing what we call skimming."[12] Director and comedian

Figure 5.4
Typical Eye Fixations Through a Reading Passage
The eyes move in fits and starts—both backward and forward—through a textbook page. *Source:* Kevin Larson "The Science of Word Recognition," Microsoft typography, available at http://www.microsoft.com/typography/ctfonts/WordRecognition.aspx.

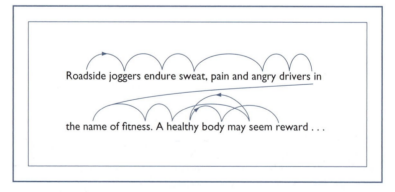

[9]John M. Henderson and Fernanada Ferreira, "Effects of Foveal Processing Difficulty on the Perceptual Span in Reading: Implications for Attention and Eye Movement Control," *Journal of Experimental Psychology: Learning, Memory and Cognition* 16, no. 3 (1990): pp. 417–429.

[10]Quackwatch, http://www.quackwatch.org/02ConsumerProtection/FTCActions/trudeau.html

[11]Robertson, "Speed-Reading Between the Lines," p. A1.

[12]Ibid.

Woody Allen once echoed Cunningham's point but in predictably humorous fashion: "I took a speed-reading course and read *War and Peace* in twenty minutes. It involves Russia." (Leo Tolstoy's classic novel is more than 1,000 pages long. But yes, it *does* involve Russia.)

Listen to Your Silent Speech

What is subvocalization?

There's another factor that affects reading speed: your voice. Reading experts refer to this as *subvocalizing* or "silent speech." It seems that all of us use our voices in one way or another as we read, even when we're reading silently. Some of us move our lips, some of us actually whisper the words, while others move only our vocal cords or simply think the sound of each word as we read it. Here's a case where the speed-reading advocates may be right. *Subvocalizing* actually *does* seem to decrease your reading speed. But they overlook a key point: No matter what form our subvocalization takes, it appears to be an important part of the reading process. This means speed-reading courses that train you to resist vocalizing may be interfering with your ability to understand and remember what you're reading. Recent reading research suggests that as you're silently reading a word, you're simultaneously sounding it out. This provides a kind of double-check for each word as you identify it visually. Your eyes attempt to identify the word while the sounds you process confirm that you've identified that word correctly. And if for some reason you aren't able to recognize the word visually, the sounds may jump in and identify it for you instead.[13]

IT'S YOUR Q

Over the decades, countless experiments done with increasingly sophisticated equipment have all come to the same conclusion. Although you may be able to stop moving your lips or whispering your words, you can't completely suppress this silent speech. According to internationally known linguist Robert A. Hall, Jr., "No act of reading takes place without a certain amount of subvocalization."[14] Medical tests done by Åke Edfeldt, of the University of Stockholm Institute of Reading Research, not only echoed Hall's results, but went a step further, concluding that "it seems quite clear that all kinds of training aimed at removing silent speech should be discarded."[15] In fact, engineers at the U.S. National Aeronautics and Space Administration (NASA) not only recognize the inevitability of silent speech, but have embraced it as a potential communications breakthrough. By attaching sensors under a subject's chin, they are able to do more than just measure the presence of silent speech; they are able to understand it. According to Chuck Jorgensen, a member of the NASA team, "A person using the subvocal system thinks of phrases and talks to himself so quietly, it cannot be heard, but the tongue and vocal cords do receive speech signals from the brain."[16]

[13]Carol Fraser, "Reading Fluency in a Second Language," *UTP Journals* 56 (1999).

[14]Robert A. Hall, Jr., *New Ways to Learn a Foreign Language* (New York: Bantam Books, 1966), pp. 28–29.

[15]Åke W. Edfeldt, *Silent Speech and Silent Reading* (Chicago: University of Chicago Press, 1960), p. 154.

[16]"NASA Develops System to Computerize Silent, 'Subvocal Speech,'" http://www.nasa.gov/home/hqnews/2004/mar/HQ_04093_subvocal_speech.html

Don't Forget Comprehension

What does recent
research tell us about
how the mind handles
words?

Even if you could take in words at a phenomenal rate, would it do any good? Probably not. After all, the primary reason for reading is comprehension. Just because you *see* doesn't mean you *understand*. Research at the Massachusetts Institute of Technology concluded that "even the skilled reader has considerable difficulty forming a perception of more than one word at a time."[17] What's more, as researchers Just and Carpenter discovered, your eyes continue to fixate on a word not simply until you *recognize* that word but until you *understand* it.[18]

Why does it seem
that we read words in
rapid succession?

But how can this be? After all, most of us get the feeling as we read that we are taking in words in a smooth and rapid sequence with no fits or starts. In that respect, reading is almost like watching a movie. Although each film frame is a still picture, you "see" motion and action when the film is projected at a rate of 24 frames per second. Similarly, words projected on the brain at the rate of seven or eight words per second give the impression of living, moving ideas. Nevertheless, the brain is "viewing" only one word at a time.

How can you improve
your reading speed?

With all of these factors putting the brakes on your reading speed, how can you ever hope to read faster? Your hope lies not in lengthening your saccades, shortening your fixations, or even lessening subvocalization. Your best chance of success depends on the all-important comprehension step. If you can reduce the time it takes to extract meaning from what you're reading, you'll boost your comprehension and increase your speed, the very essence in almost everybody's book of improving your reading. You can do this by reading in clusters and by strategically adjusting your pace according to the nature and importance of the text.

Read in Clusters

CLUSTERING — SUMMARIZING

How does clustering
relate to the way in
which we learn to read?

We group our letters into words without even thinking about it. Remember back to when you were first learning to read, how you sounded out a word one letter at a time until you ultimately came to recognize a growing number of words without having to break them down into their component parts? Given the size of the textbook assignments you probably face today, reading them one letter at a time would be almost unimaginable. But is reading an assignment one word at a time all that much better? If you consider a 10-page assignment with an average of 300 words per page, that's 30,000 words to keep track of and comprehend.

How can clustering be
used to help improve
your comprehension?

Although, as we've learned, you can't really transcend the eye's limitations of one or two words per fixation, you can make it easier to grasp what you've read by clustering those words into larger and thus fewer groups. If instead of moving word by word, you

---

[17]Paul A. Kolers, "Experiments in Reading," *Scientific American* 227, no. 1 (July 1972): pp. 84–91.

[18]M. A. Just and P. A. Carpenter, "Theory of Reading: From Eye Fixations to Comprehension," *Psychological Review* 87, no. 4 (1980): pp. 329–354.

work on understanding your assignments a phrase at a time, a paragraph at a time, and even a page at a time, you'll find that your level of comprehension improves considerably.

Read a Phrase at a Time

What role can intonation play in helping you read better?

As we've seen, research has shown that some level of vocalization is inevitable. So, why not use it to improve your reading instead of interfering with it? The most efficient use of vocalization, to read faster with a high degree of comprehension, is through *intonation*, which is the rise and fall of the voice in speaking. Intonation provides a natural means for combining individual words into meaningful mental "bites" that are a little larger than the word-sized ones we're used to taking. To use this system, read silently but with expression. In doing so, you will be replacing the important *rhythm*, *stress*, *emphasis*, and *pauses* that were taken out when the words were put into written form. This allows groups of words to hold together in clusters in a way they couldn't when the expression was removed. To make silent intonation a regular habit, start by reading aloud in the privacy of your room. Spend 10 or 15 minutes on one chapter from a novel. Read it with exaggerated expression, as if you were reading a part in a dramatic play. This will establish your own speech patterns in your mind, so that you will "hear" them more readily when you read silently. Using this sort of intonation encourages what is known as "reading fluency." By naturally arranging the words in meaningful bites, it enables you to decode passages more quickly and automatically, allowing your brain to focus on all-important comprehension instead.[19]

Read a Paragraph at a Time

How do you read when you approach an assignment in terms of paragraphs?

Intonation helps you cluster words into meaningful phrases. You can expand those clusters to paragraph size by stopping at the end of each textbook paragraph to summarize and condense it down to a single sentence. To do this, you must understand the functions of the three main types of sentences: the topic or controlling-idea sentence, the supporting sentences, and the concluding sentence. Figure 5.5 shows these three types of sentences in an actual paragraph.

What is the purpose of the topic sentence?

The *topic* sentence announces the topic (or the portion of the topic) to be dealt with in the paragraph. Although the topic sentence may appear anywhere in the paragraph, it is usually first—and for good reason. This sentence provides the focus for the writer while writing and for the reader while reading.

What role do the supporting sentences play?

The bulk of an expository paragraph is made up of *supporting* sentences, which help explain or prove the main topic. These sentences present facts, reasons, examples, definitions, comparisons, contrasts, and other pertinent details. They are important because they sell the ideas.

What is the function of the concluding sentence?

The last sentence of a textbook paragraph is likely to be a *concluding* sentence. It is used to sum up a discussion, to emphasize a point, or to restate all or part of the topic sentence so as to bring the paragraph to a close.

[19]Carol Fraser, "Reading Fluency in a Second Language," *UTP Journals* 56 (1999).

Figure 5.5
The Three Elements of an Expository Paragraph

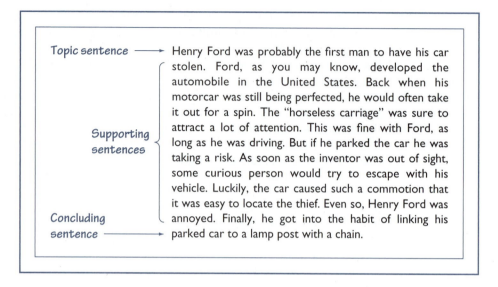

Topic sentence ⟶ Henry Ford was probably the first man to have his car stolen. Ford, as you may know, developed the automobile in the United States. Back when his motorcar was still being perfected, he would often take it out for a spin. The "horseless carriage" was sure to attract a lot of attention. This was fine with Ford, as long as he was driving. But if he parked the car he was taking a risk. As soon as the inventor was out of sight, some curious person would try to escape with his vehicle. Luckily, the car caused such a commotion that it was easy to locate the thief. Even so, Henry Ford was annoyed. Finally, he got into the habit of linking his parked car to a lamp post with a chain.

Supporting sentences

Concluding sentence

How does it help to understand the three basic sentence types?

An understanding of these three sentence types leads in turn to an understanding of each paragraph as a whole. Suddenly, instead of viewing things in terms of words, phrases, or sentences, you're clustering by paragraph, improving your comprehension and even your speed as a result.

Read a Page at a Time

What was Thomas Babington Macaulay's predicament?

Imagine the embarrassing predicament of Thomas Babington Macaulay (1800–1859), a learned English statesman, historian, and poet and author of *The History of England*, which when it was published actually outsold all books except the Bible. Macaulay had been reading voraciously since the age of three. But after consuming shelf after shelf of books, he suddenly came to a discouraging realization: Although he understood every word of every book he'd read, he was often unable to summarize the ideas presented or even describe, in general terms, what the writer had written. Macaulay described his solution to this problem as follows:

> At the foot of every page I read I stopped and obliged myself to give an account of what I had read on that page. At first I had to read it three or four times before I got my mind firmly fixed. But I compelled myself to comply with the plan, until now, after I have read a book through once, I can almost recite it from the beginning to the end.

What was Macaulay's simple solution?

There's something very basic, honest, and refreshing in the Macaulay way. His simple solution was to make the page his fundamental unit of meaning. There are no complicated formulas to follow. You simply stop at the bottom of a page and ask yourself, "In brief, what did the writer say on this page?" And as you'll see in Chapter 11, clustering by page is also a bedrock technique in reviewing your textbook assignments.

Adjust Your Speed

REFRAMING

How should your goals influence your reading speed?

It's a waste of time to read everything with the same attention to detail. Different texts and different situations require different types of reading. There are some situations in which simply scanning will do, in which you move through the text at a brisk pace, just slow enough to be able to spot a name, date, word, or phrase, without paying any real attention to its meaning. There are others in which you'll need to move a little slower, to skim the text to glean the meanings that the letters hold. Skimming at this level comes in handy if you're searching for clues in your text or trying to gain the gist of an article or book. And, finally, there are occasions when speed takes a back seat to comprehension as you strive to grasp the meaning of every word, combining each to fully understand the sentences, paragraphs, and pages of your text. For the most part, the greater the meaning, the slower the speed.[20] In other words, it's a trade-off. That's why it's important to establish your purpose in reading a particular passage and then choose your speed accordingly.

Scan to Look for Specific Words

When does scanning come in handy?

If you want to find a specific name, date, word, or phrase in a textbook or an article, you need to focus on individual words. Searching may be used because it is recognition, not comprehension, that will give you the answer. To ensure that you do not overlook the word or fact you seek, concentrate on it, keeping it in mind as your eyes run over the pages. Concentration will trigger your mind to pick it out of the sea of words. Once you have located the specific word or fact, pause and read the sentence or paragraph surrounding it at a normal rate to make sure, through context, that you have found what you were looking for.

Skim to Search for Clues or Get the Gist

What is the purpose of skimming?

When you are seeking specific information but do not know in what words the information may appear or when you are looking over a passage or chapter to glean its basic idea, you must use a slower reading method. In this case, you're looking for more than just characters; you're searching for meaning.

How do you skim to search for clues?

In this kind of searching, you must infer the answer. For example, after reading an article about Paul Bunyan, a legendary giant lumberjack and folk hero, a student was asked a question about Paul Bunyan's birthplace. The answer was Canada, yet nowhere

---

[20]R. P. Carver, *Reading Rate: A Review of Research and Theory* (San Diego, CA: Academic Press, 1990).

in the article did the word *Canada* appear. The answer had to be inferred from a sentence that stated that Paul Bunyan was born at the headwaters of the St. Lawrence River. Because the student discovered on a map that the headwaters are in Canada, she could answer the question.

To get the gist of an article, read both introduction and summary rapidly. Then skim any paragraphs that have topic sentences indicating that they contain important data. To get the gist of a book, look at its TOC, or select a chapter with a title related to your topic, and skim it for its outstanding ideas. This skimming method can help when you have a term paper to write. After you've arrived at a list of books that seem related to your topic, skim through each to eliminate those that are not pertinent and to keep those that are. Obviously, you would waste time and energy if you attempted to read all the books on your list. But if you skim them instead, you should glean just enough meaning to determine which of the books will require closer reading.

IT'S YOUR Q

When should you raud instead of scan or skim?

Read with the Goal of Comprehension

With scanning, you look only for a letter combination, whether it is a particular word or a name. With skimming, you seek out meaning, either to ferret out clues from a chapter or passage or to gain the gist of an article or book. The majority of the reading you'll do, however, will be what most of us associate with normal, ordinary reading. You'll be gleaning the meaning of individual words and then piecing them together into complete thoughts. Your goal will be complete comprehension. The influential educational psychologist and reading researcher Ronald Carver called this type of reading *rauding* in order to distinguish it from scanning and skimming, both of which he considered types of reading as well. How fast does a typical college student raud? Carver measured the rate at roughly 300 standard words per minute, where a standard word is considered to be 6 letters long.[21] As we've seen, reading in clusters (see p. 152) and drawing from experience (see p. 134) may help you to pick up the pace of your normal reading, but in general, if you are reading for the purpose of comprehension, you're going to be reading relatively slowly.

What's the best approach for supplemental readings?

Take a Different Approach for Supplemental Readings

In many courses, although assignments usually focus on a single textbook, instructors often assign additional readings to supplement the main text. You aren't usually expected to master such supplementary material as thoroughly as you master your primary text. Nevertheless, once the assignment has been made, you must cope with it. Here are some suggestions for doing so:

1. *Understand the assignment.* Try to figure out why the book was assigned. You might ask the instructor. If you find out, then you can skim the book, looking for pertinent material and disregarding the rest.

[21]Ibid.

2. *Read the preface.* As you already know from earlier in this chapter, the preface provides inside information. It may tell you how this book is different from your textbook.

3. *Study the TOC.* Notice especially the chapter titles to see whether they are like those in your textbook. If the chapters with similar titles contain the same information as the chapters in your textbook, read the chapters that do not duplicate your textbook's coverage.

4. *Find the pattern.* If you have not yet found an "angle," read the summarizing paragraph at the end of each chapter. Make brief notes on each chapter from the information thus gained. With these notes spread out before you, try to see the overall pattern. From the overall pattern, come up with the author's central thesis, principle, problem, or solution.

5. *Get to the point.* Don't put the book away with only a vague notion of what it is about. You must come up with something so definite that you can talk about it the next day or write about it two weeks later. Do not waste time on details, but be ready to answer general questions: What was the author's central approach? How was it different from that of your textbook? How was it the same? Look for the central issues around which everything else is organized.

6. *Have the courage to think big.* If you lack courage, you'll waste time on minor details that you won't remember. Select the big issues and concentrate on them.

FINAL WORDS

What constitutes victory for readers?

If you're frustrated by the slow pace of your reading, that's understandable. Keep working, and you should steadily improve. We live in a world where everyone wants to get there first. Even so, it pays to remember the famous fable about the tortoise and hare. Slow and steady will often win the race. Fast readers may move through the assignment at a faster pace, but victory comes with comprehension and true understanding, not speed.

CHAPTER CHECKUP

Complete the following sentences with one of the three words listed below each sentence.

1. The pauses your eyes make as they read are known as _____.

   saccades   **fixations**   **stops**

2. Words such as *next, thus,* and *finally* often function as _____.

   signposts   **diversions**   **intonation**

3. Intonation helps you cluster words in terms of meaningful _____.

   phrases   **pages**   **paragraphs**

In each blank space in the left column, write the letter preceding the phrase in the right column that matches the left item best.

_____ 1. Lookup time   a. Encouraged by reading with intonation
_____ 2. Preface   b. Helps you cluster words into meaningful phrases
_____ 3. Signposts   c. Slows down your overall reading speed
_____ 4. Fluency   d. Mnemonic for surveying a textbook chapter
_____ 5. Ties up   e. Often reveals a textbook's overall organizational plan
_____ 6. Background   f. Imperceptible backtracks your eyes make as you read
_____ 7. Regressions   g. Most crucial prerequisite for learning
_____ 8. Intonation   h. Provide clues for the organization of a chapter

Circle T *beside the* true *statements and* F *beside the* false *statements.*

1. T F The first few pages of a textbook should usually be skipped.
2. T F Daniel Webster prepared for reading by drawing up lists.
3. T F You're seldom expected to read supplemental materials as thoroughly as your textbook.
4. T F Research suggests that as you recognize each word, you sound it out as well.
5. T F One sign of a speedy reader is a good "recognition vocabulary."

MULTIPLE CHOICE

Choose the word or phrase that completes each sentence most accurately, and circle the letter that precedes it.

1. When your eyes are in motion, the words on the page
   a. are clearer.
   b. seem larger.
   c. are a blur.
   d. seem smaller.

2. Surveying a textbook chapter can provide
   a. advance organizers.
   b. magnetic centers.
   c. familiar landmarks.
   d. all of the above.

3. The goal when you cluster by paragraphs is to come up with a single, summarizing
   a. word.
   b. sentence.
   c. paragraph.
   d. idea.

4. Subvocalization is sometimes called
   a. silent speech.
   b. skimming.
   c. saccades.
   d. undertone.

5. The bulk of an expository paragraph is made up of
   a. topic sentences.
   b. supporting sentences.
   c. concluding sentences.
   d. prepositional phrases.

REFLECTION

Think about the ideas outlined in this chapter and then draw upon your own opinions and experiences to answer each question fully.

1. As the chapter points out, many speed-reading claims can be readily debunked by scientific data. And yet many students still enroll in speed-reading courses. Imagine you have a friend who is thinking of taking a speed-reading course. Write a note to that friend

www.cengage.com/success/Pauk/HowToStudy11e

explaining in your own words what you've learned about speed-reading from this chapter.

2. The chapter uses a navigator, a surgeon, and an investigative reporter as three models for reading preparation. Which model seems to suit your particular needs? Explain.

3. Which level of clustering what you read—phrases, paragraphs, pages—seems to be the most promising for improving your reading comprehension? Explain why and how you hope to add it to your reading routine.

IT'S YOUR Q

The Q System uses marginal questions to encourage active reading. You'll notice that most but not all paragraphs in this chapter are accompanied by marginal questions. Now it's your Q. Scan the chapter for any paragraph that is missing a question, reread the paragraph, establish the main idea, and then arrive at a question that elicits it. Use the questions in the surrounding paragraphs as models for your own marginal questions.

VOCABULARY IN ACTION

To expand the horizons of your understanding and to refine the precision of your thought, the three exercises that follow are designed to help you grow, strengthen, and maintain your own vocabulary.

SAY WHAT?

From the three choices beside each numbered item, select the one that most nearly expresses the meaning of the italicized word in the quote. Make a light check mark (√) next to your choice.

We can work together for a better world with men and women of goodwill, those who *radiate* the *intrinsic* goodness of humankind.

—Wangari Maathai (1940–2011), Kenyan environmentalist and Nobel Peace Prize Laureate

1. *radiate*	convey	irradiate	warm up
2. *intrinsic*	implied	essential	internal

Definitions are the guardians of *rationality*, the first line of defense against the *chaos* of mental *disintegration*.

—Ayn Rand (1905–1982), Russian-American novelist and philosopher

3. *rationality*	reason	thrift	limitation
4. *chaos*	complexity	disorder	swirl
5. *disintegration*	fragmentation	demolition	decentralization

VOCAB-U-LADDER

Use your knowledge of word synonyms and roots to connect the word at the top rung to the word at the bottom rung, using the words listed below.

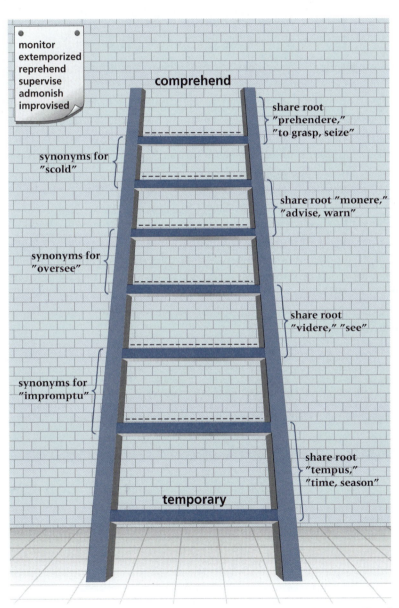

monitor
extemporized
reprehend
supervise
admonish
improvised

comprehend

share root
"prehendere,"
"to grasp, seize"

synonyms for
"scold"

share root "monere,"
"advise, warn"

synonyms for
"oversee"

share root
"videre," "see"

synonyms for
"impromptu"

share root
"tempus,"
"time, season"

temporary

www.cengage.com/success/Pauk/HowToStudy11e

Here's the story behind a word that figures prominently in the chapter you've just read.

Fixation **Where your eyes are glued**

fixation fĭk-sā′ shən *n*. 1. The act or process of fixing or fixating. 2. An obsessive preoccupation. 3. Psych. A strong attachment to a person or thing.*

Some words have simple meanings and yet a seemingly endless number of interpretations. The *fix* that lies at the root of *fixation* is a classic example. As we've seen, eye fixations are the points during reading where your eyes stop moving long enough to take in a few words of your text. Fix comes from a Latin word for "to fasten," and the "fix" in eye fixations was actually one of the word's earliest meanings in English. When the poet John Lydgate wrote more than 500 years ago, "Hyr eyen she fixethe on him," he was basically talking about the same sort of unwavering gaze that is a part of our reading. Of course, the eyes of the heroine in Lydgate's poem weren't literally fastened to her man any more than your eye fixations physically glue you to your textbook page. This symbolic tone has stuck with subsequent meanings of fix throughout the word's history. When a navigator *gets a fix* on a plane, she is able to attach the craft to a specific location. When you *fix breakfast*, you are taking all the components for the morning meal and putting them together. When you *fix a broken piece of pottery*, you may actually use glue, but you can fix other things with string or a screwdriver instead. If you find yourself *in a fix*, it seems as though you're stuck. And if an addict *craves a fix*, he probably feels as though he needs the drug just to hold him together. Even a *prefix* (literally "fix in front") sticks with the pattern. It's fastened to the beginning of a word. Now that you know the story behind fixation, there's a good chance it will stick with you.**

*Adapted from "fixation." *The American Heritage Dictionary of the English Language*, 4th ed. (Boston: Houghton Mifflin, 2000), http://dictionary.reference.com/browse/fixation (accessed May 1, 2009).
**Based on information from "fixation." *The American Heritage Dictionary of the English Language*, 4th ed. (Boston: Houghton Mifflin, 2000); "fixation." *Online Etymology Dictionary*. Douglas Harper, Historian, http://www.etymonline.com/index.php?search=fixation (accessed May 1, 2009); "fixation." *Oxford English Dictionary*, 2nd ed. 20 vols. (Oxford: Oxford University Press, 1989).

"I have learned a great deal from listening carefully. Most people never listen."

Ernest Hemingway
(1899–1961), American author and journalist

What do statistics tell us about listening?

According to the International Listening Association, students spend 45 percent of their day listening and are expected to acquire 85 percent of their knowledge through listening, and yet only 2 percent of the population ever receives formal listening training.[1] It might seem logical to suggest that because we've been doing it for so long that listening comes easily. But listening is hard! During the course of a single lecture, you are expected to comprehend what's being said, retain information in memory, integrate it with what follows, and constantly be ready to adjust and readjust your overall understanding as new information is introduced.[2] And that doesn't even consider the ongoing struggle to concentrate. According to Kay Lindahl, author of *The Sacred Art of Listening*, 75 percent of the time that we are listening, "we are distracted, preoccupied, or forgetful" and that most of us have an average listening attention span of only 22 seconds![3]

Based on those statistics, it seems almost miraculous that we are able to learn anything at all through listening. Although the numbers appear to be working against you, there are some basic things you can do to improve the quality of your listening and help bring lectures to life. Start by preparing properly, work to remain engaged during the course of the lecture, and use Triple-A listening to strengthen the attitude, attention, and capacity for adjustment that are the hallmarks of successful listeners.

Prepare Properly

Prepare Properly

Check the Syllabus

Assi

Review Your Notes from the Previous Lectu

How does your experience affect your ability to comprehend a lecture?

Just as it is for reading, your basic background of knowledge can have a major impact on your listening comprehension. Background includes not only your working vocabulary and your experience with attending to information provided in a lecture form, but also your familiarity with the subject matter itself. The more you know in advance about the substance of a lecture, the greater your rate of comprehension is likely to be. In one study, students were surveyed about their knowledge of two subjects: gold rushes and rock groups. The study found the students knew more about rock groups than about gold rushes and that this had a measurable, positive effect on their listening comprehension. Conversely, when you don't have a suitable background, your attempt to overextend what little you know can have a detrimental effect on comprehension.[4] Although you

---

[1]Cited in Bonni F. Boschee, Floyd A. Boschee, Bruce M. Whitehead, and Allan A. Glatthorn. *Curriculum Leadership: Strategies for Development and Implementation*, 3rd ed. (Los Angeles: Sage Publications, 2011), p. 437.

[2]Nobuko Osada, "Listening Comprehension Research: A Brief Review of the Past Thirty Years," *Dialogue* 3 (2004): pp. 53–66.

[3]Quoted in Nancy Ancowitz, "Listen Your Way Up the Ladder," *Psychology Today* (January 4, 2012), http://www.psychologytoday.com/node/85978

[4]Joan Rubin, "A Review of Second Language Listening Comprehension Research," *The Modern Language Journal* 78, no. ii (1994): p. 209.

can't be expected to become an instant expert on a subject that may be new for you this semester, you can take some significant steps to prepare for an upcoming lecture.

You can zero in on the upcoming lecture by marshaling the available information to provide a context for what the speaker will talk about. Of course, lectures aren't like textbook chapters; unless they've been written down or recorded already, you can't survey them in advance. But in most courses, there is enough available information supporting the lecture that it should enable you to effectively prepare for it. Each lecture can be viewed as a piece of a puzzle. The more pieces you have in place, the more you know about the shape and size of the pieces that remain. The course syllabus, the notes from your last lecture, and related reading assignments can all function as these puzzle pieces as you prepare for a lecture.

What information can you use to help prepare for an upcoming lecture?

Check the Syllabus

OVERVIEWING

How can you use your course syllabus to prepare for an upcoming lecture?

Assuming that your instructor is sticking to the syllabus, you should be able to read the list of lecture topics to get a broader sense of where this latest lecture will fit in. Pay especially close attention to the title and any description of the previous lecture, the upcoming lecture, and the one that will follow. Encourage active thinking about the lecture topics by transforming each title into a question and then answering your question in cases where the lecture has already been delivered or by speculating on the answer in cases where the lecture is still to come.

Review Your Notes from the Previous Lecture

OVERVIEWING — SUMMARIZING

Why is it helpful to prepare for an upcoming lecture by reviewing your notes from the previous lecture?

Each lecture will normally build on the concepts from the lectures that came before it. Most instructors will assume that you attended, understood, and can remember the previous lecture. After all, time will rarely permit a rehash of ideas that have already been fully explained. Although the upcoming lecture will often have some ties to all the lectures that came before it, the bond will typically be strongest with the most recent one. In fact, in some courses, each lecture is like the next episode of a continuing story. To understand what's going on in Chapter 2 in a novel, you often must understand and remember Chapter 1. Lectures often work in a similar way.

Do the Assigned Reading

OVERVIEWING

How do reading assignments relate to the upcoming lecture?

Some instructors will assign readings as background for an upcoming lecture. Others will give you readings designed to follow up on what you've just heard and learned in a lecture. In either case, surveying these readings can help provide advance organizers that will make it easier to understand and remember an upcoming lecture. Surveying is especially helpful when the lecture uses names or terms you might not otherwise be familiar with.

www.cengage.com/success/Pauk/HowToStudy11e

Remain Engaged

How can you remain engaged in a lecture?

Even the most dedicated and interested student is likely to be distracted numerous times during the course of a single lecture. What frequently distinguishes successful listeners from unsuccessful ones is the ability to notice when their attention is distracted and to make a conscious effort to regain their focus. Although no one can completely eliminate potential distractions, you can work to remain engaged in a lecture by adopting an inquisitive mindset and by actively seeking out signs that will help you to stay on track.

Be Inquisitive

QUESTIONING

What does it take to be inquisitive?

You can't really expect to do a good job of gleaning the most important information from a lecture unless you are paying attention. And while getting enough sleep and sitting up straight can help promote alertness, the real secret to being an active participant is to maintain an inquisitive mindset. Formulating questions, whether silently or aloud, will unlock the meaning of information in a way that listening passively just can't approach.

What are the roles of the speaker and listener in a lecture?

Although the communication may seem one-sided, both the speaker and the listener play important roles in a classroom lecture. The speaker's responsibility is to make points clearly. The listener's responsibility is to understand what the speaker says. If a speaker's message is not clear and the listener asks a clarifying question, both the speaker and the listener benefit. The speaker is encouraged and gratified to know that the audience is interested. The listener can concentrate on what the speaker has to say and feel good about raising a question that other, more timid members of the audience might have been hesitant to ask.

IT'S YOUR Q

As vital as questions can be to comprehension, they often go unasked. A professor at the University of Virginia who conducted a survey found that 94 percent of her students had failed to understand something in at least one class lecture during the semester. Seventy percent of the students had not asked clarifying questions even though they knew they could. When she asked them why they had remained silent, they answered with such statements as "I was afraid I'd look stupid," "I didn't want to make myself conspicuous," "I was too proud to ask," and "I was too confused to know what question to ask." The way to dispel the fear of asking is to remember that the only dumb question is the one that is never asked. The way to dispel confusion is to acknowledge it by saying, "I'm confused about the last point you made" or "I'm confused about how the example pertains to your main point." In this situation, as in most, honesty is the best policy.

What if you are unable to ask the speaker questions?

Although you won't always have the ability to directly address the speaker, being inquisitive goes far beyond simply asking questions. It also means remaining alert and intellectually curious as you actively listen to a lecture. The linguist David Nunan sees the listener as a "meaning builder."[5] You are taking each idea from the lecture and mentally reconstructing it in your own brain. Prediction means constantly anticipating where the lecturer is going and where each new idea will belong. You may not always be correct, but this "educated guessing" can only be done when you are following the lecture closely and when you have prepared yourself for the lecture. Whether you guess right or wrong, predicting the course of the lecture will maintain your inquisitive mindset and is almost guaranteed to keep you paying attention.[6]

Stay on Track

FOCUSING

What is the role of a road map on a cross-country journey?

Look at a road map of the United States and you will discover that you can take Interstate 90 from Boston all the way to Seattle, traveling east to west and crossing through a total of 13 states. This big-picture view of a 3,000-mile journey won't tell you when to turn left or right or even when you've exited one state and entered another, but it will provide a broad and helpful framework for your overall trip.

What do macro markers do?

Elements known as "macro markers" play roughly the same role with a lecture that a route marked off on a map plays for a cross-country trek. They tell you where the lecture has started, where it's going, and how it's going to get there. With a basic sense of a lecture's direction and the route that the speaker will be taking, you'll find it much easier to comprehend—and remember—the important concepts and to distinguish them from information along the way that may be interesting but is a little off the beaten path.

What is the purpose of micro markers?

Of course, anyone who has made a cross-country journey by car knows that a large map provides only part of the picture. There are lots of smaller decisions to make along the way. You need to know which lane to be in and which exit to take in order to avoid getting lost. This is where the "micro markers," the signposts of a lecture, come in. In order to get the most out of a lecture, you need to stay on track, both by reading the map and by following the signs.

Read the Map

How does it help to recognize a lecture's organizational pattern?

Like a cross-country route, a lecture's organizational course can sometimes follow a spatial pattern. But unlike routes to a geographical destination, lectures aren't limited to a directional approach. Speakers have a number of other options for arranging their information. A content analysis of close to 50 introductory college lectures in the social sciences and humanities found that nearly all of the lectures followed just five basic patterns—Topic–List, Time–Order, Compare–Contrast, Cause–Effect, Problem–Solution—or a combination

[5]Pauline Gibbons, *Scaffolding Language, Scaffolding Learning* (Portsmouth, NH: Heinemann, 2002), p. 103.

[6]Official Languages and Bilingualism Institute of the University of Ottawa, *Introduction: Applying the Strategies of Good Listeners*, transcript of podcast (www.olbi.uottawa.ca/files/podcast1.pdf).

of them.[7] (The Topic-List pattern is basically the Deductive pattern, which is explained on p. 146 of Chapter 5.) As a listener, it is important to be familiar with these patterns. Once you've identified the particular route that the speaker has chosen, use it as a framework for understanding, organizing, and remembering the landmarks of a lecture. Chapter 5 provides an explanation for most of the organizational patterns you're likely to encounter that are used by authors and speakers, although speakers will often adapt these patterns to meet the special needs of a listening audience.

What additional navigational aids do skilled speakers include in their lectures?

Experienced lecturers are aware of the special challenges that listeners face. They realize that you don't have the same sort of control over a lecture that you have with a textbook assignment. After all, unless the lecture has been recorded, you can't rewind and replay a point you didn't fully understand the first time you heard it. Nor can you slow things down during parts of the lecture that seem especially difficult to grasp or particularly important. For these reasons and others, lecturers will often include additional navigational aids, such as road maps, recaps, and redundancy, all of which are designed to help you stay on track.

What sort of road maps do some speakers provide?

Road maps. Although alert listeners are usually able to detect a lecture's overall organizational pattern by listening for key words and phrases, some speakers make it easier for everyone by supplying this information in advance in the form of an outline or set of talking points that they print out and distribute or display on a board or screen, enabling you to refer to it whenever you need to regain your bearings. As a rule of thumb, if the instructor goes to the trouble of furnishing you with a road map, you can be confident that it is essential to the overall understanding of the lecture.

What is the value of lecture recaps?

Recaps. Because spoken information can be much more difficult than text to remember and retain, speakers will frequently include internal summaries within their lectures that recap one important point before moving on to another. This not only gives you another chance to see if you understood each point, but also makes the relationship between points a little clearer.

In what way are lectures sometimes redundant?

Redundancy. Restating the previous point before making the next is just one common example of a lecturer's use of deliberate redundancy in order to ensure that listeners are still following. Whereas textbooks may mention a person's name in the first reference and then subsequently refer to him or her with a pronoun for the rest of the paragraph or even the page, speakers are aware that you may lose track of to whom that pronoun is referring and will often restate the name in full each time so the connection remains clear. They will typically take the same approach to important locations, concepts, or terms, mentioning them again and again instead of requiring you to remember what "it" refers to. This sort of treatment might seem unnecessarily repetitive in text, but is usually a welcome source of clarification in lectures.

[7]Kay L. Lopate, "The Organization of College Lectures in Selected Introductory Level Courses" (1987). *Dissertations from ProQuest.* Paper 1626, http://scholarlyrepository.miami.edu/dissertations/1626

Follow the Signs

What signs
help improve
comprehension of
lectures or readings?

Throughout the course of a lecture, there are usually signs that help direct you down the road to comprehension. Both the intonation of the words and the way they are organized provide clues about the speaker's purpose and approach.

Pay Attention to Intonation

How does intonation
affect the meaning of
words?

Consider the dramatic effect that intonation can have on the meaning of even a simple phrase, such as "Excuse me." Depending on the tone of voice, these two words can sound polite, tentative, argumentative, or downright resentful. In each case, the words are identical, but the delivery is different. If you pay attention only to the words when you're listening to a lecture but ignore their delivery, you may be missing a critical component of their meaning.

Most college lecturers speak about 120 words per minute, which means that in a 50-minute lecture you hear roughly 6,000 words. Listening for signals in a lecture is especially helpful because, unlike in reading, you don't have the luxury of retracing your steps if you discover that you're lost. In addition to words, intonation—variations in the lecturer's voice—is the most significant signal in spoken language. Intonation has three components: volume, pauses, and cadence.

IT'S YOUR Q

Volume. In general, the introduction of a crucial idea is preceded by a change in volume; the speaker raises or lowers his or her voice.

Pauses. Pausing before and after main ideas sets these ideas apart from the rest of the lecture. Pauses achieve a dramatic effect and, on a practical level, provide note takers with extra writing time.

Cadence. The rhythm of a lecturer's speaking patterns can be particularly helpful. Often, like the bulleted lists you find in textbooks, the speaker lists a series of important ideas by using a steady speaking rhythm, sometimes even beginning each idea with the same words or phrase.

Listen for Signposts

What is the role of
signposts in a lecture?

Unlike the "macro markers" that establish the overall organization of a lecture, "micro markers" provide smaller signposts that emphasize particular points or lead you from one point to the next. Phrases such as "This is important," "Remember this," "You'll see this again," and "This is a pitfall" practically advertise the fact that what follows belongs in your notes and is likely to wind up on your test. In addition, words and phrases such as "however," "for example," and "furthermore" play the same basic role in lectures that they play in texts, signaling smaller twists and turns in the course of the lecture, providing you with landmarks that prevent you from losing your way. Chapter 5 provides a table that lists signposts that are common in both lectures and texts.

www.cengage.com/success/Pauk/HowToStudy11e

Use Triple-A Listening

The skills you need to listen effectively are pretty straightforward but are often overlooked. Figure 6.1 presents a short quiz to help you learn where you stand as a listener.

Figure 6.1

Listening Habits

Source: Adapted from Ralph G. Nichols and Thomas R. Lewis, "Listening and Speaking", by Dr. Lyman K. Steil, Communication Development, Inc., St. Paul, MN. Reprinted with permission of Dr. Steil and the Unisys Corporation.

How often do you find yourself engaging in these ten bad habits of listening? Check the appropriate columns.

How often do you ...	Almost always	Usually	Sometimes	Seldom	Almost never	Score
Decide that the topic is boring?						
Criticize the speaker?						
Overreact by disagreeing?						
Listen only for bare facts?						
Outline everything?						
Fake attention?						
Yield to distractions?						
Avoid listening to tough technical information?						
Let emotion-laden words arouse personal antagonism?						
Waste thought speed by daydreaming?						
Total score						

Tally your score as follows:

Almost always	2
Usually	4
Sometimes	6
Seldom	8
Almost never	10

Interpret your score as follows:

Below 70	Need training in listening
70 to 90	You listen well
Above 90	Extraordinarily good listener

All you need to do is recognize the habits of a poor listener as well as the techniques used by a good listener. Then, knowing the good techniques, apply them in all your daily activities. You can make a fresh and immediate start today by referring to Figure 6.2, which lists the ten most important keys to effective listening.

What does it take to be a good listener?

Being a good listener means being fully engaged. It is a conscious activity that grows out of three basic skills: *a*ttitude, *a*ttention, and *a*djustment. These skills are known collectively as *triple-A listening*.

Figure 6.2
Ten Keys to Effective Listening
Source: Reprinted by permission of Unisys Corporation.

Keys to Effective Listening	The Poor Listener	The Good Listener
1. Find areas of interest	Tunes out dry topics.	Seizes opportunities: "What's in it for me?"
2. Judge content, not delivery	Tunes out if delivery is poor.	Judges content, skips over delivery errors.
3. Hold your fire	Tends to enter into argument.	Doesn't judge until comprehension is complete.
4. Listen for ideas	Listens for facts.	Listens for central themes.
5. Be a flexible note taker	Is busy with form, misses content.	Adjusts to topic and organizational pattern.
6. Work at listening	Shows no energy output, fakes attention.	Works hard; exhibits alertness.
7. Resist distractions	Is distracted easily.	Fights or avoids distractions; tolerates bad habits in others; knows how to concentrate.
8. Exercise your mind	Resists difficult expository material; seeks light, recreational material.	Uses heavier material as exercise for the mind.
9. Keep your mind open	Reacts to emotional words.	Interprets emotional words; does not get hung up on them.
10. Thought is faster than speech; use it	Tends to daydream with slow speakers.	Challenges, anticipates, mentally summarizes, weighs the evidence, listens between the lines to tone of voice.

www.cengage.com/success/Pauk/HowToStudy11e

A₁: Maintain a Positive Attitude

Why do you need a positive attitude to listen effectively?

You can take many steps to improve your listening, but the primary prerequisite to effective listening is a positive mental attitude. A positive attitude sets the stage for the open-mindedness that is essential to learning and comprehension. As businessman and author Kevin J. Murphy says in *Effective Listening*, "Minds are like parachutes; they only function when open."[8] Whether you're sitting in a classroom or listening to a video lecture, you should be convinced that you will acquire new information and insights and learn things of real value.

How do you cultivate a positive attitude?

Cultivating a positive attitude isn't always easy. But it is worth the effort. If you're struggling to do so, try finding areas of interest in what others have to say, judge the content of their points instead of the delivery, and hold your fire if you're inclined to lash out at those things you don't agree with.

Find Areas of Interest

How can you find areas of interest in "boring" ideas?

It doesn't take any talent to tune out a lecture or brand it as "boring." Anyone can do that. Most speakers work hard to make their lectures informative and interesting. But they can't do it alone. It requires some effort on your part as well. Don't waste time by ignoring the instructor or by leafing through your textbook when you should be giving the speaker your full attention. You can often find an element or an aspect of the lecture topic that appeals to your personal interests.

IT'S YOUR Q

Of course, you can't always immediately find something that captures your interest. Remember the James–Lange theory from Chapter 3? Although we usually think that emotions trigger physical reactions (when you're happy, you smile), a number of recent studies have turned this idea on its head. In other words, smiling can sometimes make you happy. In the same way, acting interested in something that doesn't immediately interest you can sometimes lead to genuine interest! Pay close attention, take notes vigorously, and show interest by your facial expression. In time, real interest may emerge where none existed.

Judge Content, Not Delivery

What's the most important aspect of a discussion comment?

Listeners are sometimes terribly rude or downright cruel to people whose delivery fails to measure up to some preconceived standard. Keep in mind that great thinkers aren't always excellent orators. Try to approach each lecture with a humane attitude, and concentrate on what the lecturer is saying, not on how it's being said. If you do, you'll emerge with a positive self-image. You will also learn something.

[8]Kevin J. Murphy, *Effective Listening: Hearing What People Say and Making It Work for You* (New York: Bantam Books, 1987), p. 28.

Hold Your Fire

What should you do if someone writes or says something you don't agree with?

In college you're bound to be exposed to ideas that are different from or even contrary to those you hold. When this happens, your knee-jerk reaction may be to speak up immediately to defend your position. Hold your fire! Try to fully grasp the differing viewpoint even if you strongly disagree with it. If you shift all your focus to rebutting a point you don't agree with, you'll be unable to concentrate on the rest of the lecture. In a war of words of this type, understanding is often the first casualty.

A₂: Strive to Pay Attention

FOCUSING — SELF-DIRECTION

Why is attention important?

Attention is the path that will lead you into the wonderful state of concentration. Without concentration there is no focus, and without focus there is almost no learning. If you pay attention and concentrate, you will become an active listener able to synthesize new information with facts and ideas you've already known.

How can you build anticipation?

Attention often thrives on anticipation. Before class, look over your notes from the last lecture, and take a minute to speculate about what your instructor is going to talk about today. Once the lecture starts, let your mind dart ahead (during pauses) to anticipate what's coming next. You'll be alert, engrossed in the material, and concentrating 100 percent.

What should your attention be focused on?

Of course, as we learned in Chapter 1, you cannot attain concentration by concentrating on concentration. Your attention must focus on the lecture, not on the act of concentration itself. Deep cognition, or deep thinking, is vital. When you hear a lecture, the words enter your working memory, where they have to be swiftly processed into ideas to avoid getting dumped from your memory altogether. Active listening ensures the words' survival. If you process them into ideas, those ideas will be stored in your long-term memory almost instantly.

How can you foster the kind of attention that leads to concentration?

You can foster the kind of attention that leads to concentration by focusing on ideas instead of facts, by working to stay fully engaged, by tuning out distractions, and by using the natural lag between speech and thought to forge ahead in your mind in order to consider the current point and anticipate the next one.

Listen for Ideas

What's the drawback of listening for facts instead of ideas?

Don't imitate the detective who says, "The facts, ma'am, just stick to the facts." Sure, facts are important. And it's true that they're often what you'll be tested on. But facts in isolation don't hold together well. In order to organize information both in your notes and your memory, look to the ideas that lie behind the facts. Strive to uncover the principle or idea that each fact is supporting. Try to see how the pieces of the puzzle fit into the big picture.

Work at Listening

How do you work at listening?

Listening isn't a passive activity; it requires true participation. Good listeners are fully engaged, outwardly calm, but inwardly dynamic; and they sit toward the front of the classroom. While taking notes, the listener may nod in agreement or look quizzical when the presentation becomes unclear. These sorts of gestures aren't just for effect. Such activity actually promotes comprehension and learning by the listener and provides feedback to the speaker.

Resist Distractions

How can you resist distractions during a lecture?

There are distractions aplenty in the classroom: antics of other students, whispering, the speaker's dress and mannerisms, outside noise, and outside views. In some classes, students may actually be browsing the Web or sending text messages while the lecturer is speaking! The best way to resist distractions and maintain your concentration is to rivet your eyes on the speaker when you have a chance and focus on taking notes the rest of the time. This is another reason to consider sitting close to the front. The level of distraction tends to increase as you move farther away from the instructor, especially in large lecture halls.

Use Your Thought Speed

How can you take advantage of thought speed?

In a race of ideas, thought is swifter than spoken words. Most of us can grasp the gist of a point faster than someone can express it. This "thought speed" leaves a bit of a lag during which your mind is apt to wander. Rather than using this time to daydream or to dart off on mental side trips, devote it to thinking more deeply about what has just been said. Mentally enumerate the ideas that have been expressed and summarize them until it's time to shift your focus back to the comments. Keep alternating in this fashion throughout the lecture.

A₃: Cultivate a Capacity for Adjustment

SELF-DIRECTION — REFRAMING

IT'S YOUR Q

Even though most speakers try to indicate what they intend to cover in their lectures, you still need to be mentally limber enough to follow a lecture regardless of the direction it may take. Sometimes a speaker says, "This event had three important results," but then goes on to discuss four or five. Other times a question from the audience suddenly shifts the speaker's focus. In such cases, you can't simply tune out the parts of the lecture that don't fit with your expectations. You have to be able to "roll with the punches." That's why adjustment is such an important component of active listening. You can cultivate your capacity for adjustment by remaining flexible while taking notes, by exercising your mind by sitting in on subjects that you are unfamiliar with, and by keeping your mind open to ideas and information that you may initially want to tune out.

Be a Flexible Note Taker

What is the key to being a flexible note taker?

Flexibility in note taking depends on informed listening. Informed listening means being able to identify the organizational patterns used by the speaker. Organizational patterns are easily recognizable if you know their basic structures in advance. Once you have detected a pattern, you'll have a framework you can use to anticipate the form of the message and adjust the way you record your notes. Similarly, when the speaker shifts gears and adopts a different pattern, a flexible note taker should be able to adjust and reframe accordingly.

Exercise Your Mind

How can you exercise your mind to become a better listener?

From time to time, try to sit in on lectures in fields that you know very little about or that you may even consider to be "over your head." When you do, make a serious effort to follow the chain of thoughts and ideas. True, some parts may be unintelligible to you, but you're bound to understand other parts. Such listening can be hard work, but in the same way that hard work at a gym can strengthen your muscles, the hard work of following strange or difficult ideas will strengthen your will to concentrate and your power to persist.

Keep Your Mind Open

What can you do to prevent highly charged words from interfering with your participation?

It's hard to believe that a single word or phrase can cause an emotional eruption. But all of us can be susceptible to these reactions from time to time. In class, such words can raise the blood pressure or even trigger an outburst. Notorious hot-button words include *activist, fundamentalist, liberal, conservative, evolution, creationism, feminist, abortion, pro-life,* and *free market*. Dealing with highly charged language is similar to dealing with a fear or phobia. Often, the emotional impact of the words can be decreased through a frank and open discussion. Don't be so inflexible as to totally shut out opposing ideas, as incendiary as they may seem at first. Genuinely listen to the other point of view. You might learn something that you didn't know before.

FINAL WORDS

What special technique do experienced documentary filmmakers often use?

Artists of all types traditionally feel a strong drive to communicate, to express themselves on stage, on the page, in notes, in paint, and on screen. Documentaries, which often pack a powerful message, would seem to be an especially conspicuous example of this artistic drive. And yet experienced documentary filmmakers frequently use a technique that might surprise you. When interviewing people for their movies, they don't typically pepper them with questions. Instead, they turn the camera on, ask a simple, open-ended question, and patiently let the subjects speak for themselves, often for as long as they like. Thus, the lessons we learn from many insightful documentaries don't come from the filmmakers' abilities to speak their own minds but grow out of their extraordinary capacity for listening.

CHAPTER CHECKUP

SENTENCE COMPLETION

Complete the following sentences with one of the three words listed below each sentence.

1. A good listener places emphasis on the speaker's _____.

   delivery   **appearance**   **ideas**

2. Each lecture can be thought of as part of a _____.

   textbook   **discussion**   **puzzle**

3. In listening to a lecture, attention often thrives on _____.

   appearance   **anticipation**   **agreement**

MATCHING

In each blank space in the left column, write the letter preceding the phrase in the right column that matches the left item best.

_____ 1. Delivery   a. Helps provide context for an upcoming lecture

_____ 2. Pauses   b. May distract some listeners from the content of a lecture

_____ 3. Intonation   c. Can set main ideas apart from the rest of a lecture

_____ 4. Road maps   d. Can dramatically change the meaning of a simple phrase

_____ 5. Recaps   e. Helps listeners keep track of whom or what the speaker is talking about

_____ 6. Redundancy   f. Moves at a faster rate of speed than writing or speech

_____ 7. Thought   g. Internal summaries that may accompany shifts from one idea to another

_____ 8. Syllabus   h. Outlines or talking points that provide listeners with the lecture's structure

TRUE-FALSE

Circle T *beside the true statements and* F *beside the false statements.*

1. T   F   Students typically acquire 85 percent of their knowledge through listening.
2. T   F   In one study, 94 percent of students failed to understand something in at least one class lecture during the semester.
3. T   F   Most students don't hesitate to ask questions when there is something in a lecture that they don't understand.
4. T   F   Micro markers are used to emphasize particular points or to lead you from one point to the next.
5. T   F   One way to exercise your mind is by sitting in on lectures in fields you know little about.

MULTIPLE CHOICE

Choose the word or phrase that completes each sentence most accurately, and circle the letter that precedes it.

1. Most college lecturers speak about
   a. 55 words per minute.
   b. 120 words per minute.
   c. 300 words per minute.
   d. none of the above.

2. In general, the introduction of a crucial lecture idea is preceded by a change in
   a. temperature.
   b. direction.
   c. attitude.
   d. volume.

3. The words "however" and "furthermore" are examples of
   a. bias.
   b. signposts.
   c. macro markers.
   d. cadence.

4. The primary prerequisite to effective listening is
   a. a positive mental attitude.
   b. systematic note-taking skills.
   c. a thorough hearing examination.
   d. all of the above.

5. When you disagree with a lecturer's statement,
   a. begin rehearsing your rebuttal.
   b. automatically decide he or she is misinformed.
   c. take his or her stand as a bias.
   d. make a note of it, but keep listening.

REFLECTION

Think about the ideas outlined in this chapter and then draw upon your own opinions and experiences to answer each question fully.

1. Do you already prepare for lectures in the way that the chapter suggests? If so, explain which part of your preparation has proven to be the most valuable. If not, which part do you think will turn out to be the most helpful? Explain.

2. Given the importance of listening in college, speculate on why it is taught so rarely.
3. Of the three A's in Triple-A listening, which do you consider the easiest to adopt and why? Which do you consider the hardest?

IT'S YOUR Q The Q System uses marginal questions to encourage active reading. You'll notice that most but not all paragraphs in this chapter are accompanied by marginal questions. Now it's your Q. Scan the chapter for any paragraph that is missing a question, reread the paragraph, establish the main idea, and then arrive at a question that elicits it. Use the questions in the surrounding paragraphs as models for your own marginal questions.

VOCABULARY IN ACTION

To expand the horizons of your understanding and to refine the precision of your thought, the three exercises that follow are designed to help you grow, strengthen, and maintain your own vocabulary.

SAY WHAT?

From the three choices beside each numbered item, select the one that most nearly expresses the meaning of the italicized word in the quote. Make a light check mark (√) next to your choice.

Any reviewer who expresses rage and *loathing* for a novel is *preposterous*. He or she is like a person who has put on full armor and attacked a hot fudge sundae.

—Kurt Vonnegut (1922–2007), American writer

1. *loathing*	resentment	contempt	hatred
2. *preposterous*	absurd	stupid	misleading

Let's not be so *elitist* that we can't honor good, hard, dignified, *ennobling* work.

—Van Jones (1968–), American civil rights leader and environmentalist

3. *elitist*	condescending	wealthy	narrow-minded
4. *ennobling*	royal	honorable	manual

There is always an easy solution to every human problem—neat, *plausible* and wrong.

—H. L. Mencken (1880–1956), American editor and critic

5. *plausible*	reasonable	smart	advantageous

VOCAB-U-LADDER

Use your knowledge of word synonyms, prefixes, and roots to connect the word at the top rung to the word at the bottom rung, using the words listed below.

recurrent
assemble
repeated
collect
simultaneous
concurrent

lecture

share root "legere," "to gather, pick out, choose"

synonyms for "gather"

share root "simulare," "to make like"

synonyms for "coincident"

share root "currere," "to run"

synonyms for "continual"

share root "petere," "to go toward, seek"

petition

Here's the story behind a word that figures prominently in the chapter you've just read.

Listen The word with the letter you can't even hear

listen līs′-ən *intr.v.* 1. To make an effort to hear something. 2. To pay attention; heed.*

Was there ever a better cautionary tale for the pitfalls of listening—things can sometimes get garbled and be difficult to hear—than the story of the word *listen* itself? After all, it's spelled with a "t" you never hear and probably got that way hundreds of years ago when two similar Old English words grew slightly entangled.

Although quite a number of English words include a silent t, the backstory for *listen* is a little bit different. (Most of the others, such as *moisten* or *soften*, lost the t sound in order to make them a little bit easier to pronounce, while *often*, where the t sound is optional, would appear to be a kind of missing link.) Once upon a time, there were two Old English synonyms, *hlystan*, which meant "to harken or hear" and *hlysnan*, which meant "to listen." The former, t intact, evolved into the now obsolete *list*, a verb that meant basically the same thing as its ancestor. Then when *hlysnan* made its way into modern English as *listen*, it took on the spelling of cousin *list* but retained its own historically t-less pronunciation. By the way, there's also some suggestion that a *listing* boat and a *listening* person are tied together by their shared tendency to tilt. Although we haven't yet been able to confirm whether that particular story is sound, we'll keep our ears open!**

*Adapted from "listen." *The American Heritage Dictionary of the English Language*, 4th ed. (Boston: Houghton Mifflin, 2000), p. 1021.
**Based on information from "listen." *The American Heritage Dictionary of the English Language*, 4th ed. (Boston: Houghton Mifflin, 2000), p. 1021; "list." *The American Heritage Dictionary of the English Language*, 4th ed. (Boston: Houghton Mifflin, 2000), p. 1021; "listen." *Online Etymology Dictionary*. Douglas Harper, Historian, http://www.etymonline.com/index.php?search=listen (accessed May 28, 2012); "list (v.2)." *Online Etymology Dictionary*. Douglas Harper, Historian, http://www.etymonline.com/index .php?search=listen (accessed May 28, 2012); "Why Is 't' Often Silent?," *The Grammarphobia Blog* (January 2, 2012), http://www .grammarphobia.com/blog/2012/01/silent-t.html

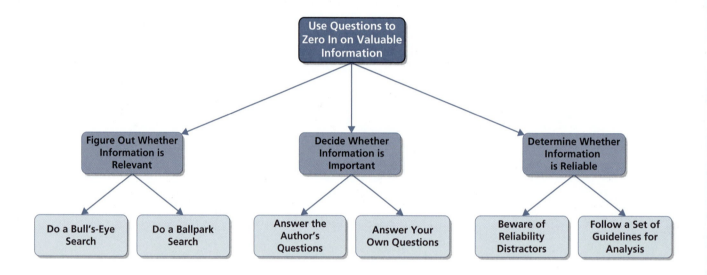

Use Questions to Zero In on Valuable Information

You can't possibly hold on to all the information you're bombarded with on a given day. You have to make some choices. That's why it's essential to be able to use questions to zero in on the most valuable information. This chapter explains how to use questions to

- **Figure Out Whether Information Is Relevant**
- **Decide Whether Information Is Important**
- **Determine Whether Information Is Reliable**

In this chapter

Why is so much information so readily available?

There has never been a time when more information has been more readily available than right now. Thanks primarily to the Internet but also to a wealth of electronic documents and databases, many of us have at our fingertips what students in the past had to walk or drive miles to gain access to. But this mountain of available information has its drawbacks. Author David Shenk calls it "data smog." As Shenk explains, "We thrive on the information, and yet we can also choke on it."[1]

How can you prevent information overload?

So, how can we benefit from all this information without being asphyxiated by it? Questions are the key. Questions turn you from a passive learner into an active one. They provide the engine that drives the whole understanding process. Humans have realized the power of questions for more than 2,400 years when the Greek philosopher Socrates (469–399 BC) found that instead of simply lecturing, he could pose a series of carefully directed questions that enabled the students who answered them to arrive at their understandings or conclusions themselves.

How do questions aid learning?

Students have been using questions ever since to activate their learning and make sense out of their studies. Time and time again, questions have provided a needed breakthrough for those who had been struggling with a subject. Instead of expecting meaning to simply pop up magically like a jack-in-the-box, active learners take the initiative, using their own questions to extract meaning from readings and lectures.

How do you pinpoint the most valuable information?

By employing this questioning method, you should be able to pierce the thick haze of data to pinpoint what's truly valuable in the things you read and hear. With questions as your laser beam, you can focus your attention on the information that is relevant, important, and reliable—in other words, on the stuff that's worth retaining.

Figure Out Whether Information Is Relevant

How can you tell if information is relevant?

Relevant information has a connection to your focus. If you're living in Los Angeles, today's weather in New York probably isn't relevant. That's because it has no obvious connection to your life in Los Angeles. On the other hand, the temperature in Los Angeles and the traffic conditions there will probably be relevant, particularly if you're venturing outside.

What's wrong with irrelevant information?

Irrelevant information is a little like the distractions described in Chapter 1. It can gum up the works of understanding, making it difficult to concentrate properly, to think clearly, or to make decisions quickly and effectively. Math instructors frequently assign word problems that deliberately contain some irrelevant information. For example, a problem designed to see if you can calculate the distance that a person will be able to travel at a particular rate of speed in a set amount of time may describe the color of the person's shoes or running shorts. Neither of these details is relevant, because they have

[1]David Shenk, *Data Smog: Surviving the Information Glut* (New York: HarperCollins, 1997), p. 22.

nothing to do with the focus of the problem, namely, how far someone can travel at a given speed in a given amount of time.

How can you reduce irrelevant information?

The sharper your focus, the more readily you'll be able to discard irrelevant information. If you want to learn everything you can about the Empire State Building, then the height of the building (1,454 feet) is relevant. But if your purpose is to find what you need to know to visit the Empire State Building, your focus is sharper and the height is no longer relevant. What *is* relevant is the location of the building and how to get there, its hours, and how much it will cost to visit. That's because all of this information has a connection to your purpose: visiting the Empire State Building.

How do you find relevant information?

You can't tell whether information is connected unless you know what it's connecting to. That normally requires a clearly articulated focus. This is where questions come in. The more specific your question, the sharper your focus is likely to be. Asking a question is like pointing a camera at a field of facts. All those facts you can see in the viewfinder are relevant. All those that you can't see are not.

How do you find relevant information using a search engine?

There are lots of books and websites devoted to search engine tips. Most of them devote a fair amount of time to the individual idiosyncrasies of particular search engines, the symbols and keywords that certain engines recognize that will help you focus your search. These details are helpful, although most of them are typically explained in the particular search engine's "advanced search" area. What's more important and more fundamental is to know what you're searching for before you begin searching. Back before the Web was commonplace, it was often possible to do computer-based searches of online databases with the help of a librarian or other trained researcher. These searches took time and in some cases they cost money. Both factors tended to discourage the casual, hit-or-miss approach that has gradually become more common.

What are the differences between a bull's-eye search and a ballpark search?

In general, there are two types of searches: bull's-eye and ballpark. With a bull's-eye search, you are looking for a specific document or fact. With a ballpark search, you are seeking information on a particular topic, but you don't have a specific fact or document in mind.

Do a Bull's-Eye Search

FOCUSING — QUESTIONING

How should you do a bull's-eye search?"

With a bull's-eye search, your best approach is to be as specific as possible. After all, if you know exactly what you're looking for, there's no real value in being vague about it.

How do you do a bull's-eye search in a book?

Searching in a book. If you're doing a bull's-eye search in a book, begin with the index. If the index is detailed and your search is sufficiently specific, you should be able to find an entry that takes you straight to the page or pages you're looking for. If the index is sparse or doesn't list what you're searching for, try the table of contents (TOC). Based on the chapter titles, find the chapter most likely to contain the information you're looking for, turn to that chapter, and then skim the pages until you locate the information you need.

How do you do a bull's-eye search in a magazine or journal?

Searching in a magazine or journal. Individual magazine or journal articles are rarely indexed. To do a bull's-eye search in these articles, your only real option is to concentrate on the information you're seeking and then skim the article intently in search of it. If the article uses subheadings, they can help to narrow your search. Skim the subheadings first and find the one that seems most likely to contain the information you're searching for. Then focus your attention on that section with your bull's-eye search.

Searching online or other electronic text. Doing a bull's-eye search in a specific online or other electronic text is comparatively easy. Most applications that read electronic documents (Web browsers, word processors, portable document readers) have a Find command that should enable you to type in the name, word, or phrase you're seeking and then go straight to it. By the way, these tools don't care if you've typed in the entire word or phrase; they just take the characters you've typed and find a match within the document. So, for example, if you're not sure how to spell the name of German composer Ludwig van Beethoven, you'd be safer searching for a part of his name—such as "hoven"—rather than run the risk of spelling it wrong. (A search for "Ludvig von Baythoven," for example, would turn up nothing.) On the other hand, if you've spelled your search words correctly and there are several occurrences of them within the text, most tools will normally take you to the first instance of their occurrence and enable you to search again for others.

Do a Ballpark Search

OVERVIEWING — QUESTIONING

What approach should you use for a ballpark search?

A ballpark search differs from a bull's-eye search in that you don't know exactly what you're looking for. You just have a general idea. Perhaps you're searching for information on Beethoven, but for some reason you don't remember his name. However, you know the person you are thinking of was German and a composer. The more clues you can assemble for a ballpark search, the more focused your search will be. But you have to be careful. If you include a clue that turns out to be incorrect, you may leave the ballpark entirely.

How do you do a ballpark search in a book?

Searching in a book. If your ballpark search is in a book in hard-copy format, you'll need to skim not simply for a specific term as you did with the bull's-eye search but for any context that could lead to the information you are looking for. Once again, you can start with the index to see if you can find any clues, although it's less likely this time that you'll be able to find something this way. Then move on to the TOC to see if there's a chapter title that will put you in the ballpark. For example, if you were skimming a book called either "Famous Germans" or "Famous Musicians," you might find a chapter that would help to refine your search further (perhaps "Germans in Music" in the former and "German Composers" in the latter). If you're lucky enough to be searching a particular chapter, you may be able to zero in even further by reading the chapter subheadings for additional clues. Beyond that point, you must be alert for context that might be likely to surround the information you're seeking.

How do you do a ballpark search in a magazine or journal?

Searching in a magazine or journal. Because a magazine or journal probably won't have an index, your only real hope of further narrowing a ballpark search in a magazine or journal article would be in its subheadings. Beyond that, you'll have to let the context lead you to the information you're searching for.

How can you do a ballpark search for an online document or in an electronic text?

Searching a single online or other electronic text. It's unlikely that a ballpark search of a specific online or other electronic text document will take you exactly where you want to go. But it may get you in the vicinity. The Find tool in a browser, word processor, or other document reader is not as sophisticated as an Internet search engine. If you're searching for the name of a German composer, it's best to search for either "German" or "composer" in the hopes of finding who you're looking for. (If you were to search for "German composer," you would be successful only if the two words occurred consecutively in the text.) Once the Find tool has you in the right ballpark (and it may take several attempts), clues from context should take you the rest of the way.

How do you do a ballpark search through multiple documents on the Internet?

Doing a ballpark search on the Internet. Although the Find tools you can use to search the pages in a single electronic document are limited, if you're searching several documents and they are all available on the Internet, then you should be able to do more sophisticated searches. Search engines allow you to refine your search by combining several searches into one. This approach, known as Boolean searching, allows you to establish a relationship between two or more search terms (see Figure 7.1). The rules for particular search engines may vary slightly, but in general, if you search using the words "German" and "composer," the search engine will return all the documents that contain "German," all the documents that contain "composer," and, most important (and normally at the top of the list), all the documents that contain "German" *and* "composer."

Figure 7.1
How Boolean Searching Works
Boolean searching can refine your searches by providing the intersection of two or more sets of data.

Decide Whether Information Is Important

How does important
information differ from
relevant information?

Of course, just because information is relevant doesn't necessarily mean it's something you want to hold on to. Valuable information is normally both relevant *and* important. Even if you've managed to discard irrelevant information, you may still be left with information of different weights competing for your time and attention. For example, if you had a to-do list that listed "Empty garbage" and "Complete research paper," both tasks would be relevant but they clearly wouldn't have the same weight or importance.

How do you determine
which information is
the most important?

The most important information is the information that responds most directly to a particular question. If you ask, "How do I get to the Statue of Liberty from midtown Manhattan?" the most important information is "To get to the Statue of Liberty from midtown Manhattan, take the subway to the South Ferry station and then catch the Liberty Ferry at Battery Park." But if you asked instead, "Where did the Statue of Liberty come from?" information about the subway and ferry routes would no longer be important. In fact, it wouldn't even be relevant. The most important information would be that "The Statue of Liberty was created by Frederic Auguste Bartholdi and was presented to the United States in 1865 as a gift from France."

What happens when
you find an answer to
the question?

Few answers mark an automatic end point. Every answer has the potential to generate new questions. An answer such as "The Statue of Liberty was created by Frederic Auguste Bartholdi and was presented to the United States in 1865 as a gift from France" might prompt you to ask "Who was Bartholdi?" and "Why did France give the United States a statue?" If the authors have anticipated your questions, the sentences or paragraphs that follow may answer them. Or it may turn out that you and the authors hit a fork in the road and move in different directions.

How do you determine
what's important?

To find what's important, ask questions and then seek to answer them. You can be driven by the engine of the author's questions or by questions of your own.

Answer the Author's Questions

QUESTIONING

Where do you find the
author's questions?

A book can be thought of as the answers to a series of invisible questions. Granted, you can't usually see these questions, but they're there. If this sounds like some sort of fairy tale, think again. Questions are actually built into the unit that organizes almost everything we read. What unit is that? The paragraph. According to its definition, a paragraph "typically deals with a single thought or topic."[2] Everything in a paragraph points to that thought or topic. All the other sentences in that paragraph are there to

---

[2]*The American Heritage Dictionary of the English Language*, 4th ed. (Boston: Houghton Mifflin, 2000), p. 1274.

support it. If you read a paragraph and ask, "What's important here?" your answer will be the controlling idea and that should lead you to the invisible question.

> The Empire State Building is an impressive symbol of early twentieth century industrial achievement. At 1,454 feet, this massive two-acre office building is the tallest in New York City and the ninth tallest in the world. Started in 1930, it took a total of 7,000,000 work-hours and a little more than a year of almost nonstop work to complete. It weighs 365,000 tons, has 6,500 windows, and boasts a total of 1,860 steps leading from the street level to the 102nd floor.

How are the controlling ideas arranged?

Most information is organized hierarchically. A chapter or an article has a single controlling idea or "thesis," which answers the question, "What's the point?" All other ideas grow out of that idea. On a smaller scale, each individual paragraph has its own controlling idea, with the rest of the paragraph acting to support it. Just as the controlling idea of the article answers the question "What's the point?" for the article, *these* controlling ideas answer a similar question, but for each individual paragraph this time.

How do the chapter maps show the controlling idea relationships?

The maps that open each of the chapters in this book provide a good example of how this arrangement works. Each idea, like each node in the map, is supported by the ideas beneath it. The controlling idea provides the answer to a question; the ideas beneath provide examples and evidence to support it. This pattern of questions, answers, and support is repeated from article to section to paragraph. With more space, the maps could be expanded to include every paragraph in a chapter. The maps would be much bigger, of course, but the basic arrangement would be the same.

To find the most important information in an article or chapter, look for the controlling ideas in each paragraph. These ideas in turn are likely to cluster around a controlling idea for a particular section. And those ideas should all support the chapter or article's controlling idea. Often, the first paragraph of each section provides the controlling idea for that section, and the introductory paragraph for the chapter provides the controlling idea for the entire chapter. Some articles or chapters are better organized than others, but in many cases you should be able to create a framework of controlling ideas that resembles the maps that begin each chapter in this book.

IT'S YOUR Q

Answer Your Own Questions
QUESTIONING

What provides the framework for a chapter or article?

Of course, your view of what's important may differ from the author's view. Just as the Empire State Building was built around a steel framework, an article or chapter is constructed by the author around a framework of controlling ideas. But these important ideas don't necessarily have to be *your* important ideas.

How do you find
what's important to
you?

The way to find the information that is important to you is by asking a focused question and then zeroing in on the area that provides the answer. Depending on the scope of your question, that area might be a sentence, a paragraph, a section, a chapter or article, or even an entire book. The next most important information will be the information that directly supports your original answer.

How can you be sure
what you've found is
the most important?

Unlike relevance, which has to do with whether a connection exists or doesn't, importance is a relative thing. It has to do with the scope of your topic or question. If relevance can be seen as where the camera lens is pointed, importance is influenced by how far you zoom in or zoom out. The larger something is relative to the other facts around it, the more important it's likely to be. So, if your question asks, "How tall is the Empire State Building?" then its height is likely to be the most important piece of information in your answer. If, on the other hand, your question asks, "How big is the Empire State Building?" then its height would presumably compete with its other dimensions for importance.

What happens to
information that is
interesting but not
important?

Keep in mind that what is important is not always the same as what is interesting. A lot of information (such as the number of steps in the Empire State Building) falls under the general heading of *trivia*. Trivia fascinates some students and bores others. Regardless, it's rarely important. At best it provides support for a controlling idea. If you think trivia is interesting, you may find this motivates you to remember it. It's still better to focus your attention on the important ideas though. When you do, the details that interest you will often remain in the picture. If, on the other hand, you focus on trivia instead, the controlling ideas may be pushed out of frame.

Determine Whether Information Is Reliable

IT'S YOUR Q

Questions activate your learning and help you to determine which information is relevant and which information is important. But they play one more especially vital role. They help you put the reliability of information to the test. Compared to finding information that's relevant or deciding which information is important, determining whether information is reliable can be a real challenge. It helps to beware of things that can frequently distract from your ability to determine whether information is reliable and to arrive at some guidelines you can use consistently to analyze information for its overall reliability.

Beware of Reliability Distractors

QUESTIONING

Most of us would like to think that we can determine the reliability of information. However, certain factors such as the echo chamber, confirmation bias, and logical fallacies can sometimes distort our perception of reliability.

The Echo Chamber

What is the echo chamber?

The echo chamber describes a situation in which information is amplified by constant repetition. If the information is false, it may be mistaken as true. If the information is true, it may appear to be more relevant or important than it actually is. The satirist H. L. Mencken's "bathtub hoax" offers an interesting insight into the echo chamber run amok, whereas urban legends provide more commonplace examples. And because the echo chamber isn't just for false information, it helps sometimes to take a good look at the "news" that everyone is buzzing about.

What was the bathtub hoax?

The Bathtub Hoax   In 1917, the reporter and satirist Henry Louis Mencken wrote a whimsical, entirely fictional piece for the *New York Evening Mail* called "A Neglected Anniversary," a meticulously fabricated history of the evolution of the bathtub in America and its introduction in the White House during the Millard Fillmore administration in 1850. Unfortunately, many of the people who read the piece must not have been active learners because the joke was lost on them. Soon, Mencken's fictional account of the first White House bathtub made its way into respectable history and reference books. Once the "fact" was available in other sources, the echo chamber effect took hold and the story of the first White House bathtub started popping up in numerous books as though it were the truth. Mencken, who had a distinctly mischievous side, claimed to be astonished by the longevity of his hoax, but given his temperament, he was probably amused by the impact of his stunt, which was an especially colorful illustration of the echo chamber effect.

IT'S YOUR Q

Urban Legends   Urban legends are modern myths that once depended almost entirely on word of mouth for their dissemination but have gotten an extra boost with the advent of e-mail. Either method of communication provides the echo chamber. Classic urban legends include the fancy sports car that gets sold for $50, the unsuspecting tourist in Mexico who buys what he or she thinks is a Chihuahua but once home discovers that the little dog is actually a rat, the well-meaning but absent-minded woman who tragically tries to dry off her wet poodle in a microwave, and the passing motorist who picks up a hitchhiker in a prom dress but learns later that the girl he drove home died several years before on that very night. None of these stories is true, and yet you're likely to hear many of them told again and again as true, albeit with some variations that either bring them up to date or associate them with local landmarks.

What makes urban legends convincing?

   What makes urban legends convincing, among other things, is that they are usually told by someone you know who insists that he or she knows someone who knows the person the incident actually happened to. For this reason, urban legends are sometimes called FOAF or "friend of a friend" stories. Ironically, the same thing that initially makes urban legends seem convincing is what ultimately gives them away as false.

How can you detect an urban legend?

If you hear a story from someone who knows someone who has a friend the story "really happened to," that's usually a dead giveaway. Urban legends almost never hold up to scrutiny if you try to trace them back to the source. Even in those situations in which the legend is based on truth, it inevitably gets distorted or exaggerated. Although e-mail has done a lot to increase the spread of urban legends, the Internet has made it easier to debunk them. Several websites, including snopes.com, track urban legends. The websites provide regularly updated listings of legends and, in most cases—although not always—proof that they aren't true. This can be valuable because people who unwittingly pass on an urban legend can often get quite irritable if the reliability of their story is questioned. Actual evidence instead of unsubstantiated disbelief is usually enough to convince most people.

How does the echo chamber affect information that is true?

The Dangers of Summer   Not all information that gets amplified in the echo chamber is false. Sometimes stories are true but they get blown out of proportion. A good example was the widespread fear of shark attacks and the spread of the West Nile virus a few summers ago. From the nervous reactions of some vacationers, you might've gotten the impression that if "Jaws" didn't get them, then the West Nile would. Were the fears of ferocious sharks and a mosquito-borne virus justified? Not according to an article and graphic in the *New York Times* that compared the relative dangers of what it called "The Real Dangers of Summer."[3] The greatest risks, according to the piece, were skin cancer and food poisoning. The former would strike 1 in 200 people, the latter 1 in 800. But what of the West Nile virus and sharks? The *Times* statistics showed that these were actually the lowest risks of all summertime hazards, affecting 1 in 68,500 and 1 in 6 million, respectively. So why the hysteria? Additional statistics in the same graphic provided a clue. Whereas only 359 newspaper articles had been written the previous summer about the dangers of skin cancer and food poisoning, during the same period a whopping 2,516 articles had dealt with either the West Nile virus or the hungry sharks.

Confirmation Bias

What happens with confirmation bias? What influences whether we tune in or tune out information?

Some information that's unreliable may be embraced while other information that's reliable may be overlooked. Why? It's called confirmation bias.

Have you ever had the experience of learning the meaning of a word, only to find that suddenly everyone around you seems to be using that same word? Of course, if the word you learned *is* actually a new word (also known as a *neologism*), then it may well be that the number of people using that word is increasing. But if it's a word that's only new for you, it's unlikely that others have suddenly decided to use it more often on your account. What's more plausible is that you've just become more attuned to that word. As we move through our daily lives, the sheer magnitude of information we confront means it's almost inevitable that we will tune in some information and tune out

[3]David Ropeik and Nigel Holmes, "Never Bitten, Twice Shy: The Real Dangers of Summer," *New York Times* (August 9, 2003), p. A11.

some other. When the information relates to something you already know or believe, you're more likely to tune it in. And if the information doesn't relate to something you already know or believe, you're more likely to tune it out.

When is selectivity harmful?

In the case of learning a new word, this tendency is relatively harmless. But the same phenomenon can act to reinforce your particular viewpoint or bias at the expense of other information that may actually contradict or modify your beliefs. This is known as confirmation bias. In the journal *Review of General Psychology*, psychologist Raymond S. Nickerson defines confirmation bias as "the unwitting selectivity in the acquisition and use of evidence."[4] So, although selectivity is an essential tool in reducing the glut of information you're exposed to, it can also have a negative effect by shielding you from vital information or depriving you of the complete picture.

What did Forer's experiment show?

One of the most famous demonstrations of confirmation bias was an experiment conducted by a psychology professor named Forer, who administered a personality profile test to his students. When Forer received the completed tests, he promptly threw them all out and instead, unbeknownst to the students, returned the identical personality profile to each member of his class, asking each student to read his or her profile and then rate its accuracy on a scale of 0 to 5, with 5 meaning "excellent" and 4 meaning "good." Incredibly, the personality profile, even though it was written without any of the students in mind, still received a cumulative average of 4.26 for accuracy. What the students didn't realize—until he told them—is that Forer had clipped the profile out of a newspaper horoscope column. The profile was ambiguous but vaguely complimentary. The criticisms were mild. Thanks to confirmation bias, most of the students who read the profile related to its positive elements, ignored those elements that were too negative or didn't relate specifically to them, and then concluded that it was an accurate assessment of their particular personality traits![5]

What can you do to avoid confirmation bias?

All of us are susceptible to confirmation bias. It's important to be aware of this tendency and to keep your mind open for differing evidence and information that might change your viewpoint. Also, it doesn't hurt to have a set of consistent guidelines that you use to gauge the validity of information.

Why is it risky to make decisions based on your "gut"?

Many people make a decision whether or not to trust information based on their "gut." And it's true that our hunches and instincts do seem to provide us with clues, although there is very little scientific data to support this. Unfortunately, emotional appeals have a way of short-circuiting common sense. It happens to nearly all of us at times. Articulate, charismatic liars can sometimes trigger a positive response while honest but awkward writing or speaking can sometimes put us on guard.

[4]Raymond S. Nickerson, "Confirmation Bias: A Ubiquitous Phenomenon in Many Guises," *Review of General Psychology* 2, no. 2 (1998): pp. 175–220.

[5]Robert Todd Carroll, "Forer Effect," *The Skeptics Dictionary*, http://www.skepdic.com/forer.html

Logical Fallacies

What are logical
fallacies?

Although your own biases can affect the way you select and interpret information, there are also elements embedded in some arguments that can lead you to unknowingly accept a false conclusion as fact. Usually there is a flaw in an otherwise reasonable argument that renders it invalid. These are commonly known as logical fallacies and are used by writers and speakers sometimes accidentally but often on purpose to lead you to a desired conclusion.

What is an example of
a logical fallacy?

One of the best-known logical fallacies has to do with ice cream sales. It suggests that because an increase in ice cream sales seems to correspond with an increase in crime, ice cream must cause crime. What's tricky about a fallacy is that it's usually made up of a true premise or premises that reach a false conclusion. Therefore, a person who isn't listening or reading critically may notice the true statements but overlook the logical leap that leads to a false outcome. It's true that ice cream sales and crime often increase at the same time. But it's not true that one causes the other. (It's more likely that hot weather causes the increase in both.)

Another common fallacy is known as the straw man. That's a situation in which the writer or speaker uses an opposing example that is either weak or imaginary in order to make his argument appear to gain legitimacy or strength. The straw man is often called "some" or "some people" to present the appearance of a real opposition without ever naming it. So, if the authors of a study skills textbook wanted to appear more courageous and defiant than they actually are, they might write: "Although there are some who may want to do away with study skills textbooks altogether, we were determined to make sure that our book was published." A person who read this might feel increased respect and admiration for these brave authors and might even be tempted to purchase an additional book or two just to spite those who want to do away with study skills textbooks altogether. But there's only one problem. The enemy is never specified. It's a phantom. And that is how the straw man fallacy works.

IT'S YOUR Q

Where can you learn
more about fallacies?

There are numerous books and websites devoted to fallacies. All of them are informative, and many are quite entertaining.

Books

Capaldi, Nicholas. *The Art of Deception: An Introduction to Critical Thinking: How to: Win an Argument, Defend a Case, Recognize a Fallacy, See Through a Deception*. Prometheus Books, 1987.

Damer, T. Edward. *Attacking Faulty Reasoning: Practical Guide to Fallacy-Free Arguments*, 5th ed. Wadsworth, 2004.

Engel, S. Morris. *With Good Reason: An Introduction to Informal Fallacies*, 6th ed. St. Martins, 1999.

Gula, Robert J. *Nonsense: A Handbook of Logical Fallacies*. Axios, 2002.

Whyte, Jamie. *Crimes Against Logic*. McGraw-Hill, 2004.

Websites

Fallacies: The Internet Encyclopedia of Philosophy. http://www.iep.utm.edu/fallacy/
Fallacies: The Nizkor Project. http://www.nizkor.org/features/fallacies/
Logical Fallacies: The Fallacy Files. http://www.fallacyfiles.org/
Logical Fallacies and the Art of Debate. http://www.csun.edu/~dgw61315/fallacies.html

Follow a Set of Guidelines for Analysis

PLANNING

How can you avoid being swayed by unreliable information?

Given all the potential ways in which information can be misleading, how do you establish what's reliable and what isn't? One of the most effective ways to guard against being swayed by unreliable information in one instance but unaffected by it in another is to consistently apply standards that allow you to subject everything to the same analysis or test. You can use a test for analyzing all types of information or tailor your analysis for a specific area, such as Internet sites. What's important in either case is to keep your approach systematic and consistent.

Evaluate Information

What are the four steps for Ruggiero's comprehensive thinking strategy?

Critical thinking authority Vincent Ruggiero has defined a four-step "comprehensive thinking strategy."[6]

1. *Identify facts and opinions.* If the information is common knowledge or easily verifiable, it's likely to be factual. If not, treat it as opinion.
2. *Check the facts and test the opinions.* If the information is factual, can you verify it? Did the author or speaker seem to leave out anything important? If it's opinion, do the speaker's views stand up to scrutiny or are they easily refuted?
3. *Evaluate the evidence.* If the author or speaker has offered support for any opinions, is this support reasonable and sufficient?
4. *Make your judgment.* Based on the facts and the evidence, rather than your gut feelings or preferences, decide whether you consider the information reliable.

Evaluate Internet Sites

What special challenge does Internet information create?

One of the Internet's greatest strengths—its wide-open, inclusive nature—is also a potential weakness. With a few days' work and very little money, a talented person can put together a website that superficially resembles one of the top professional news and information sites and yet ignores the standards for quality and accuracy that traditional news organizations live by. Although the following questions may be especially

[6]Vincent Ryan Ruggiero, *Becoming a Critical Thinker*, 5th ed. (Boston: Houghton Mifflin, 1999), pp. 26–27.

important to ask about Internet sites, they can also apply to traditional TV, radio, magazines, and newspapers.

1. *Who owns them?* More and more news and information operations are owned by companies whose emphasis is on something other than news. This may affect their tone or approach. Others aren't news organizations at all but lobbies or think tanks organized to promote a particular product or viewpoint but whose publications are designed to look like news. With newspapers, magazines, and websites, you can usually find information about the ownership in the paper or magazine or on the site. With television or radio stations, it can take a little more digging. Most news operations try to maintain a wall (see #3) between their business and editorial operations, but it isn't always possible.

2. *How do they make their money?* A key rule of investigative journalism is to "follow the money," and to some degree these special journalists are professional critical thinkers. Almost no publication or website relies solely on money from subscribers to exist. As disillusioning as it is to realize, financial obligations to owners or advertisers can sometimes influence what a publication or broadcaster does and doesn't cover. For example, a newspaper that relies heavily on automobile ads may be reluctant to cover a scandal at a car dealership, whereas a magazine that runs ads for a local restaurant may feel pressure to give that restaurant a good review. Advertisements are usually pretty easy to notice and the nature of the advertising can sometimes be illuminating. It can tell you something about the viewers, readers, or listening audience and may give you an idea of what topics could test the organization's editorial independence.

3. *Can you tell the difference between news, opinion, and advertising?* In the past, publications and broadcasters have gone to great lengths to distinguish between news and paid advertising, feeling that it serves the public better to make sure that this distinction is clear. In newspapers, this is commonly known as "the wall." Journalists are normally well aware of this wall and are proud of its existence. The wall between news and opinion isn't always as clear, and that can be a problem when one is mistaken for the other.

4. *Where do they get their information?* Some small news operations rely heavily on national and international news wires for most or even all of their information. Larger operations have their own staffs of reporters and columnists. Over time, if you pay attention, you should be able to get a sense of a particular news service or journalist's track record for reliability.

5. *How well presented is the information?* Crudely written or clumsily delivered words can occasionally pack a wallop, but, in general, sloppy writing or speaking should set off alarm bells in your head.

6. *What other information is presented?* You can sometimes learn about the reliability of an article from the company it keeps. This is especially true on the Internet. If someone sends you a link to a news story, see if you can navigate back to the homepage of

the site where the story came from. The "mix" of a site's stories can be a tip-off. For example, a White House exclusive may not look very reliable if you discover that it's running alongside a story about a dog with two heads and an article about a miracle weight-loss product.

What is a simpler way for determining whether something is reliable?

A simpler way to determine whether information is reliable or not is basically no different than the strategy for zeroing in on all valuable information: Stay alert, think about your thinking, and above all, ask questions!

FINAL WORDS

What surprising result can zeroing in on valuable ideas sometimes produce?

Not only will zeroing in on what's valuable enable you to extract the most relevant, important, and reliable information from what you read and hear and make it a part of your personal web of knowledge, but it will also produce a result that may surprise you: It will help you to derive real pleasure out of thinking!

CHAPTER CHECKUP

SENTENCE COMPLETION

Complete the following sentences with one of the three words listed below each sentence.

1. Author David Shenk calls the glut of information _____.

   data mining   **databases**   **data smog**

2. Information in an article or chapter is usually organized _____.

   hierarchically   **collectively**   **repeatedly**

3. In newspapers, the distinction between news and advertising is commonly known as _____.

   "the gap"   **"the tower"**   **"the wall"**

MATCHING

In each blank space in the left column, write the letter preceding the phrase in the right column that matches the left item best.

_____ 1. Ballpark   a. Used questions and answers to promote understanding

_____ 2. Socrates   b. Wrote a fictional story that was adopted as historical fact

_____ 3. Fallacy   c. The engine that drives the whole understanding process

_____ 4. Mencken   d. Method of searching for information when you're not exactly sure what you're looking for

_____ 5. Forer   e. Method of searching when you know exactly what you're looking for

_____ 6. Boolean   f. Conducted an experiment with his class that demonstrated confirmation bias

_____ 7. Bull's-eye   g. Method that lets you define a logical relationship between two or more search terms

_____ 8. Questions   h. A flaw in an otherwise logical argument

TRUE-FALSE

Circle T *beside the true statements and* F *beside the false statements.*

1. T   F   In the process of understanding, questions are the engine.
2. T   F   Questions change you from an active learner to a passive one.
3. T   F   Sharks and West Nile virus are the greatest summertime hazards.
4. T   F   Math instructors are careful to keep irrelevant information out of the word problems they assign.
5. T   F   Most programs that read electronic documents have a Find command.

MULTIPLE CHOICE

Choose the word or phrase that completes each sentence most accurately, and circle the letter that precedes it.

1. Valuable information should be
    a. relevant.
    b. important.
    c. reliable.
    d. all of the above.

2. Many books can be thought of as a series of
    a. answers to invisible questions.
    b. clues to unsolvable mysteries.
    c. episodes from timeless stories.
    d. conclusions to unspoken introductions.

3. The most important information in a paragraph is
    a. the controlling idea.
    b. a question.
    c. the last sentence.
    d. a detail.

4. The story of the Chihuahua that turned out to be a rat is an example of
    a. confirmation bias.
    b. an urban legend.
    c. a logical fallacy.
    d. a controlling idea.

5. A key rule of investigative journalism is
    a. know thyself.
    b. trust but verify.
    c. follow the money.
    d. none of the above.

REFLECTION

Think about the ideas outlined in this chapter and then draw upon your own opinions and experiences to answer each question fully.

1. Explain the distinction between relevant, reliable, and important information. Which of the three poses the biggest challenge for you? Why?
2. Do you use particular tricks or shortcuts to improve your Internet searching? If so, explain your approach in a way that would be useful for others. If not, suggest

www.cengage.com/success/Pauk/HowToStudy11e

ideas you've gleaned from this chapter that may help improve your searching in the future.

3. Cite an example of an urban legend, a case of confirmation bias, or an instance of the echo chamber that fooled you at first, and then explain how you eventually realized that it was unreliable.

IT'S YOUR Q

The Q System uses marginal questions to encourage active reading. You'll notice that most but not all paragraphs in this chapter are accompanied by marginal questions. Now it's your Q. Scan the chapter for any paragraph that is missing a question, reread the paragraph, establish the main idea, and then arrive at a question that elicits it. Use the questions in the surrounding paragraphs as models for your own marginal questions.

VOCABULARY IN ACTION

To expand the horizons of your understanding and to refine the precision of your thought, the three exercises that follow are designed to help you grow, strengthen, and maintain your own vocabulary.

SAY WHAT?

From the three choices beside each numbered item, select the one that most nearly expresses the meaning of the italicized word in the quote. Make a light check mark (√) next to your choice.

When strangers start acting like neighbors, communities are *reinvigorated*.

—Ralph Nader (1934–), American lawyer, consumer advocate, and presidential candidate

| 1. *reinvigorated* | given new leaders | given old standards | given new life |

It's *stasis* that kills you off in the end, not *ambition*.

—Bono (1960–), Irish musician

| 2. *stasis* | apathy | inactivity | paralysis |
| 3. *ambition* | drive | enthusiasm | greed |

Diplomacy is the art of saying "nice doggie" until you can find a rock.

—Will Rogers (1879–1935), American actor and humorist

| 4. *diplomacy* | trickery | cleverness | tact |

The gambling known as business looks with *austere* disfavor upon the business known as gambling.

—Ambrose Bierce (1842–1914), American author

| 5. *austere* | stern | enormous | particular |

VOCAB-U-LADDER

Use your knowledge of word synonyms and roots to connect the word at the top rung to the word at the bottom rung, using the words listed below.

desultory
germ
germane
salient
sporadic
spore

relevant

synonyms for "related"

share root "germen," "sprout, bud"

synonyms for "seed"

share root "sporas," "scattered"

synonyms for "haphazard"

share root "salire," "to leap"

synonyms for "prominent"

conspicuous

Here's the story behind a word that figures prominently in the chapter you've just read.

Critical **Critical words aren't always critical words.**

critical crĭt′ ĭ-kəl. *adj.* 1. Inclined to judge severely and find fault. 2. Characterized by careful, exact evaluation and judgment. 3. Of, relating to, or characteristic of critics or criticism. 4. Forming or having the nature of a turning point; crucial or decisive.*

"May I be critical?" Ask someone that, and you're apt to be faced with a frown or maybe even a full-fledged "fight-or-flight" response. These days, that question can be about as welcome as a punch in the solar plexus. It's a confusing world as far as words are concerned. In some circles, *bad* can mean "good," *cool* can mean "hot," and calling something *sick* can be seen as a compliment. The English language is in an almost constant state of flux. When architect Christopher Wren completed St. Paul's Cathedral in 1710, the Queen told him she thought it was awful. In other words, she loved it. *Awful* meant "awe-inspiring" in Wren's day but now it generally means "*horrid*." Although somewhere along the way the word critical has acquired a primarily negative connotation, it hasn't always been this way. The words critical and criticism come from the Greek word *krĭnein*, which means "to separate, judge, or decide." Both of these words in turn are descendants of crisis, which has met a similar fate. A *crisis* is a crossroads, a critical point where paths may separate or when it's time to judge or decide. The welcome end to a high fever is a crisis; a thoughtful, detailed analysis of a novel is criticism; and a large supply of water can be *critical* on a long hike. But a hurricane is a crisis, insults can be *criticism*, and if you thoughtlessly fail to bring water on that hike, the person who scolds you may be accurately described as *critical*. Yes, English words can have slippery meanings. And critical is a classic example. A lot depends on the time, the context, and the intentions of the person who uses them. So the next time that someone asks, "May I be critical?" hold your fire, take a deep breath, and think critically before you answer.**

*Adapted from "critical." *The American Heritage Dictionary of the English Language*, 4th ed. (Boston: Houghton Mifflin, 2000), http://dictionary.reference.com/browse/critical (accessed May 26, 2009).
**Based on information from "critical." *The American Heritage Dictionary of the English Language*, 4th ed. (Boston: Houghton Mifflin, 2000), http://dictionary.reference.com/browse/critical (accessed May 26, 2009); "critical." *Online Etymology Dictionary*. Douglas Harper, Historian, http://www.etymonline.com/index.php?search=critical (accessed May 26, 2009); "critical, *a.*" *Oxford English Dictionary*, 2nd ed. 20 vols. (Oxford: Oxford University Press, 1989).

Learn
Chan

*If you wish to advance
into the infinite, explore
the finite in all directions.*

**Johann Wolfgang von
Goethe** (1749–1832), German
author, painter, philosopher,
scientist, and politician

Instructors d
in the same
Some, like w
others, like g
traditional ro
tune in to th
to enhance y
personal lear

-
-
-
-
-

In this

- ▶ A simpl
  rise. (p.

- ▶ Why yo

- ▶ There a

How will an understanding of learning styles affect your success in college?

Although we may sit in the same classrooms or log on to the same websites, we don't all learn in the same way. Instructors are well aware of this, and most students have at least a vague sense that this is true. Unfortunately, despite the diversity of learning styles, course information is still primarily conveyed on two basic channels: as symbols and as shapes. The symbols are the words and numbers we read and hear. The shapes are the graphs, charts, maps, and other illustrations that often accompany those numbers and words. First, it helps to have a good sense of what kind of learner you are. Then, in order to learn and succeed, you must develop strategies to deal with the dominant channels of symbols and shapes and when possible use your preferred learning styles to provide additional support.

Deal with the Dominant Channels

What are the dominant learning channels?

It's rare that you'll take a college course that doesn't have text you need to read and images you're expected to understand and interpret. With few exceptions, to succeed in college you will need to learn to operate on these dominant channels, to understand your assigned texts to the best of your ability, and to make sense out of any accompanying charts, graphs, and illustrations.

Cope with Difficult Texts

REFRAMING

Why are some textbooks so difficult to understand?

Sometimes you and the required text for your course may not "hit it off." There are several factors that can make a textbook seem difficult. Here are three of them:

Writing style or tone. As we saw in Chapter 5, most books have a distinctive style or tone, one that usually reflects the voice of the author or authors. Some books are chatty and informal. Others are staid and scholarly. You may not feel as though you are in sync with the way the authors choose to express their ideas. If so, that can make reading the assignments more challenging and even aggravating. Try to stick it out, though. The style may seem jarring at first, but there's a good chance you'll grow accustomed to it over time.

Vocabulary. If a book seems to be "over your head," a primary reason for this will often be its vocabulary level. If you're having trouble with a textbook because you don't understand what the words mean, then you probably should be reading two books at once—your text and your dictionary—until you've grown accustomed enough to the vocabulary that you can keep reading without stopping to look something up. With some books, the new and challenging words never end, but more often it's just a matter of getting up to speed. Once you learn the lingo, you'll be fine.

Organization. Trouble with the way a book is organized may indicate a conflict between the author's writing style and your personal learning style. As Felder and Soloman explain,[1] *sequential learners* process things methodically, step by step, relating each new piece of information to the facts that came before it as though following a recipe. *Global learners* learn in bursts and insights, grabbing huge handfuls of seemingly unrelated information and then suddenly (and often unexpectedly) establishing connections between ideas in one great big "Aha!" If you're a sequential learner and you run into that rare textbook that's written globally, your best defense is to search first for some sort of summary at the end of the chapter that will pull things together and provide you with a road map for your wild ride. If the author writes sequentially and you learn globally, you might as well get used to it. The vast majority of courses and texts are delivered in a sequential fashion. Global learners can adjust to a sequential text and add some unaccustomed structure to their way of looking at things by taking a few moments to systematically survey a reading assignment (see Chapter 5) before diving in.

Keep in mind that most relationships, even those between a student and a textbook, take work and time. But if there truly seems to be a disconnect between you and your book, you may want to find a supplementary text or "read" the original book in a different form.

Use a Supplementary Text

If for whatever reason you're having difficulties understanding the course's primary textbook and you've already sought help from the instructor or a tutor, then a supplementary textbook can sometimes help you gain a better grasp of the subject. In some instances, you may be able to find another textbook that covers the same topic that your course textbook does, but it's more likely that you will have to use different supplementary texts for different parts of your course text. It's important to stress that this is a *supplementary* textbook, not an alternate one. Your instructor still has every right and reason to expect you to be studying from the required text. Therefore, any reading you do in a second text will be in addition to your regular text, not instead of it. Once you have a better grasp of the subject or ideas you were struggling with, return to the regular text and see if it is easier to understand.

Listen Instead of Reading

What is the value of listening instead of reading?

Auditory learners comprehend better when they hear information instead of reading it on a page or screen. This means that although lectures are helpful, reading assignments can sometimes be a struggle. The organization Recording for the Blind and Dyslexic (RFB&D) provides audio versions of a large number of textbooks (http://www.rfbd.org).

---

[1]Richard A. Felder and Barbara M. Soloman, "Learning Styles and Strategies," http://www.ncsu.edu/felder-public/ILSdir/styles.htm

In addition, many popular books—both fiction and nonfiction—are released in audio form by commercial publishers and are often available from your college or public library for free. It's important to stick with the unabridged versions, however, or you may miss a part of the book that is stressed in class and on your tests but is absent from the copy you listened to.

Understand Visuals

REFRAMING — OVERVIEWING

Why is it important to understand visuals?

All of us are taught to read words at an early age. But when are we taught to read pictures? When you read words, you're cracking a code. That code is the English language, and its message is the meaning you extract from words, sentences, and paragraphs. Although we spend a great deal of time decoding language, most of the codes around us are visual. We can decode a smile, for example, and know how its meaning differs from that of a frown. Visual materials in textbooks use codes as well to supply messages that are often as important as the meanings contained in sentences and paragraphs. For that reason, they must be read every bit as carefully. Like reading a paragraph, reading a picture simply means extracting its message.

Use the OPTIC System

What is the purpose of the OPTIC system?

Many students mistakenly give visuals only a quick glance or even skip over them entirely. But these graphic materials should be scrutinized as carefully and as systematically as paragraphs. The OPTIC system will help you take an organized approach to this task.

What do the five letters in OPTIC stand for?

The five letters in the word *OPTIC* (which means "pertaining to the eye") provide you with a simple system for remembering the five elements of analyzing a visual:

O is for *overview*.
P is for *parts*.
T is for *title*.
I is for *interrelationships*.
C is for *conclusion*.

What are the five steps of the OPTIC system?

Using these five elements as cues, you can conduct a meaningful analysis of almost any diagram, graph, or illustration by following these steps:

1. Begin by conducting a brief *overview* of the visual. See if you can grasp its basic message without paying attention to the details.
2. Then zero in on the *parts* of the visual. Read all labels, and note any elements or details that seem important.
3. Now read the *title* of the visual so that you're clear on the subject it is covering.
4. Next, use the title as your theory and the parts of the visual as clues to detect and specify the *interrelationships* in the graphic.

5. Finally, try to reach a *conclusion* about the visual as a whole. What does it mean? Why was it included in the text? Sum up the message of the visual in just a sentence or two.

Learn the Language of Graphs

What are the most common types of graphs?

You are most likely to encounter three general types of graphs: circle graphs, bar graphs, and line graphs. The purpose of a circle graph is unique, whereas bar and line graphs perform the same basic function.

What is the purpose of the circle graph?

Decode Circle Graphs. The purpose of a circle graph, also known as a pie chart, is to proportionally show the relationship of parts (slices) to a whole (the pie). Although these graphs are relatively rare in highly technical books, they regularly appear in newspapers as well as in textbooks on topics other than mathematics and science. The popularity of the circle graph is mainly due to its simplicity. In most cases, you can tell at a glance the proportions the graph illustrates—that is, the various-sized slices of the pie. For example, in Figure 8.1, the circle graph gives you a clear picture of the population distribution in the United States.

How do you decode bar and line graphs?

Decode Bar and Line Graphs. The purpose of a bar or line graph is to illustrate the relationship of a set of dependent variables to a set of independent variables. *Variables* are numbers that can change. For example, the number we use to refer to the year

Figure 8.1

U.S. Population by Region

Circle graphs (pie charts) show the relationship of several parts to a whole. *Source:* U.S. Census Bureau.

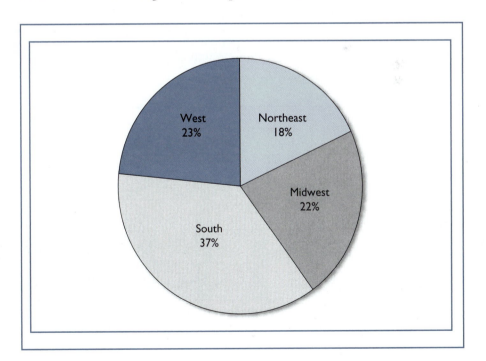

is a variable. It increases by one every twelve months. Population is another variable. It changes when someone is born or dies, when someone becomes a citizen, or when someone leaves the country. Years and dates in general are called *independent variables* because they change on their own. The population of the United States does not influence the fact that a new year begins every 365 or 366 days. Quantities such as population are called *dependent variables* because their change occurs in relation to another variable, such as the year. For example, we measure the changes in the U.S. population every ten years when the census is taken.

How do bar and line graphs differ?

Although bar and line graphs both show how a dependent variable such as population increases or decreases in relation to an independent variable such as the year, each takes a slightly different approach. Bar graphs (see Figure 8.2) focus on specific changes; line graphs (see Figure 8.3) illustrate long-term trends. One way to visualize this distinction is to think of bar graphs as snapshots and line graphs as movies. If you were to take successive snapshots of a long jumper, you would have a series of photographs showing successive stages of the jump. If you were to film the same jump with a movie camera, you'd have a continuous record of the entire jump. Figure 8.4 illustrates this idea.

What are the relative strengths and weaknesses of bar and line graphs?

Like snapshots and movies, each type of graph has strengths. Bar graphs are good for comparing the individual sizes or amounts of items, and they provide clear comparisons of several sets of data at once. Line graphs are useful for showing changes in data over long periods of time. For instance, if you wanted to examine a country's population increase over a brief period of time, or if you wanted to compare it with the population of another country, you would probably use a bar graph. Figure 8.2 shows that the growth in U.S. population was relatively steady from 1950 through 2010, whereas Canada's population growth surged during the 1950s and 1960s and then again at the

Figure 8.2
Population Growth in the United States and Canada, 1950–2010
Bar graphs show sizes of individual items and illustrate comparisons. *Source:* U.S. Census Bureau; Statistics Canada.

beginning of the twenty-first century. But if you wanted to show the percentage increase in U.S. population since the eighteenth century, a line graph would be a better visual. Figure 8.3 shows that the growth in U.S. population has generally slowed since 1850.

Regardless of whether the graphic is a circle, bar, or line graph, once you understand the language of the particular graph, you can methodically extract its meaning in the

Figure 8.3

Percentage Increase in U.S. Population, 1800–2010

Line graphs show long-term trends in data.

Source: U.S. Census Bureau.

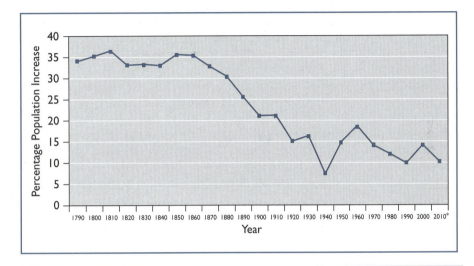

Figure 8.4

Snapshots Versus Movies: Bar Graphs and Line Graphs

A bar graph can be compared to a set of snapshots, whereas a line graph is more like a movie.

Source: Track and Field Omnibook, Fourth Ed., 1985, by Ken Doherty, Tafnews Press (Track and Field News), Mountain View, Calif. Reprinted with permission.

same way you would with a picture or diagram—by using the OPTIC system. Figure 8.5 analyzes a graph using this system.

Watch Out for Distorted Data

How can you avoid being misled by pictures?

Pictures, like words, can occasionally be misleading. Whereas many readers have learned to detect deceptive phrases or sentences, not everyone is quite as sophisticated about detecting distortions in pictures or other kinds of graphic materials. When you consider a graph, illustration, or chart, it helps to do so with a critical eye, paying particular attention to the format, the scale, and the overall context.

How does the way that data are formatted affect their meaning?

Format. Factual data—especially statistics—can be placed in graphic formats that distort the information. The book *How to Lie with Statistics* exposes some of the devious tricks that are used and is also fun to read.[2] For example, you should be wary of the word average, and you should try to find the highest and lowest figures that went into each average. Two companies may have an average salary of $29,000. But if the range of salaries in one company is from $6,000 to $90,000, and the range in the other company is from $20,000 to $35,000, the salary policies of the two companies are quite different.

What effect does scale have on a graphic?

Scale. Changing the scale of a graphic can instantly turn a gentle slope into an alarming rise. For example, units of $100 can make a line much steeper than units of $1,000. Don't be overly impressed by the steepness of the lines in graphs. Always convert what

Figure 8.5
Using the OPTIC System to Analyze a Graph
Source: U.S. Dept. of Labor, Bureau of Labor Statistics.

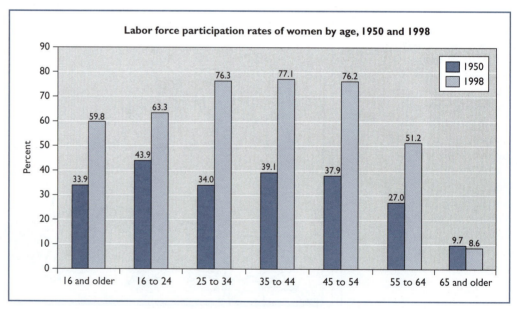

[2]Darrell Huff, *How to Lie with Statistics* (New York: W. W. Norton, 1993).

Figure 8.5
(*Continued*)

OVERVIEW
A graph with seven pairs of vertical bars.

PARTS
• Each pair of bars compares women in the labor force in 1950 and 1998.
• Seven age ranges are listed at the bottom of the graph.
• The height of each bar represents the percentage of participating women from each age range.

TITLE
The title makes it clear that the graphic will be comparing working women, both by age groups and time periods.

INTERRELATIONSHIPS
• In every pair of bars except the last one, the percentage participation of women in the labor force has increased between 1950 and 1998.
• The first pair of bars represents a cumulative total for the six that follow.
• In 1998, the age group with the most women in the labor force was 35–44.
• In 1950, the age group with the most women in the labor force was16–24.

CONCLUSION
Although the title of the graphic draws no conclusions, the bars make it clear that by percentage more women were working in 1998 than were in 1950. The graphic doesn't provide an explanation for this increase. Nor does it offer insights as to why the peak age range for participation was 16–24 in 1950 but 35–44 for 1998.

you see into words; otherwise you'll remember the steepness or flatness but not the real information that is being presented.

How does context affect the meaning of a graphic?

Context. Remember that visual relationships can be tricky. The frame around a diagram can actually change the way you see the diagram. For example, this is a diamond-shaped figure:

But notice that when the same figure is placed in a frame,

it looks like a square. The size and shape of a chart or graph can also affect what you see. Data that may be quite neutral or ordinary can be made to appear startling by the form and scale of the graphic. If you read graphics carefully, you'll see them properly, rather than as someone else may expect—or want—you to see them.

Change the Channel

What can you do to supplement difficult courses with more comfortable learning approaches?

If you're fortunate, your course textbook will be easy to follow and any graphs, charts, or illustrations will make sense to you. However, if you're struggling with the standard way your class is being taught, you can try these other approaches to learning to help the course make sense. If you don't have difficulties with the instructor's approach, you can still use additional learning styles to add extra dimensions to your understanding.

Converting words into pictures. Even though visual communication is one of the predominant channels for information, visually oriented students can use their graphical way of thinking to actually rethink information that may not have been conveyed visually in the first place.

Working in groups. Nearly all students, but especially those who demonstrate an inter-personal intelligence, should find it helpful to work in groups.

Gaining hands-on practice. Active, practical, hands-on learners, who may be impatient with abstractions, can reinforce concepts that might have been difficult to grasp in lectures or readings by trying out examples and drills that should make ideas clearer.

Convert Words into Pictures

REFRAMING — SUMMARIZING

How do visual learners incorporate pictures into normally nonvisual areas?

Whereas some students find it difficult to extract meaning from images, many others are predominantly visual and actually prefer the picture perspective. They not only find it easy to analyze graphs and illustrations, but often incorporate visual thinking into other normally nonvisual areas. For example, a visual learner who is listening to a lecture may simultaneously be creating a mental picture of what the speaker is saying. Students who think visually may even find it important to be able to see the speakers during the lecture while listening to them speak.[3] If you are predominantly visually oriented (and even if you're not), you may find it helpful to add an extra dimension to your learning by writing in pictures.

We now know that reading a visual means studying a diagram or a graph and turning its message into a sentence or two. When you write in pictures, you simply reverse the process. You convert the sentences you've read or heard into a diagram or graph.

If the information you encounter is concrete, your task is fairly simple. The objects you sketch in your diagram represent real, tangible things. If, however, the ideas you read or hear are more abstract, such as information about the characteristics of amphibians, your approach needs to be a bit more involved. Instead of drawing sketches of the animals, which doesn't tell you much about their characteristics, you need to create a concept map. Although your approach to abstract ideas is different from your approach to concrete ones, your goal is the same: to turn something you can read into something you can see (see Figure 8.6).

Add Illustrations to Your Notes

As you read your textbook or go over your lecture notes, don't just jot down the key ideas in words; sketch some of them as well. In some subjects this sketching will come naturally. Science courses, for example, are full of information that can be drawn. The parts of a one-celled organism or the connections in a computer network are much easier to understand if you put little diagrams of them in your notes. Sometimes the drawing is done for you. If the instructor puts a sketch on the board or screen, or if the textbook author includes diagrams in the chapter, add these pictures to your notes in the same way that you would jot down important examples. When a drawing doesn't exist, make one of your own.

A history course may not feature easily drawn elements, but it does include plenty of concrete data that can be translated into picture form. A series of important dates, for example, can be turned into a timeline, and individual historical facts can be visualized almost as easily.

Here is an example of how words can be converted into a picture. The following paragraph describes an experiment conducted by the English physicist and chemist Michael Faraday (1791–1867):

> In 1831, Michael Faraday, one of Britain's greatest scientists, did the experiments which completely demonstrated the close relationship between electricity and magnetism. One of his famous experiments was to take a coil of wire and connect the ends across an instrument capable of measuring tiny currents. By quickly pushing a bar magnet through the coil he was able to produce a small current in the coil and to measure that current. What he was really doing was to change the strength of the magnetic field in the coil by inserting and removing the magnet. The more rapidly he changed the field the more current he could generate.[4]

[3]Available at http://marciaconner.com/books/learn-more-now/learn-your-nature/

[4]J. D. Jukes, *Man-Made Sun* (New York: Abelard-Schuman, 1959), p. 33.

www.cengage.com/success/Pauk/HowToStudy11e

IT'S YOUR Q

When should you add illustrations to your notes?

What should you do in subjects where elements aren't easily drawn?

Figure 8.6
A Concept Map of
Text Information

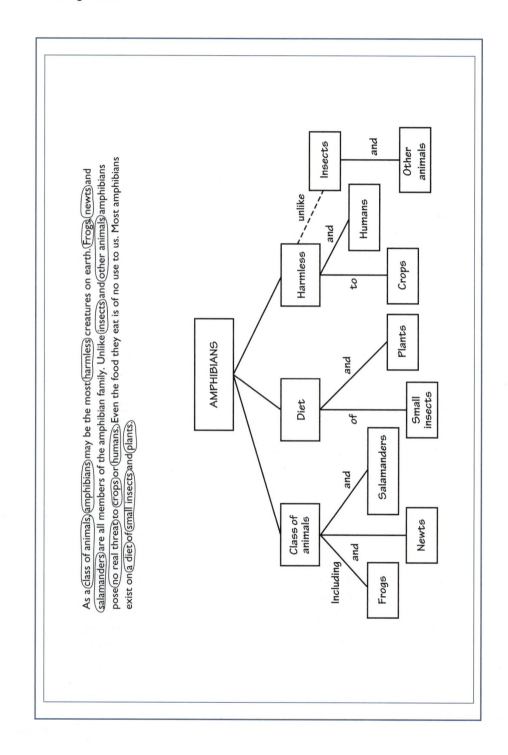

As a (class of animals) (amphibians) may be the most (harmless) creatures on earth. (Frogs,) (newts) and (salamanders) are all members of the amphibian family. Unlike (insects) and (other animals) amphibians pose (no real threat) to (crops) or (humans). Even the food they eat is of no use to us. Most amphibians exist on (a diet) of (small insects) and (plants).

Figure 8.7
A Descriptive Paragraph Made Visual

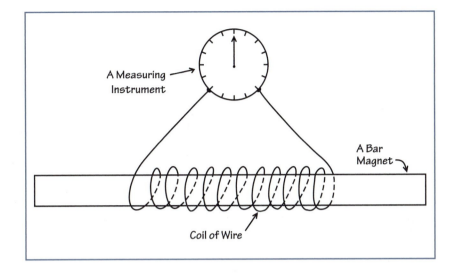

Figure 8.7 is an example of how one student converted this descriptive paragraph into a diagram, which helped the student not only to understand the described process but to visualize and remember it as well. If a question about Faraday's experiment appeared on a test, it is not hard to imagine how well a student with this picture in mind would do.

Why is it helpful to add diagrams to your notes?

You don't have to be Michelangelo or Leonardo da Vinci to draw diagrams in your notes. The important point is to tap into the right side of your brain, where most of our visual thinking is done. In his influential "dual coding" theory, Allan Paivio from the University of Western Ontario concluded that information is more readily recalled when it is learned as both pictures and words.[5] Thus, if you make both a verbal and a visual effort to recall something you've learned, your memory will have two places in which to search for the information instead of just one. With your full mind at work, you will increase your brain power, regardless of whether your drawing looks like doodling or a priceless work of art.

Turn Abstract Ideas into Maps

How do you turn more abstract ideas into pictures?

Abstract ideas don't lend themselves quite as easily to diagrams as do concrete ideas. For example, you can draw a rough sketch of farmland, a field worker, and a tractor, but how would you diagram economic production, a procedure that involves all three? That's where a concept map comes in. Concept maps are used to diagram abstract processes and relationships. Creating a concept map based on a set of abstract ideas is

[5]Allan Paivio, Mary Walsh, and Trudy Bons, "Concreteness Effects or Memory: When and Why?" *Journal of Experimental Psychology: Learning, Memory and Cognition* 20, no. 5 (1994): pp. 1196–1204.

similar to drawing a road map based on a set of hard-to-follow directions. In both cases, the map will make the idea easier to visualize, understand, and remember. Although the simplest way to create a concept map is with a pencil and paper, there are a number of mapping applications (many of them free) that enable you to perform the entire process onscreen instead of on paper.

Here are the steps for mapping a textbook passage:

1. Determine the topic of the passage you are planning to map. Put the topic at the top of a sheet of paper (or document page), and circle it.
2. Go back to the passage and circle or list the concepts involved.
3. Find the two to five most important concepts on your list. These are the key concepts. List them on your map in a row beneath the circled topic. Circle these key concepts as well.
4. Cluster the remaining concepts under the key concepts to which they relate. After adding them to your map beneath the key concepts they support, circle these new concepts.
5. Draw lines connecting related concepts. Along each line, you may want to specify the relationship that connects the concepts.

What is the simplest way to master a map?

Master the Map. Drawing a concept map, like taking notes, does a great deal to help cement important ideas and concepts in your memory. And like your notes, your maps can be mastered. Although there are several systems for mastering your map, the simplest and most effective is to look it over carefully and then, without peeking at the original passage, write a short summarizing paragraph explaining the key concepts and how they relate. The result is like writing your own textbook. You start out with the same concepts the textbook uses, but the words are your own instead of the author's. Figure 8.8 shows a map and its summary paragraph.

What are some other ways to use a concept map?

Concept maps are flexible study aids. They don't lock you into a single method or approach. Here are some additional ways you can use a concept map to improve your studying:

Use the concepts for recitation. Take one circled concept from your map and explain out loud and without looking at the rest of the map how it relates to the map as a whole.

Add to your map. New ideas frequently connect with old information. Take a moment to think about how the concepts in your map relate to ideas you already know. Add the appropriate old ideas to your map, and connect them to what you've just learned.

Redraw your map. There's no right or wrong way to draw a concept map. The same information can be mapped in a number of ways. Look over your original map, and see if you can organize the concepts a little differently. Looking at the information from a different angle often makes some of the concepts clearer. Also, creating a second map

Figure 8.8
Mastering a Concept Map

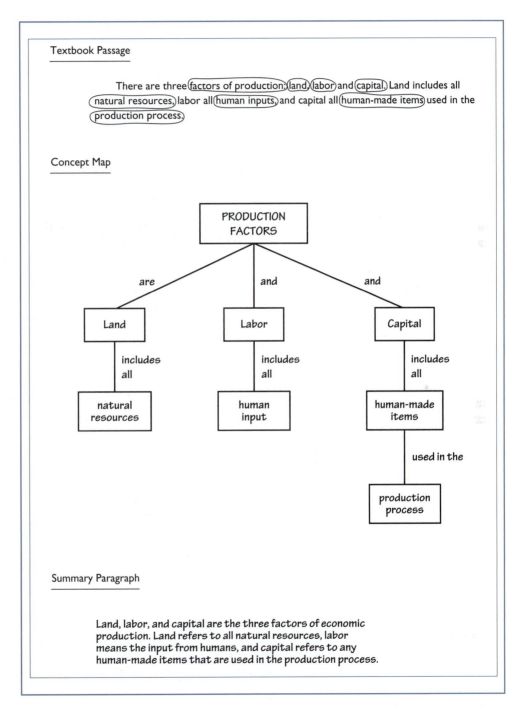

Textbook Passage

There are three factors of production: land, labor and capital. Land includes all natural resources, labor all human inputs, and capital all human-made items used in the production process.

Concept Map

PRODUCTION FACTORS

are · and · and

Land · Labor · Capital

includes all · includes all · includes all

natural resources · human input · human-made items

used in the

production process

Summary Paragraph

Land, labor, and capital are the three factors of economic production. Land refers to all natural resources, labor means the input from humans, and capital refers to any human-made items that are used in the production process.

of the same information means that the concepts will be stored in your memory an additional time.

IT'S YOUR Q

Use Maps for Summaries. Although a map of every concept in a chapter would be huge, and a concept map for even a small book would likely be about the size of a bill-board, you can use mapping to summarize the key concepts from chapters, articles, and books. The procedure for summarizing information with a concept map is identical to the one you just followed for mapping a single paragraph from your textbook or section from your notes, except that you cover more ground. Instead of containing information from one paragraph, a summary map may draw from dozens of paragraphs. For this reason, summary maps do not include as much detail as maps created for more specific sections. The maps at the beginning of each chapter in this book are good examples of summary maps. Notice how they include the most important concepts from the chapters they illustrate.

How can you use concept maps to help plan a paper or report?

Use Maps as Planning Strategies. Concept maps can be used to plan a paper or an oral report. First, start your map with a single concept: the topic you've chosen for your paper. Then, after you have done a bit of preliminary research and have come up with several main concepts, add these to your map, and connect them to your topic with lines. Finally, fill out your map with any supporting ideas you've acquired, making sure to cluster them under the main concepts to which they refer. Once again, draw connecting lines to show how each piece fits into the puzzle. Here is the step-by-step procedure for mapping a paper or an oral report:

1. Do some preliminary research on your subject.
2. Write or type the topic you've chosen at the top of your map.
3. Add two to five main ideas that you plan to cover, and link them to the topic on your map.
4. Cluster sub-ideas under the main ideas that they support. Link them with lines.
5. Survey your map in order to decide whether its branches are evenly developed.
6. If your map seems lopsided, rearrange it or add information so that all its branches are balanced.
7. Use your map as a guide to do in-depth research on the concepts you plan to cover. Add to your map if necessary.

At the very least, your finished concept map can function as an outline, supplying you with all the main ideas and sub-ideas you plan to include in your paper or oral report. In addition, the map can be used as a guide to help you do your more detailed research as systematically as possible.

How are maps unlike outlines?

Unlike a conventional outline, a map enables you to see your structure instead of just reading it. In general, a well-organized report looks fairly symmetrical when you map it. If your map has a lopsided appearance, your report may need to be more evenly balanced. Adding some concepts or clustering your existing topics in a different arrangement should do the trick. Once you're happy with the look of your map, it can serve as a plan for further research.

Work in Groups

REFRAMING

What has research shown about working in groups?

Concepts that make you wrack your brain and tear your hair out when you listen to lectures or study alone may seem more manageable and understandable when they're handled in a group context. Research has shown that students learn more, retain more, and are generally more satisfied with a course if they are given an opportunity to learn actively, rather than just taking notes in lectures or readings.[6] Group work is an excellent example of this sort of active learning.

What does Gardner say about working well with others?

MIT's Howard Gardner arrived at a groundbreaking theory to suggest that instead of possessing one single type of intelligence, we have the potential for nine distinct intelligences. Gardner argues that one of these "frames of mind" is interpersonal intelligence, which is essentially the ability to work well with others.[7]

What should you do if your class doesn't incorporate group work?

Thanks in part to Gardner's research and to their own eyewitness observations, many instructors are well aware of the value of groups. As a result, some of your classes may already include group work as part of the curriculum. If they don't and you find that you learn better with group interaction, it is important to take the initiative yourself and see if you can encourage several of your classmates to join you. Try to limit your group to four or five members, though, to assure that everyone participates actively. One of the advantages (and challenges) of working in a small group is that it's not as easy to just "fade into the woodwork" as it can be in some larger classes.

Group work offers several benefits that you're unlikely to gain from working on your own:

IT'S YOUR Q

Explanations from your peers. Although instructors are experts and often trained "explainers," you may find there are concepts you struggle with from lectures or readings that become clearer and easier to understand when a classmate explains them.

Encouragement and support. Study groups are also support groups. If you work on assignments on your own, you have only yourself and any grades you might get to encourage you. In a group, the other members have faced the same challenges you have and should be able to share in your success. This is an aspect of collaborative study that transforms group work into teamwork.

[6]Available at http://teaching.berkeley.edu/bgd/collaborative.html

[7]Howard Gardner, *Frames of Mind: The Theory of Multiple Intelligences*, 10th anniversary ed. (New York: Basic Books, 1993).

www.cengage.com/success/Pauk/HowToStudy11e

Structure for your study. If you have an assignment to read or some notes to master, it's much easier to simply let things slide when you are working alone. But if you are part of a group, your sense of obligation is extended to several other people. Groups don't work unless everyone pulls his or her own weight. The sense of obligation to a group can provide a powerful motivation to study and keep up for students who might otherwise fall behind.[8]

Multiple perspectives. Unless your group consists entirely of students who think the same way you do, you will probably find that someone in the group will tackle a topic with a fresh approach that hadn't occurred to you. This is the essence of what is sometimes known as "reframing." Almost any time that you can examine an idea or issue from multiple angles you have a greater chance of understanding and retaining it.

Of course, one common type of group activity is a class discussion. In class or online, these discussions not only provide the benefits of group work but may also be a component of your grade. Chapter 13 deals with these in more detail.

Gain Hands-On Practice

REFRAMING — SELF-DIRECTION

How can you gain hands-on practice from a class made up mainly of abstractions?

Many students are bored, dissatisfied, or intimidated by courses that deal primarily with abstractions and concepts. They seek hands-on, real-world relevance with details and concrete examples. In fact, some research suggests that the majority of high school seniors are so-called "concrete active" students who fit this description.[9] If you're that kind of student and you find yourself in a class that doesn't seem to play to your strengths, you can often supplement your class' core materials by completing the end-of-chapter exercises, by using any ancillary materials associated with your text, by looking for related workbooks or programmed software, and by physically manipulating those abstract ideas and concepts.

Do the Chapter Exercises

Why is it helpful to do the end-of-chapter exercises?

Depending on the nature of your class and the preferences of your instructor, you may or may not be assigned the questions and exercises that often come at the end of a textbook chapter. If you haven't already been assigned these end-of-chapter materials, it still helps to try them, especially if you're finding the course or the text to be a struggle. Once again, it will take you out of the realm of the theoretical and into the realm of the practical. Also, because end-of-chapter exercises often echo the sort of approach that

---

[8]A. Kohn, *No Contest: The Case Against Competition* (Boston: Houghton Mifflin, 1986).

[9]Charles C. Schroeder, "New Students—New Learning Styles," *Change* 25, no. 5 (September/October 1993): pp. 21–26.

your exams and quizzes are likely to take, you'll get an early, no-risk indication of how well you'll perform when a grade is at stake.

Use Your Text's Ancillary Materials

What is the value of ancillary materials?

Many textbooks (including this one) come with an array of additional materials known as ancillaries that are commonly posted on a website, the address of which is usually provided along with the book, either as part of the purchase price or for a nominal fee. Tests, drills, and exercises included in such materials are usually interactive, which means that you are provided an almost instantaneous assessment of how well you understand what you've read. Using these materials can encourage active learning and can provide an early heads up if you've got textbook troubles that require the help of a tutor.

Look for Programmed Materials and Workbooks

What is the advantage of programmed materials and workbooks?

If your skills don't seem to match the requirements of a course, you may need some extra practice. Programmed materials furnish questions and problems closely followed by their answers, thereby enabling you to teach yourself each incremental step of a lesson. These days, the most common programmed materials are found on websites or in specialized software, although some books operate using the programmed format as well. Workbooks provide exercises that apply the ideas explained in your textbooks. These study aids can help minimize the anxiety that arises from feeling uncertain about putting newly learned ideas to use. They can also stimulate your interest by helping you take what you've learned a step further. Unless your text comes with its own programmed materials or workbook, the difference between these and the ancillary materials is that the content may not match your textbook exactly. As a result, you may find yourself spending time on information that won't be covered in your course and perhaps, more important, the programmed or workbook materials may skip over information that will be covered in your text and might even wind up on a test or quiz. So be careful!

Work with Your Hands

What sort of approach do tactile or kinesthetic learners prefer?

Some students are kinesthetic or tactile learners. They understand better when they are able to move things or touch them. This sort of approach can be a natural with some courses in engineering or the sciences, where you are often able to pick up and examine specimens, construct or disassemble apparatuses, or pour things from one container to another. But there usually aren't a lot of hands-on opportunities in courses such as history or English, where the emphasis is on the conceptual instead of the concrete.

How can you use kinesthetic or tactile learning with abstract concepts?

Luckily, there's a relatively simple way that you can add an active hands-on element to abstract courses. That's by jotting key dates, themes, or concepts on sticky notes and then arranging and rearranging them in different ways. This is basically a low-tech version of creating a concept map, but if you are a kinesthetic learner, being able to physically arrange and rearrange these concepts with your hands instead of on a screen, on a page, or in your head may make them easier to understand and retain. Another variation on this theme is to transfer some of the key ideas from your notes or text to index cards, putting the term or concept on one side of the card and its defini-tion or explanation on the other. (This is similar to the procedure for creating Frontier Vocabulary cards, explained in Chapter 4.) And while shuffling a pack of index cards may not be quite as active or engaging as peering into a microscope, looking under the hood of a car, or examining the integrated circuits inside a computer, it should help to involve you more fully with a subject.

FINAL WORDS

Why are nondominant learning channels worth pursuing?

The notion that we use only 10 percent of our brains has been repeated so often and attributed to so many experts that despite the absence of actual data, it's read-ily accepted as fact. There's still something about it that rings true. If you think about it, reading and writing words have been a mandatory element of your education. But other than art, music, and physical education classes, which are often underemphasized and in some schools optional or even nonexistent, there are very few nonverbal equiv-alents to the elementary school reading group or to those early lessons in handwriting. It's true that we've had a head start with words, but that doesn't mean we shouldn't build up our other learning channels. Like boosting your vocabulary, sharpening your other learning skills will strengthen your thinking. And as someone who approaches learning from a variety of different directions, you're bound to be a better-balanced, more successful student.

CHAPTER CHECKUP

SENTENCE COMPLETION

Complete the following sentences with one of the three words listed below each sentence.

1. Most textbooks are organized _____.

   globally   **sequentially**   **kinesthetically**

2. MIT's Howard Gardner suggests that there are nine distinct types of _____.

   intelligence   **memory**   **textbooks**

3. When presented as a map, a well-organized report is usually _____.

   detailed   **unbalanced**   **symmetrical**

MATCHING

In each blank space in the left column, write the letter preceding the phrase in the right column that matches the left item best.

_____ 1. Circle graphs	a. Type of learning that favors "hands-on" approach
_____ 2. Global	b. Used to diagram abstract relationships and processes
_____ 3. Peers	c. Illustrate the relationship of parts to a whole
_____ 4. OPTIC	d. One way to think of the function of line graphs
_____ 5. Kinesthetic	e. Sometimes provide more meaningful explanations than experts
_____ 6. Snapshots	f. Learning style that often comes in bursts and insights
_____ 7. Movies	g. One way to think of the function of bar graphs
_____ 8. Concept maps	h. Method for systematically analyzing graphic materials

TRUE-FALSE

Circle T *beside the* true *statements and* F *beside the* false *statements.*

1. T F Tactile learning is encouraged in English and history classes.
2. T F Line graphs can provide an effective illustration of long-term trends.
3. T F The OPTIC system can be used for analyzing both pictures and graphs.
4. T F Artistic ability isn't necessary for drawing pictures to help you study.
5. T F Group study can provide encouragement and support.

www.cengage.com/success/Pauk/HowToStudy11e

MULTIPLE CHOICE

Choose the word or phrase that completes each sentence most accurately, and circle the letter that precedes it.

1. Research has shown that students learn more, retain more, and are generally more satisfied in a course where they are
    a. required to take notes.
    b. allowed to learn actively.
    c. permitted to use textbooks in tests.
    d. encouraged to work independently.

2. A circle graph is also known as a
    a. Venn diagram.
    b. color wheel.
    c. pie chart.
    d. lookup table.

3. The simplest way to master a concept map is by
    a. erasing it.
    b. summarizing it.
    c. highlighting it.
    d. redrawing it.

4. Summary maps should be drawn with
    a. less detail than standard maps.
    b. a black marking pen.
    c. independent variables.
    d. concrete concepts.

5. When used with a paper or an oral report, a map can function as
    a. a guide for research.
    b. a visual outline.
    c. a taking-off point.
    d. all of the above.

REFLECTION

Think about the ideas outlined in this chapter and then draw upon your own opinions and experiences to answer each question fully.

1. What is your dominant channel for learning? Explain how you know this and what if anything you have done differently as a result.

2. Choose a diagram, graph, or illustration in this book or another and use the OPTIC system to analyze it.
3. Do you add illustrations to your notes? If so, which of your classes lend themselves well to illustrated notes? If not, suggest some types of information in your notes that you might consider illustrating in the future.

IT'S YOUR Q

The Q System uses marginal questions to encourage active reading. You'll notice that most but not all paragraphs in this chapter are accompanied by marginal questions. Now it's your Q. Scan the chapter for any paragraph that is missing a question, reread the paragraph, establish the main idea, and then arrive at a question that elicits it. Use the questions in the surrounding paragraphs as models for your own marginal questions.

VOCABULARY IN ACTION

To expand the horizons of your understanding and to refine the precision of your thought, the three exercises that follow are designed to help you grow, strengthen, and maintain your own vocabulary.

SAY WHAT?

From the three choices beside each numbered item, select the one that most nearly expresses the meaning of the italicized word in the quote. Make a light check mark (√) next to your choice.

We still think of a powerful man as a born leader and a powerful woman as an *anomaly*.

—Margaret Atwood (1939–), Canadian author

1. *anomaly*	exception	subordinate	deviant

Don't be afraid to take a big step. You can't cross a *chasm* in two small jumps.

—David Lloyd George (1863–1945), British statesman and prime minister

2. *chasm*	river	gorge	peak

It always seemed strange to me that the things we admire in men, kindness and generosity, openness, honesty, understanding and feeling are the *concomitants* of failure in our system. And those traits we detest, sharpness, greed, *acquisitiveness*, meanness, *egotism* and self-interest are the traits of success. And while men admire the quality of the first, they love the produce of the second.

—John Steinbeck (1902–1968), American writer

3. *Concomitants*	accompaniments	requirements	definitions
4. *Acquisitiveness*	materialism	wealth	greed
5. *Egotism*	confidence	self-importance	pride

www.cengage.com/success/Pauk/HowToStudy11e

VOCAB-U-LADDER

Use your knowledge of word synonyms and roots to connect the word at the top rung to the word at the bottom rung, using the words listed below.

acquiesce
comply
dormant
provide
quiescent
supply

visual

share root
"videre," "to see"

synonyms for
"equip"

share root
"plere," "to fill"

synonyms for
"obey"

share root "quies,"
"rest, quiet"

synonyms for
"inactive"

share root
"dormire,"
"to sleep"

dormitory

Here's the story behind a word that figures prominently in the chapter you've just read.

Channel From straw to stream to TV screen

channel chăn′əl *n.* 1. The bed of a stream or river. 2. The deeper part of a river or harbor, especially a deep navigable passage. 3. A broad strait, especially one that connects two seas. 4. A trench, furrow, or groove. 5. A tubular passage for liquids; a conduit. 6. A course or pathway through which information is transmitted.*

The ancient Sumerians had a bit of a problem. They liked to drink beer—in fact, they invented it—but they didn't enjoy getting a mouthful of grainy yeast and other brewing by-products each time they tried to take a sip. So they used hollowed pieces of straw to suck up their favorite batch of brew. It didn't take long for these innovative people (who were also pioneers of written language) to see that the idea of routing liquid through a thin pipe had ramifications that went well beyond beer-drinking. Primitive plumbing systems first used larger kinds of hollow grasses, such as bamboo and sugarcane (from the Latin canna for "reed") before making the transformation to non-vegetable materials, like clay, lead, or stone. In Rome, these stronger, more sophisticated pipes were still called canalis in recognition of the cane from which they came. The word *canalis* became *chanel* in France before traveling to England as channel, where it described a stream or trough of running water. Although channels originally carried liquids, with the advent of the telegraph, the word was first adopted to name the routes for electrical transmission. As communication systems became more sophisticated, so did the meaning of the word *channel*, which now is used to describe a wide variety of information pathways, including diplomatic negotiations, TV transmissions, and Internet video streams.**

*Adapted from "channel." *The American Heritage Dictionary of the English Language*, 4th ed. (Boston: Houghton Mifflin, 2000), http://dictionary.reference.com/browse/channel (accessed May 12, 2009).
**Based on information from "channel." *The American Heritage Dictionary of the English Language*, 4th ed. (Boston: Houghton Mifflin, 2000), http://dictionary.reference.com/browse/channel (accessed May 12, 2009); "channel." *Online Etymology Dictionary*. Douglas Harper, Historian, http://www.etymonline.com/index.php?search=channel (accessed May 12, 2009); "channel, n1." *Oxford English Dictionary*, 2nd ed. 20 vols. (Oxford: Oxford University Press, 1989); "A Brief History of the Drinking Straw, Part 1: From Sumer to Stone," *Perpenduum* (2008), http://perpenduum.com/2008/01/a-brief-history-of-the-drinking-straw-part-1-from-sumer-to-stone/ (accessed May 12, 2009); Horst Dornbusch, "Which Came First... the Bread or the Beer?" *Beer Advocate* (June 23, 2004), http://beeradvocate.com/articles/595 (accessed May 12, 2009).

PART

III

Gaining | **Retaining** | Explaining

Retaining Information

Now that you've got it, don't lose it! It would be a shame—not to mention a waste of time—to take all the hard-earned information you've gained and let it slip through your fingers. But if you don't counteract the inevitable toll that time takes on all that we learn, that's just what will happen. This part helps you to retain what you've gained. It tells you how to

9 Fight Back Against Forgetting

10 Take Notes You Can Actually Use

11 Turn Your Notes into Knowledge

Fight Back Against Forgetting

Forgetting doesn't fight fair. In fact, the moment you acquire new information is the moment that forgetting starts trying to take it away. Unfortunately, you can't stop forgetting anymore than you can stop time. But you can fight back, reinforcing what you've learned and strengthening your memories in the face of forgetting's relentless attack. To aid in your defense, this chapter focuses on how to

- **Make an Effort to Remember**
- **Organize Your Information**
- **Strengthen Your Memories**
- **Allow Time for Consolidation**

In this chapter

Why is forgetting the biggest enemy of academic success?

There's a battle going on in your brain. You may not always be aware of it, but your memory is under constant assault from forgetfulness, the biggest single enemy of your academic success. Forgetting works both massively and rapidly to undo learning. In fact, research has shown again and again that when you learn something new you are likely to forget most of it in a matter of days.

What have experiments shown about forgetting?

In one experiment, people who read a textbook chapter forgot 46 percent of their reading after 1 day, 79 percent after 14 days, and 81 percent after 28 days. In other words, subjects could remember slightly more than half of what they'd read the previous day; after less than a month, the information they were able to retain from their reading had dwindled to 19 percent.

Why is it harder to remember what you've heard than what you've read?

Although reading is forgotten quickly, the rate of forgetting for things you hear occurs even faster. This has to do with the way the short-term or *working memory* is designed. The working memory is a way station. All new information passes through there before some of it is sent on to more permanent storage in your long-term memory. Your working memory essentially has two front doors. There's an entrance for the things you see and another for the things you say or hear. Solid evidence suggests that when you read words in a book, you are both seeing and hearing them at once. Images of the words combine with the sounds of those words that you hear in your "inner ear" to make the memories stronger.[1] Contrast that with listening, where there's normally nothing to see, and you can understand why the key points from speech may be easier to forget than the main ideas in a chapter. Besides, when you read, you have an opportunity to set your own pace. You can slow down, pause, reflect, and, if necessary, reread. Listeners have no such luxury; they usually have just one chance to catch spoken words and ideas.

What determines whether information in working memory will be saved to long-term memory?

Almost nothing is a shoo-in for your long-term memory. Anyone who has forgotten a name just moments after hearing it or had to look up a phone number a second time just a few minutes after reading it knows from experience that forgetting can be instantaneous and complete. The way to make memories stick, the way to move them from your working memory to your long-term memory is through rehearsal. The word *rehearse* comes from an old French word that means "to plow again." (For more on the history of this word, see "Backstory" at the end of the chapter.) Each time you repeat or rewrite what you've read or heard, you're rehearsing it; you are deepening and strengthening its memory trace, just like a tractor plow that deepens the furrow in a farmer's field. If you make sure the path is deep, it should last. But if you only plow a shallow path, it can vanish in the first heavy wind or driving rain. It's the same with unrehearsed information.

How quickly does forgetting occur?

Experiments have shown that unrehearsed information is sometimes forgotten in as little as 20 seconds.[2] In a classical experiment, Hermann Ebbinghaus (1850–1909),

---

[1]Alan Baddeley, *Your Memory: A User's Guide* (Garden City Park, NY: Prion, 1993), p. 41.

[2]Douglas A. Bernstein, Edward J. Roy, Thomas K. Srull, and Christopher D. Wickens, *Psychology* (Boston: Houghton Mifflin, 1988), p. 293.

a German psychologist and pioneer in the modern study of memory, found that almost half of what is learned is forgotten within an hour.[3] More than a century after Ebbinghaus conducted his original experiment, psychologists continue to affirm his findings.

The following true story further confirms the rapidity and scope of forgetting. Three professors eating lunch in the faculty lounge had this conversation:

Clyde: Did you hear last night's lecture?
Walter: No, I was busy.
Clyde: Well, you missed one of the best lectures in recent years.
Leon: I agree. The four points that he developed were gems.
Clyde: I never heard anyone make his points so clearly.
Walter: I don't want you to repeat the lecture, but what were those four points?
Leon: (Long silence) Clyde? (Passage of two or three minutes; seems like an hour.)
Leon: Well, I'd better get back to the office.
Clyde: Me, too!
Walter: Me, too!

What can we learn from the Leon and Clyde story?

Both Leon and Clyde were brilliant men, yet neither was able to recall even a fragment of any point made in the previous night's lecture. Each had forgotten the four points because neither had transferred those points from working memory to long-term memory by reciting them. Instead, both had recited that the speaker was clear, forceful, and wise and that he had made four points—and they remembered only what they had recited.

What does research show about lecture recall?

These two learned men were by no means exceptions. Their story has been borne out time and again in traditional research. For instance, in a classic experiment, researchers secretly recorded a seminar held by the Cambridge Psychological Society.[4] Two weeks later, the society members who had attended the seminar were asked to write down all they could recall of it. The results were shocking. More than 90 percent of the points from the lecture had been forgotten or confused with the passage of time. The average proportion of specific points each member correctly recalled was 8.4 percent! Much of what members recalled was at odds with what had actually been said. Events were mentioned that never took place; casual remarks were embellished; points were reported that had only been hinted at. This eminent group of psychologists forgot 91.6 percent of the specific points made in the seminar.

How can you defend your memories from forgetting?

When you consider how much resistance your memories face, it's folly to assume that something you've learned will still be there when you need it. You need to put up a fight. You can defend your memories by making an effort to remember, by organizing

[3]Alan J. Parkin, *Memory: Phenomena, Experiment and Theory* (Cambridge, MA: Blackwell, 1993); Hermann Ebbinghaus, *Memory* (New York: Dover, 1964), p. 76.

[4]Ian M. L. Hunter, *Memory: Facts and Fallacies* (Baltimore: Penguin, 1957), p. 83.

www.cengage.com/success/Pauk/HowToStudy11e

your information, by working to strengthen your memories, and by allowing time for consolidation.

Make an Effort to Remember

How does effort affect your memory?

Memory isn't automatic. To remember something, you have to make a conscious effort to learn it. If you don't, it isn't really yours to forget. And even if you *do* learn new information, it won't stay with you very long unless you're convinced that it's worth hanging on to. Your initial effort determines whether you'll remember what you've heard or read for a lifetime or forget it in a matter of seconds.

Avoid Pseudo-Forgetting

SELF-DIRECTION

IT'S YOUR Q

Whenever you cannot remember a name, a telephone number, a fact, an idea, or even a joke, it's quite natural to say, "I forgot." Yet forgetting may have nothing to do with your problem. You may never have learned the information in the first place. This phenomenon is known as pseudo-forgetting. The prefix *pseudo* means "false" or "phony." Thousands of instances we blame on forgetting are actually a result of this "phony forgetting." As Dr. Russell Poldrack, an associate professor of psychology at UCLA, explains, "The best thing you can do to improve your memory is to pay attention to the things you want to remember."[5] Or, as the poet and physician Oliver Wendell Holmes succinctly put it more than a century before Poldrack, "A man must get a thing before he can *forget* it."

How can you guard against pseudo-forgetting?

If an idea or a fact is to be retained in your memory for any length of time, it must be impressed on your mind clearly and crisply at least once. A record of that idea or fact must be laid down in your brain before you can truly recall or forget what you've learned. You can create this record by jotting the new information down or by repeating it aloud. If you are accustomed to meeting a lot of new people, perhaps you already know the technique of repeating the name of the person to whom you've just been introduced. Instead of saying "Pleased to meet you," you say "Pleased to meet you, Mr. Brown." Not only is this approach personable, but it also provides an easy way to counteract pseudo-forgetting.

[5]Stewart Wolpert, "Don't Talk to a Friend While Reading This; Multi-Tasking Adversely Affects the Brain's Learning Systems, UCLA Scientists Report," http://newsroom.ucla.edu/portal/ucla/Don-t-Talk-to-a-Friend-While-Reading-7212.aspx?RelNum=7212

Find a Motivation

What effect does motivation have on memory?

It's easier to remember something when you have a clear motivation for doing so. In a carefully designed study, researchers showed how motivation can influence the life span of a memory. Two groups of students were asked to master identical material. The only difference was that those in the first group were told to remember the material for only a single day, while those in the second group were instructed to master it for recall after two weeks.[6] The difference in instructions had a noticeable effect. Although the two groups studied the same material in a similar fashion, after two weeks the students who were motivated to remember for the long term retained more than those who were told they only needed to remember the information for a day.

What is the strongest source of motivation for remembering?

Of all the sources of motivation, interest is the strongest. If you could study all your subjects with a motivated interest, you probably wouldn't have to worry about your final grades. When you are naturally interested in a subject, remembering comes easily. This explains why a student who may have an encyclopedic memory for baseball batting averages can still struggle in a class where statistics are emphasized. If you are not naturally interested, try to counteract this by artificially creating interest. Once you begin to learn something about a new subject, the chances are great that you will find it genuinely interesting. Use the power of interest to work *for* you, not against you.

Whether genuine interest or simple academic survival serves as your motivation, when you hear or read information you want to hold on to, there are ways to strengthen your intention to remember, so that what you've learned will be recalled:

IT'S YOUR Q

Pay attention. It's difficult to remember anything when you're distracted. Therefore, make a point of minimizing distractions (see Chapter 1) as you read your assignments or listen to lectures.

Get it right the first time. False ideas and misunderstood facts can hang on as tenaciously as information you learn correctly. Therefore, it pays to be attentive when you learn something new. For example, many people incorrectly pronounce the word *nuclear* (NEW-clee-er) as "NEW-cue-ler." One look at the word shows you that this pronunciation is incorrect. But if you learn a word incorrectly, you'll have difficulty replacing the old memory with the correct pronunciation.

Make sure you understand. Ideas that aren't clear to you when you initially read or hear them won't miraculously jell and become clearer in your memory. You cannot fashion a lucid, correct memory from a fuzzy, poorly understood concept. Therefore, don't hesitate to ask the instructor to explain any point that confuses you. And don't be

[6]H. H. Remmers and M. N. Thisted, "The Effect of Temporal Set on Learning," *Journal of Applied Psychology* 16 (June 1932): pp. 257–268.

reluctant to read and reread a passage in your textbook until you're sure you fully grasp its meaning.

Interestingly, the same motivation that enables you to remember can also help you forget. It can be used in a positive way to clear your mind of information you no longer need to retain.

This conscious intention to forget is well demonstrated by servers in restaurants. They exhibit a remarkably good memory for what their customers have ordered up to the moment the bill is paid. Then experienced servers jettison the entire transaction from their minds and give their full attention to the next customer. Just as they intend to remember, so they intend to forget.

This idea of intending to forget explains why Albert Einstein, unquestionably one of the great minds of the twentieth century, was nonetheless unable to provide his home telephone number from memory. He saw no point in clogging his mind with simple numbers that could easily be stored in an address book, so he purposely forgot them.

Organize Your Information

Why is your memory like a small box filled with desktop belongings?

You can't simply sweep the entire contents of your desktop into a small box and expect to be able to find anything easily later. For starters, the box may not be big enough. And even if it is, the items will probably be arranged so haphazardly that you will have to search for a while to find what you were looking for. Your memory faces similar problems. There's a limit to how much you can remember at once. And unless you arrange your memories in a meaningful way, they will be difficult to retrieve when you need them.

What did G. A. Miller determine about our memory's capacity?

How many memories can we hold onto at once? In 1956, psychologist G. A. Miller conducted groundbreaking research that provided us with an answer. In his article "The Magical Number Seven, Plus or Minus Two," Miller points out that most people are able to hold only seven items at a time in their short-term or working memory. If that seems like a terribly small number, it is. Luckily, there's an important refinement to Miller's conclusion that buys us all some extra space. The size of each of the seven items can be virtually unlimited as long as the information in it is meaningfully organized. For example, you couldn't expect to remember the following 31 items:

aabceeeeeeeilmmmnnnoorrrssttuvy

How does organization help memory?

But if you organized these items in a meaningful way—as words—you could reduce the number of items to seven and increase your chances of remembering them. Here are the same 31 letters reorganized in a far more meaningful way:

You	can	learn	to	remember	seven	items
1	2	3	4	5	6	7

As Miller explains, "Our language is tremendously useful for repackaging material into a few chunks rich in information."[7]

What has recent
research revealed
about memory spans?

Since Miller's breakthrough in establishing the limits of memory, other psychologists have gone on to refine our understanding of what has come to be known as *memory span*. Although complex information can be retained in short-term memory if it is "chunked" into roughly seven items, research indicates that it can actually be harder to recall long words than it is to remember shorter ones. It seems that even when we are reading words on a printed page, "silent speech" (see Chapter 5) still plays a role in how we retain them. Because longer words take longer to say, they increase the likelihood that a memory trace will fade. As a rule of thumb, we can hold on to as many words at once as we can say in two seconds.[8] Or, as British psychologist Alan Baddeley explains it, "short words or fast talking gives rise to long spans."[9]

What lesson we can
learn from Miller and
his successors?

The lesson from research on memory span is this: Improve your chances of remembering by being selective, by limiting what you choose to learn, and by making sure that what you do choose to remember is meaningfully organized.

Limit What You Choose to Learn

FOCUSING

What were the
conclusions from
Ebbinghaus' most
famous experiment?

Long before Miller's discussion of the "magical number seven," Hermann Ebbinghaus conducted perhaps the most famous experiment in the history of memory research. He counted the number of trials required to learn a series of six nonsense syllables (such as *bik*, *luf*, *tur*, *pem*, *nif*, and *wox*). He then counted the number of trials required to learn a series of 12 such syllables. Ebbinghaus' tabulations yielded surprising results: The number of trials required to memorize 12 syllables was 15 times greater than the number required to learn 6 syllables.[10] So, for example, if it took 4 minutes to memorize 6 syllables, it would take 1 hour to memorize 12.

What does
Ebbinghaus' research
tell us about mastering
textbook and lecture
material?

Granted, Ebbinghaus dealt only with nonsense syllables, but his careful research still teaches us a valuable lesson: To improve your chances of remembering what you've learned, you must condense and summarize. In practical terms, this means picking out the main ideas from your lecture and textbook notes and leaving the

[7]G. A. Miller, "The Magical Number Seven, Plus or Minus Two: Some Limits on Our Capacity for Processing Information," *Psychological Review* 63 (March 1956): pp. 81–97.

[8]Alan Baddeley "The Fractionation of Working Memory," *Proceedings of the National Academy of Sciences of the United States of America* 93, no. 24 (November 26, 1996): pp. 13468–13472.

[9]Ibid.

[10]Matthew High Erdelyi, "Commentary: Integrating Dissociations Prone Psychology," *Journal of Personality* 62, no. 4 (1994): pp. 669–680.

supporting materials and examples aside. Once you have selected the important points from what you've read, you should be able to memorize them in a manageable amount of time.

How does limiting what you learn help to strengthen your understanding?

Another beneficial by-product that comes from limiting what you learn is that in making the choice of what to keep and what to discard, you'll be strengthening your overall understanding of the material. In other words, you can't really tell what idea is worth saving and what is worth deleting without having a basic understanding of both. As you'll see in Chapter 11, a method for condensing your notes called the Silver Dollar System provides an opportunity to make what you've learned a permanent part of your knowledge.

Arrive at Meaningful Patterns

CLUSTERING

How does organizing affect retrieval?

The papers on your desk (or the files on your computer desktop) are easier to keep track of if you organize them into groups and put them into folders. A textbook is easier to understand because its information has been divided into chapters. A single item is easier to find in a store because the products have been grouped together and arranged in different aisles. If you had to look for a jar of peanut butter in a supermarket where the items were randomly placed, you might give up the search.

How should you organize a list of items you need to remember?

The same idea applies to memories. When you have a large list of items to remember, try to cluster similar items around a natural heading or category. Once clustered and categorized, the items will resist the decaying power of forgetting. Just as the stem holds together the individual grapes, so categories and clusters hold together individual facts and ideas. This hanging together is especially useful during an exam: Remembering one item from a cluster can often be the key to remembering all the items. For example, it would take a long time to memorize by rote the following words, which you might encounter in a geology course:

slate	diamond	sapphire
bronze	lead	aluminum
iron	marble	silver
emerald	steel	brass
gold	limestone	ruby
granite	platinum	copper

But when these words are organized into categories and are clustered as shown in Figure 9.1, memorization is relatively easy and remembering is strong.

CHAPTER
9

Figure 9.1

The Category and Cluster System of Organizing Items

Source: Figure from *Psychology: An Introduction*, Sixth Edition, by Jerome Kagan. Copyright © 1988. Reprinted with permission of Wadsworth, a division of Thomson Learning: www.thomsonrights.com. Fax 800-730-2215.

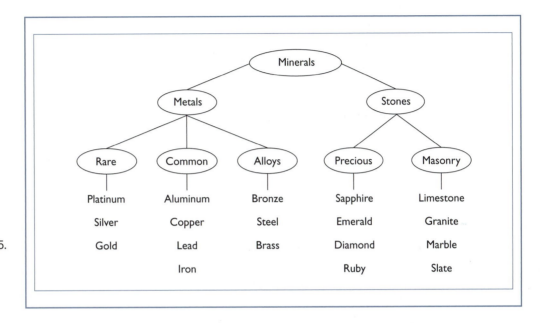

Strengthen Your Memories

What can you do to help strengthen your memories?

The stronger a memory is, the longer it lasts. If you reinforce new ideas by connecting them to ideas already in your memory, and if you conscientiously use recitation to rehearse what you've learned, that result should be strong enough to stand up to forgetting.

Connect New Memories to Old

CLUSTERING

What is the role of association in memory?

The famous line "No man is an island" applies to memories as well. An idea that stands alone is not likely to be recalled. The ideas you remember are woven into a network that connects a single memory with hundreds and often thousands of other memories. The more connections there are in the network and the stronger those connections are, the better the chance for recall.

When are connections made automatically?

Sometimes connections are made automatically, as in the case of traumatic events. Most people easily recall, for example, exactly where they were and what they were doing when they learned of the attack on the World Trade Center in 2001. Previous generations have a similar reaction when recalling the assassination of President John F. Kennedy or Martin Luther King Jr. In these cases, you instantly connect the memory of the event with the memory of where you were.

What can you do to deliberately create associations?

But in normal circumstances, relying on your memory to automatically make these connections is risky. If you want to improve your chances of remembering something, you must make a real effort to link what you've learned to your memory network. You can strengthen the staying power of information when you add it to your memory by consciously making either logical or artificial connections.

Make Logical Connections

How do you establish logical connections for memories?

Consider how you can recall the written directions to a friend's house by keeping in mind a map you once saw or how you can strengthen your memory of the bones of the body by recalling a diagram of a human skeleton. These are examples of logical connections you make to improve your recall. The best ways of strengthening your memory network through logical connections are by building on your basic background and by using images to support what you're trying to remember.

IT'S YOUR Q

Build on Your Basic Background. The principle behind basic background is simple but powerful. Your understanding and memory of what you hear, read, see, feel, or taste depend entirely on what you know, on what you already have in your background. Some of this information has been with you for years, whereas other parts of it may be just seconds old. When listening to a speaker, you understand her points as long as you can interpret them in light of something you've already learned. When you make connections this way, you increase the power of your memory.

Here are some concrete steps to help you build a solid background:

Why are basic courses so important?

Give basic courses the attention they deserve. Many students make the mistake of thinking that the basic courses they take in their first year of college are a waste of time. Similarly, a house without a foundation looks just fine, that is until the first heavy gust of wind blows it away. Introductory courses provide a solid foundation that is essential for all the courses that follow. Indeed, a student's professional life often begins with first-year courses.

How can you consciously link new information to old?

Make a conscious attempt to link what you learn to what you already know. When you learn something new, ask yourself questions such as "How does this relate to what I already know?" and "How does this change what I already know?" These questions will help you to fit new information within the framework of your existing knowledge.

How can your instructor help your background?

Ask an instructor to explain what you don't understand. At times, an entire class can hinge on a single point. Miss that and you miss the purpose of the class. Don't feel hesitant or shy about asking an instructor to go back over a point you can't quite get a fix on. After all, the instructor is there to help you learn.

How do pictures strengthen memories?

Strengthen Memories with Pictures. Another way of logically reinforcing what you've learned is by creating a picture of it. In fact, many students are more visual than

Figure 9.2
Structure of the Amoeba

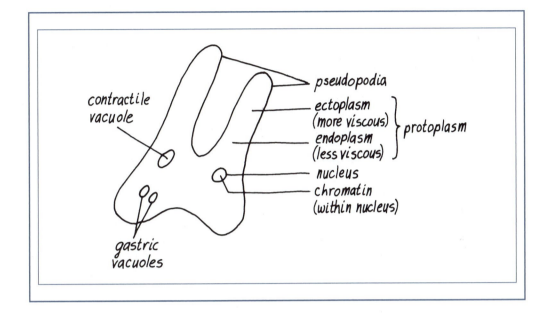

verbal in the way they learn (see Chapter 8). Whether you draw the new information on paper or simply visualize it in your mind, you add an extra dimension to your memory. After all, one part of your brain thinks in words and another part thinks in pictures. When you convert words into pictures, you are using more of your brain.

A student who attended a lecture on amoebas included a sketch of this one-celled organism in her notes (see Figure 9.2). The combination of words and picture gave her a clearer understanding of the subject than she would have gained from relying exclusively on written information. When a question about amoebas appeared on a test, the student handled it easily by recalling the picture she had drawn.

What do you do with material that doesn't seem to lend itself to drawing?

Even when material doesn't seem to lend itself to drawing, you can still devise a mental image. According to Dr. Joseph E. Shorr of the Institute of Psycho-Imagination Therapy in Beverly Hills, California, "The human memory would be worthless without the capacity to make mental pictures." Almost any memory can be turned into a mental image. If you need to remember, for example, that Abraham Lincoln was born in 1809, you can picture a log cabin with "1809" inscribed over the doorway. The image you recall doesn't have to be especially detailed; it only has to be strong enough to jog your memory.

Make Artificial Connections

What is an example of an artificial memory connection?

The connections you make don't always have to be logical. They just need to be memorable. A classic example of an artificial connection is the time-honored practice of tying a string around a finger as a reminder. (The custom originated with the Anglo-Saxons, who supposedly believed the string would literally keep a memory from escaping.) Perhaps you needed to remember to take out the garbage, to pick up your dry cleaning, or to bring your textbook to class. None of these things has anything logically to do with a piece of string, and yet when you look at your finger and say to yourself, "What's this string for?" there's a good chance that you'll recall the task you were trying to remember. You can make equally effective connections to words, to images, and even to locations.

How are words used to make artificial memory connections?

Because words are portable, readable, and usually recognizable, they can be used to store more complicated or difficult-to-remember information. But just as a string has nothing inherently to do with remembering something, the connection between a word and the thing it's designed to remind you of can be artificial. After all, what natural link is there between the word *face* and a group of musical notes? Yet many beginning music students rely on this word to help them recall the notes written in the spaces of the treble clef (F, A, C, E).

How do images aid memory?

Our amazing human ability to generate vivid and often nonsensical images also comes in handy when you're trying to remember something. Suppose you have just been introduced to a man named Mr. Perkins. To remember his name, you immediately associate it with a coffeepot *perking*. You even visualize the perking pot and smell the aroma of freshly brewed coffee. And if you really want to make the picture memorable, you imagine the pot where Mr. Perkins' nose normally is. (In most cases, a silly image is actually easier to remember than a logical one, so don't feel an obligation to have your image make sense.) What you have done is tie *new* information (Mr. Perkins) to *old* information (perking coffeepot) that is already well established in your memory. When you meet Mr. Perkins at some future time, you will recall the perking coffeepot (try not to stare at his nose though!), which will prepare you to say, "Hello, Mr. Perkins. Nice to see you again."

IT'S YOUR Q

Another system, known as the loci method, also relies heavily on our ability to conjure up images. The loci method was developed in ancient Greek and Roman times and is still widely used today. The word *loci* is the plural for the root of the word "location," and that is the key to this system. With loci, you remember items by associating them with locations in a familiar physical space, such as your house, apartment, or dorm room. By creating mental pictures of the names or items you want to remember and then associating them with objects in your chosen location, you can then take a tour of the space in your mind's eye and recall each name or item as you encounter it. For example, to remember key physicists who were involved in the top-secret atomic bomb initiative known as the Manhattan Project, you might step into your room and mistakenly trip over J. Robert Oppenheimer, sit down on your couch and disturb Edward Teller, who is napping there, and go over to your dresser, open the top drawer, and be startled when Enrico Fermi pops out. The layout of your room becomes the organizing principle that makes it easier to retain these names. Once again, the comical aspect strengthens those memories further.

What are some less ridiculous uses of the loci method?

Of course, loci connections don't *have* to be outrageous or comical. An instructor who assigns seats in her class may be using a variation of the loci method. Granted, she may have a seating chart with all the names of her students listed, but it is the position of the students in the classroom that makes it easier to recall their names without consulting the list. That's why it has been a time-honored prank of some students to switch seats in the class of a brand-new instructor.

What do most memory tricks rely upon?

Although we make a lot of logical connections to remember things, the majority of so-called "memory tricks" (also known as *mnemonic devices*) rely on artificial connections, like the ones just mentioned.

How prevalent are mnemonic devices?

Use Classic Mnemonic Devices. Nearly everyone employs at least one or two mnemonic devices to recall specific hard-to-remember facts and information. Probably the most widely used mnemonic device is the old jingle by which many of us keep track of the irregularities in the calendar:

> Thirty days hath September,
> April, June, and November.
> All the rest have thirty-one,
> Except February alone.

Rivaling this days-in-the-month mnemonic is one for spelling:

> *i* before *e* except after *c*
> or when sounding like *a*
> as in *neighbor* and *weigh*

Many people have their own personal mnemonics, such as "Surround the *r* with *a* for the word *separate*."

Why do mnemonics work?

As we've already learned, the cardinal rule for dealing with masses of information is to make sure the information is organized in a meaningful way. A mnemonic device is an organizational system, pure and simple. It is an ordinary means to an important end. Gerald R. Miller conducted a study to evaluate the effectiveness of mnemonic devices as aids to study.[11] He found that students who used mnemonics raised their test scores by as much as 77 percent!

What is the risk of using mnemonics?

Miller acknowledges that the use of too many mnemonics can overload the memory. Nevertheless, he argues that learning a large number of mnemonics well creates no greater hazard than learning a large amount of material in the traditional way. Here's a sampling of some classic mnemonics you may have encountered:

Spelling. The greatest number of mnemonic devices are aids to spelling. Here's how to remember the correct way to spell two words that confuse many students:

> A princi<u>pal</u> is a <u>pal</u>.
> A princi<u>ple</u> is a <u>rule</u>.

[11]Gerald R. Miller, *An Evaluation of the Effectiveness of Mnemonic Devices as Aids to Study*, Cooperative Research Project no. 5-8438 (El Paso: University of Texas Press, 1967).

Biology. The first letters of the words in the following sentence stand for the major categories and subdivisions of the animal world—kingdom, phylum, class, order, family, genus, species, and variety:

K̲ings P̲lay C̲ards O̲n F̲airly G̲ood S̲oft V̲elvet.

Geometry. Here's a clever way of remembering the first six decimal places of pi. Just count the number of letters in each word of this rhyme.

How I wish I
could calculate Pi!
(3.141592)

Astronomy. Most people, when pressed, can name the eight planets. But how about listing them in order? (Mercury, Venus, Earth, Mars, Jupiter, Saturn, Uranus, Neptune.)

M̲y V̲ery E̲conomical M̲other J̲ust S̲erves U̲s N̲oodles.

Zoology. Naturalists may automatically know the difference, but many of us get the African and Indian elephants confused.

India's big, but Africa's bigger,
The same as their elephants—easy to figure!

History. The royal houses of England (Norman, Plantagenet, Lancaster, York, Tudor, Stuart, Hanover, Windsor) are difficult to remember without the help of a mnemonic device:

N̲o P̲lan L̲ike Y̲ours T̲o S̲tudy H̲istory W̲isely.

Medicine. Even doctors and pharmacists use memory systems to help keep certain chemicals straight. To distinguish between cyanates, which are harmless, and cyanides, which are extremely poisonous, they use this device:

-ate, I ate; *-ide*, I died.

Why is it especially important to memorize mnemonics thoroughly?

If you use classic mnemonic devices to help recall information, make certain you memorize the sentence, word, or jingle thoroughly. The slightest error can throw you off completely. For example, some algebra students use the FOIL method to remember the order for multiplying a binomial: F̲irst, O̲uter, I̲nner, L̲ast. But if you recall the wrong word instead, say, FILE, you wind up hopelessly confused.

Devise Your Own Mnemonics. Associating new information logically is generally better than doing so artificially, and truly knowing something is always better than using a system to remember it. But if you're required to learn facts that you can't connect with your memory network and that have no classic mnemonic, you may want to invent your own mnemonic device to help yourself remember.

Keyword mnemonic.[12] Connecting a man named Perkins with a perking coffeepot provides a good example of a *keyword mnemonic* in action. The procedure for devising a keyword mnemonic has two steps, a verbal step and a visual step.

1. *The verbal step*. Find a familiar word or phrase that sounds like the word you are trying to remember. This is your keyword. For the name *Perkins* the keyword is *perking*.
2. *The visual step*. Connect your keyword with what you want to remember. For example, form a mental image of Mr. Perkins' face on a perking coffeepot. Then when you see him again, you'll recall that image, which will remind you of his name.

The keyword system isn't limited to helping you remember the names of people you meet. It also comes in handy for remembering vocabulary from a foreign language. For example, if you want to recall the French word for "butter," *beurre*, connect it with a keyword like *burr*, or *brrr*, and then link the two with a visual image, a pat of butter covered with burrs or a stick of butter wearing a parka and shivering (brrr!).

Create-a-word mnemonic. The letters of a "created" word can be used to help you remember important information. What if you needed to remember the Great Lakes, for example: Lake Superior, Lake Erie, Lake Michigan, Lake Huron, and Lake Ontario?

To devise a *create-a-word mnemonic*, proceed as follows:

1. Underline the keyword in each item. (Superior, Erie, Michigan, Huron, Ontario.)
2. Write down the first letter of each keyword. (S, E, M, H, O.)
3. Create a word or several words from the first letters of the keywords. If the order of the elements isn't important, try rearranging the letters until they spell a word or words. (HOMES.)
4. If possible, make a link between your keyword and the idea for which it acts as a mnemonic. ("The HOMES along the Great Lakes must have a beautiful view.")

Your mnemonic may be a real word or a word you just made up. If you use a made-up word, be sure you have some means of remembering it.

---

[12]The keyword mnemonics section is based on a discussion in K. L. Higbee, *Your Memory: How It Works and How to Improve It*, 2nd ed. (New York: Prentice-Hall, 1988).

www.cengage.com/success/Pauk/HowToStudy11e

*Side notes:*

What can you do to remember information that doesn't have a common mnemonic device?

What are the two steps for creating a keyword mnemonic?

What is involved in the verbal step?
What do you do in the visual step?

What are some common uses for keyword mnemonics?

What is a create-a-word mnemonic?

What are the steps in creating a mnemonic word?

In what cases is a create-a-sentence mnemonic preferable to a create-a-word one?

What are the steps for a create-a-sentence mnemonic?

Create-a-sentence mnemonic. If the order of the items you want to remember is important, the create-a-sentence mnemonic is often more flexible than the create-a-word mnemonic. For example, if you need to remember the Great Lakes from west to east (Lake Superior, Lake Michigan, Lake Huron, Lake Erie, Lake Ontario), HOMES won't help you. But a create-a-sentence mnemonic will.

Here are the steps for devising a create-a-sentence mnemonic:

1. Underline the keyword for each item. (Superior, Michigan, Huron, Erie, Ontario.)
2. Write down the first letter of each keyword. (S, M, H, E, O.)
3. Construct an easy-to-remember sentence using words whose first letters are the same as the first letters of the keywords. (Super Machine Heaved Earth Out.)
4. Devise a sentence that relates to the information you want to remember. ("Five large lakes in the middle of the country almost make it seem as though a super machine heaved earth out.")

Why is creating a sentence mnemonic sometimes easier than creating a word or two?

In general, creating a simple sentence is easier than taking the first letters from your keywords and turning them into a word or two, especially if the order of the points has to be maintained. Of course, if the initial letters are mainly consonants, both methods can be difficult. To circumvent the problem of having too many consonants, try to choose some keywords (or synonyms of the keywords) that begin with vowels.

Use Recitation to Rehearse

SUMMARIZING

Why is recitation so vital to strengthening your memory?

No single activity is more important in strengthening your memory than recitation. That's because recitation forces you to think seriously about what you've read or heard. This deep thinking (experts call it *deep cognitive processing*) is the key to making memories last. To reap the benefits of recitation, you need to know what reciting involves. It also helps to learn why reciting works.

What Recitation Involves

What does reciting involve?

Reciting simply involves reading a passage in a book or a line of your notes and then repeating it from memory, either out loud or by writing or typing it. Whether you recite out loud or in writing, your goal should be to use your own words rather than parroting what you've just read. Recitation isn't about memorizing words. It's about comprehending ideas. Chapter 11 explains in detail how you can use recitation to master the notes you've taken from lectures or textbook assignments.

Why Recitation Works

What is the secret behind recitation?

Whether you recite by speaking or by writing, the effect on your memory is basically the same. Recitation strengthens the original memory trace by prompting you to think actively about the new material, thus keeping it in your working memory. It gets both your body and your mind involved in the process of learning. It supplies immediate feedback so you can test yourself and check your progress. And it motivates you to continue reading.

IT'S YOUR Q

Reciting Encourages Participation.   Reading is not the same as comprehending. By the time that most of us are college-aged, the process of decoding words on a page has long since become automatic. It's possible, for example, to read a book aloud to a child without paying attention to the story. Likewise, if you're having a tough time concentrating, you can read every word on a page and still not understand or even recall what you've read. To truly comprehend what you've read, you need to know both what the words say and what they mean. When you recite, you make yourself stop and wonder, "What did this just say?" You're transformed from a detached observer into an active participant. The physical activity of thinking, pronouncing, and hearing your own words involves your body as well as your mind in the process of learning. The more physical senses you use in learning, the stronger the memory will be.

How does recitation provide feedback?

Reciting Provides Feedback.   Reciting not only gets you involved in your reading, it also demonstrates how involved you are. Rereading can give you a false and dangerous sense of confidence. It takes a lot of time and leaves you with the feeling that you've been hard at work, yet it provides no concrete indication of what you're learning. When test time comes, you may blame your mental blanks on test anxiety or on unfair questions when the real culprit is ineffective studying. Unlike rereading, reciting lets you know right away where your weaknesses lie. As you finish each paragraph, you find out whether you understand what you've just read. This gives you a chance to clarify and solidify information on the spot, long before you're tested on it.

How does recitation supply motivation?

Reciting Supplies Motivation.   Because it gets you involved and checks your progress regularly, recitation provides motivation for studying. And, as we've just seen, motivated interest promotes a stronger memory. If you struggled to extract the information from a paragraph you just read, you may be motivated to grasp the point of the next paragraph more readily. If you had no trouble finding the meaning in that paragraph, the momentum of your reading may serve as motivation.

Allow Time for Consolidation

Why don't new ideas instantly become part of your memory?

The fact that recitation helps new information jell hints at another aspect of memory: New ideas don't instantly become part of your long-term memory. Your memory needs time to consolidate what you've learned.

How did a mountain
climber's injury
demonstrate
consolidation?

A dramatic illustration of memory's need to consolidate comes in a story of a mountain climber who fell and hit his head. Although the man was not permanently injured, he couldn't remember falling. In fact, he couldn't recall anything that had happened to him in the 15 minutes *before* the accident. Why not? According to the principle of consolidation, the climber's memories before the accident had not had a chance to consolidate. As a result, when the climber hit his head, those unfinished memories were lost.[13]

What are the
similarities between
human memory and a
computer's memory?

Although analogies between humans and machines can only be taken so far, your working memory shares some interesting similarities with DRAM, the dynamic random access memory (often just referred to as RAM) of a personal computer. If your computer crashes a few minutes after you started typing a paper or letter, there's a chance that most of your work up to that point will be lost. That's because it existed only in dynamic memory and had yet to be saved to a disk. When you save a file, you move the information from the short-term temporary storage of DRAM to the long-term storage of a disk. Similarly, when you allow time to consolidate your memories, you move them from the limbo of your short-term working memory to the stability of your long-term memory.

What does
consolidation tell us
about study strategies?

This principle helps explain why, in most cases, the most effective way to study is in short blocks of time instead of in one long stretch. Also, an understanding of consolidation will help you live through those frustrating times when you don't seem to retain what you're studying.

Break Up Your Study Sessions

FOCUSING

What is distributed
practice?

In *distributed practice*, you engage in relatively short study periods broken up by rest intervals. In *massed practice*, you study continuously until the task is completed. A number of studies have demonstrated that several short "learning sprints" are more productive than one grueling, uninterrupted study session. This is sometimes known as the "spacing effect."

What effect did
distributed practice
have on learning
French vocabulary?

For example, Kristine Bloom and Thomas Shuell gave two groups of high school French students 20 new vocabulary words to learn. The first group used massed practice, studying all the words in a single 30-minute session. The second group spent the same amount of time on the words but spread the sessions over three consecutive days, studying ten minutes per day. When tested immediately after they had completed their practice, both groups remembered roughly the same number of words (16). But when the test was readministered four days later, the massed group had forgotten nearly half of the words, while the distributed group was able to recall all but five.[14]

[13]R. S. Woodworth and H. Schlosberg, *Experimental Psychology*, rev. ed. (New York: Holt, Rinehart & Winston, 1954), p. 773.

[14]Kristine C. Bloom and Thomas J. Shuell, "Effects of Massed and Distributed Practice on the Learning and Retention of Second-Language Vocabulary," *Journal of Educational Research* 74, no. 4 (1981): pp. 245–248.

How does distributed practice affect comprehension?
What are some other advantages of using bite-sized study sessions?

In an extensive experiment, researchers D. Krug, T. B. Davis, and J. A. Glover examined the effects of massed and distributed practice on a reading comprehension task and found that distributed practice led to better performance.[15]

The memory's need to consolidate information seems to play a key role in explaining why distributed practice is superior to massed practice. Other advantages also support these bite-sized study sessions:

Periodic "breathers" discourage fatigue. They refresh you both physically and emotionally.
Motivation is stronger when you work in short blocks of time. The end of each session marks a mini victory that provides momentum and a sense of accomplishment.
Distributed practice wards off boredom. Uninteresting subjects are easier to take in small doses.

When is massed practice superior to distributed practice?

In spite of all the advantages of distributed practice, massed practice is superior in a few cases. For instance, when you are writing the first draft of a paper, massed practice is often essential. You have organized your notes in stacks; discrete bits of information are waiting in your mind like jigsaw-puzzle pieces to be fitted together; and the organizational pattern of your paper, though dimly perceived, is beginning to take shape. To stop working at this point would be disastrous. The entire effort would collapse. In such a circumstance, it is far more efficient to overextend yourself—to complete that stage of the process—than to take a break or otherwise apply the principle of distributed practice.

Come to Terms with Plateaus

SELF-DIRECTION

What are learning plateaus?

No two people learn at exactly the same rate, yet the learning patterns of most people are similar. We all experience lulls in our learning. Progress is usually slow and steady at first; then for a period of time there might be no perceptible progress even though we are making a genuine effort. This "no-progress" period is called a *learning plateau*. After days, weeks, or even a month of effort, a surprising spurt in learning suddenly occurs and continues until another plateau is reached.

What is the best way to deal with a learning plateau?

When you reach a plateau, do not lose heart. Plateaus are a normal part of learning and are often an indicator of long-term consolidation. You may not see any progress, but learning is still occurring. Once everything is in place, you'll be rewarded for your effort.

[15]D. Krug, T. B. Davis, and J. A. Glover, "Massed Versus Distributed Repeated Reading: A Case of Forgetting Helping Recall?" *Journal of Educational Psychology* 82 (1990): pp. 366–371.

FINAL WORDS

How has Alzheimer's
disease affected
our attitude toward
memory?

Alzheimer's disease has recently shifted a great deal of attention to human memory. People—especially older people—worry even more than they once did when a name or a piece of information slips their minds. Some make changes in their diet or lifestyle in the hope of forestalling or turning back the dreaded disease. The fear is understandable, and the attention to health and good habits is commendable. But the preciousness and precariousness of memory is nothing new. Memory has always been a vital component of our humanity, and it deserved our care, our respect, and our attention long before the emphasis turned to Alzheimer's. That is something we should never forget.

CHAPTER CHECKUP

Complete the following sentences with one of the three words listed below each sentence.

1. G. A. Miller's Magical Number Seven theory teaches the importance of _____.

   numbers   selectivity   reciting

2. Your brain's short-term working memory can be compared to a computer's _____.

   mouse   monitor   DRAM

3. No single activity is more important in strengthening your memory than _____.

   reviewing   reciting   reflection

In each blank space in the left column, write the letter preceding the phrase in the right column that matches the left item best.

_____ 1. Listening   a. Enables large amounts of information to be more readily remembered

_____ 2. FOIL   b. Illustrated by the story of the injured mountain climber

_____ 3. Interest   c. Even more susceptible to forgetting than reading is

_____ 4. Einstein   d. Measured the time it took to remember a series of nonsense syllables

_____ 5. Clustering   e. Used in math to remember the order for multiplying a binomial

_____ 6. Ebbinghaus   f. Provided when you recite information either out loud or on paper

_____ 7. Feedback   g. Strongest form of motivation for remembering information

_____ 8. Consolidation   h. Used motivated forgetting to free his mind of unnecessary information

Circle T *beside the* true *statements and* F *beside the* false *statements.*

1. T   F   When you learn something new, you are likely to forget most of it in a matter of days.
2. T   F   To remember something, you have to make a conscious effort to learn it.

3. T F   Incorrect information can last as long in memory as correct information.
4. T F   Strong, memorable connections between ideas always have to be logical.
5. T F   The loci method uses geometrical figures as memory aids.

MULTIPLE CHOICE

Choose the word or phrase that completes each sentence most accurately, and circle the letter that precedes it.

1. Restaurant servers frequently use
   a. working memory.
   b. motivated forgetting.
   c. pseudo-forgetting.
   d. mnemonic devices.

2. The "basic background" memory principle reinforces the importance of
   a. getting it right the first time.
   b. introductory classes.
   c. pseudo-forgetting.
   d. condensing and summarizing.

3. Memory acquires an extra dimension when information is
   a. written on note cards.
   b. drawn or visualized.
   c. reread or recited.
   d. condensed or reduced.

4. Mnemonic devices are
   a. computer programs.
   b. memory aids.
   c. research instruments.
   d. learning theories.

5. Reciting should always be done
   a. out loud.
   b. silently.
   c. from memory.
   d. on paper.

REFLECTION

Think about the ideas outlined in this chapter and then draw upon your own opinions and experiences to answer each question fully.

1. Explain some things that have motivated you to remember in the past and suggest some other ways that you can be motivated to remember in the future.
2. Have you made artificial connections to help you remember information? If so, explain some of the connections you've made. If not, think of some areas in your coursework where such connections would be helpful and provide some ideas on how you can make them.
3. What is your greatest personal obstacle to remembering more? Using the systems and methods discussed in this chapter, provide some specific ideas on how you will set out to improve your rate of remembering.

IT'S YOUR Q

The Q System uses marginal questions to encourage active reading. You'll notice that most but not all paragraphs in this chapter are accompanied by marginal questions. Now it's your Q. Scan the chapter for any paragraph that is missing a question, reread the paragraph, establish the main idea, and then arrive at a question that elicits it. Use the questions in the surrounding paragraphs as models for your own marginal questions.

VOCABULARY IN ACTION

To expand the horizons of your understanding and to refine the precision of your thought, the three exercises that follow are designed to help you grow, strengthen, and maintain your own vocabulary.

SAY WHAT?

From the three choices beside each numbered item, select the one that most nearly expresses the meaning of the italicized word in the quote. Make a light check mark (√) next to your choice.

Destiny is a name often given in *retrospect* to choices that had dramatic consequences.

—J. K. Rowling (1965–), British author of the *Harry Potter* books

1. *destiny*	favor	fortune	fate
2. *retrospect*	hindsight	reverse	nostalgia

Focusing your life solely on making a buck shows a certain *poverty* of *ambition*. It asks too little of yourself. Because it's only when you hitch your wagon to something larger than yourself that you *realize* your true potential.

—Barack Obama (1961–), 44th president of the United States

3. *poverty*   lack of money   deficiency   emptiness
4. *ambition*   desire to achieve flexibility of motion energy or exertion
5. *realize*   understand   achieve   invent

VOCAB-U-LADDER

Use your knowledge of word synonyms and roots to connect the word at the top rung to the word at the bottom rung, using the words listed below.

observe
tenacious
commemorate
persistent
reserve
retain

memory

share root
"memor," "mindful,
remembering"

synonyms for
"honor"

share root
"servare," "to
watch, keep safe"

synonyms for
"keep"

share root
"tenere,"
"to hold"

synonyms for
"determined"

share root
"sistere,"
"to stand"

subsist

www.cengage.com/success/Pauk/HowToStudy11e

Here's the story behind a word that figures prominently in the chapter you've just read.

Rehearse Of memory and the funeral wagon

rehearse re-hearse' *v.* 1. a. To practice in preparation for a public performance. b. To direct in rehearsal. 2. To perfect through repetition. 3. a. To retell or recite. b. To list or enumerate.*

If you think that the act of practice through repetition has nothing to do with the vehicle that carries a coffin to a cemetery, you're half right. *Hearse* and *rehearse* aren't directly related, although the two share a common ancestor and an interesting story. The word *hearse* comes from the French word *hercier* for harrow, which was originally a farm implement with a series of sharp teeth attached to a triangular wooden frame. A farmer or his farm animal would drag the *hercier* through the fields, allowing the teeth to dig up the soil in preparation for planting. Death in those days, just as now, was treated with great solemnity and ceremony. Candles were lit and placed on a triangular frame just above where the coffin was resting. Because the frame with the candles resembled an upended harrow, the word *hearse* was soon used to describe it. As time went on and the construction around the coffin grew more elaborate, it still retained the word *hearse*, even though it no longer resembled the original rake. Eventually it acquired wheels and, with the advent of the automobile, an engine. And yet to this day it's still called a hearse. But what of the *hearse* in *rehearsing*? That too refers to the original harrow. *Rehearse* literally means "to re-plow or rake again," in short, to go back over the same territory. And that's pretty much what we do when we rehearse something in an effort to remember it better.**

*Adapted from "rehearse." *The American Heritage Dictionary of the English Language*, 4th ed. (Boston: Houghton Mifflin, 2000), http://dictionary.reference.com/browse/rehearse (accessed April 9, 2009).
**Based on information from "rehearse." *The American Heritage Dictionary of the English Language*, 4th ed. (Boston: Houghton Mifflin, 2000), http://dictionary.reference.com/browse/rehearse (accessed April 9, 2009); "rehearse." *Online Etymology Dictionary*. Douglas Harper, Historian, http://www.etymonline.com/index.php?search=rehearse (accessed April 9, 2009); "rehearse, *v.*" *Oxford English Dictionary*, 2nd ed. 20 vols. (Oxford: Oxford University Press, 1989).

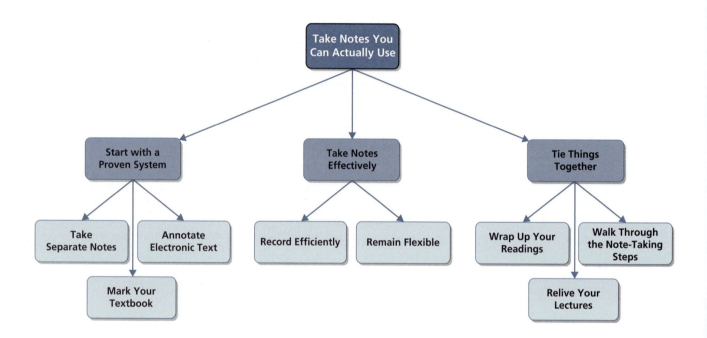

CHAPTER

10

Take Notes You Can Actually Use

Learn, compare, collect the facts!

Ivan Petrovich Pavlov
(1849–1936), Russian physiologist

The lectures you hear and the assignments you read are a potential gold mine. Both include valuable nuggets of knowledge. Because you spend so much of your academic life accumulating information, it's unwise to do so haphazardly. After all, anybody can take notes, just as anyone can doodle. But it's crucial for your notes to go beyond mere busywork. The key is to end up with notes you can actually use. This chapter maps out a practical, useable note-taking strategy and shows you how to

- **Start with a Proven System**
- **Take Notes Effectively**
- **Tie Things Together**

In this chapter

► One common note-taking format that you'll want to avoid. (p. 265)

► Take a tip from an old-fashioned technology to speed up your modern-day note taking. (p. 275)

► The time when your notes are like wet clay, and what you should do about it. (p. 279)

What are the elements
of successful note
taking?
Taking notes doesn't simply mean scribbling down or marking up the things that strike your fancy. It means using a proven system and then effectively recording information before tying everything together.

Start with a Proven System

What is the Cornell System?

All of the methodical preparation you've done before attending a lecture (see Chapter 6) or beginning a textbook assignment (see Chapter 5) will be wasted if you just wing it when you start to take notes. Instead of taking a chance on a haphazard, seat-of-the-pants method of taking notes, you need a proven note-taking system. The Cornell System, which was developed at Cornell University almost 50 years ago, has been embraced by countless colleges and universities in the United States and throughout the world. It can be used for taking separate notes, for marking your textbook, and even for annotating electronic texts. The system is flexible and far-reaching, but its secret is simple: Wide margins on the outside and the bottom of the text area are the key.

Take Separate Notes

PLANNING

How are notes worth more than a textbook?

The notes you jot down can become a handwritten textbook. In fact, in many instances they are more practical, meaningful, and up-to-date than a textbook. If you keep your notes neat, complete, and well organized, they will serve you splendidly.

What are the principal components of Cornell-style note paper?

Cornell-style note paper is available at some college bookstores and office supply stores. In addition, several enterprising individuals have created Cornell-style templates in a number of document formats that you should be able to locate fairly quickly with a Web search. Or, if you prefer, you can easily use a pen and ruler to transform standard loose-leaf paper into Cornell-style sheets. First, draw a vertical line down the left side of each page two-and-one-half inches from the edge of the paper; end the line two inches from the bottom of the sheet. This creates the *cue column*. Next, draw a horizontal line two inches from the bottom of the page. This is the border for your *summary area*. The large space to the right of the cue column and above the summary area is where you write your notes. Figure 10.1 shows a Cornell note sheet.

What are the cue column and summary area used for?

As you're taking notes, the cue column should remain empty, as should the summary area. But when the time comes to review and recite what you've jotted down, you'll use the cue column for questions to help clarify meanings, reveal relationships, establish continuity, and strengthen memory. The summary area will be used to distill a page's worth of notes down to a sentence or two.

How does the Cornell System adjust?

The information that goes in the largest space on the page varies from class to class and from student to student. Different courses come with different demands. The format

Figure 10.1
The Cornell Note Sheet

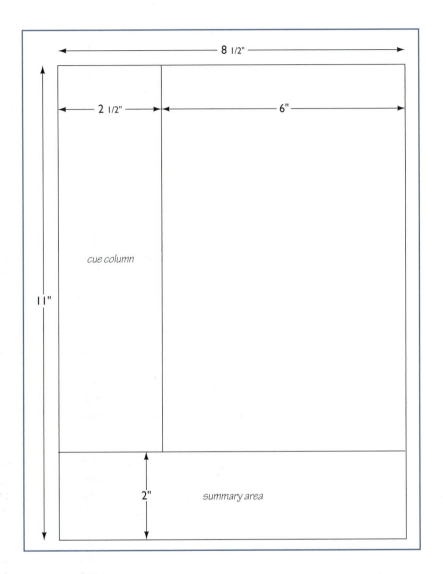

cue column

11"

8 1/2"

2 1/2"   6"

2"   summary area

you choose for taking your notes and the ideas you jot down are almost entirely up to you. If you have a special way of jotting down your notes, you should be able to use it with the Cornell note sheet.

Why is the outline format discouraged?

About the only format you should be wary of is the outline. As crisp and neat as they may look at a glance, outlines have a way of tying your hands and forcing you to squeeze information into an unforgiving framework. When you're taking notes—especially in a lecture—the last thing you want to be worrying about is

Roman numerals. As Edward W. Fox, Cornell's great teacher, lecturer, and historian, explained:

> Elaborate arrangements tend to confuse, and the traditional topical form, the use of Roman numerals, capital letters, Arabic numerals, and small letters, etc., with much indentation, has a fatal tendency to imply a logical analysis rather than elicit one.[1]

If outlines are a bad idea, what sort of note-taking format should you use instead?

Outlines are the tail that wagged the dog. You should be concentrating on the information itself, not on its numbering scheme. Whatever works for you is best. You can take notes in sentence or paragraph form, in lists, as definitions, by adding drawings, or by using a combination of these formats.

How do sentences in your notes differ from traditional sentences?

Sentences. Take key ideas from a lecture or reading and jot them down in your own words. If you're taking notes in a lecture, you probably won't have time to write out complete sentences. Instead, write telegraphically, leaving out articles such as *a, an,* and *the,* and abbreviating words you use often. Figure 10.2 provides an example.

Figure 10.2
Sentence Notes

	Oct. 10 (Mon.) – Soc. 102 – Prof. Oxford

What's animism?	A. Animism
	    1. Object has supernatural power
	    2. Power called mana (not limited to objects)

What's mana?	a. Objects accumulate mana
	            Ex. Good canoe – more mana than poor one.
	        b. Objects can lose mana

How to gain mana?	c. People collect objects w/lots of mana
	        d. Good person's objects collect mana
	        e. People, animals, plants have mana, too.
	            Ex. Expert canoe builder has mana –
	                imparts mana to canoe

Who has mana?	f. Chief has lots of mana – dangerous to get too close to chief – mana around head.

[1]Edward W. Fox, *Syllabus for History* (Ithaca, NY: Cornell University Press, 1959). Reprinted by permission of the author.

How do paragraphs in your notes differ from traditional paragraphs?

Paragraphs. Cluster related sentences in a block of text, often under a heading or label that serves to tie them together. As you see in Figure 10.3, these are not traditional paragraphs where one complete sentence flows smoothly to the next. Your sentences in paragraph-style notes will usually be telegraphic, and smooth transitions are not important. However, these paragraphs share one important thing with traditional paragraphs: All the sentences should relate to the same main idea.

What do definition-style notes look like?

Definitions. Write a name or term, add a dash or colon, and then provide a succinct explanation or elaboration. Figure 10.4 provides an example.

How do you make items stand out in list-style notes?

Lists. Start with a topic, name, term, or process, and then list phrases or telegraphic sentences that relate. Avoid numbering the items unless the numbers are relevant to the list. If you want to make the items stand out in your notes, consider beginning each with an asterisk or a bullet point. Figure 10.5 shows what these lists are apt to look like.

What is the advantage of using drawings in your notes?

Drawings. Drawings and diagrams can succinctly sum up information that may be difficult to explain in words alone. A sketch can often convey locations or relationships more effectively than a sentence or two. Moreover, a single visual can often act as a powerful cue for a huge amount of underlying verbal information. The adage "A picture is worth a thousand words" can be especially meaningful in the context of note taking. Figure 10.6 shows the sort of diagram that a biology student might include in her notes.

Figure 10.3
Paragraph Notes

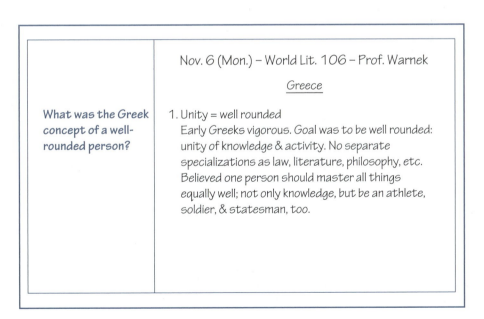

Nov. 6 (Mon.) – World Lit. 106 – Prof. Warnek

Greece

What was the Greek concept of a well-rounded person?

1. Unity = well rounded
Early Greeks vigorous. Goal was to be well rounded: unity of knowledge & activity. No separate specializations as law, literature, philosophy, etc. Believed one person should master all things equally well; not only knowledge, but be an athlete, soldier, & statesman, too.

Figure 10.4
Definition Notes

What are main types of note-taking formats?	Mar. 14 (Fri.) – Ed. 103 – Prof. Pauk Types of note-taking formats sentence - Notes written in sentences, but telegraphically: w/ abbrevs. for common wds. Articles ("a", "an", etc.) left out. paragraph - Like real paragraphs, clustered around main idea, but sentences telegraphic & transitions left off definition - name or term, followed by dash or colon and explanation list - word or phrase heading, followed by series of items. No numbers unless relevant. Use bullet pts. instead. combination - mix of other formats

Figure 10.5
List Notes

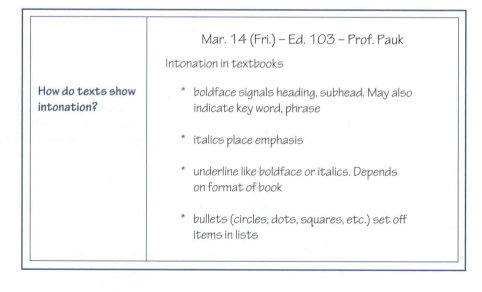

How do texts show intonation?	Mar. 14 (Fri.) – Ed. 103 – Prof. Pauk Intonation in textbooks * boldface signals heading, subhead. May also indicate key word, phrase * italics place emphasis * underline like boldface or italics. Depends on format of book * bullets (circles, dots, squares, etc.) set off items in lists

Figure 10.6
Diagramming as a
Study Aid

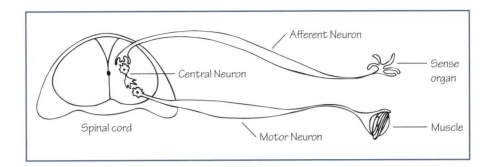

Combination. Some chapters and a few lectures may fit into a single note-taking format, but it's unlikely that most will. Good note takers must remain flexible, shifting quickly from one format to another to capture key information as efficiently and meaningfully as possible. Knowing when to shift from one format to another and deciding to do so is often a sign that you are thinking deeply about what you are reading or listening to. In a large-scale study at the University of Michigan, researchers concluded that students who engaged in this sort of deep processing were more likely to receive better grades on individual assignments as well as on courses as a whole.[2] Above all, it's important to choose the right tool for the job. Figure 10.7 shows notes that combine several formats.

When will you need a combination of formats for your notes?

Mark Your Textbook

PLANNING

What happens to the key Cornell components when you choose to mark your text instead of taking separate notes?

Although the Cornell System can work as well with readings as it does with lectures, when you're taking notes for a textbook assignment, you also have the option of putting those notes directly on the pages of your book instead. When you choose to take notes directly in your textbook, the outside margin of the textbook page becomes the substitute for the cue column, and the spaces at the bottom or top of each page become the summary area. Of course, because a textbook page is already filled with text, you obviously can't put traditional notes where the text already is. What may at first seem like a disadvantage can actually be a great boon. Rather than jotting down your notes from scratch, you can mark the words or phrases in your textbook that make up the most important ideas.

Figure 10.8 contains 12 suggestions for marking textbooks. Notice especially the use of single and double underlines; the use of asterisks, circling, and boxing for important items; and the use of the top and bottom margins for long notations or summaries. If

[2]P. Pintrich and T. Garcia, "Self-Regulated Learning in College Students: Knowledge, Strategies, and Motivation." In P. Pintrich, D. Brown, and C. Weinstein (Eds.), *Perspectives on Student Motivation, Cognition, and Learning: Essays in Honor of W.J. McKeachie* (Hillsdale, NJ: Erlbaum, 1994), pp. 113–133.

www.cengage.com/success/Pauk/HowToStudy11e

Figure 10.7
Notes That Use
a Combination of
Formats

Mar. 14 (Fri.) – Ed. 103 – Prof. Pauk

Organizational patterns

How do org.
patterns help
make books,
lectures easier to
follow?

Where is this going? Org. patterns provide guidance
in lectures & texts. Tell you where author, speaker is
headed. Learning common patterns can make it
easier to follow both. Also, <u>signposts</u> (next, finally,
thus) can provide clues about path.

What are
movement
patterns?

<u>Movement patterns</u> systematically travel through
time, space, process. Can be easiest pattern to
follow. Several types:

Examples?

   * time or chronological pattern - events
     presented in order.

   * place or spatial pattern - info presented
     based on location or arrangement. Ex:
     descrip. of geog. features of U.S., outline of
     company setup

   * process pattern - steps or events lead to
     desired situation or product. Ex: recipe.

some of these ideas appeal to you, work them into your marking system. Be sure to use them consistently so that you will instantly remember what they mean.

What advantage does textbook marking have over separate notes?

IT'S YOUR Q

One key advantage of marking up your textbook directly is that your notes and your textbook travel together as a unit. Whenever you need clarification for a sentence or phrase you have marked, you have an entire book's worth of supporting material, including a table of contents, an index, and often a glossary, at your fingertips.

Of course, a potential disadvantage of textbook marking is that it doesn't require your complete concentration. Unlike taking separate notes, in which you have to consciously choose to add each idea, you can annotate your textbook without a true understanding of what you've marked. Drawing lines and boxes and inserting symbols and question marks can give you a false sense of accomplishment if you're not thinking deeply about what you read. It can also result in overmarking, which can undermine the original value of marking. When you mark your text, you need to do so sparingly, with both discipline and forethought. Keep in mind that the "you" who reviews the marked book will likely be more knowledgeable than the "you" who marked the book originally. Think

Figure 10.8
A System for Marking Your Textbooks

EXPLANATION AND DESCRIPTION	SYMBOLS, MARKINGS, AND NOTATIONS
1. Use double lines under words or phrases to signify main ideas.	<u><u>Radiation can produce mutations</u></u> . . .
2. Use single lines under words or phrases to signify supporting material.	<u>comes from cosmic rays</u> . . .
3. Mark small circled numbers near the initial word of an underlined group of words to indicate a series of arguments, facts, ideas—either main or supporting.	Conditions change . . . ① <u>rocks rise</u> . . . ② <u>some sink</u> . . . ③ <u>the sea dashes</u> . . . ④ <u>strong winds</u> . . .
4. Rather than underlining a group of three or more important lines, use a vertical bracket in the margin.	had known . . . who gave . . . the time . . . of time . . .
5. Use one asterisk in the margin to indicate ideas of special importance, and two for ideas of unusual importance. Reserve three asterisks for principles and high-level generalizations.	* When a <u>nuclear blast</u> is . . . ** People <u>quite close</u> to the . . . ***The main <u>cause of mutations</u> . . .
6. Circle keywords and key terms.	The ⟨genes⟩ are the . . .
7. Box words of enumeration and transition.	[fourth,] the lack of supplies . . . [furthermore,] the shortage . . .
8. Place a question mark in the margin, opposite lines you do not understand, as a reminder to ask the instructor for clarification.	? The latest . . . cold period . . . about 1,000,000 . . . Even today . . .
9. If you disagree with a statement, indicate that in the margin.	Disagree Life became . . . on land only . . . 340 million years . . .
10. Use the top and bottom margins of a page to record ideas of your own that are prompted by what you read.	Why not use carbon dating? Check on reference of fossils found in Tennessee stone quarry.
11. On sheets of paper that are smaller than the pages of the book, write longer thoughts or summaries; then insert them between the pages.	Fossils Plants = 500,000,000 years old Insects = 260,000,000 " " Bees = 100,000,000 " " True Fish = 330,000,000 " " Amphibians = 300,000,000 " " Reptiles = 300,000,000 " " Birds = 150,000,000 " "
12. Even though you have underlined the important ideas and supporting materials, still jot brief cues in the side margins.	Adapt – _____ fossil – _____ layer – _____

ahead, so that weeks or months later when you look back at chapters you marked, your marks will still be meaningful and won't seem excessive.

How can you make sure your marks are meaningful and not excessive?

There is a simple but powerful way to manage your marking: recitation. Rather than marking each paragraph as you go, read it through completely and then recite its main idea in your own words. Then return to the paragraph and mark the words or phrases that express this main idea. This step will move you out of the realm of simple recognition and into recall. Recalling your notes is the way to help make information your own.

Figure 10.9 provides an example of an appropriately marked textbook page. Notice how numbers are used to highlight the five basic types of supporting materials and how a box has been drawn around each of those types so they're easy to discern. The rest of the passage is marked sparingly, with the underlined phrases primarily forming the answers to the marginal questions. This type of organization not only aids in comprehending and remembering the main points of the page, but also helps immensely when you're studying for an examination and time is short.

Annotate Electronic Text

PLANNING

IT'S YOUR Q

These days, many of the texts we read are no longer printed pages. Instead, they take some electronic form, such as webpages, Portable Document Format (PDF) files, word processor documents, or electronic slides from presentation software such as Microsoft PowerPoint. Any one of these formats can be printed out and then marked up as though they were pages from a textbook, although you may find that you don't have enough space for your marginal cues if you simply print them out "as-is." However, there are adjustments you can make to accommodate Cornell-style margins.

How can you make room for Cornell margins on printed webpages?

Webpages. To add the space you need for note taking at the left and the bottom of each webpage, choose Page Setup from the File menu of your browser. Once you do, you should be able to change your browser's default margins to Cornell margins by typing the new dimensions into the appropriate text boxes. Enter 2.5 in the box for the left-hand margin and 2 in the box for the bottom. The text of the webpages will not be reduced. Instead it will be squeezed into the smaller text space to make room for the oversized margins.

What are your options for annotating PDF files?

How do you resize PDF files?

PDF files. With PDF files, you have two options: You can resize the pages to accommodate marginal notes and then print those pages out to allow handwritten annotations or, depending on the application you use for reading your files, you can do your annotating electronically.

Resizing your PDF files can be done by fooling your printer into thinking that you are printing standard 8.5×11 sheets onto smaller sized paper. Your options may vary,

Figure 10.9
Use of Enumeration in Textbooks
Source: Stephanie J. Coopman and James Lull, *Public Speaking: The Evolving Art,* p. 188. Copyright © 2009 by Cengage Learning.

How many types of supp. materials? Purpose of narratives?	There are <u>five basic types of supporting materials.</u> ① Narratives <u>dramatize a topic</u> and <u>help</u> your <u>audience identify</u> with it. A speech might include your own stories, stories about others, organizational stories, or cultural stories. Telling a good story requires having a sense of timing and drama.
How do examples help? Types of examples?	② Examples <u>make ideas less abstract and personalize a topic.</u> (General) examples are broad and provide <u>little detail.</u> (Specific) examples provide greater detail. (Hypothetical) examples are based on supposition--the audience imagines the circumstances--and must seem plausible to be effective. Examples <u>help listeners better understand the topic,</u> yet an example can mislead if it doesn't accurately represent the larger class to which it belongs.
Why use definitions?	③ Definitions establish a common meaning between the speaker and the audience. Speakers use definitions to <u>clarify concepts and identify the boundaries of a topic.</u> Definitions may <u>explain how something functions</u> or <u>offer analogies</u> for a word or concept. Specialized dictionaries can provide more descriptive and technical meanings for a word than standard dictionaries can. In using definitions as supporting materials, speakers must recognize that the audience likely will associate connotations with words, no matter how those words are defined.
What makes testimony effective?	④ <u>Experts, celebrities,</u> and <u>laypeople</u> may provide testimony or their experiences about a topic. The effectiveness of testimony rests on the degree to which <u>audience members perceive the person as a credible source</u> of information about the topic.
What is appeal of facts and stats?	⑤ Facts and statistics clearly <u>appeal to an audience's logical thinking processes.</u> These supporting materials show listeners the scope of a problem and can <u>demonstrate a topic's importance.</u> Including too many facts and statistics, especially without using presentation media to show all the numbers and figures, can overwhelm the audience. In addition, facts and statistics may be interpreted--and misinterpreted--in many ways.

but the paper size that comes closest to providing the proper margins you need on the side and the bottom is called "B5(JIS)." This will usually give you just the right amount of space for the cue column and maybe a bit more than you need at the bottom for the summary space.

If your PDF reader has annotation capabilities, you should be able to electronically duplicate most of the features that you would normally have on printed pages by activating the annotation toolbar. Most annotation toolbars on PDF readers allow you to underline and highlight your text, even permitting you to use a number of different colors if you like. There's also a sticky note feature that will automatically expand the size of the left-hand margin to accommodate any notes you choose to include. These notes can accommodate your Q System questions when the time comes. About the only important Cornell System feature you can't easily duplicate electronically with PDF files is the summary space, although you can dedicate the last sticky note on each page for that purpose.

Presentation slides. Presentation software typically is designed so the slides can be printed out in a way that allows room for notations. In addition, if the slideshow is editable, you may be able to add your notations onscreen without even printing out the slides.

Word processor documents. Of all the electronic documents you may want to annotate, word processor documents are probably the best suited and most flexible. If you prefer to handwrite your marginal jottings, you can change the margins in the document (just as you did with the webpages) to accommodate both the cue column and the summary space. With most word processing applications, you do this by choosing Page Setup from the File menu, clicking on the tab for margins, and increasing the size of the left and bottom margins. When you print out the pages, you should have ample room at both the left and the bottom of each printed page.

Word processor documents also make it relatively easy to type your jottings onscreen instead of writing them down by hand. You do this by converting the text of your document into a one-column table, with one paragraph per row. Highlight the text of your document and then choose the item in the Table menu that converts your text to a table. Once you're satisfied that each paragraph occupies its own table row, go back and add an additional column to your table, just to the left of the original one. This should create a blank cell to the left of every paragraph in your document that you can use for typing in your marginal questions. Adding a summary area is a little trickier—particularly if you want to be sure that each summary winds up at the bottom of a page. To do so, highlight the last row on a page, choose Insert from the Table menu, and add a row below the one you've selected. Then select the newly created two-column row and choose Merge Cells from the Table menu. This should provide you with a summary space that spans the two columns of your note-taking table. To add a space to the next page of your notes, simply repeat the process.

CHAPTER 10

Take Notes Effectively

What can you do to be fully engaged as you take notes?

Whether you are taking notes on sheets of paper, making marks in your textbook, or typing your notes onscreen, you need to be fully engaged. To avoid drifting into the sort of robotic routine that adds little to learning, it is important to take your notes efficiently and flexibly.

Record Efficiently

PLANNING

How can you take notes efficiently?

Depending on whether you're taking lecture notes or textbook notes, you may find that you are short on space, short on time, or both. Of course, if you scribble down information too quickly, your notes may be illegible. The way to circumvent these problems and record legible, useful notes at a reasonable speed is to adopt the modified printing style and use telegraphic sentences.

Use Modified Printing

What is modified printing?

Poor handwriting need not keep you from taking legible notes. The easy-to-master *modified printing style* combines the rapidity of writing with the legibility of printing. Your words still have a cursive look, but the periodic breaks between letters that are normally characteristic of printing prevent your writing from deteriorating into an unreadable blur.

$$a\ b\ c\ d\ e\ f\ g\ h\ i\ j\ k\ l\ m\ n\ o\ p\ q\ r\ s\ t\ u\ v\ w\ x\ y\ z$$

Figure 10.10 shows how modified printing looks in a typical paragraph.

Take Notes Telegraphically

IT'S YOUR Q

The best way to take notes is telegraphically. Long before e-mail and the fax machine were invented, important business and personal messages were sent by telegraph. The sender paid by the word; the fewer the words, the lower the cost. A 3-word message such as "Arriving three pm" was much less expensive than an 11-word message: "I will arrive home promptly at three o'clock in the afternoon." Of course, taking notes doesn't cost money, but it does cost time. To save time when you're taking notes, leave out unnecessary words such as articles (*a, an, the*), abbreviate words you use often (see Figure 10.11), and streamline definitions by using a colon (:) or a dash (—). Two examples of this telegraphic style are shown in Figure 10.12.

Figure 10.10
Modified Printing Style

> There are four advantages to using this modified printing style. First, it is faster than cursive writing; second, it is neater, permitting easy and direct comprehension; third, it saves time by precluding rewriting or typing; and fourth, it permits easy and clear re-forming of letters that are ill-formed due to haste.

Figure 10.11
Typical Technical Abbreviations
Source: Reprinted by permission from G. H. Logan, "Speed Notes for Engineers," *Product Engineering,* September 30, 1963. Copyright © 1963 by Morgan-Grampian, Inc.

anlys	analysis	*pltg*	plotting
ampltd	amplitude	*reman*	remain
asmg	assuming	*rsnc*	resonance
cald	called	*rltnshp*	relationship
cnst	constant	*smpl*	simple
dmpg	damping	*smpfd*	simplified
dmnsls	dimensionless	*stfns*	stiffness
dfln	deflection	*systm*	system
dfnd	defined	*sgnft*	significant
dstrbg	disturbing	*ths*	this
eftvns	effectiveness	*trnsmsblty*	transmissibility
frdm	freedom	*thrtly*	theoretically
frcg	forcing	*valu*	value
gvs	gives	*wth*	with
hrmc	harmonic	*whn*	when
isltr	isolator	*xprsd*	expressed
isltn	isolation		

Figure 10.12
Examples of Tele-graphic Sentences

Lecture's words

In marketing, we try to understand customers' needs and then respond to them with the right products and services. In the past, firms often produced goods first and tried to fit the customer's needs to the goods. Today's world-class marketers pride themselves on their customer orientation. We begin with the customer and build the product or service from there. A good example is McDonald's, the fast-food chain, which tailors its menus to local tastes and customs when it opens fast-food outlets in Moscow and other international locations.

Student's telegraphic sentences

Marketing understands customers' needs first.
- In past, firms produced goods first, then fit them to customers.
- World-class = having customer orientation.
- Ex. McDonald's in Moscow

Lecture's words

The US Patent Office has granted numerous patents for perpetual motion machines based upon applications with complete detailed drawings. Some years ago, though, the patent office began requiring working models of such a machine before a patent would be granted. Result: No patents granted for perpetual motion machines since that time.

Student's telegraphic sentences

Perpetual motion machine (drawings) = many patents.
Required working model = no patents since.

Remain Flexible

How should you
remain flexible as
you're taking notes?

Although modified printing and telegraphic sentences will help increase your speed, the goal is not to end up like some sort of note-taking machine. It's important to be thinking actively all the time, making spur-of-the-moment decisions about what belongs in your notes and what can be left out, and remaining ready to adjust your strategies if the speed of your note-taking can't keep up with the pace of a fast-moving lecture. You can increase your flexibility by taking notes selectively and by using a separate system for especially fast-moving lectures.

Take Notes Selectively

IT'S YOUR Q

With textbook note taking it's impractical to jot down every word. In lectures, it's impossible. Notes are not supposed to be a transcript. Your emphasis should be on the ideas, not the words. And you don't want all the ideas, either, just the key ones (as Figure 10.13 shows), along with any details or examples you need to make those ideas easier to understand. Use the organizational patterns and signposts that provide the framework for both lectures and texts to make intelligent decisions about what belongs in your notes and what can be safely left out.

Use the Two-Page System for Fast-Moving Lectures

How does the two-
page system work?

When you need to scramble to keep up with a fast-talking lecturer, try the two-page system. Lay your binder or notebook flat on the desk. On the left-hand page, record

Figure 10.13
Selective Note Taking

What's sympathetic
magic?

What's
contagious magic?

Oct. 10 (Mon.) – Soc. 102 – Prof. Oxford

A. Two kinds of magic
 1. Sympathetic — make model or form of a
  person from clay, etc. — then stick pins into
  object to hurt symbolized person.
 2. Contagious magic
  a. Need to possess an article belonging to
   another person.
  b. Ex. Fingernail clippings. By doing harm to
   these objects, feel that harm can be
   transmitted.

main ideas only. This is your primary page. On the right-hand page, record as many details as you have time for. Place the details opposite the main ideas they support. After the lecture, remain in your seat for a few minutes and fill in any gaps in your notes while the lecture is still relatively fresh in your mind.

Tie Things Together

Why is it a waste to end your note taking abruptly?

Many students squander the most valuable part of a note-taking session. As a lecture draws to a close or a chapter comes to an end, there's a temptation to just pack up and move on. That may be understandable, but it can prove to be a great waste of an especially valuable time. At this point, the ideas from the lecture or reading are like wet clay. You have only a brief time to shape them into something meaningful. If you wait too long, they won't be nearly as pliable.

Wrap Up Your Readings
OVERVIEWING

How do you conduct a quick overview of a reading assignment?

After you've completed a reading assignment, step back and quickly overview what you've just read. Here are two ways to do so:

1. *Reread the abstract, introduction, or summary.* Any of these three common elements provides a brief overview of what you've just read and puts the ideas you've picked up in an appropriate framework or context.
2. *Reread the title and headings.* If the text doesn't include an obvious overview, create one yourself by rereading the title, headings, and subheadings. In combination, these elements can help you mentally organize the information you've just learned. Don't spend too much time doing this rereading. The primary purpose is to refresh your memory of the important points so that you'll be able to focus more carefully on them later. If you find you have questions, jot them down so you can ask them in class.

Relive Your Lectures
OVERVIEWING — SUMMARIZING — QUESTIONING

What should you do at the end of a lecture?

The closing minutes can sometimes prove to be the most important part of an entire lecture. Speakers who do not pace themselves well may have to cram half the lecture into the last five or ten minutes. Record such fact-packed finales as rapidly as you can. After class, stay in your seat for a few extra minutes to write down as much as you can remember.

What should you do once you've left the lecture room?

As soon as you leave the lecture room, while walking to your next class, mentally recall the lecture from beginning to end. Visualize the classroom, the lecturer, and any chalkboard work. After mentally recalling the lecture, ask yourself some questions: What was the lecturer getting at? What was the central point? What did I learn? How does what I learned fit with what I already know? If you discover anything you don't quite understand, no matter how small, make a note of it and ask the instructor to explain it before the next class.

Walk Through the Note-Taking Steps

PLANNING

What are the basic steps in taking lecture and textbook notes?

Despite some obvious differences, the core concepts that underlie taking lecture notes, taking textbook notes, and marking up your textbook are remarkably similar. If you are careful to devise a system and stick with it, to gather information actively, efficiently, and flexibly, and to pull things together conscientiously at the end of a note-taking session, the handful of steps that follow should put you in a powerful position to master your notes and make them your own.

How to Take Lectures Notes

Figure 10.14 is a flow chart of this process.

1. *Record.* Put the lecturer's ideas and facts (along with any relevant diagrams) in the six-inch column of your Cornell System note sheet.
2. *Remember.* As soon as class is over, take a moment to mentally recall the entire lecture from start to finish.
3. *Refine.* Looking over your note sheets, add words, phrases, and facts you may have skipped or missed, and fix any difficult-to-decipher jottings.

How to Take Textbook Notes

Figure 10.15 shows how this process works for textbook marking and separate notes.

1. *Focus.* As you read through each section, turn the headings and subheadings into attention-getting questions that help stimulate your thinking and your curiosity as you read on.
2. *Read.* Move through the assignment a paragraph at a time, striving to understand the meaning of the current paragraph.
3. *Question.* Before you move on to the next paragraph, take a moment to ask yourself, "What's the main idea?" or "What is the author saying?"
4. *Recite.* Recite the answer to the question you just asked, in your own words and preferably out loud.
5. *Record.* If you're marking your textbook, find the words or phrases in the paragraph that support your recited answer and mark them. If you're taking separate notes, jot down the answer you've just recited in the six-inch column of your Cornell System note sheet. Then repeat the entire process until you have completed the assignment.

Figure 10.14
Taking Lecture Notes

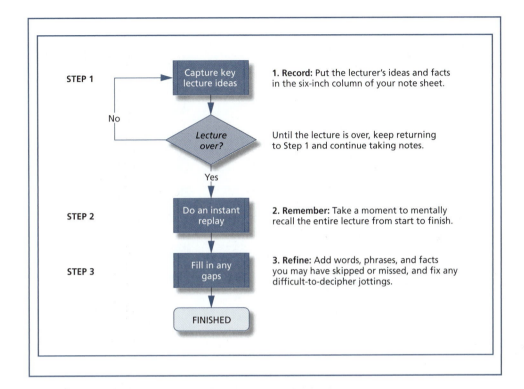

FINAL WORDS

What is the final step
that makes your note
taking effective?

Despite indisputable benefits, taking effective notes can be difficult for many students. Of course, most students take some sort of notes when they attend lectures; and a smaller number do so when they're reading. But in each case, the students who take notes often come close but don't quite reach the point where their notes are truly effective. Taking effective notes requires work; it requires time; and it forces you to be actively engaged in what you're reading or listening to. This can be a little daunting, especially when you may already have a false sense of accomplishment from half-baked notes or markings. Take that final step. Cross that threshold and make your note taking truly effective. You'll be working harder initially, it's true. All new skills require a little extra effort at the outset. But the benefits you derive will materialize almost immediately when you begin to master the notes that you have taken and make your new knowledge permanent instead of just fleeting.

Figure 10.15
Taking Textbook Notes

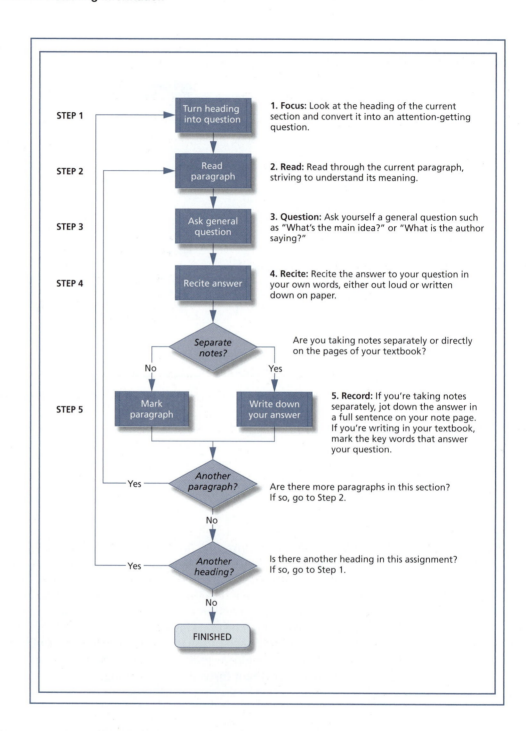

STEP 1   Turn heading into question   **1. Focus:** Look at the heading of the current section and convert it into an attention-getting question.

STEP 2   Read paragraph   **2. Read:** Read through the current paragraph, striving to understand its meaning.

STEP 3   Ask general question   **3. Question:** Ask yourself a general question such as "What's the main idea?" or "What is the author saying?"

STEP 4   Recite answer   **4. Recite:** Recite the answer to your question in your own words, either out loud or written down on paper.

Separate notes?   Are you taking notes separately or directly on the pages of your textbook?

No   Yes

STEP 5   Mark paragraph   Write down your answer   **5. Record:** If you're taking notes separately, jot down the answer in a full sentence on your note page. If you're writing in your textbook, mark the key words that answer your question.

Another paragraph?   Are there more paragraphs in this section? If so, go to Step 2.

Yes   No

Another heading?   Is there another heading in this assignment? If so, go to Step 1.

Yes   No

FINISHED

CHAPTER CHECKUP

SENTENCE COMPLETION

Complete the following sentences with one of the three words listed below each sentence.

1. Effective note taking requires building a background and creating a _____.

   context   **summary**   **memory**

2. Each lecture can be thought of as part of a _____.

   textbook   **discussion**   **puzzle**

3. The margin area at the outside of each page should be reserved for _____.

   reminders   **questions**   **definitions**

MATCHING

In each blank space in the left column, write the letter preceding the phrase in the right column that matches the left item best.

_____ 1. Ties Up   a. Helps provide context for an upcoming lecture

_____ 2. Drawings   b. Mnemonic for surveying a textbook chapter

_____ 3. Summary area   c. Can put what you've read into an appropriate frame-
                              work or context

_____ 4. Telegraphic   d. Used for distilling a page's worth of notes down to a
                              few sentences

_____ 5. Two-page   e. The only note-taking format that is explicitly discouraged

_____ 6. Outline   f. Can provide a cue for a great deal of verbal information.

_____ 7. Abstract   g. System for taking notes in especially fast-paced lectures

_____ 8. Syllabus   h. Note-taking style that employs only the most essential
                              words

TRUE-FALSE

Circle T *beside the* true *statements and* F *beside the* false *statements.*

1. T F The Cornell System provides a rigid set of rules for taking notes.
2. T F Of all the electronic texts you annotate, word processor documents are
         probably the most flexible.
3. T F It's unlikely that a chapter or lecture will fit into a single note-taking format.
4. T F A sketch can rarely convey locations or relationships as clearly as a few sentences.
5. T F You're seldom expected to read supplemental materials as thoroughly as
         your textbook.

www.cengage.com/success/Pauk/HowToStudy11e

MULTIPLE CHOICE   *Choose the word or phrase that completes each sentence most accurately, and circle the letter that precedes it.*

1. To take notes you can actually use, you need
   a. a loose-leaf notebook.
   b. a proven system.
   c. sheets of unlined paper.
   d. several fundamental questions.

2. As you're taking notes, the cue column should
   a. remind you.
   b. get wider.
   c. remain empty.
   d. be filled.

3. One advantage of taking notes directly in your textbook is that
   a. your book is more valuable when you sell it at the end of the semester.
   b. your notes and your textbook can travel together as a unit.
   c. you can use a highlighter to single out important ideas and concepts.
   d. as the term progresses, your knowledge is likely to grow.

4. PDF files typically enable you to use all Cornell System features except
   a. the cue column.
   b. the summary space.
   c. highlighting.
   d. underlining.

5. Modified printing is
   a. speedy, like writing.
   b. neat, like printing.
   c. easy to learn.
   d. all of the above.

REFLECTION   *Think about the ideas outlined in this chapter and then draw upon your own opinions and experiences to answer each question fully.*

1. Why do you take notes? Analyze your own reasons for note taking and then explain how this chapter has affected those reasons.
2. To what extent does your handwriting influence the quality of notes that you take or your choice of note-taking methods? What effect will the knowledge of modified printing have on your present note-taking strategies?

3. Do you plan to take notes on readings by marking them directly in your textbook or by writing them on separate sheets of paper? Explain the thoughts behind your choice.

IT'S YOUR Q

The Q System uses marginal questions to encourage active reading. You'll notice that most but not all paragraphs in this chapter are accompanied by marginal questions. Now it's your Q. Scan the chapter for any paragraph that is missing a question, reread the paragraph, establish the main idea, and then arrive at a question that elicits it. Use the questions in the surrounding paragraphs as models for your own marginal questions.

VOCABULARY IN ACTION

To expand the horizons of your understanding and to refine the precision of your thought, the three exercises that follow are designed to help you grow, strengthen, and maintain your own vocabulary.

SAY WHAT?

From the three choices beside each numbered item, select the one that most nearly expresses the meaning of the italicized word in the quote. Make a light check mark (√) next to your choice.

One of the wonderful things about learning is that knowledge not only translates from one area to another but is also an *avenue* that leads to understanding and *insight*.

—Benjamin Carson, M.D. (1951–), American neurosurgeon

1. *avenue*	sign	passage	boulevard
2. *insight*	wisdom	visibility	provocation

Preservation of one's own *culture* does not require *contempt* or disrespect for other cultures.

—Cesar Chavez (1927–1993), American labor leader and civil rights activist

3. *preservation*	tradition	protection	isolation
4. *culture*	society	specimen	refinement
5. *contempt*	rejection	ignorance	disdain

VOCAB-U-LADDER

Use your knowledge of word synonyms and roots to connect the word at the top rung to the word at the bottom rung, using the words listed below.

alleviate
altitude
ecstasy
elevation
exaltation
mitigate

system

share root "histanai," "cause to stand"

synonyms for "joy"

share root "altus," "high"

synonyms for "height"

share root "levare," "lighten, raise"

synonyms for "lessen"

share root "agere," "make, drive, do"

navigate

Here's the story behind a word that figures prominently in the chapter you've just read.

Survey A view from above

sur-vey sûr'vā' *n.* 1. A detailed inspection or investigation. 2. A general or comprehensive view.*

Once you know the history of the word *survey*, you'll find that describing it as a "35,000-foot view" is pretty appropriate. In fact, that's almost literally what it means. *Survey* comes from the Old French word surveeir, which hails from a combination of two extremely useful Latin roots, super and vidēre. *Vidēre* is Latin for "to look" or "to see" and is the source of a huge number of *"vision"* words you should recognize, including vision itself, as well as *video, view, vista, voyeur,* many words ending in -*vise*, such as *advise* and *revise,* and, of course, *survey,* along with its relatives, convey and purvey. All these variations exist because the spellings change slightly as the words journey from one language to another. The same fascinating sort of garbling happened to super, which, although it sometimes gets shortened to *sur* (as in *surmount, surpass,* and, of course, *survey*), has also managed to make it from Latin to English intact (*superscript, superlative, supervise*), as well as in other forms that come closer to its original primitive Indo-European source, *uper,* which meant "over or above." If that word *uper* looks familiar, it should. Thanks once again to spelling changes through the centuries, we get upper, over, and *hyper* from it. Although the additional s makes *super* look a little different, it's actually the little brother of this trio. So, you see, with *vidēre* meaning "see" and *super* "above" you now have the big-picture story of how *survey* came to mean "a view from above" and ultimately, "a general or comprehensive view."**

*Adapted from "survey." *The American Heritage Dictionary of the English Language,* 4th ed. (Boston: Houghton Mifflin, 2000), http://dictionary.reference.com/browse/survey (accessed June 17, 2009).
**Based on information from "survey." *The American Heritage Dictionary of the English Language,* 4th ed. (Boston: Houghton Mifflin, 2000), http://dictionary.reference.com/browse/survey (accessed June 17, 2009); "survey." Douglas Harper, Historian, http://www.etymonline.com/index.php?search=survey (accessed June 17, 2009); "survey, n." *Oxford English Dictionary*, 2nd ed. 20 vols. (Oxford: Oxford University Press, 1989).

Turn Your Notes into Knowledge

You've reached a crossroads. Now that you've conscientiously taken notes, you can let all that hard work go to waste. Or you can put in some extra effort to retain all that valuable information and transform what you've read and heard into a permanent part of your knowledge. Congratulations. You've taken the right path. This chapter tells you how to

- **Review to Cement Understanding**
- **Recite to Strengthen Memories**
- **Reflect to Add Wisdom**

In this chapter

How do you master
your notes?

If you've taken notes thoroughly and conscientiously, you have every right to feel good about your efforts. But taking notes is not an end in itself. In fact, it is only the beginning. Far too many students jot down their notes and then forget about them until exam time rolls around. They leave them neglected in a desk drawer or repeatedly pass over their detailed textbook markings as they move on to subsequent chapters. This is a tragic mistake and a great waste of time and effort. The only way to take advantage of all the information you've jotted down or marked up and highlighted—to master information that you've worked so hard to understand—is to review it carefully, recite it regularly, and reflect on it deeply until it becomes a permanent part of your knowledge.

Review to Cement Understanding

What's wrong with
reviewing notes just
by looking them over?

What do you gain
by conducting an
immediate review?

Most students review their notes by reading them over and perhaps by asking themselves a question or two to see what they remember. This spot-check approach may be common, but it's also haphazard. A systematic approach not only makes your review worthwhile, but also enables you to gain a clear sense of how you're doing.

The purpose of the immediate review is to cement your understanding of what you've just read or heard. As you learned in Chapter 9, memory can be fleeting. Chances are that when you were taking notes, especially in a lecture, you were taking in information an idea at a time. You probably didn't have the opportunity to make sure you truly understood everything you'd marked or written down, and you almost certainly didn't have the chance to step back and see how things all fit together. That's where the immediate review comes in. By targeting key ideas with the Q System, you are able to verify that you understand your notes. And by pulling things together in summaries, you gain a valuable big-picture perspective.

Target Key Ideas with the Q System

QUESTIONING   SUMMARIZING   PLANNING

What is the
Q System?

The left-hand margins of your Cornell System paper or the outside margins of your text should have remained blank up to this point. Here's your chance to put them to good use. At your earliest opportunity, move systematically through the notes you've just taken or the assignment you've just marked up, and come up with a question for each important idea. This is known as the Q System. Each question you write will provide a cue for the answer it addresses. Figure 11.1 provides a diagram of the Q System process.

How do you arrive at
Q System questions
for each important
idea?

When using the Q System, don't formulate yes-or-no questions. Aim instead for questions that prompt you to recall key information. Arriving at a suitable question is a little like playing the popular TV game show in which contestants are given the answers and asked to supply the questions. And it's almost identical to the process you went through

Figure 11.1
Using the Q System to Review Your Notes
Whether you're reviewing textbook notes, lecture notes, or markings you've made directly in your textbook, the Q System is your best bet.

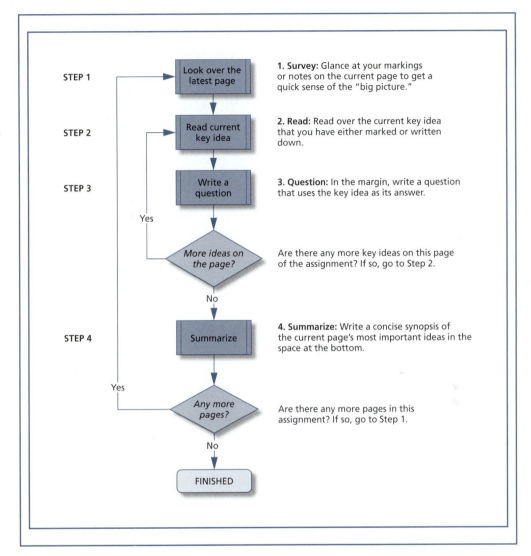

as you were reading an assignment and converting the headings into questions. The only real difference is that this time you're using ideas from your notes or the lines you underlined in your textbook as the starting point. The goal is to pose a question whose answer most effectively sums up the entire key idea or paragraph. Jot (or type) the question down in the margin alongside the information it refers to. Figure 11.2 shows some marginal questions for a textbook passage.

Figure 11.2
Using the Q System with a Textbook Assignment

WRITING GOOD PAPERS IN COLLEGE

What 2 aspects lead to success?

The techniques of writing a good paper are easy to follow. You should remember two important aspects that lead to success. First, start work early on the paper. Second, if you have a choice, choose a subject that you are interested in or that you can develop an interest in.

What 3 elements might make up a paper?

Much of your work in college involves absorbing knowledge; when it comes to writing papers, you have the opportunity to put down on paper what you've learned about a subject, and perhaps your opinions and conclusions on the subject.

What's the key in choosing a topic?

Writing is an important form of communication. To communicate well you must have something you really want to say. So if you have a choice of topics, choose one that intrigues you. If it isn't one that everyone else is writing on, all the better.

If not sure of a topic, do what?

If you're not sure about your choice of topic, do a little preliminary research to see what's involved in several topics before you make a final decision. Remember the caution about allowing yourself enough time? Here's where it comes into play. Take enough time to choose a topic carefully.

What form should your marginal questions take?

Repeat the process of formulating questions and putting them in the margin as you systematically move through all the paragraphs in your text or notes from your note paper. It's OK to abbreviate your question, especially if you are short on space. (Figure 11.3 shows an excerpt from some classroom notes with abbreviated questions in the margins.) But be certain there's nothing ambiguous about what you've written down. After all, you'll want to be able to read these questions throughout the semester. A badly abbreviated question may make sense to you now, but it could leave you scratching your head later on. The same applies to your handwriting. Make sure you can read it. You may want to use the modified printing style (explained in Chapter 10) to help you write quickly and legibly.

What should you do if there's no space for your questions?

Properly ruled Cornell System note paper should provide plenty of room for your Q System questions. But if you've marked up your textbook and it has skinny margins, you have a handful of options to adjust for the limited space.

Try the Sticky Note Method

How does the sticky note method work?

Jot down the same sort of question that you would have written in the margin, but put it on a "sticky note" instead (using one sticky note per question). When you've finished writing the question, affix it near the paragraph it refers to. Because your sticky notes

Figure 11.3
Using the Q System
with Classroom Notes

Who purchased Alaska?
When? Cost?
Rough dimensions of
mainland?
How long is the Yukon River?
Name kinds of minerals?

How are the forests?

Two most numerous fish?

Name several kinds of fur?

What's the highest mt. in
No. America?
When admitted as state?

Who designed the state flag?

Sept. 10, 2007 (Mon.) – History 101 –
Prof. A. Newhall

A.   Some facts about Alaska
       William H. Seward, Sec. of State –
       fr. Russia in 1867 – $7,200,000.
       Size – mainland: length = 1,500 mi. –
       width = 1,200 mi.
       Yukon River – 1,979 mi. long
       Minerals – oil, gold, silver, coal,
       chrome, iron, etc.
       Forests – commercial timber =
       85 billion board feet
       Fish – world's richest in salmon
       and halibut
       Furs – seal, mink, otter, beaver,
       fox, etc.
       Mt. McKinley – 20,320 ft. –
       highest in No. America
       Statehood – Jan. 3, 1959 –
       49th State
       State flag – designed by 13-year-old
       Benjamin Benson

may come unstuck, it's often a good idea to put a circled number in the margin of your textbook next to the paragraph your question is intended for and to number your sticky note to match, adding the page number as well in case you renumber with each new page.

Use the Bookmark Method

What does the
bookmark method
involve?

One method that many students swear by is to jot their questions on slips of scrap paper that resemble extra-wide bookmarks (about two-and-a-half inches wide, the same dimension as the margin in Cornell System paper). Use one bookmark for each pair of facing pages, keeping a running list of the questions for the left-hand page on one side and putting the questions for the right-hand page on the other. Just as you did with the sticky note system, number each question and put a corresponding number in the margin alongside the paragraph it refers to. When you've written all of the questions for the two pages, you can lodge the slip in the book at just the right spot, the same way you would an ordinary bookmark.

Take Separate Notes

What is the advantage of using separate notes?

Of course, if your textbook doesn't offer an accommodating set of margins, it might be simpler to take separate notes. You'll miss some of the advantages of taking notes directly in your book (see Chapter 10), but you'll be able to carry the notes for your assignment (even stash them in a pocket or purse) without having to lug around the book.

What do you accomplish by writing marginal questions?

Regardless of the method you choose when using the Q System, you will be accomplishing something vital. The straightforward process of formulating questions should provide you with a thorough and immediate review of your material. Although it's possible to do so, it's unnecessarily difficult (not to mention pointless) to "fake" questions for each idea. Ask questions that truly get to the heart of the information. To be able to turn an idea into a meaningful question, you need to have a genuine grasp of that idea.

See the Big Picture with Summaries

SUMMARIZING — PLANNING

How do summaries aid understanding?

In the same way that questions from the Q System provide you with a better grasp of the important ideas from your notes, summaries help supply the context. It's surprisingly easy to get caught up in the details of your notes and lose the grand scheme of things in the process. Writing a summary is a sure-fire way to force yourself to think about and come to grips with the broader ideas, trends, lessons, and themes that run through notes like a thread. Summaries supply a straightforward answer to the question, "What is this page about?" This cut-to-the-chase aspect of summaries should be especially handy when you're studying for an exam or doing research for a paper and want to go straight to the key information in your notes without having to read through every note on every page to find it. Although boiling down an entire page of notes into a couple of sentences can be challenging, the process of summarizing encourages you to reflect on your notes and decide which ideas are the most important.

The Standard Summary

IT'S YOUR Q

The standard system for summaries is to write one at the bottom of every page. Figure 11.4 shows an example. If you're taking notes directly in your textbook, you may find that there's more room to write at the top of each page than at the bottom. Either place is fine. Regardless of whether you're taking notes in your textbook or on separate sheets, don't pen an epic; you probably don't have the time, and you definitely don't have the room. Just come up with a concentrated sentence or two that efficiently pulls together the key information on the page. If space permits, it's a good idea to use complete sentences for your summaries. This reinforces your goal of articulately expressing what's important on the page. It can be a little too easy to

Figure 11.4
Summarizing a Page of Lecture Notes in Two Sentences

Psych. 105 – Prof. Martin – Sept. 14 (Mon.)

<u>MEMORY</u>

Memory tricky – Can recall instantly many trivial things of childhood, yet forget things recently worked hard to learn & retain.

Memory Trace
— Fact that we retain information means that some change was made in the brain.
— Change called "memory trace."
— "Trace" probably a molecular arrangement similar to molecular changes in a magnetic recording tape.

Three memory systems: sensory, short term, long term.
— <u>Sensory</u> (lasts one second)
   Ex. Words or numbers sent to brain by sight (visual image) start to disintegrate within a few tenths of a second & gone in one full second, unless quickly transferred to S-T memory by verbal repetition.
— Short-term memory [STM] (lasts 30 seconds)
   • Experiments show: a syllable of 3 letters remembered 50% of the time after 3 seconds. Totally forgotten end of 30 seconds.
   • S-T memory — limited capacity — holds average of 7 items.
   • More than 7 items — jettisons some to make room.
   • To hold items in STM, must rehearse — must hear <u>sound</u> of words internally or externally.
— Long-term memory [LTM] (lasts a lifetime or short time).
   • Transfer fact or idea by
      (1) <u>Associating</u> w/information already in LTM.
      (2) <u>Organizing</u> information into meaningful units.
      (3) <u>Understanding</u> by comparing & making relationships.
      (4) <u>Frameworking</u> – fit pieces in like in a jigsaw puzzle.
      (5) <u>Reorganizing</u> – combining new & old into a new unit.
      (6) <u>Rehearsing</u> – aloud to keep memory trace strong.

How do psychologists account for remembering?

What's a "memory trace"?

What are the three memory systems?

How long does sensory memory retain information?

How is information transferred to STM?

What are the retention times of STM?

What's the capacity of the STM?

How to hold information in STM?

What are the retention times of LTM?

What are the six ways to transfer infomation from STM to LTM?

Three kinds of memory systems are sensory, which retains information for about 1 second; short-term, which retains for a maximum of 30 seconds; and long-term, which varies from a lifetime of retention to a relatively short time.

The six ways (activities) to transfer information to the long-term memory are associating, organizing, understanding, frameworking, reorganizing, and rehearsing.

disguise your confusion in an abbreviated sentence. Now is the time to make sure you grasp what you've written down or read. If you don't understand things at this stage, there's a good chance that they will grow murkier with time. Make the effort right now to see clearly. If you still don't understand, you have time to get help from a tutor or instructor. If you wait, it may be too late.

The Wrap-Up Summary

What is the approach for the wrap-up summary?

Rather than summarizing each page, you may choose to write a longer summary at the very end of your lecture notes or textbook assignment. Depending on the length or importance of the assignment, this method may be enough, but in general it's not recommended, at least not in isolation. Even if you write several paragraphs for your wrap-up summary, you probably can't expect to approach the level of insight and detail that you gain from summarizing each page. However, if the lecture is especially brief or the reading assignment is a supplemental one that doesn't require a great deal of attention (see Chapter 10), a wrap-up summary may suffice.

The Split-Level Summary

Why is the split-level approach best for summarizing your notes?

The best way to review and summarize your notes is to combine the standard summaries with the wrap-up summary. Start with the standard summary, summarizing each page with a sentence or two. Then, rather than rereading all of your notes to arrive at a wrap-up summary, simply reread the summaries you've written for each page and come up with a summary of your summaries. This two-level approach makes your notes extremely useful and flexible. If you just need a reminder of what a single assignment or lecture was about, you can read the wrap-up summary. If you need more detail, you can go to the next level and read the summary on a particular page. If you're still perplexed, you can reread the key ideas from that particular page.

What else do questions and summaries provide besides an immediate review?

Formulating questions for each important idea in your notes and then coming up with summaries not only provides an extremely directed and effective means of review, but it also sets the stage for recitation, the most valuable technique you can use to help commit your notes to memory.

Recite to Strengthen Memories

What is the role of reciting?

Now that you've added Q System questions (and brief summaries) to each page and conducted a thorough review in the process, how are you going to hold on to all that valuable information? After all, forgetting never lets up. It works continuously to expel from memory what you worked so hard to put there. Luckily, you can bring forgetting almost to a standstill by using the power of recitation.

How does reciting work?

Reciting forces you to think, and this thinking leaves a neural trace in your memory. Reciting promotes concentration, forms a sound basis for understanding the next paragraph or the next chapter, provides time for consolidation, ensures that facts and ideas are remembered accurately, and supplies immediate feedback on how you're doing. Moreover, experiments have shown that the greater the proportion of reciting time to reading time, the greater the learning. Students who spent 20 percent of their time reading and 80 percent reciting did much better than students who spent less time reciting and more time reading.

What is the process for reciting?

The process of reciting is relatively straightforward. Go back to the first page and cover it with a blank sheet of paper, exposing only your Q System questions. (If you used the sticky note method, you should still be able to obscure the text while reading your questions. If you chose the bookmark method, you can use your marker to cover the text. If your notes and Q System questions are in a computer file, open the file and then create a new, empty document and use it as an electronic version of a blank sheet of paper to cover your text.) Read the first question, and answer it in your own words. Slide the blank sheet down to check your answer. If your answer is wrong or incomplete, try again. Do this until you get the answer right. Go through the entire assignment this way. (See Figure 11.5 for a diagram of the entire process.) Your aim is to establish an accurate, crystal clear impression in your memory, because that's what you want to return to during an exam. If the impression in your memory is fuzzy at this time, it will be even fuzzier three or four weeks later (see Chapter 9).

Recite Out Loud

SUMMARIZING

How do you recite out loud?

The traditional way to recite is out loud and in your own words. When you recite aloud, speak clearly so there's no mistake about what you are saying. Express the ideas in complete sentences, using the proper signal words. For example, when you are reciting a list of ideas or facts, enumerate them by saying *first*, *second*, and so on. Insert words such as *furthermore*, *however*, and *finally*. When you do so in oral practice, you will do so more naturally in writing during an exam. One of the best ways to recite out loud is in a group study or discussion (see Chapter 13), where there are people who can alert you right away should you answer seem unclear or incorrect.

Recite by Writing

SUMMARIZING

IT'S YOUR Q

If you are reluctant or unable to recite aloud, you can recite by writing out (or typing) your answers instead. This method is slower than traditional reciting, but it provides added benefits. Even more than reciting aloud, reciting by writing supplies solid proof that you can answer your questions. After all, you have a written record. And it provides excellent practice for essay and short-answer tests. To recite by writing, move through your notes a question at a time just as you would normally. But instead of speaking your answers, write them down on a separate sheet of paper. Then uncover the page and compare each answer you've just written with the one in your notes.

www.cengage.com/success/Pauk/HowToStudy11e

Figure 11.5
The Process of Reciting Your Notes

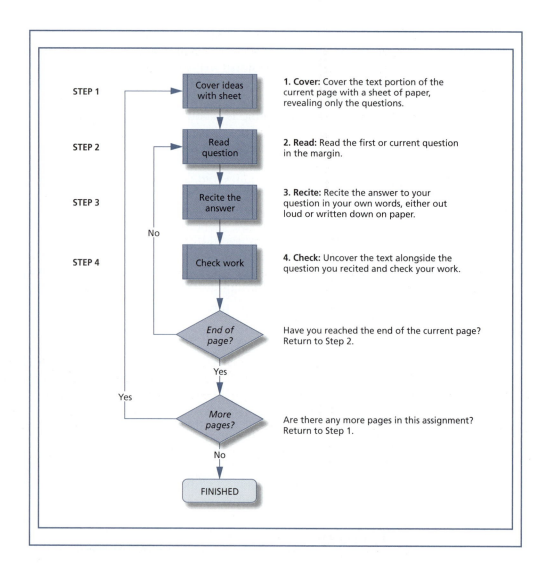

STEP 1 — Cover ideas with sheet
1. Cover: Cover the text portion of the current page with a sheet of paper, revealing only the questions.

STEP 2 — Read question
2. Read: Read the first or current question in the margin.

STEP 3 — Recite the answer
3. Recite: Recite the answer to your question in your own words, either out loud or written down on paper.

STEP 4 — Check work
4. Check: Uncover the text alongside the question you recited and check your work.

End of page? — No / Yes
Have you reached the end of the current page? Return to Step 2.

More pages? — Yes / No
Are there any more pages in this assignment? Return to Step 1.

FINISHED

Reflect to Add Wisdom

What is reflection?

After you learn facts and ideas through reviewing and reciting, take some time to mull them over. Use your innate sense of curiosity to speculate or play with the knowledge you've acquired. This is called *reflection*. To engage in reflection is to bring creativity to your learning. Ask yourself such questions as these: What is the significance of these facts and ideas? What principle or principles are they based on? What else could they be applied to? How do they fit in with what I already know? From these facts and ideas, what else can I learn? When you reflect, you weave new facts and ideas into your existing knowledge and create a fabric of genuine wisdom. History's greatest thinkers have relied on reflection for their breakthroughs. They make a strong case for reflection as a vital skill. With a technique or two to get you started, you can begin using reflection on your own to master your notes and gain lasting learning and genuine insight.

Learn Why Reflection Is Vital

REFRAMING

What did Bethe say about reflection?

Professor Hans Bethe, Cornell University's famous nuclear physicist and Nobel Prize winner, talked about reflection as used by a scientist:

> To become a good scientist one must live with the problem he's working on. The problem must follow the scientist wherever he goes. You can't be a good scientist working only eight hours a day. Science must be the consuming interest of your life. You must want to know. Nothing matters more than finding the answer to the question or the problem you are engaged in.[1]

What is the connection between reflection and creativity?

Professor Bethe went on to say that students who go only as far as their textbooks and lectures take them may become proficient, but they will never be creative. Creativity comes only with reflection. That is, seeing new material in the light of what you already know is the only road to original ideas, for having an idea is nothing more than discovering a relationship not seen before. And it is impossible to have ideas without reflecting.

What was Whitehead's position on reflection?

Alfred North Whitehead, famous British philosopher and mathematician, strongly advocated reflection. He, too, spoke about the knowledge that grows out of throwing ideas "into fresh combinations." He viewed reflection as taking what one already knows and projecting one's thought beyond familiar experience—considering new knowledge and ideas in the light of the old, and the old in the light of the new.

What was Schopenhauer's point about reflection?

The famous German philosopher Arthur Schopenhauer had exceptionally strong views on the importance of reflection:

> A library may be very large, but if it is in disorder, it is not so useful as one that is small but well arranged. In the same way, a man may have a great mass of knowledge, but if he has not worked it up by thinking it over for himself, it has much less value than a far smaller amount which he has thoroughly pondered. For it is only when a man looks at his knowledge from all sides, and combines the things he knows by comparing truth with truth, that he obtains a complete hold over it and gets it into his power.
>
> Reflections should not be left vague. Pursue the problem until ideas take definite shape. If you need more information, an encyclopedia or a standard book on the subject will often give you what you need to bring fuzzy ideas into focus.[2]

[1]Interview with Professor Hans Bethe, May 19, 1960.
[2]Essays of Arthur Schopenhauer, selected and translated by T. Bailey Saunders (New York: A. L. Burt, 1892), p. 321.

www.cengage.com/success/Pauk/HowToStudy11e

What is the connection
between reflection and
the subconscious?

The subconscious plays an important role in creative thinking and discovery. Many of us have had the experience of being struck as if by lightning by an exciting idea or even the solution to a problem at a time when we weren't consciously thinking about it. The great Hungarian physicist Leó Szilárd came up with the solution to the nuclear chain reaction while crossing a London street. Archimedes arrived at the principle of displacement while sitting in his bathtub. The mind continues to work on concepts even when you aren't aware of it. The process that initiates much of this deep thinking is reflection.

Use Techniques to Help You Reflect

REFRAMING — PLANNING

What is a big
advantage of
reflection?

A great advantage of reflection is its flexibility. It can be molded to fit your imagination. You can take it with you wherever you go and make use of it in spare moments. You can reflect while walking from one class to another, standing in line, waiting for a friend, or riding a bus.

What is a drawback of
reflection?

But reflection's flexibility can also be a disadvantage if you're unsure of how to get started. This uncertainty prompts some students to skip over the reflection step completely. Although there are no specific reflection steps like those you might find for reviewing or reciting, there are a number of strategies you can use to ease into a reflective mindset.

Use the Silver Dollar System

IT'S YOUR Q

You can reflect on the information from your notes and make it more manageable by using the Silver Dollar System:

1. Read through your notes and make an *S* in the margin next to any idea that seems important. Depending on the number of pages of notes you read, you'll probably wind up with several dozen *S*'s.
2. Now read only the notes you have flagged with an *S*. As you go through these flagged notes for a second time, select the ideas that seem particularly important, and draw a vertical line through the *S*'s that are next to them. Your symbol will look like this: $.
3. Make a third and final pass through your notes, reading only those ideas that have been marked $. Out of these notes, mark the truly outstanding ideas—there will be only a handful of them—with another vertical line so your markings look like dollar signs: $.

How does the Silver
Dollar System
stimulate reflection?

The Silver Dollar System stimulates reflection by helping you compare the relative weights of the ideas you have noted. It shows you at a glance which ideas are crucial to remember and which are not. The $ sign alerts you to the truly important ideas, the "Silver Dollar" ideas that should receive most of your attention. Next come the $ ideas; they are worthy but shouldn't clutter up your memory if you have a lot to remember in a limited amount of time. Finally, the *S* ideas can be ignored. Although you flagged these as potentially important ideas, since then you've twice marked ideas that were even more important.

Rearrange Your Information

How is rearranging your information helpful?

You almost always gain insight when you *reframe* information, that is, when you look at it from a different framework or perspective. If, for example, you've been studying countries geographically, you might want to consider grouping them by their systems of government, by their predominant religions, or by comparing them chronologically. You may want to group existing information under categories such as "pros" and "cons" or "before" and "after," depending on the nature of the information you are mastering.

Use Software

IT'S YOUR Q

Software can provide most of the benefits of manual rearranging but without the drudgery and time expense. Some applications can take a split second to reconfigure information that would take hours to rearrange by hand. Most word processor and spreadsheet applications allow you to sort a table of information by one or more of its columns. More sophisticated tools found in many spreadsheet programs allow you to take an existing table and turn it into a brand-new table that clusters the information in any number of ways of your choosing. Thus, if you had a table that listed all the presidents of the United States, the years they took office, their political parties, and their states of birth, you would be able to see, for example, all the presidents from Ohio, all the presidents who were members of the Whig Party, or all the presidents who took office between 1800 and 1850. These clusters could trigger any number of reflective questions: What happened to the Whig Party? What other political parties no longer exist? Why are so many presidents from Ohio? Who was the first president from Ohio? Who is the most recent president from Ohio? Which state has produced the most presidents? How does the number of presidents between 1800 and 1850 compare with the number of presidents between 1900 and 1950? And so on. Because a computer performs it, the actual rearranging teaches you nothing. But the questions you ask as a result will stimulate reflection and strengthen your memories by allowing you to remember things in a variety of ways. In a similar fashion, the tagging that is commonly used in blogs and on other Internet sites provides an extremely helpful means of quickly and dynamically grouping information in different ways to add context, broaden understanding, and aid reflection.

Put It in Context

Why is context an important factor in reflection?

Few ideas are meaningful when viewed in isolation. They need context to establish them in a realm that you can truly understand. For example, if you read about a scientific discovery from a certain time period, consider examining other events from the year the discovery was made or the place where the discovery occurred. Was this before or after the Civil War, World War II, or the war in Iraq? Had the telephone, the radio, or the computer been invented? Were people traveling by horse, by car, or by jet? These investigations supply a basic background (see Chapter 9) that will often yield a deeper understanding.

Ask More Questions

Why is it helpful to ask additional questions?

In press conferences, the follow-up question is sometimes more insightful than the original question. If you've been using the Q System, each idea in your notes or paragraph in your reading assignment has an accompanying question. Come up with a follow-up to the original question and see if your notes or your text can provide the answer. If not, you might want to dig deeper for clues.

Think Visually

How can concept maps be used as a reflection tool?

Chapter 8 explains how concept maps can be used to work out problems, explore possibilities, and establish connections. These are exactly the sorts of issues that reflection addresses. Take the key concepts from your notes or from a chapter assignment, put them in ovals on a plain sheet of paper, and try numerous ways of arranging and connecting them. If you do, you will almost certainly learn something that wasn't clear to you when those concepts were merely isolated words on a page. If you're more comfortable creating your concept maps on a computer screen instead of a sheet of paper, there are a number of concept- and mind-mapping applications available, some of which are free.

Combine Textbook and Lecture Notes

How do you combine textbook and lecture notes?

Although the classroom lectures you attend should presumably relate to your reading assignments, you won't always see the connections clearly until you can actually place notes from both side by side. Using the format shown in Figure 11.6, jot down the most important information from a textbook assignment in the middle column of the three-column note sheet. Then add any lecture notes that deal with the same topic in the right column, alongside the textbook notes they pertain to. Finally, just as you did with your original notes, use the Q System to arrive at a question for which the textbook note *and* any related information from the lecture is the answer. It's impossible to predict in advance what you'll learn from this experience, but by combining two sets of notes you'll almost certainly arrive at an answer that is greater than the sum of the parts. This is the essence of reflection.

FINAL WORDS

How do a scholar and a student differ?

There's a huge difference between proficiency and creativity. You can become proficient by studying your textbooks and lecture notes, but you will never be creative until you try to see beyond the facts, to leap mentally beyond the given. If your object is simply

Figure 11.6

Cornell System Format for Combining Lecture and Textbook Notes

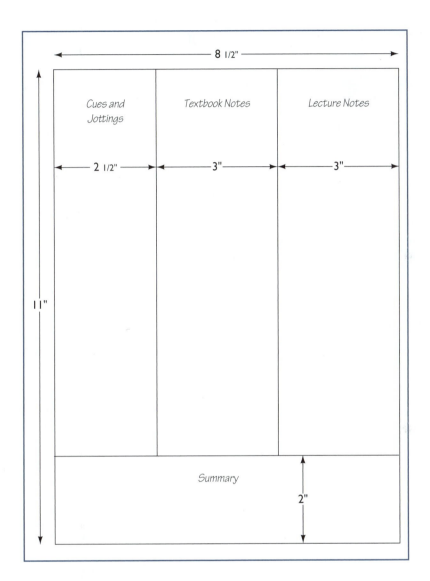

to tackle tests, pass your courses, and emerge from college with a degree and reasonably good prospects for employment, this book should serve you well. But if your aspirations aim higher, this book will serve you even better. The things that distinguish a scholar from a mere student are perpetual curiosity and an unquenchable thirst for learning. Reviewing and reciting should help you reach your modest goals. Reflection will enable you to reach for the stars.

www.cengage.com/success/Pauk/HowToStudy11e

CHAPTER CHECKUP

SENTENCE COMPLETION

Complete the following sentences with one of the three words listed below each sentence.

1. You can bring forgetting almost to a standstill with _____.

   summaries   **recitation**   **questions**

2. Creativity comes only with _____

   practice   **reflection**   **summaries**

3. Ideas in your notes that you have marked with an *S* can be _____.

   saved   **difficult**   **ignored**

MATCHING

In each blank space in the left column, write the letter preceding the phrase in the right column that matches the left item best.

_____ 1. Reflecting
a. Method that summarizes an entire assignment as well as each page

_____ 2. Reciting
b. System that allows you to reduce and reflect on your note sheets

_____ 3. Split-level
c. Used as an alternative to the traditional method of reciting your notes

_____ 4. Bookmark
d. Using your innate curiosity to consider ideas in new and different ways

_____ 5. Rereading
e. Alternate Q System method when your textbook margins are too narrow

_____ 6. Silver Dollar
f. Provided when you add questions and summaries to your notes

_____ 7. Reviewing
g. Mistakenly thought to be an effective method of reviewing

_____ 8. Writing
h. Repeating key information from memory and in your own words

TRUE-FALSE

Circle T *beside the* true *statements and* F *beside the* false *statements.*

1. T F Most students review their notes by reading them over.
2. T F When using the Q System, try to come up with yes-or-no questions.
3. T F It's OK to abbreviate your Q System questions.
4. T F If your notes are in a computer file, you will be unable to recite them.
5. T F Although reciting by writing is slower than traditional reciting, it provides added benefits.

MULTIPLE CHOICE   *Choose the word or phrase that completes each sentence most accurately, and circle the letter that precedes it.*

1. The primary purpose of an immediate review is to
   a. cement your understanding.
   b. spot-check your notes.
   c. look up words or terms you don't know.
   d. make sure your notes are legible.

2. If your textbook's margins are too narrow for Q System questions, you can use
   a. the sticky note method.
   b. the bookmark method.
   c. separate notes.
   d. all of the above.

3. Adding summaries to your notes helps you
   a. zero in on key ideas.
   b. gain a broader perspective.
   c. anticipate multiple-choice questions.
   d. include questions you couldn't fit in the margins.

4. The traditional way to recite is
   a. out loud.
   b. in your own words.
   c. from memory.
   d. all of the above.

5. One strength and weakness of reflection is its
   a. cost.
   b. repetitiveness.
   c. flexibility.
   d. imagination.

REFLECTION   *Think about the ideas outlined in this chapter and then draw upon your own opinions and experiences to answer each question fully.*

1. Both the Q System and summaries help you master your notes but from two different perspectives. Which approach do you think will be easiest for you to adopt? Which approach will be the most valuable for you? Explain why in each case.

www.cengage.com/success/Pauk/HowToStudy11e

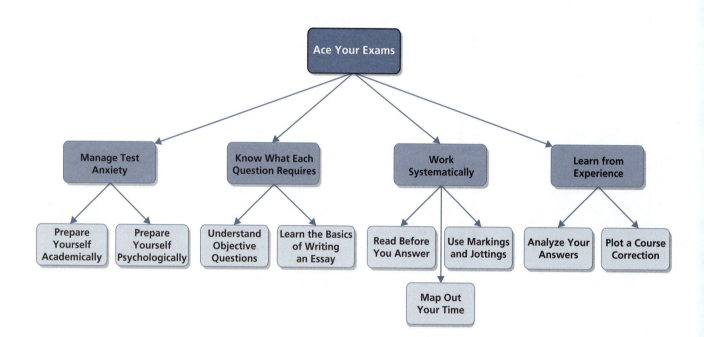

CHAPTER

12

Ace Your Exams

The real purpose of exams is to test your knowledge, not to try your
patience. Yet when faced with the prospect of answering true-false,
multiple-choice, matching, sentence-completion, or essay questions,
many students would prefer to choose "none of the above." If you're
well prepared, methodical, and thoughtful, then taking a test doesn't
have to be traumatic. This chapter shows you how to

- **Manage Test Anxiety**
- **Know What Each Question Requires**
- **Work Systematically**
- **Learn from Experience**

In this chapter

► The three items that belong in every exam-week schedule. (p. 314)

► A valuable test preparation technique that's so obvious you probably
never considered it. (p. 319)

► Objective tests and pasta may have more in common that you realize.
(p. 320)

What are the two basic categories of test questions?

Most of the test questions you'll be expected to answer in college fall into one of two categories: essay questions and objective questions. Essay questions take a broader view of a subject and generally emphasize your ability to recall and organize what you've learned and to write about it. Objective questions focus more on details and on your ability to recognize, rather than recall, them.

What does performing well on a test involve?

Performing well on a test involves managing test anxiety through preparation, understanding each question type, moving systematically through a test, and learning from experience.

Manage Test Anxiety

What is the simple cure for test anxiety?

The best cure for test anxiety is simple but powerful: preparation. Advance preparation is like a fire drill: It teaches you what to do and how to proceed, even in a high-stress situation, because you've been through the procedure so many times that you know it by heart. To manage the anxiety that often arises at test time, you can prepare yourself both academically and psychologically.

Prepare Yourself Academically

OVERVIEWING — CLUSTERING — SUMMARIZING

How can you prepare yourself academically for a test?

To be prepared academically, start early, stay on top of your coursework, and organize yourself and your studying plan. Even if you're forced to cram for a test, do so as sensibly and methodically as you would if there were no time constraints.

Start Early

What can you do to get a head start on your courses?

The pressure is almost nonexistent at the start of a new term. Take advantage of this calm before the storm. Get a head start in a course by picking up your textbooks, looking over your syllabus, and learning where and how to get academic help. Picking up your textbooks right away instead of waiting until the last minute will give you time to build a foundation of understanding. You'll be able to look through the text in a leisurely manner to get a sense of where the book and the course will be headed. In the same way that surveying your textbook gives you a sense of the book as a whole, reading the syllabus from start to finish at the earliest opportunity provides a valuable overview of the course and makes preparing for tests much easier. And finally, take a few minutes before the semester begins to find out where your campus tutoring service is located and how to arrange for a tutor. This information is often available on the campus website or in the materials you receive during orientation. Then, if you should find that you are struggling with a course and need help, all the research will have been done in advance. You'll be able to arrange for a tutor without delay rather than putting things off until the tutors' schedules are full and your situation has reached a crisis.

Stay on Top of Your Coursework

When the time comes to start focusing on an exam, you can seriously endanger your performance if you have to spend valuable time getting caught up. If you stay on top of your assignments throughout the semester—by taking notes as you read or listen and by mastering those notes at the earliest possible opportunity—they won't come back to haunt you when it's time to study for finals. Taken conscientiously throughout the semester, your Cornell-style notes will provide a valuable storehouse of knowledge and an excellent start in your preparation for upcoming exams. If you took notes using the Q System (see Chapter 11), you'll not only have used the powerful tool of recitation to embed your course's important ideas into your memory, but you will have already set up a format for your notes that allows you to study in a way that closely matches the format of your exams!

IT'S YOUR Q

Organize Yourself

How can you organize yourself?

The work you put into preparing yourself academically by starting early and by keeping up with your classes and assignments can be best used if you organize both your time and your notes.

What kinds of schedules help prepare you for exams?

Organize Your Time with Schedules Scheduling is important throughout the term. Three-part scheduling plans (explained in Chapter 2) allow you to set aside time for reviewing material so that you won't get caught off guard by a quiz or test. As you near the end of a term or semester, scheduling your time becomes even more crucial. If you haven't been using schedules, now's a good time to start. If you have been, you probably feel on top of things already. In either case, it's a good idea to organize your time with a "homestretch schedule" specifically designed to help you tie up loose ends and get you through that all-important last week before exams begin. When exam week arrives, devise another schedule that specifies when each of your tests takes place and that includes time for meals, sleep, and recreation, which are particularly crucial during exam week.

What items belong in a homestretch schedule?

Make up a homestretch schedule. Use the format in Figure 12.1 for your homestretch schedule. (This schedule uses the grid discussed in Chapter 2.) Start by filling in the time blocks that will be taken up by meals, sleep, job, and recreation. Next, fill in your classes. Do not miss classes for any reason at this stage; you will want to be there to hear the instructors' answers to students' questions about exams. Finally, fill in the time you will need for completing term papers and other assignments. Make sure you get them done before exam week. You don't want unfinished business to interfere with your studying or distract your thinking during exams. Use any time remaining at the end of the week to study for your exams. Fill in the exact study times and subjects. Instead of writing "Study" in the time blocks, write exactly what you plan to study: "Study economics, chaps 1 to 10" or "Summarize sociology notes." Make a schedule that you'll be able to follow, and then be sure to follow it.

Figure 12.2
A Standard Summary Sheet

<u>Steps in Writing</u>

What are four elements of college writing?

<u>Writing must have:</u> basic premise, logical development of ideas, support in paragraphs, good word choice

What are steps in prewriting?

<u>Prewriting</u>
  Brainstorm about a subject — generate ideas
  Narrow to a topic — use list or concept map
  Focus on a basic premise — ask a meaningful
    question that makes a point
  Plot a pattern — organize points into a
    framework

What is the basic structure?

<u>Writing</u>
  Structure — use introduction, body
    paragraphs, and conclusion
    – write body first

What should a body paragraph contain?

  Body Paragraphs — begin each with
    topic sentence that supports basic
    premise (controlling idea)
    – support points with good examples
      and detail

What is the purpose of introduction?
What does it reveal?

  Introduction — first paragraph — states
        basic premise
    Reveals: — topic of essay
      – opinion about topic
      – organization pattern
        you'll use

How do you conclude?

  Conclusion — should leave reader with
    a feeling of completion
    Either: summarize basic premise
      or main points — state your opinion

What are the two main facets of revising?

<u>Revising</u>
  Strengthen support — data, examples, etc.
  Edit for transitions, spelling, and
    grammar errors.

Figure 12.3
An Advanced Summary Sheet for Classroom Lecture Notes

	Sociology 103 – Dr. Lund	
	19th Century	20th Century
How is family governed?	1. Patriarchal, Father head of family.	1. Individualistic, democratic
Difference in stability?	2. Family stable	2. Family less stable
Status of extended family?	3. Many children and relatives under one roof – extended family	3. Smaller in size. Only 2 generations (parents & children)
Changes in mobility?	4. Non-mobile. Rarely moved. "Old family homestead."	4. Mobility increased & residences changed often
Relationship between women & work?	5. Women: housework & children	5. Women: work outside & care for children after hours
Attitude toward sex?	6. Puritanical on sex	6. Increasingly liberal
Variance in family types?	7. Family types in community alike	7. Greater variability in family type
Family's function?	8. Family had many functions: political, religious, economic	8. Family for procreation & socialization

Cram Systematically

If you're forced to cram, how do you cram systematically?

Proper academic preparation usually eliminates the need for cramming. But if you find yourself unprepared for an exam, sometimes cramming can be an unfortunate necessity. To cram systematically, the key words to remember are *selectivity* and *recitation*. Resist the temptation to try to learn everything. It's too late for that now. Instead, comb through your readings and lecture notes for only the essential facts, write them in your own words on summary sheets, and then use as much of your time as possible for remembering them. Don't make the mistake of reading and rereading this material. To make these notes your own, you must recite, recite, and recite. Begin by reading each fact you've

www.cengage.com/success/Pauk/HowToStudy11e

Figure 12.4
An Advanced Summary Sheet from a Textbook Chapter

Economics 102 – Professor Maxwell

I. Single

What are
two advtgs?

What are
two disadvtgs?

I. Single proprietorship
<u>ADVANTAGES</u>
1. Can do what desires
2. All profit goes to owner
<u>DISADVANTAGES</u>
1. All losses hurt owner (unlimited liability)
2. Commerical banks ordinarily will not provide "venture capital"

II. Partner--

What are
three advtgs?

What are
two disadvtgs?

II. Partnership
<u>ADVANTAGES</u>
1. Pool wealth, profits, losses
2. "Vertical integration" = gain control of resources, become own wholesaler
3. "Horizontal integration" = buy out competitors; add products; improve products
<u>DISADVANTAGES</u>
1. Each time a member dies or leaves, a new partnership needs to be formed
2. Unlimited liability, even if own a small share

III. Corporation

What are
four advtgs?

What are four
advtgs to society?

III. Corporation
<u>ADVANTAGES</u>
1. Easy to form (legal permission needed)
2. Issue stock to raise capital; banker underwrites stock issue and sells to public
3. Limited liability – Corp., distinct from its owners; can sue and be sued
4. "Perpetual succession," or existence. Board of directors
<u>ADVANTAGES TO SOCIETY</u>
1. Technical efficiency – production of goods & services
2. Pool business risks – continuation of production
3. Creates further capital for expansion or finance new
4. It is taxed

chosen and devising a question you can jot down in the margin of your summary sheet for which that fact provides the answer. This will function as written recitation. Then, once you have a question for every idea, cover up the answers and test yourself by reading each question and reciting the answer from memory, again and again, until you know the information cold. By judiciously selecting the very top ideas and by using your own set of questions to help memorize them, you will have a chance of passing the exam. You may not remember much once the test is over, but for now the objective is to survive the battle so that you can come back next term and continue the war.

Prepare Yourself Psychologically

OVERVIEWING — SELF-DIRECTION

What role should psychological preparation play in getting ready for an exam?

When it comes to getting ready for an upcoming exam, there's no substitute for academic preparation. But even if you know your material inside out, there's still an advantage to be gained from putting yourself in the proper mindset. Some students who experience test anxiety claim that even when they've studied hard, they still freeze when the test is placed in front of them. Although academic preparation is essential, a little psychological preparation can help take the sting out of an exam. If you take time to find out all you can about the exam, get yourself acquainted with the test site or a similar site, and work at maintaining a positive attitude, you're more likely to escape the test-taking anxiety that plagues unprepared students.

Find Out About the Exam

How can you lessen the fear of the unknown that contributes to test anxiety?

Fear of the unknown can be a great contributor to test anxiety. You can dispel some of this fear and its resulting anxiety by asking the instructor directly about the nature of the exam and by looking over previous exams for further clues. Asking the instructor seems so obvious that it's surprising how many students fail to do it. And yet, in many cases, instructors are not at all hesitant to discuss what the test will involve. Ask about the types of questions (objective, essay, or both), the length of the exam, and the materials (textbooks, notes, calculators) you'll be allowed to bring with you into the exam room. You can gain further clues about the nature of your upcoming exam by looking at exams from previous semesters and noting how each test was written and what the questions covered. When you do finally sit down to take the exam, you're less apt to be knocked off balance by surprises.

Get Acquainted with the Test Site

How can you get acquainted with your test site?

Exams may be held in auditoriums, large lecture halls, or ordinary classrooms. To be psychologically prepared for an exam, get acquainted with the site where the test will take place or with a similar location. A week or two before the exam, study for a few hours each evening at the site where you will be taking the test. Your familiarity with the room and the sense of control you feel while studying will help establish a link between working in this room and succeeding on the exam. If you can't study at the site of the test, you can still prepare yourself for the atmosphere of the test by studying in a quiet area, by practicing at a chairdesk if you know that's what you'll be sitting at for the exam, and by timing yourself as you work to get used to the challenge of performing under a deadline.

Maintain a Positive Attitude

How do you cultivate a positive attitude about an upcoming exam?

Of course, the ideas and strategies for managing stress (see Chapter 3) can be helpful throughout the semester. But often it's not until exam time that these techniques are truly put through their paces. It is essential to address the stress of a test with a can-do approach. Exam-anxious students often sabotage their own efforts by preparing themselves for failure. To counteract this inclination and to cultivate an optimistic attitude, use deep breathing and progressive muscle relaxation to help you relax, use affirmative statements to counter any negative self-talk, and use visualization to help chart a course for your success. Take a moment to review Chapter 3 to find the techniques that will work best for you.

Know What Each Question Requires

What should you know before you take a test?

Even natural athletes can falter in competition if they don't know the rules. Although the most important things you can do to gear up for a test are to master your material and be psychologically ready for the challenge, you also need to be well acquainted with the rules of the game. Depending on the nature of your test or quiz, that means understanding objective questions, learning the basics of writing an essay, or both.

Understand Objective Questions

PLANNING

Why are objective questions like pasta?

Objective questions are a bit like pasta in its various shapes. Each type may look different and many of us prefer one over another, but they're all basically made up of the same stuff. The primary ingredients of pasta are flour and water. The primary ingredients of objective questions are true and false statements. In the strictest sense, there are no real tricks for taking objective tests. The requirement for taking any test is basically the same: Know your material. Even so, it helps to understand how each question type works, to know the characteristics that will sometimes make it more complicated, and, finally, to be aware of certain rules and techniques that may not give you the answer, but can sometimes make answering a little easier.

True-False Leaves No Room for Ambiguity

How do true-false questions work?

The basic idea behind a true-false question is simple: Faced with a single statement, your job is to decide whether it's true. And when we say true, we mean true. The statement must be 100 percent true, not 50 percent or even 99 percent true. A partially true statement is still a false statement. Consider this example:

1.   T   F   In 1787, the year the United States ratified the Constitution, Washington, D.C., became the nation's capital.

The statement is false. Although the Constitution was ratified in 1787 and the nation's capital is Washington, D.C., the United States had no federal capital until 1790, when Congress chose Philadelphia. Washington didn't officially become the capital until June 10, 1800.

What makes true-false questions difficult?

Understanding What Makes Them Difficult One word can be all it takes to turn a true statement into a false one. For example, consider the impact of a word like *always* on a true-false statement or how words like *no* and *not* can radically change a statement's meaning. Words like *always*, *no*, and *not* are known as qualifiers. Other qualifiers include *all*, *some*, *most*, *many*, *usually*, *never*, and *none*. Simply adding one of these words can turn a true statement into a false one or a false statement into a true one. For that reason, you need to be extra sensitive to any qualifiers you encounter in a true-false statement.

Learning Techniques That Can Make Answering Them Easier

How can you make true-false questions easier?

Mark or circle each qualifier. Qualifiers can have such a huge impact on the meaning of a true-false statement that it's crucial not to overlook them. As you read through each statement for the first time, underline or circle any qualifiers. If you aren't sure whether a statement is true or false, try reading it without the qualifier or by swapping in a different qualifier. Comparing and contrasting the statements in this way can sometimes make it clearer whether the original was true or false.

Mark "True" if you're stumped. Because instructors would rather leave true information in your mind, they tend to stack true-false tests with more true statements than false ones. You shouldn't guess right away on a true-false question, but if you're stumped and pressed for time, the odds are in your favor if you choose true over false.

Be suspicious of longer statements. Remember the importance of context, and remember that true-false statements must be 100 percent true. Each word added to a true-false statement increases its chances of being false. All it takes is one incorrect word to make the statement false.

Multiple Choice Is a Cluster of True-False Statements

How do multiple-choice questions work?

A multiple-choice question normally begins with an incomplete sentence known as a *stem*, followed by a series of choices, known as *options*, for completing that sentence. In a typical multiple-choice question, your job is to find the option that completes the stem and makes the resulting statement true. In that sense, a classic multiple-choice question is like a cluster of true-false statements, each one beginning the same way but ending a little differently.

> In 1787, the year the United States ratified the Constitution,
> a. George Washington became the country's first president.
> b. Washington, D.C., became the nation's capital.
> c. New Mexico was admitted to the Union.
> d. the country had no official capital.

In this question, connecting option (d) to the stem results in a true statement. Linking the stem to any other option results in a false statement.

IT'S YOUR Q

Understanding What Makes Them Difficult Multiple-choice questions inherit the aspect that makes true-false statements harder. Just as a qualifier can transform a true statement into a false one (or vice versa), it can turn a correct option into a wrong one. Also, because a multiple-choice question is more complex than its true-false ancestor, it acquires some additional aspects that can make it a little more difficult to answer.

Varying directions. Some multiple-choice directions tell you to pick more than one correct option; others ask you to mark the one option that is *incorrect*. Be sure to read the directions carefully and go over all the options before you mark your selection.

Divided context. Because each choice in a multiple-choice question is usually divided into stem and option, you have to mentally connect the two components to determine whether an option is correct. Correct answers aren't always obvious, even when you know your material.

Differing format. Most multiple-choice questions follow the incomplete stem and option format. In some cases, however, the stem may be made up of an entire sentence. A setup of this sort can take you by surprise if you're expecting a standard multiple-choice question, but in general this variation is easier because you don't have to work with a divided context.

Learning Techniques That Can Make Answering Them Easier

How can you make multiple-choice questions easier?

Use the true-false technique. If you know your material but have a mental block about the multiple-choice format, you can gain a new perspective by treating the question as a series of true-false statements instead. Construct each statement in your head (or on paper) and decide whether it is true or false. The true statement you find in the true-false statements you create should contain the correct multiple-choice option. Here's an example:

Before becoming president in 1857, James Buchanan was
a. married and divorced.
b. secretary of state.
c. prime minister of Canada.
d. secretary of defense.

This question and its options can be thought of as four true-false statements:

1. T   F   Before becoming president in 1857, James Buchanan was married and divorced.
2. T   F   Before becoming president in 1857, James Buchanan was secretary of state.
3. T   F   Before becoming president in 1857, James Buchanan was prime minister of Canada.
4. T   F   Before becoming president in 1857, James Buchanan was secretary of defense.

Viewing the question this way can sometimes make it easier to spot the correct answer. (In this case, the correct answer is b.) The true statement you find in the true-false statements you create usually contains the correct multiple-choice option.

Discard foolish options. Not all of the options in a multiple-choice question provide a plausible way of completing the stem. Some of the options are downright silly. If you spot one of these foolish options, known as *distracters*, you can eliminate it right away, and choose your answer from the options that remain. Any time you can reduce your possible choices in a multiple-choice question, you improve your odds of selecting the correct answer. In that sense, a foolish option can be considered a gift.

Choose the middle number from a range of numbers. Test writers usually include at least one number lower than the correct answer and one number higher. Using this "rule," you can often eliminate half the options in a four-option question. If you know the correct answer, then by all means pick that one. But if you're stumped by the question and have no other information to go on, you can increase your odds of guessing correctly by choosing a number in the middle.

Pick "all of the above" if you're in doubt. As the purpose behind a quiz or exam is not only to test but also to teach, "all of the above" becomes an attractive choice for the test maker because it allows a single question to convey several facts instead of just one. So, if you don't know the correct answer in a multiple-choice question and "all of the above" is an option, choosing "all of the above" can be a pretty safe bet.

Do a double-check when you choose "all of the above." You don't normally have to confirm that all of the options are correct when you choose "all of the above." You just have to verify two. If you are unsure whether one particular option is correct, but you know that the other two are, then you should have all the information you need to choose "all of the above."

www.cengage.com/success/Pauk/HowToStudy11e

How do matching
questions work?

Matching Is a Multiple, Multiple Choice

Items in a matching test are usually divided into two columns and arranged in random order. Using a relationship that is normally explained in the directions, you systematically match the items in one column with the items in the other.

Groundbreaking Women of Science

Directions: Match the name of the scientist in the left-hand column with her discovery or distinction in the right-hand column by writing the proper letter in the space provided alongside each scientist's name. Use each item from the right-hand column only once.

Scientist	Discovery or Distinction
_____ 1. Rachel Carson	a. Created the first programming language
_____ 2. Mary Leakey	b. Devised the system for classifying stars by brightness
_____ 3. Marie Curie	c. Garnered a Nobel Prize for her groundbreaking work in genetics
_____ 4. Margaret Mead	d. Earned fame for children's books but gained respect as a mycologist
_____ 5. Jane Goodall	e. First female physics instructor at Princeton University
_____ 6. Grace Hopper	f. Best known as an actress, she patented the technology that makes WiFi possible
_____ 7. Georgia Rooks Dwelle	g. First woman elected to the National Academy of Sciences
_____ 8. Caroline Herschel	h. First American woman in space
_____ 9. Florence Sabin	i. Founded the first hospital for African American women
_____ 10. Hedy Lamarr	j. Invented the compiler, a critical element in most computer programs
_____ 11. Chien-Shiung Wu	k. Studied chimpanzees as a means of understanding human evolution
_____ 12. Beatrix Potter	l. Popularized anthropology with her book *Coming of Age in Samoa*
_____ 13. Barbara McClintock	m. Received two Nobel Prizes for her work on radioactivity
_____ 14. Annie Jump Cannon	n. Uncovered fossils that helped unlock the origins of humankind
_____ 15. Sally Ride	o. Founded the contemporary environmental movement
_____ 16. Ada Byron King	p. Teamed up with her brother to discover the planet Uranus

Answers: 1. o   2. n   3. m   4. l   5. k   6. j   7. i   8. p   9. g   10. f
11. e   12. d   13. c   14. b   15. h   16. a

CHAPTER
12

(Consider the test shown on the previous page.) Matching tests work like multiple-choice questions with an added dimension. You're faced with a *multiple*, multiple choice. Instead of one stem and several options, you have several stems and several options.

Understanding What Makes Them Difficult Answering a matching question is a bit like filling in a crossword or doing a jigsaw. If you make one mistake, it can sometimes lead to a chain reaction of errors. Therefore, you need to be confident that each match you make is correct before you move on to the next match.

Learning Techniques That Can Make Answering Them Easier

IT'S YOUR Q

Mark off matches to avoid redundancy. Each time you correctly match two items, cross them off or mark them with a circle or an X. If you're taking your test on a computer screen you might want to keep a running tally on a piece of scratch paper, crossing off the number and letter of each match you make. That way, when you move on to the next match, you'll have fewer items to read, and you won't be confused about which items you've chosen and which ones you haven't.

Match shorter items to longer ones. In most matching tests, the items in one column are usually longer than the items in the other. For example, a typical matching test might contain a column of terms and a column of definitions. In cases like these, you can save yourself some time if you set out in search of matches for the longer items instead of the reverse. In other words, the column you keep reading and rereading contains the shorter items. That way you need to read each long item only once. It's a case of the dog wagging the tail instead of the other way around.

Sentence Completion Is Multiple Choice Without the Choice

How do sentence-completion questions work?

Sentence-completion questions work like multiple-choice questions without the choice. A typical sentence-completion question consists of a partial sentence and one or more blanks. Your job is to read the sentences and to use both context and recall to determine what words belong in the blanks.

What makes sentence-completion questions difficult?

Understanding What Makes Them Difficult Unlike answering true-false, multiple-choice, and matching questions, answering a sentence-completion question requires recall instead of recognition. You have to extract the answer from your memory instead of picking it out from the exam page or computer screen. Recall is almost always better from a standpoint of learning, but it can be a little harder when you're taking a test.

www.cengage.com/success/Pauk/HowToStudy11e

Learning Techniques That Can Make Answering Them Easier

How can you make
sentence-completion
questions easier?

Try to clarify any ambiguity. Sometimes a question seems to have two or more reasonable answers. In these cases, you may need to clarify the type of answer the question is seeking by raising your hand and asking a well-formulated, unambiguous question of your own to clear up the confusion.

Disregard the length of the blank. With sentence-completion questions, the length of the blank is usually irrelevant. Use the context of the sentence, not the length of the blank, to help you arrive at your answer.

Treat some sentences as multiple questions. Even students who aren't influenced by the size of one blank when answering a sentence-completion question may become flustered by a question that has two blanks. If the blanks are side by side, the question may be calling for a person's name or a place name. Paying attention to the question's context should help you confirm whether this is the case. But if the blanks in a sentence-completion question are widely separated instead of side by side, the best way to treat them is as if each occurred in a separate sentence. There may or may not be a direct relationship between the missing words, so make sure that each filled-in word makes sense in its own part of the statement. Consider this example:

1. Although corn is second only to _____ as the most widely grown crop in the world, no one in Europe had even heard about corn until _____ returned from the New World.

   In the first portion of the sentence, the word *corn* indicates that you're dealing with a grain. If you had read your textbook carefully (or if you made an intelligent guess), you'd know the answer is wheat. The second blank calls for a person's name: Columbus.

Learn the Basics of Writing an Essay

SUMMARIZING

How do you write an
effective essay?

To write an effective essay, you need to be able to understand each question with precision and provide a carefully constructed answer.

Understand Each Question with Precision

Why is it important
to understand the
questions precisely?

A precise question requires a precise answer. Read each question carefully so you understand exactly what it is asking. A good essay question is never vague or ambiguous. As you can see from Figure 12.5, words such as *criticize*, *describe*, and *interpret* have specific definitions. Therefore, if you have even the slightest uncertainty about what's being asked, don't hesitate to check with the instructor for clarification.

Provide a Carefully Constructed Answer

What are the qualities of a carefully constructed answer?

For better or worse, an essay answer provides a kind of snapshot of your thinking processes. Depending on who is reading your essay (the instructor, a teaching assistant, or someone else), this may be the only glimpse the grader gets of who you are and what you know. That's why it's important that each essay is well organized, well supported, and neatly written.

What can you do to make sure your essay is well organized?

Be Sure the Path of Your Answer Is Easy to Follow Essay exams are written in a hurry and are often read in a hurry. Graders usually have a lot of essays to read and seldom have the time or patience to untangle a convoluted answer. You have to be concise! Answer the question right at the start of the essay, choose a recognizable organizational pattern, use clear transitions, and wrap things up neatly with a summary. Wordy answers may be the refuge for unprepared students who hope to bury their ignorance under a heavy blanket of overstuffed sentences, but they seldom fool an experienced grader. This is no time for lavish flourishes or excessive subtlety. Clearly show what you know as soon as possible. Don't waste your time or the grader's with any sort of introduction. Start with the question itself, turn it into the stem of your opening sentence, and complete it with your answer. (See Figures 12.6 and 12.7 for some examples of how to do this.) Then figuratively take your reader by the hand and lead him or her along the path of your essay by organizing your answer with a recognizable pattern such as decreasing importance or comparison/contrast (see Chapter 5). Make things that much easier to follow by inserting transitional words and phrases to act as signposts whenever you change direction or introduce evidence during the course of your essay.

Then finish things off with a summarizing conclusion that ties your points together and reminds the grader of the original answer that you wrote back at the beginning. These suggestions for organizing your essay become even more compelling when you learn how essays are actually graded. Figure 12.8 takes a brief behind-the-scenes look at an essay exam grading session.

What kind of support should you include in your essay?

Devote the Bulk of Your Essay to Supporting Your Answer Instructors rarely include essay questions to learn how you *feel*. They want to find out how you *think* and what you *know*. The best way to make a good impression and earn a good grade is to write essays that are well supported. Back up your answer with solid evidence, support any general opinions, and steer clear of personal opinions unless they are specifically requested. Provide examples, details, and further evidence for your initial answer and its major points. If you can support your answer with ideas or sources that your

Figure 12.5
Keywords in Essay Questions
This alphabetical list contains keywords encountered in the directions for essay questions, along with brief explanations of what each word means.

Key Word	Explanation
Apply a principle	Show how a principle works, through an example.
Comment	Discuss briefly.
Compare	Emphasize similarities, but also present differences.
Contrast	Give differences only.
Criticize	Give your judgment of good points and limitations, with evidence.
Define	Give meanings but no details.
Demonstrate	Show or prove an opinion, evaluation, or judgment.
Describe	State the particulars in detail.
Diagram	Show a drawing with labels.
Differentiate	Show how two things are different.
Discuss	Give reasons pro and con, with details.
Distinguish	Show main differences between two things.
Enumerate	List the points.
Evaluate	Discuss advantages and disadvantages with your opinion.
Explain	Give reasons for happenings or situations.
Give cause and effect	Describe the steps that lead to an event or a situation.
Give an example	Give a concrete example from the textbook or from your experience.
Identify	List and describe.
Illustrate	Give an example.
Interpret	State the meaning in simpler terms, using your judgment.
Justify	Prove or give reasons.
List	List without details.
Outline	Make a short summary with headings and subheadings.
Prove	Give evidence and reasons.
Relate	Show how things interconnect.
Review	Show main points or events in summary form.
Show	List your evidence in order of time, importance, logic.
Solve	Come up with a solution based on given facts or your knowledge.
State	List main points briefly without details.
Summarize	Organize and bring together the main points only.
Support	Back up a statement with facts and proof.
Trace	Give main points from beginning to end of an event.

CHAPTER 12

Figure 12.6
A Paragraph-Length Essay

> *Question:* Identify three of the theories psychologists have suggested to explain forgetting.
>
> *Answer:* Three of the theories that psychologists have suggested to explain how forgetting occurs include fading theory, retrieval theory, and reactive interference theory. Fading theory defines memories as paths or traces in the brain. According to the theory, if these paths aren't used (recalled) regularly, they fade until they eventually disappear (are forgotten). Retrieval theory claims that memories never really disappear; they simply get lost or misfiled, like important information buried under piles of paper on a messy desk. Reactive interference theory says that your attitude or emotions can interfere with your memory. If you are bored with or bothered by information, there's a greater chance that you will forget it. In certain cases, evidence seems to support all these theories of forgetting. But they remain only theories. None of them can be proved conclusively.

instructor has stressed in class, you would be wise to do so. An essay that incorporates some of the instructor's "pet ideas" is more likely to be viewed in a positive light. According to respected educator Hugo Hartig, author of *The Idea of Composition*:

> An alert student can easily identify these "pet ideas" and work them out carefully in his own words. The student who does this is prepared not only to see through the instructor's questions quite readily, but he also knows exactly how to answer them, using the teacher's own methods of problem solving! Perhaps this is the very essence of grade-getting in any course that depends heavily on essay exams.[1]

Don't assume that even general opinions will unquestionably be accepted as fact. As Hartig explains,

> If you make the statement: "*Huckleberry Finn* is a masterpiece of American literature," and do not give any good reason to show that the statement is true, you get a zero for the statement.[2]

And finally, unless asked for them specifically, keep your personal opinions out of your essay. Informed or uninformed, knowledgeable or ignorant, all of us have opinions. But that's not what the instructor is looking for. The purpose of essay exams, after all, is to see what you've learned and how you can apply it.

How can you improve your essay's appearance?

Pay Attention to Appearance as well as to Content In a carefully controlled experiment mixing neatly handwritten essay answers with others in which the handwriting was poor, instructors consistently gave better grades to the neater essays, even when

[1] Hugo Hartig, *The Idea of Composition* (Oshkosh, WI: Academia, 1974), p. 32.
[2] Ibid., p. 31.

www.cengage.com/success/Pauk/HowToStudy11e

Figure 12.7
A Longer Essay Answer

Question: Compare and contrast reciting and rereading as methods of study.

Answer: Although reciting and rereading are both common methods of study, reciting is superior to rereading as a way of mastering your material. Unlike rereading, reciting (1) gets you involved, (2) supplies motivation, and (3) provides you with feedback on your progress.

1. Reciting gets you involved by compelling you to extract the meaning out of each paragraph you read. In contrast, it's possible to reread an assignment without understanding it.

2. Reciting supplies motivation because it encourages you to understand what you've read. If you had trouble grasping the meaning of one paragraph, you may be determined to have an easier time with the next one. If you understood a paragraph, you'll be motivated to continue your progress. But if you simply reread your assignment, you'll have no such incentive to succeed.

3. Because you know right away whether you've understood each paragraph, reciting provides you with immediate feedback on your progress. Potential trouble spots in your reading are brought to your attention right away. With rereading, the first real feedback you get is delayed until the test or quiz.

they were word-for-word duplicates of the sloppy ones and graders were told explicitly to grade the essays *solely on the basis of their content*. The appearance of your essay has an unconscious effect on how it gets graded. Manage that appearance by writing legibly and on only one side of the sheet, by leaving ample space around each essay, and by avoiding careless errors. Writing in pen instead of pencil will make almost any handwriting look better. If your handwriting is less than it should be, start using the modified printing style explained in Chapter 10. Write on only one side of each sheet of paper so the writing on one side won't show through to the other. Leaving a little "breathing room" around the edges of your essay will not only make your answer look tidier, but it will also provide room for any grader's comments and give you space to insert any last-minute facts or ideas. Above all, keep your essay free of needless errors in grammar or spelling, which can be every bit as costly to your grade as sloppy handwriting. As Hartig observes:

> If you misspell common words, and make clumsy errors in sentence structure, or even if you write paragraphs that lack unity and coherence, many of your instructors are going to take it as a sure sign that you are sadly lacking in basic academic ability. Once a teacher thinks this about you, you will not get much credit for your ideas, even if they are brilliant.[3]

[3]Ibid.

Figure 12.8
The Essay Grading Process

> ### Behind the Scenes at an Essay Exam Grading Session
>
> What happens after you finish your last essay, heave a sigh of relief, and hand in your exam? Although grading procedures may vary from school to school, here is how more than 200 examination booklets in a popular introductory history course are graded at one college.
>
> The day of the exam, each grader in the history department has time to scan, but not to grade, the answer booklets. Then at a meeting the next day, each grader reads aloud what he or she thinks is the one best answer for each question. A model answer for each question is then agreed on by the staff. The essential points in the model answers are noted by all the graders for use as common criteria in grading the responses.
>
> Unfortunately, simply listing all the essential points in your essay won't automatically earn you a superior score. During the reading of the answers, one grader remarks, "Yes, this student mentioned points five and six . . . but I think he didn't realize what he was doing. He just happened to use the right words as he was explaining point four."
>
> These comments reinforce the importance of crystal-clear organization in your essay. You may also want to underline the main point of the essay so it's obvious and mark off your subpoints with dark numbers. Don't forget to include transitional words to show how you got from one idea to the next. Make sure that no one thinks you just stumbled on to the correct answer.

Work Systematically

Why are students tempted to rush through exams?

When an exam is handed out, some students have difficulty resisting the temptation to jump right in. Confident students are often anxious to "get down to business" and show what they know; apprehensive test takers want to get the whole thing over with as quickly as possible. At first glance, these behaviors seem reasonable because time is limited. But if you take a few moments to plan a systematic response to the test, you'll be a lot more efficient as a result. A little preparation saves you a lot more time than it uses. You can make the most of your test-taking experience if you read before you answer, map out your time wisely, and use markings or jottings to help you move through the test more methodically and efficiently.

Read Before You Answer

What causes some students to skip over the obvious step of reading?

It may sound silly to suggest reading through the test before you begin answering. After all, the advice seems obvious. But because of anxiety and time pressure, common sense is often a casualty, and many students skip the directions and even rush through the questions without paying attention to what they say. In the long run, cutting corners on these crucial elements of a test could cost you time and points. Take a few moments to read the directions before you make a single mark on your test and then read the questions carefully as well.

Read the Directions First

Why should you read the directions first?

Exam directions often contain vital instructions for answering the questions. They may establish the length of your answers (1 paragraph, 300 words, 5 pages), the approach you should take (explain, compare, contrast, mark the two best options), the number of questions to be answered (say, half of the questions presented), or the overall time you've been allotted. If you miss such instructions, you may endanger your grade, waste a great deal of time, and even invite criticism for carelessness.

Read the Questions Carefully

IT'S YOUR Q

The text of a test question is usually very dense. If it's an objective question, it may be peppered with clauses, qualifiers, or negatives that can have a huge impact on its meaning. If it's an essay question, as we've already seen, whether it says *evaluate*, *enumerate*, or *interpret* can make a big difference in the instructor's expectations for your answer. For that reason, read each question carefully to pick up important details and context. If the questions are part of an objective test, you can read each question as you encounter it. If the questions are part of an essay test, it's best to read all of the questions before you write anything. This will give you a better sense of how to budget your time. If you have a choice among questions, you will be able to select those for which you are best prepared. If you have to answer every question, you'll know in advance which ones will require the most attention. And if several questions tackle different aspects of the same topic or issue, you'll be able to avoid including information in one answer that should have been saved for another.

Map Out Your Time

How can you map out your time?

Once you've carefully read over the directions and questions and jotted down any thoughts you may have, you should be able to get a realistic sense of how much time remains for answering the questions. Using this as a starting point, divide the time you have left by the number of questions to figure out roughly how much time you can spend on each question in order to complete the test. Stick as close to your time plan as you can, but don't become overly anxious or rigid about doing so.

Answer the Easiest Question First

A good way to get a head start is by tackling the easiest question first. Nothing inspires confidence and clear thinking more than answering one question right away. If the first question has you stumped, don't let it deflate your morale and throw off your time plan. Just pick an easier question and build on the momentum that you get from answering it to your satisfaction.

Keep Your Schedule Flexible

Of course, even with an easy question under your belt, your time schedule still may not go exactly as planned. It's important to keep your schedule flexible by developing strategies to deal with both a time shortage and a time surplus. If time is running out, zero in on any remaining easy questions and tackle them first. If you've got essay questions remaining, outline the key points you were trying to make in any unfinished questions. Instructors sometimes award partial credit when you can demonstrate that you know the material. If you finish early, use the surplus time to your advantage by going over your exam and rechecking your answers, especially any you were uncertain about. If you've answered essay questions, use any extra time to double-check your spelling and grammar, and, if necessary, insert words, phrases, and examples that may make your answers clearer.

Use Markings and Jottings

PLANNING

In some exam settings, the most underused piece of paper is the question sheet itself. Except in tests in which the question and answer sheets are the same, in tests in which writing on the question sheet isn't allowed, or when the test is onscreen instead of on paper, you can often use the question sheet as a helpful scratch pad as you're progressing through the test. You can use the back of the sheet to jot down important ideas you want to remember. You can use the front to annotate questions, cross off certain items, and highlight any questions that deserve extra attention.

Make Notes on the Back of Your Exam Sheet In the few minutes before you begin an exam, your brain may be buzzing with information you want to include or remember. Before you begin reading the test, do a quick "data dump": Unburden your mind by jotting on the back of the exam sheet the ideas, facts, and details you think you may forget. Almost like a summary of your summary sheets, these jottings act as cues for the Silver Dollar ideas you gleaned from your lectures and readings (see Chapter 11). Furthermore, the action of writing these notes involves you in the exam immediately. But remember: You are graded for what you write on the front of the exam, so don't spend more than a minute or so jotting down reminders on the back.

Annotate Each Question As you read through each question, underline or circle important words that provide clues for answering that question. With objective questions, these will likely be the qualifiers and negatives that can make a simple question more complex. With essay questions, these will be words such as *contrast, demonstrate, summarize,* or any other word or phrase that provides insights into the type of answer that is expected. If the directions ask for an essay answer, you may also want to keep track of any keywords or key phrases that come to mind by jotting them in the margin. Later, when you begin writing, use these jottings and those on the back of the exam sheet to help organize your answer.

What sorts of choices should you cross off?

Cross Off Choices You've Used or Eliminated If you're answering objective questions, you can cross off any multiple-choice options you've been able to eliminate or cross off the items in a matching question that you've already used. If you're taking an essay test and are expected to answer only some of the questions, cross off the questions you don't plan to answer. Then, as you answer the questions that remain, you can cross them off as well. In each case, whether you're answering essay questions or objective questions, crossing off items will help to simplify your job and provide the same sort of sense of accomplishment you get when you cross an item off a to-do list.

What kinds of questions should you mark?

Put a Mark Next to Questions Requiring Special Attention Annotating certain questions with a circle or a check mark can make it easier to distinguish them from the rest of the questions in the test. Which questions you choose to mark depends on your purpose. If you're taking an essay test in which you have to answer only some of the questions, you might want to mark the questions you plan to complete. If you've answered an objective question but you're not confident about that answer, you could add the mark to remind you to go back and double-check your response if you have time. Regardless of the marking strategy you use, it should make taking a test a bit more efficient and methodical.

Learn from Experience

What should you do with a test once it's been returned to you?

Once a test or quiz is over, whether you did well or you did poorly, the urge to "move on" or to "put it behind you" can be strong. Don't give in to that particular temptation. The test is more than just a score. It's an informative record of how you perform on a variety of topics and question types. Before you stash the test in a desk drawer or worse, take a few minutes to systematically survey the results. To get the most out of returned exams, analyze your answers and then, based on your analysis, adjust your strategy for taking future tests.

Analyze Your Answers

SUMMARIZING — REFRAMING

What can you learn from your test?

Unless you earned a perfect score, you missed some questions and answered others correctly. On some questions, particularly essay questions, your answer may be accompanied by comments from the grader. You can learn something valuable from your mistakes, from your correct answers, and especially from any comments on your test.

Why is essay grading like a major league strike zone?

Instructors usually try very hard to remain objective and establish a clear set of expectations, but there is almost always an element of subjectivity in the grading of essays. In that respect it's a bit like the strike zone in major league baseball. Although the official baseball rulebook describes the theoretical strike zone in considerable detail, most players know that in reality that zone may shrink or expand depending on the particular interpretation of the home plate umpire. A wise ballplayer quickly learns the boundaries of the current strike zone and makes a point to adjust. In the same way, a savvy student uses the feedback she receives from one test to help her to adjust the way that she writes her essays in subsequent tests.

What questions should you ask yourself as you analyze your mistakes?

Examine Your Mistakes Look over any objective questions you missed and, if the answer hasn't been provided for you, see if you can figure out what it was supposed to be. If the answer is provided, try to discover why you didn't choose it. Was it a case of failing to recall a detail or fact? Misunderstanding an important idea or concept? Or did you misinterpret the wording of the question? Seeking the correct answer in this way will encourage you to reflect on your answers. This reflection should help to strengthen your memory of the correct information, so it will be more readily available the next time you should need it.

What can you learn by analyzing your correct answers?

Inventory Your Correct Answers Oddly enough, wrong answers probably provide more information, but you can learn from your correct answers as well. Take an inventory of the questions you answered correctly. Is there a pattern you detect? Do you perform better on multiple-choice questions than on true-false? Are you better at essay questions than objective questions? Do you remember dates but forget names? Are you good at details but bad at concepts? Once again, these questions encourage reflection and help you to arrive at some conclusions that you can use in preparing for future tests.

Why are the grader's comments valuable?

Pay Close Attention to Comments Carefully look over any comments that the instructor or grader has added to your test sheet. What did he or she like? Dislike? Some instructors may not clearly articulate their standards or preferences in class but will convey them in comments on a test paper, especially in the case of essay questions. Analyze these comments and see if you can draw some conclusions about the instructor's expectations for test answers.

Plot a Course Correction

REFRAMING — SELF-DIRECTION

What similarities do students and navigators share?

Navigators at sea, on land, in the air, and even in space share some qualities in common: They all point their craft toward a destination and then carefully map out a route designed to get them there. That's how it's supposed to work, in theory. But in real life, the wind may shift, a road could be closed, a storm might blow in, or an engine could lose power. It's a rare route that doesn't require some sort of adjustment along the way. Navigators rely on constant feedback to determine whether a course correction is needed. In the same way, tests are your feedback as you head toward your academic goals. Depending on your own specific analysis of the test you've just taken, you may need to place greater emphasis on mastering the type of information you missed, gaining additional practice on types of questions you seem to struggle with, or working at moving through your tests more methodically. And if none of these strategies seems as though it will help to get you back on track, it might be a good idea to make an appointment to get your instructor's perspective or arrange to have a tutor provide you with the extra assistance you require.

FINAL WORDS

Exams don't have to be situations of stress. They can actually be times of great triumph. Know your material, know your test site, and know as much as you ethically can about the content of the upcoming test. But above all, know yourself. Learn to distinguish a natural sense of excitement from a damaging feeling of doom. Keep in mind that some of the world's greatest actors still feel nervous when they first walk on stage. But these actors quickly settle down when they realize the obvious: They know their lines and they know their abilities. Like an accomplished actor, with preparation and confidence you can overcome your initial hesitation and be a star.

CHAPTER CHECKUP

SENTENCE COMPLETION

Complete the following sentences with one of the three words listed below each sentence.

1. One of the most obvious but overlooked sources of information on an upcoming exam is your _____.

    instructor   **textbook**   **intuition**

2. In a test question, the qualifiers should be _____.

    avoided ˙   **circled**   **defined**

3. Key points in an unfinished essay should be _____.

    outlined   **combined**   **deleted**

MATCHING

In each blank space in the left column, write the letter preceding the phrase in the right column that matches the left item best.

_____ 1. Introduction	a. Allows for late additions as well as for instructor's comments
_____ 2. Context	b. Is provided when you read the entire question
_____ 3. "Switch hitting"	c. Statement that starts off a multiple-choice question
_____ 4. Homestretch	d. Schedule that ties up loose ends as exam week approaches
_____ 5. Reflection	e. Often provide specifics on how each question should be answered
_____ 6. Directions	f. Should be left off to ensure that your essay gets right to the point
_____ 7. Space	g. Added benefit that comes from creating advanced summary sheets
_____ 8. Stem	h. Mastering possible test material from both sides

TRUE-FALSE

Circle T *beside the* true *statements and* F *beside the* false *statements.*

1. T   F   If you've been using the Silver Dollar System, creating summary sheets should be relatively easy.
2. T   F   By finals week, the bulk of your exam preparation should be completed.
3. T   F   For a statement to be marked true, it must be entirely true.
4. T   F   With a sentence-completion question, the length of the blank dictates the size of the answer.
5. T   F   The appearance of your essay will have no influence on your grade.

www.cengage.com/success/Pauk/HowToStudy11e

MULTIPLE CHOICE   *Choose the word or phrase that completes each sentence most accurately, and circle the letter that precedes it.*

1. During exam week, it is OK to skip
   a. meals.
   b. sleep.
   c. recreation.
   d. none of the above.

2. Deep breathing can be used to produce feelings of
   a. relaxation.
   b. fatigue.
   c. anxiety.
   d. resentment.

3. A multiple-choice question can be viewed as a series of
   a. stems.
   b. qualifiers.
   c. true-false statements.
   d. decoys or distracters.

4. Jotting down notes on the back of the test sheet
   a. gets you involved right away.
   b. is usually not permitted in an essay exam.
   c. takes time that could be better spent.
   d. will often gain you partial credit.

5. Keywords in an essay question should be
   a. paraphrased.
   b. circled.
   c. discussed.
   d. replaced.

REFLECTION   *Think about the ideas outlined in this chapter and then draw upon your own opinions and experiences to answer each question fully.*

1. What is your biggest source of test anxiety? Explain how you hope to use a technique or method from this chapter to cope with that anxiety in the future.

2. Which type of objective question—true-false, multiple-choice, matching, sentence-completion—do you prefer? Which do you like the least? Why? Given what you now understand about how these questions are constructed, how do you think this will influence your preferences from now on?

3. Do you make a point of reviewing and analyzing your tests once they are returned to you? If so, can you cite a case in which doing this helped you to do better on a future test? If not, can you explain why you haven't done so up until now?

IT'S YOUR Q

The Q System uses marginal questions to encourage active reading. You'll notice that most but not all paragraphs in this chapter are accompanied by marginal questions. Now it's your Q. Scan the chapter for any paragraph that is missing a question, reread the paragraph, establish the main idea, and then arrive at a question that elicits it. Use the questions in the surrounding paragraphs as models for your own marginal questions.

VOCABULARY IN ACTION

To expand the horizons of your understanding and to refine the precision of your thought, the three exercises that follow are designed to help you grow, strengthen, and maintain your own vocabulary.

SAY WHAT?

From the three choices beside each numbered item, select the one that most nearly expresses the meaning of the italicized word in the quote. Make a light check mark (√) next to your choice.

If you are going to achieve *excellence* in big things, you develop the habit in little matters. Excellence is not an *exception*, it is a *prevailing* attitude.

—Colin Powell (1937–), American statesman and retired Army general

1. *excellence*	superiority	speed	notoriety
2. *exception*	objection	rarity	acquisition
3. *prevailing*	victorious	predominant	ordinary

Journalism is the only profession *explicitly* protected by the U.S. Constitution, because journalists are supposed to be the *check* and balance on government.

—Amy Goodman (1957–), American journalist

4. *explicitly*	expressly	obviously	suggestively
5. *check*	payment	restraint	inspection

VOCAB-U-LADDER

Use your knowledge of word synonyms and roots to connect the word at the top rung to the word at the bottom rung, using the words listed below.

educate
factual
instruct
manufacture
obstruct
produce

objective

synonyms for
"unbiased"

share root
"facere,"
"to do"

synonyms for
"make"

share root
"ducere,"
"to lead"

synonyms for
"teach"

share root
"struere,"
"to pile, build"

synonyms for
"hide"

obscure

Here's the story behind a word that figures prominently in the chapter you've just read.

Test **Exams may test your mettle, but the first tests tested metal**

test tĕst *n.* 1. A procedure for critical evaluation; a means of determining the presence, quality, or truth of something; a trial. 2. A series of questions, problems, or physical responses designed to determine knowledge, intelligence, or ability.*

Few words strike fear in the heart of students more than the word *test*. And yet *test* comes from a tool called a *testum* that was once used for a rather mundane, methodical purpose. The Latin word *testum* was a fireproof container, often made out of clay. It comes from another Latin word *testa*, which described an earthen pot or shell (which in turn grew out of another Latin word *testudo* for tortoise!). In ancient times, metals such as gold and silver were considered valuable, just as they are today. But it was necessary to determine whether a seller's silver was pure or his gold was in fact "as good as gold." As a result, experts would confirm the purity of the metals by melting a small sample in the *testum*. In time, the word for the pot used for testing your metal was expanded to include evaluations of all types, including the kind you take in a classroom with a blue book or a No. 2 pencil. By the way, what is the term used for testing metal in a *testum?* Assaying. Sound *familiar?* It should. It shares its root with "essay," still a key part of many modern-day tests.**

*Adapted from "test." *The American Heritage Dictionary of the English Language*, 4th ed. (Boston: Houghton Mifflin, 2000), http://dictionary.reference.com/browse/test (accessed May 26, 2009).
**Based on information from "test." *The American Heritage Dictionary of the English Language*, 4th ed. (Boston: Houghton Mifflin, 2000), http://dictionary.reference.com/browse/test (accessed May 26, 2009); "test." *Online Etymology Dictionary*. Douglas Harper, Historian, http://www.etymonline.com/index.php?search=test (accessed May 26, 2009); "test, *n.*" *Oxford English Dictionary*, 2nd ed. 20 vols. (Oxford: Oxford University Press, 1989).

Get the Most Out of Discussions

Do you want to raise the stakes for recitation? Do you want to do some high-quality reflection on the ideas you've learned from your lectures and texts? Some of the most valuable learning you can do comes from what is often the least valuable part of your overall grade. And yet, online or in class, discussions are a precious tool in the pursuit of knowledge. This chapter explains how to get the most out of discussions:

- **Do Your Homework**
- **Know the Ground Rules**
- **Participate Fully**
- **Follow Up Promptly**

In this chapter

Why are discussions not given more respect?

Discussions, whether held in class or online, are perhaps the most underappreciated component of any course. Why are discussions unsung? Part of it may be because their bearing on your grade—if they are graded at all—is relatively small. It may also be because discussions involve the significant participation of "ordinary people"— you and your classmates—instead of the "experts" who write textbooks or deliver lectures.

What are the benefits of discussions?

The potential benefit from discussions in fostering true understanding and long-lasting knowledge is huge. Discussions can breathe life into dormant ideas. They encourage active learning, allow for a kind of recitation that rivals most solitary study, and, perhaps most important, provide an opportunity to reflect on ideas through the perspectives of multiple minds instead of simply your own. That's why it's vital to treat discussions with the respect they deserve.

How do you get the most out of discussions?

To get the most out of a discussion, approach each one well prepared, make sure you're familiar with any ground rules your instructor has laid out, remain fully engaged throughout, and finally, review each discussion while it is still fresh in your mind.

Do Your Homework

What can you do to prepare for discussions in general?

The good thing about preparing for discussions is that, for the most part, if you've been keeping up with your assignments and reciting and reflecting on your textbook and lecture notes, then you should be well prepared already. Of course, sometimes you learn a little more about the scope of the discussion. Perhaps the instructor has set specific guidelines, such as "Read Chapter 5 and be prepared to discuss it on Monday," or has supplied one or more specific questions designed to start a discussion going. In either case, you can focus your study so you are better prepared for the discussion.

Prepare Based on Specific Readings

OVERVIEWING — PLANNING

How can you prepare for discussions based on specific readings?

If the instructor suggests that the discussion will revolve around a specific chapter or section, take your notes from that portion of the text and use them to create summary sheets similar to those discussed in Chapter 12. If you are more visually inclined, take a blank sheet of paper and write down some of the assigned text's important names, terms, and concepts, and then draw connectors between those items that are related. Annotate the connectors with brief explanations of each relationship. Your annotations might include words and phrases such as "worked with," "discovered," "invented," "opposed," and "led to." The resulting map should give you a "big picture" sense of what's important in the reading.

Prepare Based on Specific Questions

OVERVIEWING — PLANNING

How should you
prepare if you are
given the discussion
questions in advance?

If the instructor has given you one or more questions that will serve as the basis for
the discussion, it's a bit like preparing for a live-action essay test. Search back into your
notes for material that relates to the question or questions. Consolidate that material into summary sheets or create a concept map that pulls together all the important
names, terms, and concepts onto a single sheet, and then draw connectors between
related items. In either scenario, you should be able to use the resulting summary sheet
or concept map as a "cheat sheet" during the discussion, regardless of whether it takes
place in class or online.

Know the Ground Rules

What are the ground
rules for discussions?

To get the most out of class discussions, it helps to know the ground rules. That means
learning the instructor's expectations and getting acquainted with the specific discussion environment.

Learn What the Instructor Expects

OVERVIEWING

What should
you know about
your instructor's
expectations for
discussions?

Instructors' expectations for discussions can vary widely. However, you can usually
get a better handle on the role discussions play in a specific class by learning the percentage of your grade that will come from the discussion part of the course and by
reading any guidelines the instructor may have provided for taking part in discussions.

Find Out the Grade Percentage

IT'S YOUR Q

If you haven't done so already, check the class syllabus or the course website to see
how your instructor has divided up the components that make up your semester
grade. Discussions—sometimes just called "class participation"—often account for
the smallest percentage of your grade, but not always. With the increasing popularity of online discussions, some instructors are placing added emphasis on your
ability to carry on a discussion based on what you've read in your text or learned
in a lecture. At any rate, it can be risky or reckless to take this part of your class for
granted. Even in cases in which the instructor doesn't officially award any points for
discussions, your ability to successfully articulate key ideas from the course in a discussion may color the instructor's overall perception of your performance. Besides,
discussions provide an excellent "dress rehearsal" for essay tests and can sometimes
serve as an early warning sign if you are struggling with the concepts in your class.

Read Any Guidelines

What is the value
of knowing the
instructor's discussion
guidelines?

Some instructors like to keep the guidelines for the class participation portion of your grade rather vague so they have the flexibility to give you extra points (or take them away) at their own discretion. Others are very specific about the criteria they use for awarding your discussion or participation grade. Check to see if your instructor has furnished some guidelines for discussion performance. This can provide a goal you can aim for and may also alert you to any specific discussion dos and don'ts as far as the instructor is concerned.

Adapt to the Discussion Environment

REFRAMING

What should you
do to adapt to
your discussion
environment?

It wasn't all that long ago when class discussions could be understood to take place in only one environment: the classroom. But things have changed. More and more colleges and universities are conducting class discussions online. That doesn't mean that in-class discussions don't still exist. They definitely do. Some instructors may have moved their discussions online, but others continue to hold them in the classroom. Still others go with a mixture of both.

What are some key
differences between
classroom discussions
and online ones?

Many of the guidelines for discussions hold true whether you're discussing something face to face or keyboard to keyboard. But there are some conspicuous differences between the real and online discussion worlds, and just as knowing your audience is important if you're a writer or a speaker, understanding your environment is essential if you're taking part in a discussion. Figure 13.1 compares the classroom and online discussion environments.

Learn the Ropes if You're New to Discussion Software

What can you do
to become familiar
with your discussion
software?

Although the basic design for many online discussions is similar, their superficial appearance can sometimes be quite different. As a result, it's best to learn the basics of your course's particular discussion software so that you can become familiar with its layout and capabilities.

- *Follow the demo or tutorial.* Depending on the course management software you are using, there may be an interactive demo (demonstration) or tutorial available that will walk you through the functions you are most likely to use in an online discussion.
- *Get assistance from a fellow student.* If you're new to discussion software or uncomfortable using it, you may be able to find a friend at school or someone else in your class who can help you with the basics.
- *Contact your campus learning lab or skills center.* If your campus uses discussion software, it's likely that the entire school has adopted the same program. If so, someone at the learning lab or skills center should be able to help you out.
- *Ask your instructor.* If you can't figure out your discussion software on your own and have been unable to get help from a tutorial, a fellow student, or someone at the learning lab, check with your instructor. But before you do, carefully check the

Figure 13.1

How Classroom and Online Discussions Compare

	Classroom Discussions	Online Discussions
How can I keep track of the key points in a discussion?	Your notes, ears, and memory are your only real means of navigating an in-class discussion.	Threaded messages provide a helpful visual representation for organizing related comments.
What are some suggestions for planning the points I'm going to make?	Although writing cue cards or using regular notes can sometimes be helpful, delivering prewritten comments verbatim will sound awkward and obvious to all.	With asynchronous discussions, you can take your time. It's recommended but not essential to have some notes prepared in advance.
How should I handle any sources in my comment?	Paraphrasing a source is usually preferable to reading a direct quotation, although you must still be sure to attribute it.	Cutting and pasting quotations from your text or notes is usually permitted, but you must be certain to provide attribution.
What factors can affect the meaning of my message?	For better or worse, your posture, facial expression, and tone of voice are all elements of your message.	Without spoken or visual cues, careful phrasing and proper context are crucial if you don't want to be misunderstood.
When is it best to contribute my comment?	Wait for an opening. Participants aren't supposed to talk at once or interrupt each other during a classroom discussion.	Contribute when you can. Simultaneous posting is common although it can sometimes have the same effect as when letters (or e-mail messages) cross in the mail.
What happens to my comments once I've made them?	In-class comments are ephemeral. Impressions of what you said may linger, and your ideas may be retained in the notes of others, but your exact words are fleeting.	Your comments can be read and reread by others for days and weeks after you first posted them. Great insights and glaring errors are immortalized. So be careful!
What if I make a point that someone has already made?	If you've been paying attention, the chances of accidentally repeating someone else's point are quite small. Redundancy provides a sure indication that you haven't been participating actively.	The risks of inadvertently repeating a point that has already been made are greater than in a classroom discussion. Try to be sure you've read all earlier comments before posting.

instructor's syllabus or website to make sure they don't already provide advice or instructions for learning the software or a link to a site that will provide help. If no help is available, your instructor should be willing to provide some assistance. But if you ask the instructor for help that she or he has already provided elsewhere, you may start class off on the wrong foot.

- *Don't delay in getting assistance.* If your class uses discussion software, try to test it out at your earliest opportunity so you can seek help promptly if you need it. The longer you wait, the harder it may be to get help.

www.cengage.com/success/Pauk/HowToStudy11e

Participate Fully

How do you participate fully in a classroom or online discussion?

Regardless of whether your class discussions count for very little or make up a substantial part of your grade, you'll waste precious time and squander a valuable resource if you fail to participate fully in the exchange. Your full participation isn't just based on how many original points you make—although that can certainly be a factor. It begins when you listen actively and can use what you've just heard or read online to contribute your own ideas effectively.

Listen Actively

SELF-DIRECTION — PLANNING — CLUSTERING

How do you listen actively in a discussion?

Active listening is important in lectures, but it's even more vital in discussions, where the communication is by definition interactive. To listen actively in discussions, remain patient and perceptive, use notes both for recording and planning, and look for ways to connect your comments to what's already been said.

IT'S YOUR Q

Remain Patient and Perceptive

Although traditional lectures are sometimes difficult to follow, class discussions, with their multiple voices and looser structure, can be even tougher to track. Because your classmates' abilities to express their thoughts in an organized fashion are going to vary dramatically, it is essential to remain on heightened alert for any discourse cues. But above all, it is important to be patient. If you jump the gun and base your conclusion on the first few words of what a classmate contributed, you may be missing the point of what he/she said. Even a student who opens his/her answer with "I disagree" may not actually be disagreeing if you follow his/her response all the way to the end.

Take Notes

What should your discussion notes include?

Most students recognize the need for taking notes during traditional lectures. Far fewer see the value of note taking during discussions. Take notes not only to record the main ideas that participants in the discussion have contributed, but also to marshal your own thoughts so when the time comes, you can respond in a clear and organized fashion.

Look for Connections

What sorts of connections should you be looking for in discussions?

Some of the least effective discussions are little more than a series of isolated mini-lectures where each contributor seems oblivious to any other points that have already been made. You can often improve both your grade and the overall caliber of the discussion by seeking ways to attach any comments you have to points that have already been made. In instances where vivid or powerful examples or evidence have been used to support a main idea, revisiting these details from a different perspective can be an extremely effective technique. It shows not only that you've been listening carefully, but also that you can express your ideas concretely and think on the fly. Noting who said what in discussions can also add a valuable level of interaction and prove that you've been paying attention. If, for example, Rashad said something that you can refine with additional insight or evidence, it doesn't hurt to mention him by name when you make your contribution. Likewise, if Maria said something with which you disagree, you can mention her name when you make your contrasting point, as long as you're clear that your focus is her point and is not intended as any sort of personal attack. Discussions can be especially enriching when they are challenging, wide-ranging, unpredictable, and impassioned, but they should always rest on a foundation of respect for all the participants.

AIM to Make Your Points Effectively

SELF-DIRECTION — PLANNING — CLUSTERING

What should you do to truly be part of a discussion?

You can't truly be part of a discussion if you aren't participating actively. But even if you're conscientiously maintaining a positive attitude, working hard to pay attention, and nimbly adjusting to the discussion's unexpected twists and turns, you're unlikely to add anything to your grade until you take advantage of your active participation and chime in yourself.

How can you add something valuable to a discussion?

But how do you do it? You can't just jump recklessly into the fray. There's a real risk that a callous or careless contributor will do more harm to his or her grade than someone who rarely pipes up. To earn a good grade from your instructor, the respect of your classmates, and to truly add something valuable to a discussion, whether in-class or online, your AIM should be to make your points Accurate, Interactive, and Memorable.

Make Your Points Accurate

What do you need to make sure your points are accurate?

On one level, the expectations for the points you make in discussions are not all that different than those for essay answers you write. They need to be well supported and well expressed.

IT'S YOUR Q

Make Sure Your Comments Are Well Supported A discussion comment typically begins with some sort of assertion that is then fleshed out with facts. Sometimes the instructor will jump-start a discussion with an assertion of her or his own or a quotation from a respected source and then look to you and your classmates to explore its implications. Other times, you may introduce the assertion yourself. Unlike in essays, opinions are usually acceptable in discussions, but they still need to be backed up with material from your lectures or readings. It's legitimate to say either "I think Martin Luther King would be appalled by the state of the world if he were living today" or "I think Martin Luther King would be pleased by the state of the world if he were living today" as long as you can support your contention with evidence, examples, facts, and reasons.

www.cengage.com/success/Pauk/HowToStudy11e

How are comments best expressed in online or classroom discussions?

Make Sure Your Comments Are Well Expressed Even the best-supported assertions can still suffer if they are poorly expressed. Poorly expressed statements in a discussion—like bad handwriting in an essay—have a way of undermining otherwise good ideas. In online discussions, that means you should write in clear, complete, properly punctuated, grammatical sentences with words and names spelled correctly. The types of abbreviations and syntax you may be used to using on social networking websites or in text messages are generally not acceptable in an online class discussion. Because most online discussions are asynchronous, don't be in such a hurry to respond that you post something sloppy. If your course management software doesn't include a spell-checker, type your comment in a blank document of your word processor and then do a spell-check before adding it to the discussion. If you are making your comments in the classroom instead of online, it still pays to think in terms of the written word. Try to visualize the sentences as you are saying them, ending each with a period and including transitions to make your argument easier to follow. Simply visualizing such structures will almost automatically transform you into a thinking-on-your-feet kind of speaker instead of a shooting-off-your-mouth one. In sum, you'll be thinking rather than just rambling. When you come to the end of your point, a summarizing sentence—ending with a period—will be impressive.

Make Your Points Interactive

How are discussion points interactive?

The emphasis on well-supported, well-expressed points may share something in common with essay answers, but discussions are fundamentally different in one crucial respect. They're interactive. Each comment you make should connect in some way to the others, and each person who participates in the discussion should be part of the group instead of acting as a lone wolf.

What can you do to connect your comments to the rest of the discussion?

Keep the Comments Connected Skillfully integrate your comments into the general discussion by keeping to the topic at hand, steering clear of loose threads, and refraining from being a rubber stamp.

1. *Stay on topic.* Your comments may be interesting and even important, but if they're off the subject, they're irrelevant to the current discussion. Save them for the appropriate forum. If you're taking part in an online discussion, you may be able to start a new topic thread or add your comment to another existing discussion, but don't gum up the current one with needless detours or digressions. They don't reflect well on your ability to think in a clear and disciplined fashion.
2. *Avoid loose threads.* Even if your comment is on topic, it shouldn't just dangle freely. Work to weave it into the overall fabric of the discussion by referring specifically to other comments and then by supporting, refuting, or refining them.
3. *Don't be a rubber stamp.* "Me too" adds nothing to a discussion. If you agree with another comment, that's fine. But cite specific information from lectures or readings that explains why you concur. Above all, be sure to avoid making a point that has

already been made. Redundancy provides a sure sign to your classmates and, more important, to your instructor, that you haven't been paying attention.

Keep the Others in Mind Just as you want to make sure that your discussion comments fit into the topic at hand, it's also important that you make an effort to keep your classmates in mind by tying in their comments, treating them with sensitivity, keeping your voice down, and pausing for effect.

1. *Tie in the comments of others*. Even if the instructor started things off, it's good to try to relate your comment to the points made by several other classmates. Beginning your comment with a phrase such as "Although I share Anil and Julie's concerns, I am more inclined to agree with Juan that . . ." will help to make it clear that you have not only read or listened to the other comments but that you have actually *thought* about them.

2. *Be a diplomat*. There's a difference between being forceful and being rude. Don't let strong opinions overwhelm your ability to be civil and respectful. Be especially careful to steer clear of sarcasm, which may grant you a moment of supremacy but can lead to some long-term resentment. This can be tricky in online discussions in which you don't have the benefit of your facial expressions or your tone of voice to help make your intentions clear. Play it safe and make your comments constructive and straightforward.

3. *Turn the volume down*. Obviously, you need to be heard, but yelling isn't going to make your point any clearer. Let your choice of words, not their volume, provide the oomph in your assertion. Similarly, when posting to an online discussion, refrain from posting messages in all capital letters, which is generally considered to be the typographical equivalent to yelling.

4. *Take a breath*. Pauses not only give you a second to collect your thoughts and come up with a good opener, but if you're participating in a classroom discussion, the brief, unanticipated silence can actually stimulate the interest of the others. Most people view it as a signal that something important is coming. Online, you can provide the equivalent of pauses by breaking your post into paragraphs instead of adding an uninterrupted block of text.

Make Your Points Memorable

The interactive nature of discussions often provides insights and perspectives that couldn't be gained from individual study. But if your contributions are going to be a key part of the process and—from a practical standpoint—if they are going to earn you suitable recognition from your instructor and a superior grade, you need to ensure that your contributions are memorable by striving to make them easy to follow and fresh.

Make Your Points Easy to Follow We've seen how a clear organizational pattern makes it easier to follow another person's point. When it's your turn to contribute to the discussion, it helps to return the favor. State your point succinctly at the

IT'S YOUR Q

What helps to make your discussion comments memorable?

How can you make your points easy to follow?

www.cengage.com/success/Pauk/HowToStudy11e

outset. Don't make others have to read between the lines to figure out what you are saying. Then elaborate on your position by using a clear organizational pattern and including "signposts" (see Chapter 5). If you have a series of facts to support your original point, enumerate them by preceding each supporting fact with a number and by introducing your last supporting fact with the word "Finally." If you're comparing and/or contrasting your point with points made by others, begin each comparison with an obvious phrase, such as "Just as" or "In the same way" or "Like," and introduce each contrasting point with phrases such as "Unlike" or "In contrast to" or "On the other hand." A succinctly stated main point and clearly structured support supply an easy-to-follow framework that will make your comments more valuable and memorable.

What is it that makes discussion comments seem fresh?

Make Your Points Fresh Good instructors seldom want their students to behave like walking, talking versions of their lectures or readings. This robotic approach may be a simple test-passer but it rarely fosters genuine learning. That's why, in all but the most rigorous courses, instructors place a premium on fresh insights, not on rote regurgitation. In short, they are seeking creativity. You can do only so much to analyze ideas in different ways on your own. Even though it may have several facets, your thinking generally comes from a distinct perspective. Because they represent the meeting of many minds, discussions expose you to a wide variety of perspectives and provide an extraordinary opportunity for reflection. And, as Nobel Laureate Hans Bethe reminds us (see Chapter 11), creativity comes only with reflection.

Follow Up Promptly

Why is it important to promptly do a follow-up?

A good discussion may be full of fresh ideas, but those ideas will have a short shelf life if you don't make a concerted effort to reinforce them in your memory. As the Leon and Clyde episode (see Chapter 9) made all too clear, even brilliant insights can fade quickly if you don't do something to fix them in your memory.

Review In-Class Discussions

SUMMARIZING

Why are in-class discussions so easy to forget?

Discussions that take place in the classroom are especially susceptible to the ravages of forgetting. Ideas and facts spend such a brief time in your working memory that a key point at the beginning of a classmate's comment could be gone without a trace before she or he is even finished talking! And because class discussions are more interactive than regular lectures, you may not be able to take notes as thoroughly as you'd like.

IT'S YOUR Q

Some students try to solve this problem by recording class discussions electronically. This is a mistake on a number of levels:

- *It's a waste of time.* The discussion will take twice as long because you'll be compelled to replay the entire recording once you're home.
- *It's an invitation to inattention.* Recording a discussion can discourage you from remaining fully engaged because you're aware—whether consciously or not—that you can go back and catch what you missed in class by listening to the recording.
- *It's a technical gamble.* Unless you have a very good recorder or a number of microphones, you may not be able to make out all of the comments when you go back and listen to them.

What's the best note-taking strategy for discussions?

Your best strategy for following discussions is to use the two-page system (explained in Chapter 10). With the main points on one page and important details on the other, you should be able to reconstruct a lot of what went on in the discussion, providing you are careful to review your notes right away while you're still able to fill in some of the missing pieces. You can further improve your memory of the discussion by labeling each point in your notes with the name of the person who made it. Associating each idea with a name and a face will strengthen its memory. Finally, because all the comments won't be coming from the same part of the classroom, you can use the loci method (see Chapter 9) to trigger memories of the points that came from various parts of the room.

Review Online Discussions

SUMMARIZING

What are the drawbacks to reviewing online discussions?

Asynchronous online discussions aren't as susceptible to your forgetting them as are discussions that are held in a classroom setting. That's because the threads retain a record of everything that's been "said" during the course of a discussion. But online discussions have their own special drawbacks. Depending on the nature of your course management software, most of the important discussion points are at least one click away, hidden beneath a hyperlinked thread title that may not be especially informative. Also, an online discussion that is many threads deep can result in a snakelike string of links that can be intimidating to approach.

What's the best strategy for reviewing online discussions?

Your best strategy for reviewing online discussions is to do so on an ongoing basis, rather than waiting until the discussion is over. Each time you read a message, try to determine its main point right away, just as you would with a paragraph in your textbook. Then type or jot down that point. If the messages are grouped in threads, try to summarize all the comments in each thread, just as you would summarize a page of your notes (see Chapter 11). Most discussion programs automatically change the color of a link after you've read its associated post. If you make a point to capture the main idea right away, the color change will not only tell you that it's a message you've read, but also that it's one you've taken notes for. That knowledge should make a dense page of threads a little less intimidating and should actually provide encouragement as you get a visual sense of the progress you've made. Also, it should make reviewing an online discussion much easier. Instead of having to painstakingly reread each thread, you should be able to conduct a thorough review of the discussion without even logging on.

FINAL WORDS

What is an unexpected outcome of some class discussions?

Like tests, quizzes, and papers, discussions provide an opportunity to take your knowledge and explain it—in short, to show what you know. But unlike the other three, which are essentially solitary activities, discussions require interaction with others. This not only encourages insight and reflection as we've seen, but it can also result in something unexpected: friendship. This underscores the motivation for treating other participants with respect. After all, the person you're agreeing (or disagreeing) with may start out as just a classmate and wind up as a good friend.

CHAPTER CHECKUP

SENTENCE COMPLETION

Complete the following sentences with one of the three words listed below each sentence.

1. The number of colleges and universities using online discussions is _____.

   increasing   **decreasing**   **stagnant**

2. During discussions, you should use your notes both for recording and _____.

   playback   **planning**   **reciting**

3. Posting a message in all capital letters is generally considered to signify _____.

   agreement   **disagreement**   **yelling**

MATCHING

In each blank space in the left column, write the letter preceding the phrase in the right column that matches the left item best.

_____ 1. Class participation a. Provides a tool for discussion preparation

_____ 2. Sarcasm b. Should be provided when you cite sources during a discussion

_____ 3. Concept map c. Often accounts for the smallest percentage of your overall grade.

_____ 4. Attribution d. Can sometimes be an unexpected by-product of discussions

_____ 5. Redundancy e. Often indicates that you haven't been paying attention to the discussion

_____ 6. Respect f. Can provide an effective means of drawing attention to your comments

_____ 7. Friendship g. May provide a brief moment of supremacy but can often lead to resentment

_____ 8. Pauses h. Should always lie at the foundation of discussions

TRUE-FALSE

Circle T *beside the true statements and* F *beside the false statements.*

1. T F Discussions are often the most appreciated component of a course.
2. T F Discussions can provide an excellent "dress rehearsal" for essay tests.
3. T F Many of the guidelines for discussions apply whether the discussion is in class or online.
4. T F Simultaneous posting is rare in online discussions.
5. T F Your comments on an online discussion can normally be read for days after you've posted them.

www.cengage.com/success/Pauk/HowToStudy11e

MULTIPLE CHOICE   *Choose the word or phrase that completes each sentence most accurately, and circle the letter that precedes it.*

1. Discussions
    a. encourage active learning.
    b. allow for superior reciting.
    c. provide reflection from many perspectives.
    d. all of the above.

2. In-class discussion comments are usually
    a. brief.
    b. ephemeral.
    c. archived.
    d. required.

3. With in-class discussions, the meaning of your message can be affected by your
    a. facial expression.
    b. tone of voice.
    c. posture.
    d. all of the above.

4. Recording in-class discussions electronically is
    a. a technical gamble.
    b. a waste of time.
    c. an invitation to inattention.
    d. all of the above.

5. After you've read a particular discussion post, most programs automatically change its
    a. time stamp.
    b. link color.
    c. ranking.
    d. password.

REFLECTION   *Think about the ideas outlined in this chapter and then draw upon your own opinions and experiences to answer each question fully.*

1. Which format of discussions—in class or online—would you pick if you had a choice? Why?

2. Of the three keys to making your points effectively, which comes most easily for you? Why? Which one do you struggle with most? What ideas have you gleaned from the chapter for improving?

3. Do you review discussions as the chapter suggests? If so, how have you done this in the past? If not, which strategy seems as though it will work best for you? Explain.

IT'S YOUR Q

The Q System uses marginal questions to encourage active reading. You'll notice that most but not all paragraphs in this chapter are accompanied by marginal questions. Now it's your Q. Scan the chapter for any paragraph that is missing a question, reread the paragraph, establish the main idea, and then arrive at a question that elicits it. Use the questions in the surrounding paragraphs as models for your own marginal questions.

VOCABULARY IN ACTION

To expand the horizons of your understanding and to refine the precision of your thought, the three exercises that follow are designed to help you grow, strengthen, and maintain your own vocabulary.

SAY WHAT?

From the three choices beside each numbered item, select the one that most nearly expresses the meaning of the italicized word in the quote. Make a light check mark (√) next to your choice.

A team should be an *extension* of the coach's personality. My teams were *arrogant* and *obnoxious*.

—Al McGuire (1928–2001), American basketball coach

1. *extension*	mirror image	counterpart	continuation
2. *arrogant*	haughty	excitable	high-spirited
3. *obnoxious*	tough	noisy	nasty

"Involvement" in this context differs from "commitment" in the same sense as the pig's and the chicken's roles in one's breakfast of ham and eggs. The chicken was *involved*—the pig was *committed*.

—Anonymous

4. *involved*	primed	rejected	associated
5. *committed*	solicited	included	affiliated

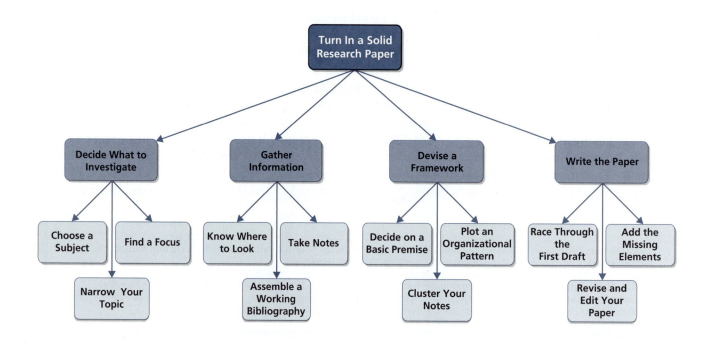

Turn In a Solid Research Paper

If your writing falls apart, it probably has no primary ideas to hold it together.

Sheridan Baker (1918–2000), professor, author of *The Practical Stylist*

From the time it is assigned until the day it is due, a research paper can occupy your mind like no other type of assignment. Although writing a research paper can be time consuming, it doesn't have to be overwhelming if you take the process one step at a time. To give you a head start in the art of the research paper, this chapter provides a calm and well-organized system to help you

- **Decide What to Investigate**
- **Gather Information**
- **Devise a Framework**
- **Write the Paper**

In this chapter

- ▶ The most common complaints about research papers. (p. 363)
- ▶ The unsung heroes of many research papers. (p. 365)
- ▶ Three short words can cut hours off the time you spend doing research. (p. 365)

How does writing
a research paper
compare to studying
your notes?

Writing even a modest research paper can take a lot of effort. Yet though the task is long, the skills it requires aren't sophisticated, and most of them aren't new. In fact, writing a paper isn't much more difficult than reading about a subject in detail, taking notes on your reading, organizing your notes, and reciting—all the activities you undertake to prepare for a test or quiz. The difference is that instead of reciting out loud, you put your recitation on paper in a form that makes what you've learned readable for others. If you realize that writing a paper is not much different from studying your notes, and if you systematically decide what to write about, gather information, devise a framework, and then do the actual writing, you may even find that writing papers can be a most absorbing way to learn about a subject.

Decide What to Investigate

What are the steps
in finding a suitable
topic?

Finding a suitable topic is often the biggest stumbling block in research. It's essential that you know how to choose a topic easily and efficiently. There are three steps in the process of selecting a topic: Begin with a general subject that interests you, narrow it down, and then sharpen it even further by finding a focus. If you follow these steps, you'll wind up with a topic that is both interesting and specific.

Choose a Subject

FOCUSING

What type of subject
should you choose?

In most cases, you'll be selecting a topic from a broad subject area. Because you'll be spending a great deal of time on the subject, your best bet is to choose one you are interested in or can develop an interest in. And if it isn't a subject that others are researching, then so much the better.

What should you do if
you can't decide on a
subject?

If you aren't sure what subject to select, do some preliminary research. Although you can sometimes get ideas by surfing the Web, the best place to do your preliminary research is still the library, where you'll have access to a variety of reference sources, both bound and computerized, a chance to browse through the section of the library stacks that matches your area of interest, and an opportunity to talk to a reference librarian, who will introduce you to an array of possible topics.

Suppose you are fascinated by natural disasters and want to learn more about them. But the subject "natural disasters" includes scores of topics: droughts, floods, tornadoes, hurricanes, volcanoes, and earthquakes, to name just a few. How can you do justice to them all? Obviously, you can't. You must narrow your topic.

Narrow Your Topic

IT'S YOUR Q

Selecting a topic that interests you is just the beginning. The most common criticism of a research paper is that its topic is too broad. A Cornell professor of English suggests this method for narrowing your topic: Put your subject through three or four significant narrowings, moving from a given category to a class within that category each time. This method is similar to the Silver Dollar System (see Chapter 11), which enables you to select the most important ideas from your notes.

For example, if you select natural disasters as the topic for a 10- to 15-page research paper, you have to narrow the scope of your topic before you can cover it in adequate depth. Three narrowings will probably reduce the subject down to a manageable size, although four may be necessary.

General Topic: Natural Disasters
First narrowing: earthquakes
Second narrowing: earthquake prediction
Third narrowing: scientific developments in earthquake prediction
Fourth narrowing: computer simulations in earthquake prediction

How can you use concept maps to help you narrow your topic?

Concept maps, which are explained in Chapter 8 and are similar to those at the beginning of each chapter, can be used to "visually" narrow a topic. Write your general subject on a blank sheet of paper and circle it. Next, write down subtopics of your general subject, circle each, and connect them with lines to the general subject. Then write and circle subtopics of your subtopics. At this point, you may have a suitably narrow subject. If not, keep adding levels of subtopics until you arrive at one. (See Figure 14.1.) The advantage of narrowing your topic with a concept map is that you provide yourself with a number of alternate topics should your original topic choice prove unworkable.

Find a Focus

What is the purpose of finding a focus for your topic?

Once you've narrowed your topic, give your research direction and purpose by developing a compelling question about that topic. The information you gather from your research can then be used to develop an answer. For the topic "The use of computer simulations in earthquake prediction," you might ask, "How helpful are computer simulations in earthquake prediction?"

Why is posing a research question important?

Whether you actually arrive at a definitive answer to your research question isn't crucial. The important thing is to focus your research efforts on answering the broad question.

Figure 14.1
**Using a Concept Map
to Narrow a Topic**

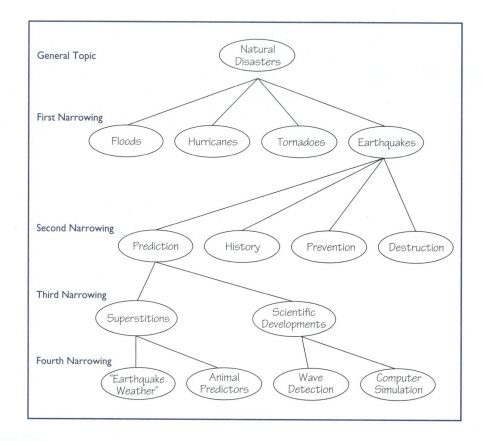

General Topic — Natural Disasters

First Narrowing — Floods, Hurricanes, Tornadoes, Earthquakes

Second Narrowing — Prediction, History, Prevention, Destruction

Third Narrowing — Superstitions, Scientific Developments

Fourth Narrowing — "Earthquake Weather", Animal Predictors, Wave Detection, Computer Simulation

Gather Information

**What does gathering
information require?**

The next step in your research is to begin gathering information. That requires knowing where to look (and knowing what you're looking for), assembling a working bibliography, and then taking detailed notes.

Know Where to Look

FOCUSING

**Where should you
look to find material
for your paper?**

Unless you're using firsthand information—from interviews or experiments—nearly all your material will come from the library (although depending on the nature of your topic, some of it may be found on the Web as well). During this stage of your investigation, the library's most valuable resources will be the reference librarian, indexes, periodicals, and books.

Get Help from the Reference Librarian

How can a reference librarian help?

Before you begin your research, as well as any time during the process when you hit a snag, seek out the reference librarian. Although librarians may not be experts on your particular subject, they *are* experts at using the library's research tools. Librarians can often suggest indexes or databases you may not have heard of, sources you didn't think to consult, and searching strategies you didn't try. Their experienced advice can save you hours of time and may provide the needed breakthrough that makes your paper a success. Librarians are the unsung heroes of many research papers.

Consult Periodical Indexes

Why is it helpful to consult periodical indexes first?

It's wise to consult the articles that relate to your paper topic before you begin to delve into books. Not only do periodicals frequently provide the most recent information on a subject, sometimes they supply the *only* information. In addition, articles often include important names and titles that relate to your subject and occasionally provide a valuable overview of your topic. There are several general and specific indexes—both computerized and bound—for periodicals.

How do computerized magazine indexes work?

Use Computerized Indexes Most libraries use computerized magazine indexes that enable you to type in the name of a subject, author, or title and receive a list of relevant articles. You should also be able to customize your search with keywords and sometimes with Boolean searching.

IT'S YOUR Q

Keyword search. Unless you know the title of a specific article, keywords usually provide the most direct route to the kinds of articles you are seeking, especially when searching by subject isn't convenient or fruitful. For example, if you want information about Gregg Toland, the cinematographer who worked with Orson Welles on the movie *Citizen Kane*, you may come up empty if you use the subjects "Toland" or "Citizen Kane" in your search. The database simply may not have enough articles on these topics to justify a separate subject heading. If, however, you search for articles under a broader subject, such as "Motion pictures—American," you may have to scan through hundreds of citations before you find appropriate ones. With a keyword search, by contrast, you can type in a word (or name) such as "Toland," and the computer will reply with every article in its database that contains the keyword you have typed.

What is a Boolean search?

Boolean search. A Boolean search uses the logical terms "AND," "OR," and "NOT" to help you to combine and refine your searches. Suppose you need information about earthquakes in San Jose. If you searched under the subject "earthquakes" or "San Jose," you would have to scan thousands of citations that have nothing to do with your particular topic. But by searching for titles that contain both keywords—"earthquakes AND San Jose"—you are likelier to pinpoint articles that deal directly with your area of interest. Because earthquakes felt in San Jose are often felt in San Francisco as well, you might want to broaden your search somewhat by using the "OR" keyword to search for information on earthquakes that occurred in San Jose OR San Francisco: "earthquakes AND (San Jose OR San Francisco)." Of course, San Jose is not only a city in Northern California, but also the capital of Costa Rica. You can use the "NOT" keyword to narrow your search, making sure you only get citations referring to California: "earthquakes AND San Jose NOT Costa Rica." Not all search engines provide all three types of Boolean searching. In addition, some engines use a "+" instead of "AND" and a "-" instead of "NOT." Luckily, most search screens, whether they're specific to your library or available on the Web, will include a link that says "Advanced Search" or something similar. Clicking on this link should provide you with more information about that search engine's particular rules and capabilities.

What is the most useful bound index?

Use Bound Indexes Despite the abundance of computerized options for searching periodicals, some bound indexes remain. The most useful of these is the *Readers' Guide to Periodical Literature*. Each volume lists by author and subject all the articles that appeared in several dozen magazines during a given year. To locate articles on your topic, consult the years in which you think those articles may have been published. Each entry in the *Readers' Guide* gives you the information you need to locate the appropriate journal or magazine.

What kinds of articles have their own indexes?

Your paper topic may pertain to a subject that has its own index. For example, if you are doing research in psychology, you can refer to several indexes that deal specifically with psychology and that include journals and magazines that aren't listed in the *Readers' Guide*. A number of other subjects, such as business and education, have their own indexes. In addition, large newspapers such as the *New York Times* publish indexes of their articles.

Consult Book Indexes

What are your search options in book indexes?

Although some libraries may consolidate their search tools, books usually have their own indexes. Like the traditional card catalogs that came before them, computer-based catalogs usually allow you to search for a book based on its subject, title, or author. In addition, most computer catalogs include advanced commands similar to those used with the periodical index that allow for keyword and Boolean searching. Most college libraries allow you to search their collections from any browser. If yours works this way, you can get a head start on compiling a list of possible references before you even set foot in the library. That should put you in a more knowledgeable position should you need to ask the reference librarian for additional assistance.

Assemble a Working Bibliography

CLUSTERING

What is a working bibliography?

As you discover books, magazines, newspapers, journals, and websites that relate to your research, add them to a *working bibliography*—a list of promising sources that you plan to consult. Be generous in compiling your list. It's better to check out several references that do not help than to miss a good one because its title isn't appealing.

How should you list your references?

Instead of listing all these references on a large sheet of paper, you can use a separate index card for each reference. Then later on, if you decide that a particular reference doesn't help, you can simply throw away its card.

What information belongs on the front of each bibliography index card?

Figure 14.2 provides an efficient format for putting your bibliography on index cards. On the front of the card, record the following information:

Library's name (optional). For sources you find at a library, write the library's name on your card.

A short title of your subject. A title will make it easier to locate a particular card and will aid in clustering your information.

A unique identifier. For books (and some periodicals), that will usually be the library call number. For sources you found on the Web, that will be the URL (Web address).

The reference information. Include the author, title, publishing data, and any page references in exactly the form that you plan to use it in the bibliographical portion of your paper. This ensures that you will include all the essential parts of the reference and that typing your paper will be much easier.

What information belongs on the back of each bibliography index card?

On the back of the card, jot down your assessment of the reference. If the source doesn't seem useful, then briefly explain why. If the source appears helpful, jot down how. Then when you have a chance to take another look at the article or book, you'll know why you thought it would or would not be useful. And if you shift the focus of

Olin Library	Theories of Memory	
Q 360 .C33	Campbell, Jeremy	
	Grammatical Man. New York: Simon & Schuster, Inc., 1982.	

Bottom-up and top-down theories of memory described in Chapter 18.

Refers back to previous chapters and is difficult to read in spots. Provides solid summary of the two theories.

Uses simple, vivid examples to explain difficult points.

Index Card with Data   **Reverse of an Index Card with Comments**

Figure 14.2
Working Bibliography: Index Card Method

your paper, you'll be able to determine whether sources you had eliminated should now be consulted and whether previously promising sources will no longer be of help.

Take Notes

What qualities should you strive for in the notes that you take?

Using your bibliography as a springboard, you can investigate your sources and begin taking notes. There's no getting around it—taking notes is time consuming. But if your notes are easy to use, neat, brief, and accurate, then the bulk of your paper will be written by the time you have completed the note-taking step.

Make Sure Your Notes Are Easy to Use

How can you make your notes easy to use?

To make your notes easy to use, jot each note on a separate index card or slip of paper rather than writing them one after the other on regular-sized sheets. Whether you use cards or slips, you will be able to rearrange them easily and often because each note is separate.

IT'S YOUR Q

Assuming you're going to write your paper on a computer, it can be tempting to take your notes on one as well. Resist the temptation. Here's why. Although software has been developed that mimics many of the characteristics of index cards, the fact is that there's no program currently available that's as flexible and as portable as a simple stack of cards or paper slips. As you're organizing your paper, you're going to want to be able to shuffle your cards easily and arrange them in stacks on the desk or table in front of you. You may want to be able to quickly shift a card from one stack to another, suddenly write a new card or slip, or tear one up and toss it in the trash. Some programmers have written thousands of lines of computer code to simulate these actions, but their programs usually cost money and don't work nearly as well as ordinary pieces of paper. It's also true that you can "write" your cards on a computer and then, depending on your printer, print them out on ordinary index cards or on special (expensive) index card paper, but this maneuver just complicates a relatively simple process. You could also conceivably just type your notes into one or more computer files and then shift them around by cutting and pasting or dragging and dropping. But there is lots of information on a regular note card that would get in the way if you had to include it in a document file along with the text of each card. When you consider both features and cost, ordinary index cards remain your best "technology" for assembling research paper notes.

What else can you do to make your notes easy to use?

Another way to make your notes easier to use is by conscientiously identifying each card or slip. In the top left corner, write the author's name or the title of the source you consulted. Then at the bottom right, jot down the specific page on which you found the information. With these two markings on every note card, you can easily verify or add to any information you've gathered for your paper. In addition, you'll have all the information you may need for your citations (see Figure 14.3).

Figure 14.3
Detailed Note Written on One Side of an Index Card

Campbell

Hemispheres of a normal brain are connected by a bundle of fibers called the corpus callosum.

p. 240

Keep Your Note Cards Neat

What can you do to keep your note cards neat?

Detailed notes are useless if you can't read them. Write your notes neatly the first time, even if it takes a little longer to do so. Use the modified printing system (see Chapter 10) to write quickly but legibly, and write in pen, instead of pencil, to avoid smears and fading.

Keep Your Note Cards Brief

Why should you keep your note cards brief?

Brevity is the secret behind a useful note card. If a note card contains several key ideas instead of just one, you're going to find it harder to organize your paper when the time comes. Get to the heart of the matter with each note you take. Make your notes concise, yet sufficiently detailed to provide accurate meaning.

What is one simple way to limit the length of each note card?

One simple way to limit the length of each note card is by abbreviating common words. For example, use *w/* instead of "with," *co.* instead of "company," and *govt* in place of "government." Develop your own abbreviations for words you commonly use. For example, if you're doing research on earthquakes, you may want to use *RS* to stand for "Richter scale" and *tct plates* to abbreviate "tectonic plates." Be careful not to go overboard with abbreviations, however. Abbreviating words may save you time to begin with, but you don't want to waste that time later trying to decipher your unfamiliar shorthand.

Strive for Accuracy

What steps can you take to ensure that your notes are accurate?

Because you're dealing in facts, you must make certain that the information you jot down is accurate. It's relatively easy to remember as you're taking notes who said what and which of the thoughts you are writing down are your own and which are the thoughts of the author. But between the time you fill your last note card and the moment you write the first line of your paper, you're liable to forget these crucial details. To counteract forgetting and to ensure the information in your paper is accurate, distinguish clearly on your note cards between quoted ideas and paraphrased ideas and between the writer's thoughts and your own.

How should you treat quotations that you add into your notes?

Copy Quotations Carefully When you quote from a book or an article, make sure that you do so carefully. Place quotation marks on your card around the exact words you copied from the reference. Compare your version with the original quotation to make sure you copied it correctly. Don't change the wording or the spelling of the author's quotation. If you find a misspelling or a grammatical error in the quotation, you may use the bracketed notation [*sic*] to make it clear to your reader that you're aware of the mistake.

How do you leave out part of a quotation?

If you leave out a section or even one word from a quote, use three ellipsis points (. . .) to indicate the omission. If the words you left out came at the end of a sentence, add a period after the ellipsis.

What is the purpose of an ellipsis?

The purpose of an ellipsis is to leave out information that doesn't relate to the point you are using the quotation to support. An ellipsis should not be used to rearrange a quotation simply to suit your needs. Ellipses are intended to abbreviate a quotation, not alter its meaning.

What happens if you come up with your own ideas as you're taking notes from a source?

Mark Thoughts of Your Own Some of your best ideas may occur as you're taking notes. Put these thoughts on paper right away, but do so on a separate card or slip marked "My Ideas" or something similar. That way you'll be sure not to confuse your original ideas with the ones you've encountered in your reading.

What should you do with notes that paraphrase material you've found in a source?

Paraphrase What You Read Although it is important to distinguish your original ideas from the ones you have read, there's nothing wrong with paraphrasing—expressing someone else's ideas in your own words—as long as you give proper credit to the source. If you paraphrase as you take notes, you'll often be able to transfer what you've written in your notes to your draft without changing a word.

Devise a Framework

How can you devise a framework for your paper?

You can devise a solid framework for your paper out of a pile of disconnected notes by deciding on a basic premise, clustering your notes under a handful of main ideas, and plotting out a clear and logical organizational pattern.

Decide on a Basic Premise

QUESTIONING FOCUSING

What is a paper's premise and how can you arrive at one?

In the same way that choosing a focus helped provide direction for your research, deciding on a basic *premise* from the notes you now have lays the foundation for your paper's organization. Potential arguments, apparent similarities, and possible theories all have a way of rising to the surface in the process of taking notes. Any of these can be used to form a basic premise, which is the fundamental approach that underlies your paper. If a premise doesn't become obvious to you as you're taking notes, go back over the information and ask yourself some hard questions. For example:

Where is this paper heading?
What are the ramifications of the information I've assembled?
What point is most important?
What am I saying?
What do I want to say?
If there's a choice of viewpoint—for or against a question, for example—which view has the most evidence to support it?

If you've done a good job of research, you should be able to decide now what you want to say in your paper, and you should have the evidence in your notes to support that view.

Cluster Your Notes

CLUSTERING — FOCUSING

How does the paper's premise influence the way you cluster your notes?

The paper's basic premise should act as a magnet for clustering your notes, which enables you to draw out the most important ideas from the dozens and perhaps hundreds of notes you have written. In most cases, a research paper should incorporate fewer than seven main ideas. These ideas will form the framework for your paper. The cards or slips that remain won't be wasted but will be used as support for the more important ideas. Of course, if a note isn't important enough to be considered a main idea and doesn't provide support for the main ideas, that note should be left out of your paper.

How do you decide on the most important ideas in your notes?

Choosing the main ideas and clustering your research notes require selectivity, the same skill you used not only in narrowing your original paper topic, but in studying conventional notes as well (see Chapter 11). In fact, if you find it difficult to pick out a handful of main ideas from a pile of notes, apply the following three-step system to help pinpoint the pillars that will form your paper's supports:

1. Read through your notes and pick out those cards or slips that seem more important than the others.
2. Now that you have two piles of notes instead of one, pick up the smaller pile and repeat the process, pulling out the most important notes and using them to make up a third pile.
3. Finally, pick up the third pile, which by now should contain only a dozen or so cards or slips, and find four or five ideas that seem to be the most important ones. These ideas will be the basis of your premise and of the pattern for your paper.

www.cengage.com/success/Pauk/HowToStudy11e

Plot an Organizational Pattern

CLUSTERING   OVERVIEWING

What are the factors that influence how you plot an organizational pattern?

Your basic premise and personal choice largely determine the pattern your paper will follow. You could use any of the organizational patterns listed in Chapter 5 as the framework for your paper. The time pattern or the process pattern is appropriate for most college papers. For some papers, however, you may be required to develop an argument. A good pattern for such papers is to begin with a statement of your premise and then support it with logical examples that build to a conclusion. This kind of organization affords more flexibility than the others.

What techniques can you use to help arrive at a pattern for your paper?

You may need to experiment with several patterns before you arrive at a framework that adequately accommodates the information you want to include in your paper. Don't be discouraged by the inevitable period of trial and error. There's no one "correct" way of plotting your paper. You may feel most comfortable using a traditional outline. Or you may find the process of mapping easier and more enjoyable.

How can you use mapping to organize your paper?

To map out your research paper, use the notes that contain your paper's main ideas and sub-ideas (or jot these ideas down on small slips of paper). On a clear surface such as a desk or a tabletop, shift these ideas around like checkers on a checkerboard, clustering them in various ways, according to the premise of your paper.

How does your paper's pattern influence the way you create your map?

If you're planning to structure your paper using the time or process pattern, arrange your ideas so they follow logically from the earliest to the latest or from the start of the process to the end. If you're structuring your paper as an argument, decide which of the major points should be made first; then arrange the remaining points in an order that will make your argument smooth, logical, and easy to follow.

What sorts of patterns do the maps that begin this book's chapters normally use?

The chapter maps in this book provide examples of the process and argument patterns. The map in this chapter, for example, uses the process pattern, spelling out in order the steps for writing a research paper. The map for Chapter 2, in contrast, develops an argument; it asserts a premise—to use your time and space effectively you need to reclaim lost time, stick to a schedule, and organize all your "stuff"—and then goes on to elaborate on each point.

When you arrive at an arrangement that incorporates your information and makes logical sense, you have found a suitable pattern for your paper. Once you have arranged the cards or slips that contain your major points in an effective order, repeat the procedure by arranging the notes that contain your minor points. Think of each major point as a premise in itself. Then arrange the minor points that support a major point in a clear and effective way.

What should you do with the notes that deal with minor points in your paper?

What if your organization has gaps? How can you make it easier to turn your notes into your paper?

If, as you arrange your notes, you find gaps in your organization, you may need to create new categories or perhaps even return to the library or the Internet to take more notes.

Finally, with all points arranged to your satisfaction, go back and number your note cards or slips according to the order in which they'll appear in your paper. This should ease the process of systematically transferring your notes to your paper's first draft. If your cards are written conscientiously and numbered properly, your first draft will practically write itself.

Write the Paper

What steps are
involved in actually
writing your paper?

You already have most of your paper worked out—information, sources, organization. Now all you have to do is put your data into sentences and paragraphs and work up a first draft of your paper. Once that is accomplished, allow yourself plenty of time to go back and revise and edit what you've written, add the missing elements, and type the final copy.

Race Through the First Draft

PLANNING

What is the best way
to start writing your
paper?

The best way to start writing is simply to write. Pausing with your pen poised over an empty page or with your fingers resting idly on a keyboard waiting for inspiration to strike is a useless endeavor. Inspiration, like concentration, seldom comes when you call it. Once your hands are engaged in the physical motions of writing, your brain will follow.

How should you
handle alternatives
that occur to you as
you're writing?

Write your first draft as rapidly and spontaneously as possible. To ensure continuity, record your thoughts as they go through your mind. Don't stop to ponder alternatives. Although you will probably write too much, don't be concerned; it's easier to cut than it is to add.

What should your goal
be when writing your
first draft?

In your first draft, your goal is simply to transfer information from your notes to your paper or computer screen. Take each card or slip in order and write. Start with major point 1. State what it is, and then use supporting evidence to show why it is so. As you use a reference from the card, note the card number on your paper. You can put the footnotes in later, taking the exact information from the card. Continue to write, following your organized and numbered notes.

Once you've finished
your first draft, what
should you do next?

Only after you've completed your first draft should you step back and take a look at what you've written. If you typed your draft using a computer, either print out a hard copy so you can jot down your comments or use the word processing program's comment function to insert any thoughts directly into your text. Regardless of the form your first draft takes, go over it carefully in search of possible changes, adding words or phrases and highlighting paragraphs you want to move or remove.

How should you
handle any changes
that you've added to
your draft?

While your annotations are still fresh in your mind, produce a clear copy that incorporates all your changes. Don't wait before adding in these corrections. If you delay even a day, you may lose a lot of time trying to recall exactly what you meant by some of your comments. And if you update your draft while it's still fresh, you may find that you do some spontaneous revision.

What should you do
with your draft once
you've updated it?

Once you have made these changes, put your draft aside for a while. To gain objectivity about what is in the paper and what is still missing, you need a cooling off period of at least a day. When you return to your paper, you should find it easier to spot errors and weaknesses in your writing.

www.cengage.com/success/Pauk/HowToStudy11e

Revise and Edit Your Paper

What should you be trying to accomplish in later drafts of your paper?

The hardest part of writing a research paper is completing the first draft. From that point on, you'll be refining what you've already written. In the next drafts—and you may write two, three, or even four drafts before you are satisfied with your paper— you'll focus on strengthening supporting evidence and fine-tuning technical details such as transitions, grammar, and spelling.

Support Your Points with Evidence

What sort of evidence should you use to support your points?

Students often state a main point and then go on to something else without support- ing it. The kinds of evidence you need to support a major point are statistics, quotations from other published works, facts, examples, comparisons and contrasts in views, expert opinion, and description. If you make statements and follow them up with gen- eralities, you will not convince your reader that your main point is true. Use what you have collected on your cards to support your points. Figure 14.4 provides an example that shows the steps you can take to develop a major point.

What should you do if you can't support one of your main points?

Be sure that all the main points are supported with this kind of evidence. If you can't find enough evidence to support one point, perhaps it's not a major one. You may need to reorganize the structure of your paper to include that point under one of the other major points.

Why won't padding work to make your paper longer?

Avoid padding. You may be tempted to add words or to rephrase a point to make the paper longer. Such padding is usually obvious to the reader, who's looking for log- ical arguments and good sense, and is unlikely to improve your grade. If you haven't enough evidence to support a statement, leave it out or get more information.

Figure 14.4
Strengthening Supporting Details

1. **State your point clearly.**
   The two sides of the human brain perform distinct functions.

2. **Develop the point beyond a brief statement.**
   According to the theory of brain laterality, the left hemisphere of the brain handles analytical thinking, while the right hemisphere is the home of abstract thought.

3. **Support with data from authorities and with statistics.**
   Drs. Michael Gazzaniga and Roger Sperry found that the cerebral hemispheres process information differently (add reference here). Subsequent research determined that the brain's left and right sides contrast information that is symbolic and conceptual versus information that is nonsymbolic and directly perceived.

4. **Illustrate with examples.**
   For example, if you were to add up a column of numbers, you would probably be using the left side of your brain. But if you were sketching a picture, you would be engaging the right side.

Figure 14.5
**Format for Footnotes
and End-of-Paper
Credits**

How does t
conclusion
the rest of y

the botto
appear at
footnotes
order in v
English u

IT'S YOU

What should go into
your bibliography?

Supply a
may inclu
paper but
listing of
rect title f
you prepa
can identi

Entries
different f
ographic :
usage, or

Ask yo
field such

The fol
for your c

What format should
you use for your
bibliography?

FINAL

How is wri
research pa
running a r

Gibaldi
Mod
The Chi
Publica
Ame

No mat
phy. Figu

What technical details
require fine-tuning?

Why are transitions
important?

IT'S YOUR Q

How can you remedy
the spelling problems
in your paper?

What are the pitfalls
of relying on a spell-
checker?

Fine-Tune Technical Details

Although awkward transitions, clumsy grammar, and poor spelling may not affect the basic meaning of your paper, they do affect the reader's perception of how you have thought about your topic and what you have written.

Provide Transitions In writing your paper, consider how to help your readers move easily from one main point to the next. If they feel that there's no connection, they will find it hard to follow the logical sequence that you have established in your own mind. You must therefore use transitional words and phrases to make your paper easy to follow. (See Chapter 5 for a list of these words.) Check carefully for transitions, and insert them where they are needed.

Correct Grammar Students who use the English language correctly get their ideas across to other people more clearly and forcibly than do those who stumble over every sentence. Moreover, students who apply the rules of grammar in their papers earn better grades. If you are unsure about these rules or careless with them, your meaning may get lost. If you feel that you could use a review of grammar, there are good texts that provide answers for most of your grammatical questions. Some of them are actually quite entertaining.

Here's a brief list of some popular books on English grammar:

Casagrande, June. *Grammar Snobs Are Great Big Meanies: A Guide to Language for Fun and Spite*. New York: Penguin, 2006.

Diamond, Harriet, and Phyllis Dutwin. *Grammar in Plain English*, 5th ed. New York: Barron's Educational Series, 2012.

Glenn, Cheryl, and Loretta Gray. *The Hodges Harbrace Handbook*, 18th ed. Belmont, CA: Wadsworth, Cengage Learning, 2013.

O'Conner, Patricia. *Woe Is I: The Grammarphobe's Guide to Better English in Plain English*, 3rd ed. New York: Riverhead Books, 2009.

Shertzer, Margaret D. *The Elements of Grammar*. New York: Macmillan Publishing, 1996.

Strumpf, Michael, and Auriel Douglas. *The Grammar Bible: Everything You Always Wanted to Know About Grammar But Didn't Know Whom to Ask*. New York: Holt, 2004.

Check Spelling If your spelling problems are not severe, you will find a dictionary helpful. If your spelling is poor, look for one of the paperback books that list the most commonly misspelled words. If you cannot recognize that you are spelling words incorrectly, have someone who is good at spelling read your paper and mark, not correct, the words that are wrong. Then look up and insert the correct spellings. If you do this conscientiously over a period of time, you will improve your spelling.

Word processing software includes a spell-checking program to pinpoint your spelling mistakes. The spell-checker compares each word you have typed with the words stored in its dictionary and calls your attention to words that don't appear there. Although

the
dict
spe
or *p*

Ad

IT'S YOUR Q

**Figu
Forn
Bibli**

Hav
will
crec
pap

Giv
To
attr

Do
the
out
not
tior
still

T
you
like
will
son
you
teac
qui
if th
so i
wo
seri

Inc
par
rial
cita
liste

How
title

Wha
infor
go ir
intro

Why
need

Wha
a cor

My First Research Paper

By Walter Pauk

Registration was like a game of chess. The smart students made their moves early. Some lined up before dawn, while others used the university's new computerized system to register from home. They registered early, not especially to get the best courses, but to avoid being "stuck" with one—the one taught by Professor Wilbur Hendricon.

The word on the grapevine was that this was a course to be avoided by the faint of heart. The chances of being forced into Professor Hendricon's course were slim but still too terrifying to take a chance. Professor Hendricon had, as the students said, "a special deal with the administration." He could handpick twenty-five students for his class, but had to take another ten at general registration.

This unusual procedure was a compromise. It came about this way: Professor Hendricon had originally taught only graduate courses; but ten years ago he decided that he would like to teach one section of English 105. So Professor Hendricon suddenly proclaimed to the dean that he would take twenty-five first-year students and turn them into scholars.

The dean was faced with a dilemma. On the one hand, the proud and sensitive Hendricon might take a negative answer as a rude rebuff. Also, the dean thought, "If he resigns, I will have to answer to the president." Hendricon was the university's brilliant light and other universities eagerly tried to woo him. On the other hand, a positive answer would be a blow to the morale of the other members of the English Department, who had no choice but to take their usual thirty-five students per class. The dean consulted her colleagues and persuaded them to accept the compromise. Needless to say, I was one of the unlucky ten.

Right from the very first day in class, I could see how well Hendricon had chosen. The twenty-five were geniuses. I later discovered that they all had straight As in high school and that they were clustered at the top of the scholarship list. Furthermore, they excelled in language and literature, while my strengths were in mathematics and music. Math skills and musical talent did not count for much in an English course.

At first I thought Professor Hendricon's legendary standards might just be rumor, but after the first test any hopes evaporated. We unfortunate ten compared notes and found our grades in the 30s and 40s. But no one questioned Professor Hendricon's honesty and sincerity. Our papers were filled with notations, symbols, and helpful comments. We did, however, question his standards. They were not for us mere mortals. Six of the ten transferred to other sections of the course immediately; the other three students transferred after the second test. Everyone knew that transferring was possible. The other instructors expected to get all ten of us in their classes within the first few weeks of term. In this way, morale was preserved, because administratively, at least, all the classes started out with thirty-five students each.

Perhaps it was the lemming instinct in me or perhaps it was Hendricon's appeal, but I decided to hang in. On the day after the last date for changing classes, I took my usual seat. The other twenty-five students, who usually chatted loudly until Professor Hendricon entered the door, were strangely silent today. You see, in all these past ten years, not one of the unchosen had ever stayed in Hendricon's class. Everyone knew this.

We could hear Hendricon's brisk but firm footsteps drawing closer to the open door. The pace was faster than usual. We saw the toe of his left foot puncture the blank space of the doorway. The blood was pounding at my temples. My breathing was fast and shallow. Hendricon always walked straight to the lectern, put down his notes, and said, "Good afternoon" to the class. As he entered today, he glanced at me with a curious look. He did not greet the class as usual. He just lectured, but more seriously. I could not keep my mind on the lecture. No one could. It seemed that I had spoiled the atmosphere of this select club. Why had I not been less foolhardy?

On Monday, however, the class resumed its normal pace and atmosphere. I was present but not accepted. The chosen twenty-five sat in a solid square. I sat outside the square, separate but linked like an appendix. But that did not bother me, for I was really fascinated by Professor Hendricon. He was a great teacher. I took copious notes and studied the assignments carefully. I occasionally forgot myself and spoke out during discussions. I worked hard on tests and examinations, but they were never quite up to standard. I could usually understand the ideas and concepts, but time always ran out. I needed more time to think. But I was not discouraged because I was enjoying the course and learning a lot.

It was just after the Christmas holidays that Professor Hendricon announced it. "It" was the research paper—3,500 words and counting for one-third of the final grade. I should have been petrified because I could not write, and yet, I was glad. This was my chance to raise my present hard-earned average of 62.7 percent to the necessary 70.

This would be the first instance where I would have an advantage over the students—I would have the advantage of time. I needed time. Time is the great equalizer; time is democratic. We all receive the same amount of it every morning. No distinction is made between the genius and the plodder. This is what I told myself; it helped me feel a little better.

There should not have been any excitement because everyone knew about the Hendricon paper. It was indeed another factor that encouraged the rush to register early for other courses. The paper was not due until after the late winter break—almost two months off. But still, there were groans and whisperings. I could hardly hear the professor's caution against plagiarism. "Use both the primary text as well as secondary critical sources," he instructed against a background of restless inattention. Very few paid attention to his next point about thinking carefully before choosing a topic. I somehow caught, "Once you have decided on your topic, it should be narrowed three or four times." What did he mean by this?

After the others had left, I edged up to Professor Hendricon, who was gathering up his lecture notes, and asked about the idea of narrowing the topic. He said, "If, for example, you were doing a history course, and you chose as your topic the 'Civil War,' you would be almost sure to fail. You simply could not do justice to such a large topic—dozens of books would be necessary to cover that subject, not an undergraduate research paper. Even a second narrowing of the topic to the 'Battle of Gettysburg,' a major engagement in the war, would still be too broad. A third stage of narrowing such as the 'Battle of Cemetery Ridge' would be more manageable, but your focus might not be sufficiently defined yet. So perhaps a further narrowing to the 'Tactical Importance of Cemetery Ridge' might be necessary. This would be an aspect of the original broad topic on which adequate information could be found to write an in-depth paper."

I was so excited about writing the term paper that I went straight to the library, eager and determined to find an interesting topic on which to use this technique of narrowing. I was surprised to find the cavernous library so empty of students. But of course, there would be time during "reading week" and the late winter break—there was no pressure yet. I went directly to the reference librarian, who showed me how to use the various special reference books. Another librarian, who joined us, had an interesting idea. She said, "If you choose a subject area carefully in your first year, and continue throughout your university years to research and write in that area, you could probably become quite an expert." This idea intrigued me.

Over the next few days I brainstormed possible topics for my paper. First, I scrutinized Professor Hendricon's course outline, mulling over his lecture themes and the prescribed authors and texts. Then I returned to the library to peruse reference books such as encyclopedias, surveys of literature, and biographical dictionaries. I developed a list of nineteen topics that interested me. I reflected on these over the weekend and after careful deliberation rejected fourteen of them.

The remaining five topics I decided to discuss with Professor Hendricon. He seemed happy to see me. In about five minutes we eliminated two. As far as the other three were concerned, he suggested that I talk about each with professors who were experts in the respective areas.

These talks were especially stimulating. I got to know three new professors from whom I received not only useful insights about narrowing the topics, but also details of important sources and prominent authorities as well. After thinking through the suggestions made by these professors, I settled on the area that was most appealing to me.

I arranged another session with Professor Hendricon to inform him of my decision and to obtain advice on the direction my assignment should take. We discussed the precise purpose of my paper, and, over a cup of tea, we juggled words and finally formulated a challenging question to launch my research. I emerged from his Dickensian study aglow with inspiration and enthusiasm. The stern and serious Hendricon of the lecture hall had a warm and sensitive side that few students had glimpsed.

So, with the topic narrowed and a clear sense of direction established, back to the library I went to search for sources and to start my research. With the first week over I was surprised to find none of the class in the library. During the first term I had learned how to use the library's computerized catalog. Why not explore other searching opportunities offered by the computer system, such as using a keyword to locate titles relevant to the focus of my research? I was amazed at the wealth of material available through the computer catalog, and soon I had an impressive list of titles in my working bibliography. Gaining confidence, I decided to use the CD-ROM databases and discovered several periodical articles pertaining to my research question.

I gathered some of my sources and began taking notes on pages of notebook paper. The reference librarian, ever helpful, wandered over and asked if I knew the advantages of recording my notes on index slips. Without waiting for an answer, she said that the ability to categorize my notes would ensure a much more efficient research system. Her specific suggestions were these:

- Record only one point, or a small cluster of related points, on one card.
- Record only information that is relevant to the purpose of your research.
- Use only one side of the card.
- Each card should indicate the author and page numbers of the source.
- Enclose all verbatim notes in quotation marks.
- Most notes should be paraphrased or summarized.
- Whenever you have a thought or insight of your own, jot it down and enclose it with brackets to signify "my own."

Noticing that I had no slips, she darted to her desk and pulled out the bottom drawer and thumped several rubber-banded stacks of cards on my table. "These are old cards left over when we converted the catalog to a computer system. They are used on only one side. You are welcome to use them for your research notes."

The card method intrigued me and, now that I had a wide-ranging list of sources, I was eager to get started on the research. I worked steadily in the library for the next two weeks, averaging two to three hours a day. It was surprisingly easy jotting down important information and ideas on cards and indicating the sources and page numbers. Rather than waste time writing out the author's name or the title on each card, I used a simple coding system to identify each source. I did not have a written outline. I had tried to prepare one after formulating my question, but I could not anticipate the material I would find. I also sensed that it would be too restricting. However, although I did not have an outline, it would be unfair to say that I selected the material for my note cards haphazardly. I selected material that had a bearing on my specific question. Once I immersed myself in the research, I began to sense what was relevant and what was not.

After two weeks, I had a shoebox full of cards. I was ready to start structuring and drafting the paper. During the course of the research I had sketched out a tentative list of sections that might serve as an outline. I stepped back from my intense two-week spell of research to reflect on the provisional outline. Keeping the research question uppermost in my mind, I modified the sections so that they would provide a structure around which I could shape my answer. Next, I read through all my note cards and moved them into categories corresponding to my outline. Having notes on each card that pertained to only one idea permitted me to place the cards in separate categories. If I had put two different notes on one card, I would have had to rewrite the information onto two separate cards now. I was glad that I had a system. It was like playing a card game.

My outline required further modification because not all the cards fit the major sections. I added another section to accommodate some of the cards, while a number of cards simply did not fit into any of the sections. So, with the cards in categories, I started to follow the second step of the librarian's advice. I began to shift the piles of cards into an order that seemed logical for my paper. It was surprisingly easy to reorder the piles of cards so that there was a logical flow in the sequence of the sections.

With the categories of cards spread out before me, I began to study each category independently to create a detailed outline. As I wrestled with sections, subsections, and supporting material, I began to see where I had gaps in data and weak spots in the argument. My detailed outline revealed plainly the areas in which my paper lacked balance and completeness. My work was cut out for the next few days since I needed specifics that the paper at that point lacked. I was glad that each card carried a reference to the source, so that I could locate not only the source but the precise page as well.

After a few hours of additional research in the library, I was able to augment my note cards. I felt that the more complete I could make my collection of cards, the more effective the first draft would be. I remembered Professor Hendricon's advice: "If you do not gather enough first-class material, you will have trouble writing a major paper." I used some of the new research information to revise and refine my detailed outline.

Finally, I was satisfied with my outline. Then I began to write the first draft. It surprised me to see how easy it is to write a long paper once the material is placed in order. I actually enjoyed the process. It took four days of writing in my spare time to complete the draft. I preferred writing my first draft in longhand because I seemed to think more clearly when writing rather than typing. On each day, I concentrated on writing one of four major parts of the paper. When I had finished, I immediately read it over and it sounded good to me—so good that I knew I would be able to enjoy the late-winter holidays—a wonderful reward. First, I had to type up my draft on the computer, and after backing it up, I printed a copy. I proudly left the copy on my desk to "cool" while I went home for the holidays.

On the last day before we departed for our week's holiday, Professor Hendricon did his duty as a teacher to remind us to work on our papers because they were due five days after our return to campus. The students fidgeted, a nervous laugh or two mingled with some of the spontaneous whispering, but no one said anything. I thought to myself that I had not seen any of the chosen twenty-five in the library; but then they could have been there at other times. Also, the thought struck me that they loved to discuss every moot point and debate hypothetical issues. They seemed to excel at writing creative papers, often at the last minute, with information they already had in their heads. Perhaps a research paper that demanded hard and dogged work was just too rigorous for their creative souls. Well, I just thought these thoughts and was a bit ashamed at my suspicious mind.

Even though I was still failing Professor Hendricon's course, the warm feeling generated by my completed draft provided the tone that I needed to enjoy my holidays. I had a good rest.

I arrived back on campus on Friday to avoid the weekend traffic. That evening, feeling proud of myself, I casually picked up my draft and, to extract the maximum amount of satisfaction from my accomplishment, I began reading. By the time I had finished page 3, my smile had vanished, and by page 10 fear had gripped me. The development of my thesis, which sounded so smooth upon completion, was now disjointed and repetitious and some paragraphs were meaningless. How could that be?

I pacified myself after the initial shock by realizing that I still had seven days, while many of the other students in the class had not even started their papers. Most of them would only arrive back on campus on Sunday evening, and that would leave them but a scant five days. As I pondered how to fix up my research paper, I realized, for the first time, the truth of the words that I had discarded as "teachers' preachings": "No paper should ever be handed in unless you have revised it. For the revision to be effective, you must always put your paper away for a few days so that you will lose some familiarity with it. Then, when you reread it, you will be better able to spot the weaknesses and the rough sections. Once these are spotted, revise, revise, revise."

My paper was certainly rough. I recalled the steps for revising: First, look through the draft to make sure the ideas are understandable and supported by details and examples. Second, make sure the organizational plan for the paper is clear and that the sections follow in logical sequence. Third, check for consistency of style, and, finally, ensure that the mechanics such as spelling and hyphenating are correct. I discovered that I had scattered throughout the paper bits of interesting information—interesting but not always pertinent. I added some of the misplaced material to the introduction and eliminated the rest. It was tough to throw away these gems that I had worked so hard to extract from my sources, but I heard ringing in my ears: "Good writers don't put everything down that is interesting. Remember the iceberg with its nine-tenths underwater and only one-tenth showing above the surface. This submerged part—your background work—gives the iceberg its strength and power."

After weeding out the irrelevant material, I concentrated on the structure of the paper and discovered that it, too, was a bit vague. Parts of the general statement that should have been at the beginning were in the body of the paper. So I sharpened the introduction by stating the thesis and then broke it down to the five main points that I had planned to establish and support. By the time I had reworked the introduction, I really knew for the first time what I was attempting to do. I was shocked to realize that my own understanding of what I was trying to do had not been clear. By the time I went to sleep on Sunday, I had hammered out a clear statement of what I was trying to establish and support.

Monday rolled around all too soon. The vacation was over. There was a lot of activity on campus as students accelerated into a faster tempo of study. Papers were due, final examinations hovered on the horizon, and most plans to complete work during the holidays had fallen through. Hendricon reminded the class of the Friday deadline. There was no whispering this time, just grim silence. I, too, contributed to the silence. I had to write not only a passing paper, but a paper good enough to earn an 85 if I was to raise my average to the passing grade of 70. I had, perhaps, counted too heavily on time and technique. Time was running out and technique was not holding up. But I still had a chance. Most of the chosen twenty-five, I was sure, had not even started.

I worked hard to strengthen the body of the paper by realigning my main sections in the same order as in the statement of thesis in the introduction. I made sure that each main section led off with a brief paragraph that introduced the section. Then I grouped the supporting information in a number of separate paragraphs all focused on the central idea of the section. As I worked through the other sections, checking the paragraph structure, I was surprised to discover that some of the supporting materials were still widely scattered even though I had carefully laid out a sequence when I grouped my note cards. By moving some of the information to more appropriate sections, I was able to eliminate repetition. I reworked each main section, especially those that seemed vague or hastily composed. Occasionally, I dug back into my collection of note cards when an idea needed additional support.

On Tuesday I fashioned a concluding summary that was not repetitious, synthesizing the thesis and key points in such a way to show mastery of the material. After dinner I printed a copy of the complete paper. I was immensely relieved and satisfied when I fell asleep that evening.

After the 9 o'clock class on Wednesday, I was free to devote the whole day to the final editing of the essay. I first read the entire paper aloud, checking for style. By reading aloud I could better detect redundant words, vague phrases, and awkward-sounding sentences. I corrected the flawed sentences so that they flowed smoothly and naturally. As part of the editing process, I made frequent use of a dictionary and a thesaurus to ensure that the vocabulary was precise. Also, I worked on internal transitions to give my paragraphs and sentences better cohesion. After I had edited the printed copy, I corrected the computer version and saved it carefully. I was meticulous in backing up each version in the event that my computer malfunctioned.

I woke early on Thursday, excited to see the final copy in print at last, and printed out my "magnum opus." I was so eager to start proofreading that I toyed with the possibility of skipping my morning lectures. But with final examinations looming, common sense won out! After lectures, I gobbled my lunch down and headed for my room and my prized paper. I proofread it meticulously, from title page to bibliography. All my thoroughness had paid off—not a single error was apparent. I was flushed with that warm feeling of satisfaction that the completion of a creative assignment brings.

This was it. This was the day! I never heard such an outpouring of incidents to a professor from frantic, frightened students who tried so hard to look and act sophisticated. "The library is so full, you can't find a table to write on." "Two other students are working on the same topic as I am and I cannot get hold of the sources." "My computer crashed." "My printer overheated and seized up." "I'll need more time, because all the typists in town are busy, and they can't get to mine until after the weekend."

Hendricon was calm but exceedingly serious. He looked around the room solemnly, making no attempt to answer any of the excuses. After a moment, he held up his hand for quiet and went on with his lecture as if nothing had happened. There was deep silence that hour. Professor Hendricon was always good, but he was especially good that day. He talked hard and earnestly. Most of the students sat glumly, motionless and glassy-eyed. Only a few had the discipline to take notes. For some reason, the professor's words seemed to be aimed at me. He was trying to make scholars of us, as well as mature men and women. About half the students handed in papers that day. Spurred by the announcement, "Five points a day will be deducted on all late papers," the rest were in on the following Monday. I was pleased and proud that mine was in on time.

With only two and a half weeks to go, Professor Hendricon lectured hard and fast, determined to complete his schedule of topics. By now, I had reconciled myself that failure was a possibility. Though I still wanted to pass the course, I was not too worried about it. I was just glad to have had the opportunity to attend Professor Hendricon's class.

On the last day of class, Professor Hendricon strode in with our research papers. "Before I hand them back to you," he said, "I want to talk about them both generally and specifically." He continued, "A few of the papers were excellent, a few poor, and the majority mediocre. The excellent ones were creative and imaginative in their use of technique; but the poor ones seemed as if they had been put together artificially and mechanically with scissors and paste."

That last remark hit me. Of course, I should have known that Professor Hendricon would be quick to see the artificial way my paper was put together: how I took notes on cards; distributed them in piles; mechanically shifted stacks of cards around; made an outline last, not first; filled gaps by digging out more material; mechanically revised; looked up words; read aloud to detect faulty intonation—all done like a "hack" in mechanical and piecemeal fashion. The rest of the class had real talent—they were truly gifted. In four or five days, they were able to write down their thoughts directly, fully developed, like true artists. And like true artists, they made good with one chance, whereas I had dozens of chances to write and rewrite.

As Professor Hendricon continued to talk about "scissors and paste," he suddenly picked up a paper to illustrate a point. I was shocked. I could tell it was my paper. I just couldn't stand the embarrassment. All I wanted to do was to get out of that room, fast! Then I suddenly realized that though I knew it was my paper, no one else did. So I steeled myself. Professor Hendricon read one paragraph after another. He jumped to the first part of the paper for a paragraph, then to the end for another. Then I noticed that the rest of the class was listening attentively, and though Professor Hendricon's voice was excited, it was kindly. As I calmed and composed myself, I heard, "Note the smooth rhythm of the prose and the careful choice of words. This is what I mean by scholarship. The technique is discernible. Yes! But put together with a scholar's love, and care, and time."

P.S. You guessed it! I passed the course.

CHAPTER CHECKUP

SENTENCE
COMPLETION

Complete the following sentences with one of the three words or phrases listed below each sentence.

1. Give your research purpose, direction, and focus by developing a _____ about your topic.

scientific	**fascinating**	**compelling**
discovery	**misconception**	**question**

2. When you are using the Web or a library's computerized indexes, a Boolean search enables you to narrow your search by _____.

using a prominent keyword	**combining multiple keywords**	**using a full sentence**

3. As you discover magazines and books that relate to your research, add them to a working bibliography that is _____.

in your notebook	**on separate cards or slips**	**kept by the reference librarian**

MATCHING

In each blank space in the left column, write the letters preceding the phrase in the right column that matches the left item best.

_____ 1. Index cards   a. Can help you find a suitable topic

_____ 2. Spell-checker   b. Synopsis found at the beginning of some journal articles

_____ 3. Abstract   c. Can be used to plan your paper visually

_____ 4. Index   d. More flexible than a computer for taking notes

_____ 5. Ellipses   e. Primary source for most of your paper's information

_____ 6. Concept map   f. Good starting point in the search for books or magazines

_____ 7. Preliminary research   g. Helpful but not infallible tool for correcting your paper's errors

_____ 8. Library   h. Indicate that part of a quotation has been omitted

TRUE-FALSE   *Circle* T *beside the* true *statements and* F *beside the* false *statements.*

1. T   F   Three or four narrowings should reduce your general topic to a suitable size.
2. T   F   The *Readers' Guide* is the best-known bound periodical index.
3. T   F   A computerized catalog usually enables you to search by subject, author, title, or keyword.
4. T   F   Paraphrasing is permitted in a research paper.
5. T   F   A conclusion isn't always necessary in a research paper.

MULTIPLE CHOICE   *Choose the word or phrase that completes each sentence most accurately, and circle the letter that precedes it.*

1. The basic skills for writing a research paper are similar to those for
    a. writing a novel or short story.
    b. preparing for a test or quiz.
    c. taking notes during a lecture.
    d. doing none of the above.

2. The most common criticism of research papers is that they are
    a. too broad.
    b. too long.
    c. poorly written.
    d. carelessly researched.

3. A research librarian is an expert on
    a. most research paper topics.
    b. the proper form for footnotes.
    c. use of the library.
    d. all of the above.

4. Your notes will be easier to use if you
    a. recopy them so they are easy to read.
    b. copy all your information verbatim.
    c. jot down each note on a separate card or slip.
    d. fit them on as few pages as possible.

5. You can avoid plagiarism by including
    a. quotation marks.
    b. citations.
    c. a bibliography.
    d. all the above.

REFLECTION

Think about the ideas outlined in this chapter and then draw upon your own opinions and experiences to answer each question fully.

1. Which do you generally find hardest to do when writing a research paper: choose a subject, find a focus, or decide on a premise? How has this chapter helped to make this easier?
2. This chapter contains a number of recommendations for taking notes for a research paper. Mention one that seems especially valuable to you and explain why.
3. In the past, what sort of system have you used to organize the writing of your paper? Which of the suggestions in this chapter seems most helpful in improving whatever organizational system you may have used?

IT'S YOUR Q

The Q System uses marginal questions to encourage active reading. You'll notice that most but not all paragraphs in this chapter are accompanied by marginal questions. Now it's your Q. Scan the chapter for any paragraph that is missing a question, reread the paragraph, establish the main idea, and then arrive at a question that elicits it. Use the questions in the surrounding paragraphs as models for your own marginal questions.

VOCABULARY IN ACTION

To expand the horizons of your understanding and to refine the precision of your thought, the three exercises that follow are designed to help you grow, strengthen, and maintain your own vocabulary.

SAY WHAT?

From the three choices beside each numbered item, select the one that most nearly expresses the meaning of the italicized word in the quote. Make a light check mark (√) next to your choice.

No one wants advice—only *corroboration*.

—John Steinbeck (1902–1968), American novelist

1. *corroboration*   cooperation   agreement   confirmation

We hold these truths to be *self-evident*, that all men are created equal, that they are *endowed* by their Creator with certain *unalienable* rights, that among these are life, liberty, and the *pursuit* of happiness.

   —Thomas Jefferson (1743–1826), third president of the United States

2. *self-evident*   genuine   effective   obvious

3. *endowed*   provided   developed   established

4. *unalienable*   lawful   intrinsic   earned

5. *pursuit*   enjoyment   search   goal

VOCAB-U-LADDER

Use your knowledge of word synonyms and roots to connect the word at the top rung to the word at the bottom rung, using the words listed below.

anthology
compendium
inflection
modulation
pensive
reflective

catalog

share root "legein," "to say, count"

synonyms for "collection"

share root "pendere," "to weigh"

synonyms for "thoughtful"

share root "flectere," "to bend"

synonyms for "pitch"

share root "modus," "measure"

modify

Here's the story behind a word that figures prominently in the chapter you've just read.

Topic **A topic was once a spot not a subject**

topic tŏp´ĭk. *n.* 1. The subject of a speech, essay, thesis, or discourse. 2. A subject of discussion or conversation. 3. A subdivision of a theme, thesis, or outline.*

With no teleprompter, index cards, or even sheets of paper at their disposal, ancient Greek and Roman orators often had to rely on their memories for holding a great deal of information. Given the limitations of memory, the points they chose to make had to be clustered in some meaningful way. A popular and quite reliable method for remembering information was known as *loci* (see Chapter 9), where *loci* was Latin for "place." It involved picking a house you knew well, imagining it in your mind's eye, and then associating the facts you wanted to recall with specific places inside of that house. Using this method, a skillful orator could mentally fill up numerous houses with the ideas he needed to recall and then simply "visit" them whenever he spoke about a particular subject. The clusters of information that speakers used routinely came to be known as commonplaces, *loci communes* in Latin and *koinos topos* in Greek. The great Greek philosopher Aristotle referred to them simply as *topos*, meaning "places." And that's how we came to use *topic* to refer to subject or grouping of information.**

*Adapted from "topic." *The American Heritage Dictionary of the English Language*, 4th ed. (Boston: Houghton Mifflin, 2000), http://dictionary.reference.com/browse/topic (accessed May 27, 2009).
**Based on information from "topic." *The American Heritage Dictionary of the English Language*, 4th ed. (Boston: Houghton Mifflin, 2000), http://dictionary.reference.com/browse/topic (accessed May 27, 2009); "topic." *Online Etymology Dictionary*. Douglas Harper, Historian, http://www.etymonline.com/index.php?search=topic (accessed May 27, 2009); "topic, *a* and *n.*" *Oxford English Dictionary*, 2nd ed. 20 vols. (Oxford: Oxford University Press, 1989).

Index